Network Routing Basics

Network Routing Basics

Understanding IP Routing in Cisco® Systems

James Macfarlane

Wiley Publishing, Inc.

Network Routing Basics: Understanding IP Routing in Cisco® Systems

Published by
Wiley Publishing, Inc.
10475 Crosspoint Boulevard
Indianapolis, IN 46256
www.wiley.com

ISBN-13: 978-0-471-77273-6
ISBN-10: 0-471-77273-9

Manufactured in the United States of America

10 9 8 7 6 5 4 3 2 1

1MA/TQ/QT/QW/IN

For general information on our other products and services or to obtain technical support, please contact our Customer Care Department within the U.S. at (800) 762-2974, outside the U.S. at (317) 572-3993 or fax (317) 572-4002.

Library of Congress Cataloging-in-Publication Data:
Macfarlane, James, 1953-
  Network routing basics : understanding IP routing in Cisco systems / James Macfarlane.
      p. cm.
  "Wiley Technology Publishing."
  Includes bibliographical references and index.
  ISBN-13: 978-0-471-77273-6 (cloth)
  ISBN-10: 0-471-77273-9 (cloth)
  1. TCP/IP (Computer network protocol) 2. Routers (Computer networks) I. Title.
  TK5105.585.M33 2006
  004.6'2--dc22
                    2005035954

To Julia

About the Author

James Macfarlane has worked in the personal computer and networking industry for over 20 years. He has worked in the capacity of consultant, network engineer, instructor, courseware developer, and technical writer.

Present and past certifications include Cisco CCNA, Microsoft MSCE and MCT, CompTIA A+ Trainer, and Novell CNE and CNI. James can be reached through his website at www.HotTrainingMaterials.com, and at routingbook@HotTrainingMaterials.com.

Technical Editor

Scott Bradner is the University Technology Security Officer at Harvard University. Scott founded the Harvard Network Device Test Lab, is a frequent speaker at technical conferences, and a weekly columnist for Network World. Mr. Bradner has served in a number of roles in the IETF, and is currently a trustee of the American Registry of Internet Numbers (ARIN).

Credits

Acquisitions Editor
Carol Long

Development Editor
Kenyon Brown

Technical Editor
Scott Bradner

Production Editor
Felicia Robinson

Copy Editor
Kathryn Duggan

Editorial Manager
Mary Beth Wakefield

Production Manager
Tim Tate

Vice President and Executive Group Publisher
Richard Swadley

Vice President and Executive Publisher
Joseph B. Wikert

Project Coordinator
Ryan Steffen

Graphics and Production Specialists
Denny Hager
Stephanie D. Jumper
Alicia South

Quality Control Technicians
Joe Niesen
Charles Spencer

Proofreading and Indexing
Tammy Todd
Johnna Van Hoose

Contents at a Glance

Contents

Acknowledgments

Thanks to each person at Wiley, both the people I worked with personally, and the many people I did not have the pleasure of meeting, for the care and effort taken to publish this book.

Introduction

A few years ago, I was preparing to teach my first introductory course on network routing. While seeking courseware material for the class, I examined a number of books on the subject but never found one I felt completely comfortable with. In the end, I chose some standardized courseware, and ended up handing out a series of "white papers" I had authored, in order to augment the books used in the course. Those white papers ultimately evolved into this book.

Routing is not rocket science, but it's a bit of a challenge to explain it in a manner that students don't find confusing. The basic idea of forwarding packets from one network to another is really not all that difficult a concept, but in the maturing, Internet-driven, multi-vendor, multi-protocol, classlessly addressed world of routing we live in today, there are a number of twists and turns when it comes to getting all those millions of packets to their destination.

In considering an addition to the various routing primers available to the reader, I saw a need for an up-to-date introduction to the subject that leaves the reader—after making the investment in studying the material—with the reward of having the confidence that they actually understand modern routing enough to go out there and put their knowledge to work. When poorly explained, routing can be a weighty, cumbersome topic. When properly understood, routing is, well . . . fun. It's a really enjoyable field to work in when you have a handle on how this aspect of networking works. There is an *art* to routing as well as a science. In other words, there's more than one way to get a packet from point A to point B. As a network engineer with a specialty in routing, you can excel in your field and gain peer recognition by playing a game called *"let's figure out the most efficient way to route packets on this network."* We're here to help you play the game well.

A primary goal in the creation of this book is to provide clear and complete information about how modern routing works. A strong emphasis has been placed on giving the student a broad enough background in each covered topic so that he or she hits *critical mass* if you will, whereby you haven't just memorized an explanation for how an aspect of routing works, you truly understand *why* it works the way it does. If, while reading this book, you find yourself saying something like "Hey, I got it!" then I have done my job.

What Material Is Covered in This Book?

Because routing is an extension of basic networking, the book starts with a review of core networking in Chapter 1. The fundamentals of networking as it relates to routing is presented, including a thorough review of network models, followed with a review of networking equipment. The concept of packet forwarding is explained, and a moderate treatment of the TCP/IP protocol suite is covered. Special attention is paid to classless addressing (subnetting, VLSMs, CIDR, and so on), because it is easily the biggest stumbling block in understanding routing. The Internet runs on CIDR addressed networks now, so it's not a topic to be brushed aside. The treatment of this subject matter will not only leave you with an understanding of classless addressing, you will be able to subnet with ease.

Chapter 2 provides the basis for understanding how routing works. The explanation starts where routing starts—at the workstation. From there, route tables and how they are populated are explained.

Chapters 3 and 4 explain how static and dynamic routing work, respectively. Chapter 4 is a pivotal chapter. Besides an in-depth primer on routing protocols, the important but elusive topics of route summarization, discontiguous networks, hierarchical addressing, and the longest match principal are covered as well.

Chapters 5 and 6 cover the two legacy routing protocols, RIP and IGRP. IGRP does not support classless addressing and was replaced by EIGRP. Its coverage is somewhat perfunctory, but there is material there that will assist you in understanding EIGRP. RIP was upgraded to support classless networking so it is still in use, but RIP does not support large networks. Regardless, read the treatment of RIP, because the coverage lays a foundation for many topics covered in subsequent chapters.

Chapters 7 and 8 cover the two contemporary routing protocols for large networks: EIGRP and OSPF. EIGRP is Cisco System's proprietary entry into the realm of routing protocols, whereas OSPF is the open standard entry, with recognition as the recommended interior routing protocol on the Internet. I have put special effort into the treatment of OSPF, and I think you will feel quite grounded with the protocol after absorbing the material in Chapter 8.

Chapter 9 provides a cursory introduction to the heady topic of the routing protocol that ties the whole Internet together, namely the Border Gateway Protocol.

Chapter 10 covers some particulars of routing that are best served up after spending some time with the routing protocols. Here, the topics of default routing and route redistribution are taken up.

What's Not Covered?

Any routing primer should give you an idea of what there is to pursue for further study after you have the basics down. Toward that end, the appendix has a list of routing topics not covered here.

An assumption is made that you know how to access a router and put it into programming mode. If that is not so, the appendix has a Web reference that will help.

Will This Book Help Me Pass a Cisco Test?

Glad you asked. This book is not written as a *pass-the-test* guide. However, the material in this book will most certainly help you in a testing environment because it is designed to help you truly understand the concepts of routing! Testing these days focuses more on understanding and troubleshooting, and less on raw facts that can be memorized. Because the book tends to give a more in-depth treatment of the topics it covers, it in fact provides a foundation for many of the Cisco certification exams.

So whether you read this book cover-to-cover, or jump right to a chapter of interest, I think you will find what you're looking for. Extensive **page-level** cross-referencing will enable you to jump to supporting topics with ease.

Best of luck to you with your routing career!

Networking Overview

Overview

The purpose of this chapter is to provide a refresher of basic networking topics related to routing. The following topics are covered:

OSI Network Model

Pop quiz. On a scale of 1–10, how well do you know the OSI network model? Come on . . . tell the truth. Don't be afraid if your number is not that high. That's what this section of the chapter is designed to help you with. The OSI network model (see Figure 1-1) provides a framework for understanding network functions, yet many folks working in the networking industry do not fully understand it. Comprehension of the OSI model, however enhances your ability to troubleshoot networking (and routing) problems.

A number of networking models have been developed over the years. This chapter gives the OSI model the most coverage because it is referenced most often. For example, a layer 3 switch refers to layer 3 of the OSI model. However the OSI model is strictly symbolic, and is less than perfect at representing today's networking technologies. It was developed in the '70s, released in the '80s and has had only minor updates. Because of that, there is a fair amount of overlap between the layers. This means a certain protocol or network service may not fit neatly into the description of a single layer.

A model that more closely reflects the modern networking environment is the TCP/IP model. This is the model that developers actually code to. At the end of this section the TCP/IP model to the OSI model are compared.

The Conundrum of Explaining the OSI Model

If you look through enough books on networking, you'll find that not every author chooses to discuss networking models up front. Some writers put the treatment of the OSI model at the beginning of the book, others place it at the end of the book, while still others intersperse a discussion of the model with networking topics. That's because the OSI model is a "chicken or egg" type thing. It's easier to understand *networking* once you understand the *OSI model*. But on the other hand . . . it's easier to understand the *OSI model* once you have a knowledge of *networking*.

	Layer Name
7	Application
6	Presentation
5	Session
4	Transport
3	Network
2	Data Link
1	Physical

Figure 1-1   Basic OSI network model.

This chapter discusses the OSI model first because it lays a foundation for how to fit routing into the broader aspects of general networking. As you read this section, keep the following in mind: The OSI model is not some "extra thing you have to learn about networking." Rather, think of it as a tool to facilitate understanding the concepts of networking. Understanding networking translates to understanding routing. Be advised that any unfamiliar networking terms used in this section are probably explained in subsequent sections (it's that chicken-or-egg thing).

Mother of All OSI Model Explanations?

The OSI reference model is based on a proposal developed by the International Organization for Standardization (ISO)[1] The model is called the ISO OSI (Open Systems Interconnection) Reference Model because it deals with allowing disparate computing platforms to communicate with each other. The OSI model allows PCs, Macs, Unix systems, Host systems, and so on to exchange information by supplying a common reference for how to apply networking technology.

Comprehending the OSI model begins with comprehending how the model came in to being in the first place. The OSI model was developed to act both as a reference for designing network components and as an aid in understanding networking technology. Think about all that is required for two computers to communicate across a network. What steps must take place to send a message from computer A to computer B?

Anatomy of a Data Communication Session

Here is an example of what must happen for two computers to communicate across a network.

Sending Side

The side originating the session has a checklist of several items that must be accomplished:

- Data from the user's application (on computer A) must be passed to the network.
- The data may need to be converted (ASCII to EBCDIC for example).
- The data may need to be encrypted and/or compressed.
- If reliable communications are desired, a communication channel with the destination computer (computer B) must be established to track each packet. In that case, a mechanism is needed to tag each packet and follow up on the delivery attempt.

- The data must be broken up into smaller chunks that can be handled by the network (you don't send a 10MB file in a single packet).

- The logical and physical addresses (IP address and MAC address respectfully) must be determined for the destination computer.

- The source and destination addresses must be added to the data packets.

- Error-detection information must be added to the packets.

- The best route to the destination host must be determined.

- The packets then need to be formatted into the particular frame type unique to the network architecture of computer A (Ethernet, Token Ring, and so on).

- The packets must be converted into electrical signals and placed on the cable.

- Access to the network cable must be managed.

- The packets may need to be repackaged along the way into a differing frame type if computer B resides on a network with a different LAN architecture.

Receiving Side

As the data stream is received, computer B has several responsibilities:

- Computer B must have a way of knowing which packets are intended for it.

- Computer B must have a way of knowing which application should receive the packets.

- Access to the network cable must be managed to retrieve the packets.

- The packets must be converted from electrical signals to bits.

- The packets must be checked for corruption.

- The packets must be checked for correct order delivery and for missing packets. Packets received out of order must be reordered.

- If reliable delivery was utilized, an acknowledgement message must be sent for packets received intact. A retransmit message must be sent for missing packets.

- The packet data needs to be rearranged into a format the receiving application can understand.

- The data may need to be decrypted and/or decompressed.

- The data may need to be converted.
- The data must be passed to the receiving application.

Phew. That's quite a lot of processing going on. A lot of things have to happen behind the scenes to pass data between computers. Each one of these processes fits into a particular layer of the OSI model and that is what helps us keep track of everything. But the question may arise: Why do I care? As long as it works, why bother about all that detail? Well, as a network engineer, you used to *not* have to care. You didn't have to worry about all that stuff. *The vendor did all the worrying for you.*

The Way Things Used to Be

Back in the old days—in the primordial era of the '60s and '70s, when the mainframe ruled the world—networks were *monolithic* in nature. One vendor provided all the hardware and software for a system, so there was no need to be concerned about all the aforementioned processes. The vendor delivered a complete solution. All aspects of communicating across the network were handled by the "solution." You bought your hardware from IBM. You bought your software from IBM. All those communication processes still had to be carried out of course, but nobody worried about it, because a single vendor handled the whole process. Interoperability was not an issue.

Things are different now. In this day and age, with hardware and software being sourced from multiple vendors, it's become important to have a method and structure for handling data communications. These days we buy our network OS from one vendor, our applications from another vendor or vendors, our network interface cards from another vendor, our cabling from another vendor, and on and on. Yet, these products must all work together. Your applications must run on Ethernet, Token Ring, FDDI, or whatever network architecture you choose to employ. You don't want to have to buy the Ethernet version of Microsoft Office, do you? The OSI reference model attempts to address this issue by providing a structure that details the responsibilities each vendor must assume to insure network communication can take place. The OSI model uses a layered system that assigns responsibility for specific portions of the data communication process to different layers of the model. *The key to the OSI model is that a vendor's product only needs to interoperate with the adjacent layers directly above and below* the layer it corresponds to.

Similar models are used frequently in the brick-and-mortar realm. The post office is a great example. If you wish to send a letter to a friend in Hawaii, do you need to know the name of the postman who will pick up the letter from the mailbox? Do you need to know the exact route the letter will take to Hawaii? Nope. Someone down the line does. The letter writer just needs to know the friend's address and the location of the nearest mailbox. The postman who picks up the letter needs to know only two things: where the mailbox is and the substation to drop the letter off. By the same token, the employees at the substation need to know only two things: where the mailman drops off the mail and which truck to load the letter on in order to get it to Hawaii. The substation employees don't care who wrote the letter, its contents, what mailbox it was picked up from, or even the return address for that matter.

It's the same with the OSI model. For example, the networking layer needs to know only how to receive data segments from the transport layer, process the segments into packets, and pass them to the data-link layer. The network layer doesn't even care if the packets reach their destination—the transport layer is in charge of that. The network layer certainly cares nothing about the data itself—the layers above it worry about that.

With the uniform set of rules provided by a networking model in place, a network-interface card manufacturer can produce a product that works with *any* application or OS. *This is because the NIC designer only needs to be concerned about communicating with adjacent layers.* Additionally, standardized APIs at the boundary of each layer provide a common set of rules that facilitate intralayer communications. As a result, product development time is greatly reduced.

Explanation of OSI Layers

Now let's examine the functions of each layer of the OSI model and how the layers interact with each other. Ultimately, the OSI network model manifests itself in the form of APIs, standards, protocols, hardware, hardware drivers, and communication technologies (Ethernet, Frame Relay, and so on). Each technology, protocol, and the like runs at a specific layer of the model, carrying out functions the layer is responsible for. Figure 1-2 illustrates the functions of each layer of the model.

WHAT IS AN API?

An application program interface, or API, is a method used by application developers to provide a standard way of accessing network services through function calls. An API supplies standardized "hooks" into a program that allow other processes to request it to do work. An API is published, thereby making access to the program's services available to any vendor. Examples of APIs are NetBIOS, WinSock, RPC, and SQL.

APIs in the OSI model allow protocols and processes to more easily interact with each other by reducing the amount of code required to perform a function.

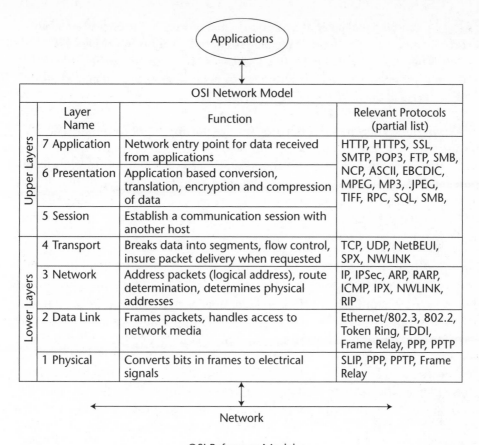

Figure 1-2 provides the OSI reference model:

	Layer Name	Function	Relevant Protocols (partial list)
		OSI Network Model	
Upper Layers	7 Application	Network entry point for data received from applications	HTTP, HTTPS, SSL, SMTP, POP3, FTP, SMB, NCP, ASCII, EBCDIC, MPEG, MP3, .JPEG, TIFF, RPC, SQL, SMB,
Upper Layers	6 Presentation	Application based conversion, translation, encryption and compression of data	
Upper Layers	5 Session	Establish a communication session with another host	
Lower Layers	4 Transport	Breaks data into segments, flow control, insure packet delivery when requested	TCP, UDP, NetBEUI, SPX, NWLINK
Lower Layers	3 Network	Address packets (logical address), route determination, determines physical addresses	IP, IPSec, ARP, RARP, ICMP, IPX, NWLINK, RIP
Lower Layers	2 Data Link	Frames packets, handles access to network media	Ethernet/802.3, 802.2, Token Ring, FDDI, Frame Relay, PPP, PPTP
Lower Layers	1 Physical	Converts bits in frames to electrical signals	SLIP, PPP, PPTP, Frame Relay

OSI Reference Model

Figure 1-2   OSI reference model.

Upper Layers (5, 6, and 7)

The upper layers of the OSI model are generally thought of as being related to applications and operating systems, whereas the lower layers are related to networking. There is much overlap of functionality in the upper layers, and this is one place the OSI model shows its age. As shown in Figure 1-2, certain protocols are mapped to specific upper layers; in fact, many of the protocols perform their functions across all three upper layers.

The upper layers are generally responsible for obtaining data from the source application (word processor, email client, data files, and so on), and passing that data to the network. The application and/or the operating system may act on the data in a variety of ways. The data may be translated so that the receiving host can understand it (PC to Mac for example), it may be compressed to speed transmission, and it may be encrypted.

> **NOTE** One potential point of confusion is that processes like encryption may occur at more than one layer of the model. Encryption at the upper layers is usually performed by the application that created the data, or perhaps by the OS, but encryption can also be performed by network protocols running at the lower layers of the model, such as the security protocol IPSec.

Bear in mind that the upper layers are the starting point to initiate communications on the *sending* computer, but they are the end point for the *receiving* computer. The communication process starts at layer 7 of the sending computer and works its way down the OSI model to layer 1. The data is then transmitted to the receiving computer, which receives the frame at layer 1 and processes it up to layer 7 where it is then made available to the receiving application.

Layer 7–Application Layer

The application layer is where the process of data communication commences. Contrary to its name, the application layer does not refer to applications themselves, but rather it is the entry point for accepting data *from* applications on the sending computer. The **redirector**, which is a part of the network client software installed on the workstation, collects the data from the application and passes it to layer 7. On the receiving side, the redirector hands off data received from the sending host to the appropriate application. The application layer also handles the setup of application-sponsored error-recovery and data-integrity procedures. Quality of service (QoS) and user authentication are also identified at the application layer.

Note that data integrity is often thought of as something to be handled by the lower layers. While that is most certainly true, the application has the option to add as many data integrity checks as it sees fit. Some applications will rely entirely on the lower layers for data integrity. For example, they can use the TCP transport protocol in layer 4. Or the application may choose to handle data integrity on its own and thus use the UDP protocol in layer 4. This will vary of course from one application to another.

> **NOTE** The OSI model is protocol neutral, but due to the pervasiveness of the TCP/IP protocol suite, TCP/IP will be used in the examples. All the TCP/IP protocols, such as TCP and UDP, are discussed in a subsequent section.

Layer 6–Presentation Layer

The presentation layer provides independence from differences in data *representation*. This is where data may be translated, converted, encrypted and decrypted, and compressed and decompressed. For example, a PC-to-mainframe session may require data be converted from native ASCII to EBCDIC, the encoding method of IBM mainframes[2]. Data formats such as MPEG and MP3 are associated with the presentation layer. Application-based encryption is another example of the presentation layer. On the sending side, data would be encrypted at this layer, and then decrypted by the corresponding layer on the receiving computer.

Layer 5—Session Layer

The session layer is where a communication connection is initiated. Sessions have a specific starting and ending point and are required by certain protocols for two-way communications to take place. The session layer is often used by client applications vis-à-vis the operating system when connections to a network or network applications are required. SQL, WinSock, RPC, and Named Pipes are examples.

This layer handles session maintenance as well. If the session is interrupted, it can be re-started. An example would be a file transfer application that automatically restarts the transfer if the connection is broken. If a service such as **NetBIOS Checkpoints** is used, checkpoints inserted into the data stream can allow the transfer to pick up where it left off. This is a *good* thing.

The session layer on the sending computer uses the lower layers to communicate with the corresponding session layer on the receiving computer to establish a connection.

Lower Layers (1, 2, 3, and 4)

As noted earlier, the lower layers are where networking actually takes place. Here the stream of data coming from the upper layers into manageable chunks determine the network (logical) and data-link (physical) addresses for both the source and destination packets, determine the best path (route) to the destination host and convert the binary data to electrical impulses, and place it on the network medium.

Layer 4—Transport Layer

The transport layer provides optional error detection and correction, end-to-end (host-to-host) error-recovery, and controls the flow of the packets. This layer provides the option for assuring data integrity independent of any integrity checks performed by the data-link layer, which usually provides error detection and correction as well.

If so-called "reliable" delivery of data is required, the TCP (Transport Control Protocol) protocol is employed at this layer. TCP numbers the outgoing packets and requires a response from the destination host confirming that each packet arrived intact. When reliable delivery of data is *not* required, the so-called "unreliable," or "best-effort," UDP (User Datagram Protocol) protocol is used for faster service. The application that sourced the data determines whether to use reliable (TCP) or unreliable (UDP) delivery.

Another important function of the transport layer is **segmentation**. The data stream from the upper layers is broken up, or segmented, into more manageable chunks. The generic term for what to call a *chunk* of data is Data Protocol Unit (DPU). A DPU is assigned a more specific name depending upon which layer of the OSI model is being referenced. In the upper layers, the DPU is simply called "data." At the transport layer, the DPU takes on the name **segment**. So at this layer you are dealing with *segments* of data.

Finally, the transport layer handles flow control. Flow control insures that data is not sent so fast that packets are dropped on the receiving side.

NOTE See the subsequent "TCP/IP Model" section for more information on these protocols.

Layer 3—Network Layer

The DPU name at this layer is **datagram** or **packet**[3]. The network layer is responsible for packet addressing, path determination (how to get to the destination network), and packet forwarding. Source and destination network addresses are assigned at this layer. Additionally, source and destination MAC (data-link) addresses are determined and passed on for use by layer 2. In a TCP/IP environment, the IP protocol handles path determination and network addressing, while the ARP protocol handles MAC address determination. Once the path is determined and the packets are addressed, they are then forwarded to their destination.

The network layer also has responsibility for insuring that packets passed down to the data-link layer are not too large for the network technology to handle. Different network technologies have varying Maximum Transmission Units (MTU). The MTU specifies the largest packet size the technology can handle. For example, the frame size for Ethernet is typically 1536 bytes (12.2KB), whereas the frame size for Token Ring is either 4KB or 16KB. The network layer is aware of which network technology is in use (Ethernet, Token Ring, and so on) and will fragment the packets into smaller units that do not exceed the MTU for the technology. The network layer on the receiving computer will reassemble the fragmented packets. This is another example of how layers in the OSI model need only be aware of adjacent layers. The network layer must satisfy the needs of the transport layer and the data-link layer, but on the other hand, it doesn't care about what the data packet contains.

Layer 2—Data-Link Layer

The data-link layer is defined by the network technology in use. For LANs, this is most often the 802.3 protocol, better known as *Ethernet*. The DPU name at this layer is **frame**. A frame includes all the data passed down from the other layers along with the source and destination MAC addresses, some information specific to the network protocol, and an added checksum for error detection.

WHAT IS A MAC ADDRESS?

MAC (Media Access Control) addresses are the unique identifying numbers burned into every network interface card (NIC) or directly into a computer if it does not have a separate NIC card. MAC addresses are known as *physical* addresses because they are permanently associated with the NIC. In the OSI reference model, the MAC address is also referred to as the data-link address because the data-link layer makes use of the physical address for communicating with another host. Communications ultimately take place between two hosts via their MAC/data-link addresses.

A MAC address is a 48-bit number expressed as six pairs of hexadecimal numbers, for example 00-20-40-70-F4-84. The first three pairs of numbers refer to the manufacturer of the NIC, while the remaining three pairs are uniquely assigned to each NIC produced. The combined numbers create a universally unique physical address that identifies a specific node on a network.

The data-link layer is only responsible for delivery and error detection on the *local* network. If the frame must be routed to a different network, the router will strip off the current frame and apply a new one based on the network protocol the packet is being forwarded to on the next hop.

Finally, the framed data is converted to a bit stream and passed to layer 1.

One question folks have when studying the OSI model regards the need for two sets of addresses: a *network address* (also known as a network ID or network number) at layer 3 and a *data-link address* at layer 2. Isn't one address enough to uniquely identify a network node? In a perfect world, a single address might be enough, but as we know all to well, it's not a perfect world. The OSI model reflects an open, flexible environment in having the ability to assign logical (changeable and hierarchical) addresses as well as physical (fixed and permanent) addresses. An analogy would be say, a Denny's restaurant at 123 Goodfood Place. If Denny's moved down the street, it would be located at a new address. The existing building, in the meantime, might become say, a Carrows (the logical address changes), but maintains the current street address (the physical address remains the same).

Dual addressing simply provides the flexibility to allow an organization to deploy any network numbering scheme it wishes (IPv4, IPv6, IPX, and so on), while maintaining a standardized, globally unique physical addressing scheme.

Layer 1—Physical Layer

The physical layer defines the electrical, mechanical, functional, and procedural characteristics used to access and send a stream of bits over a physical medium. This layer handles converting the bits in a frame into electrical signals (or light or radio signals) for transmission over the media. This is the realm of specifying maximum transmission distances and describing the physical connection to the medium (like RJ-45), and the physical media (fiber, twisted pair, and so on).

THE TWO FACES OF THE DATA-LINK LAYER

The data-link layer is actually divided into two sub-layers: The Logical Link (LLC) layer and the Media Access Control (MAC) layer.

The LLC layer is thought of as the upper sub-layer and is defined by the IEEE 802.2 standard. The LLC is a "header within a header." It frames the data received from layer 3 by applying the MAC address and a checksum header to the packet. The LLC layer can establish either a connection or connectionless session (reliable or unreliable) with the next node in the path. Frame synchronization, flow control, and error correction are all handled by this sub-layer. An 802.2 frame allows for identification of the transport protocol in use.

The MAC layer is the lower sub-layer and is associated with the various networking standards such as 802.3 (CMSA/CD or Ethernet) and 802.5 (Token Ring). The MAC layer handles communication with the network adapter and arbitrates shared access to the media.

Another Mail Analogy

With a more thorough explanation of the OSI model under your belt, let's apply another metaphor to the model. This time a more elaborate package delivery scenario will be employed. The following describes the processes involved in mailing a package from point A to point B, while at the same time associating each process to a network communications session under the OSI model (*metaphors for the OSI model are imperfect partially because the OSI model is imperfect. So just play along, OK?*)

> The boss wants to send a large quantity of confidential employee manuals to a worker named Gina at the branch office in New York. The boss has his assistant pick up the manuals.

> The assistant places each manual into the kind of binder used at the New York office and marks them as private. Some manuals need to be produced in different languages. The assistant then places a note with the name "Gina" on the binders and has a shipping clerk pick them up.

> The assistant calls the NY office and warns them to expect a package and to call her when it arrives. She then hands the manuals to the shipping clerk.

> *These processes are synonymous with the upper layers of the OSI model: receive data from the application, translate and encrypt as specified, supply the name of the destination, and inform the lower layers whether assured delivery is required.*

> The shipping clerk places the manuals into individual containers that will not exceed weight limits imposed by a local courier service that will deliver the manuals to the shipper. The clerk also checks to see if there is any room for other packages bound to the same destination. The clerk

numbers each package as 1 of 3, 2 of 3, 3 of 3, and so on. It will be the shipping clerk's responsibility to follow up on the safe delivery of the packages.

This process is synonymous with the transport layer (4): break file into smaller segments, use TCP for assured delivery, and pass the packets to layer 3.

The courier notices that the packages need to go to "Gina," so he looks up which office Gina works in. The courier also looks up the exact street address and the return address, and passes that information to a shipper that delivers to New York. In addition, the courier determines how the packages should be shipped (by air in this case). The courier may repack the items if there are any weight problems with the particular shipper chosen. The packages are driven to the airport.

This is synonymous with the network layer (3): resolve destination machine name to an IP address, add the source and destination network addresses to the datagrams, determine the best route, fragment packets as needed to accommodate the maximum frame size (MTU) for the data-link protocol in use, look up MAC address of destination, and pass the packets to layer 2.

An employee at the airport determines when a flight will be available for each package.

This is synonymous with the data-link layer (2): determine when it's time to place packets on the network media and pass the packets to layer 1.

A cargo handler loads each package he receives into a compartment on the plane and sends it on its way.

This is synonymous with the physical layer (1): NIC modulates an electric pulse onto the network cable.

Encapsulation

Encapsulation is the term used to describe adding information to packets as they are passed down the OSI model layers. If you look closely, you will notice that there's one distinct difference between what happens in the upper layers of the OSI model juxtaposed to what happens at the lower layers. In the upper layers, nothing is *added* to the data. The data itself is being acted on. It is converted or encrypted or whatever, but it's still the raw data (mostly).

In the lower layers however, information is being appended to the raw data. IP addresses, MAC addresses, tracking information, error correction code, and so on are all being added. The process by which all this network data is added to the application data is called **encapsulation**. Encapsulation adds **headers** of information to the raw data segments. As Figure 1-3 shows, most of these headers are appended to the beginning of the data.

Encapsulation in the OSI Model

	Sending					Receiving	

	DATA	7	← Application →	7	DATA		
	DATA	6	← Presentation →	6	DATA		
	DATA	5	← Session →	5	DATA		

(figure representation)

DATA | 7 | ← Application → | 7 | DATA
DATA | 6 | ← Presentation → | 6 | DATA
DATA | 5 | ← Session → | 5 | DATA
TCP Hdr DATA | 4 | ← Transport → | 4 | DATA TCP Hdr
IP Hdr TCP Hdr DATA | 3 | ← Network → | 3 | DATA TCP Hdr IP Hdr
MAC LLC IP TCP DATA FCB Hd Hdr Hdr Hdr Hdr | 2 | ← Data-Link → | 2 | DATA FCB TCP IP LLC MAC Hdr Hdr Hdr Hdr Hd
10 10 10 10 10 10 10 10 10 10 10 10 | 1 | ← Physical → | 1 | 10 10 10 10 10 10 10 10 10 10 10 10

Figure 1-3 Encapsulation adds critical networking information to each packet of data.

In the upper three layers of the sending side (7, 6, and 5), the data is passed down the OSI stack, usually without the addition of any headers. At the transport layer, the data is segmented and a header is appended to each segment. The header includes data such as source and destination port numbers.

The transport layer then passes the modified DPU to the network layer. The network layer treats the incoming segments—optional TCP/UDP header and all—as "data." This layer cares nothing about what's in the payload of each segment and does not distinguish between network data and application data. The segments are repackaged based on the LAN network type, an IP header is appended that includes information such as source and destination IP addresses and quality of service settings, and the segment is now treated as a packet.

The data-link layer receives the packet and again treats the whole packet as data. A MAC header is then appended to the packet, and, depending on the configured frame type, an 802.2, LLC header, and/or SNAP header are added as well. The DPU at this layer is referred to as a frame.

The physical layer receives the frames, converts each frame to a bit stream, and modulates the bits as electrical signals onto the medium. As before, the entire frame—headers and data—is treated as one unit.

On the receiving side, the process is reversed. Each header will be examined by the appropriate layer. The physical layer converts the electrical signals to a bit stream, recreates the frames and passes each frame to the data-link layer. The data-link layer strips off and discards the frame headers, and passes what is now a packet to the network layer, which interprets the information in the IP header. The network layer then passes the packet to the transport layer, which interprets the TCP/UDP header. Based on the destination IP address from the network layer and the destination port number from the TCP/UDP header, the segment is passed to the upper layers and to the appropriate application or service.

As shown in Figure 1-3, each layer of the OSI model communicates only with its corresponding layer on the other host. Only matching layers can interpret the headers created by their counterparts on the opposing host.

TCP/IP Network Model

The TCP/IP model describes the ubiquitous TCP/IP protocol suite. The TCP/IP model is much simpler than the OSI model. It is a four-layer model that treats all application functions as a single layer. It also combines the OSI data-link layer and physical layer into a single layer. Table 1-1 shows the two models side-by-side.

Table 1-1   TCP/IP Network Model

OSI MODEL	TCP/IP MODEL	TCP/IP PROTOCOL SUITE
Application	Application Layer	HTTP, TELNET, FTP, SMTP, DNS, SNMP
Presentation		
Session		
Transport	Transport Layer	TCP, UDP
Network	Internet Layer	IP, ARP, IGMP, ICMP
Data-link	Network Interface Layer	
Physical		

Which model should you care about? The OSI model, with all its imperfections, is imbedded in the lexicon as the reference model most used for describing networking. However, the TCP/IP model best reflects the actual protocols used in today's networks, as the model specifies strictly the TCP/IP protocol suite.

Networking Equipment

This section focuses on some of the popular networking hardware in use today. The concentration is mostly on packet forwarding equipment, with special attention paid to routers. The following hardware will be covered:

- Repeaters
- Hubs
- Bridges

- Switches
- Routers
- Layer 3 switches
- CSU/DSUs

Packet Forwarding

Before delving into packet forwarding hardware, be sure you understand what packet forwarding actually is, and how the process differs on varying types of forwarding hardware. The term "forwarding" is a generic term for transferring a packet from point A to point B. It is a "method independent" term, meaning it is used whether the packet is *routed* to a different network or *switched* to another port on the *same* network. Forwarding just refers to moving the packet along its way.

In describing forwarding, this text will usually refer to the unit of data being forwarded as a *packet*. Although the term *frame* and *datagram* are best suited to DPUs as they pass through routers (the DPU enters as a layer 2 frame and moves through the router as a layer 3 datagram, its layer 2 header having been stripped off), the term *packet* is a nice elastic one that has broader meaning in common use and can apply to forwarding at both layers 2 and 3.

Repeaters—Layer 1, Physical

Repeaters are the most basic form of forwarding devices. They are associated with the physical layer because they have no means of examining the contents of frames. Repeaters don't see the contents of headers; they simply amplify electrical signals. A repeater receives a frame, regenerates an *exact copy* of the frame, and forwards it along its way. The repeater does not scrutinize the bit pattern in any way and makes no decision about how or where to forward packets. A repeater therefore is only used for intranetwork communications. Repeaters are primarily used to extend the maximum length of a cable run. They typically have two ports: an input port and an output port. Although repeaters still have their uses, it is rare to see one used specifically for networking, partially because the advent of fiber optic cabling has extended the maximum length of cable runs. One place repeaters have seen a renaissance is as USB extenders.

Hubs—Layer 1, Physical

Hubs (also known as concentrators) are easy to define. They are simply multi-port repeaters. Whereas a repeater will have two ports (one in, one out), a hub has 24 or more ports. The concept is exactly the same though. A signal delivered to *any* port on a hub is regenerated and forwarded out *all* ports. Again, no examination of the frame is performed and no forwarding decisions are made. Every port gets a copy of the frame because the hubs are too dumb to know which port the destination node is attached to. Because hubs cannot read network addresses within a frame, they are restricted to forwarding frames within a single logical network only. Hubs do not route traffic.

Hubs have traditionally been employed on smaller Ethernet LANs to provide connections to network nodes. They are cheap and simple to deploy. However, because the Ethernet frames sent from one node is forwarded to *all* nodes, bandwidth is compromised. Ethernet is a baseband medium, meaning only one signal at a time can be placed on the network. If a second signal is placed on the wire, a collision occurs and communications must be reattempted. Hubs and repeaters therefore form what is known as a **collision domain**. All traffic on an intranetwork connected solely by hubs (or repeaters) exists within a single collision domain.

As Ethernet networks grew in size over the years, the *single collision domain* architecture became an issue because each additional node attached to the network increased the chances of a collision. Collisions happened so often on larger networks (over 50–100 nodes for example) that performance was significantly degraded. Since Ethernet looked like it was going to become a ubiquitous LAN technology, a solution was needed to somehow partition collision domains. The next three networking devices to be discussed—bridges, switches, and routers—address the issue by forming multiple collision domains.

Bridges—Layer 2, Data-Link

A bridge is a different animal than a repeater or a hub because it has the ability to examine frames. This ability is limited though in that a bridge can only "see" into the layer 2 header (the source and destination MAC addresses and checksum).

BASEBAND VERSUS BROADBAND

Most LAN technologies employ baseband signaling (also known as narrow band), which means only one signal can exist on the medium at a time. Conversely, broadband signaling allows multiple signals on the medium (such as cable TV and cable modems) at the same instant.

However, broadband is a term undergoing redefinition thanks to the huge market for high-speed Internet access. Since broadband's multi-signal capability has generally translated to higher speeds over baseband signaling, the term "broadband" has become synonymous with "fast" in the eyes of the press, and thus the public. Therefore, any technology that delivers a high-speed connection tends to be labeled broadband, regardless of the underlying signaling method.

The ability to read MAC addresses gives a bridge the ability to make intelligent decisions about forwarding packets. A bridge will build a table in memory that records the MAC address of every node connected to either port. Over a period of time, the bridge learns which nodes are connected to which of its two ports.

How can this help network congestion? A two-port bridge can be inserted between two LAN segments, thus splitting a single collision domain into two collision domains. The two segments can be literally any size and contain any number of hubs. Once the bridge learns the MAC addresses of all nodes and which port they are connected to, it will forward packets only to the port the destination node is connected to. In other words, if node 1 is connected to network segment A, the bridge will never forward traffic destined for node 1 onto segment B. That's not where it lives.

However, bridges, like hubs, are restricted to forwarding frames within the logical network because they can't discern network addresses. The capability of bridges is further enumerated in the following section on switches, which are simply multi-port bridges.

Switches—Layer 2, Data-Link

Switches are quite similar to bridges. Because of a trend away from general purpose CPUs to custom ASICs, and for marketing reasons, the *bridge* evolved into the *switch*. Switches assist packet forwarding by creating a collision domain on each switched port. As with bridges, switches track the source MAC address of all packets and maps each address to the specific port it is sourced from. A table is built containing this map, which allows the switch to forward traffic only to the port attached to the destination node (assuming only one node is connected to the port). If node 1 attached to port 1 sends a message to node 2 attached to port 2, that traffic is contained to port 1 and port 2. A node is attached to port 3 could carry on a simultaneous conversation with a node attached to port 4 without the chance of a collision. This is analogous to avoiding a traffic jam by being allocated you own personal traffic lane.

Rather than attach a single workstation to a switched port, one or more hubs could be attached to the port, although performance, as well as security, will tend to degrade.

When switches were first introduced, they were substantially more expensive than hubs, so a trade-off was made between cost and bandwidth management, and both hubs and switches were deployed on LANs.

However, as the cost of switches has come down, more and more LANs are built solely on switching technology. Moreover, the delay incurred by a switch examining each packet's MAC address has been mitigated by modern switches employing what is referred to as **wire speed** technology, which is firmware-based code whose operation does not impinge on the speed of the underlining media.

Switches are now marketed to the home networking market, typically in the form of four-port switch/Internet/router combo boxes. This is a bit silly of course, since the amount of collisions on a four-node network hardly results in a perceivable difference in performance to the end user, but sizzle tends to sell over steak. However, one computer per switched port tends to enhance security, as it makes eavesdropping quite difficult.

Due to marketing, pricing, performance, and security, switches have evolved into the most popular network component for forwarding packets within a logical network.

Routers—Layer 3, Network

The previously described networking equipment is limited in that hubs and switches can only forward packets within a single network. If packets must be forwarded to another network, a **router** is required. A router's primary function is to forward packets between networks (Chapter 2 goes into detail on this). Routers deal in network addresses and are therefore associated with the network layer (layer 3) of the OSI model. An artifact of router behavior is that they isolate **broadcast domains** as well as collision domains. Repeaters, hubs, bridges, and switches all forward broadcasts to all ports (even switched ports). Routers usually do not forward broadcast packets.[4]

What Exactly Is a Router?

A *router* is a device that forwards packets between networks. A router is simply a computer running code that determines how and where to forward packets bound for other networks. The computer carrying out routing functions may be a single purpose computer with a specialized operating system (for example, a Cisco router) or a computer running a general purpose operating system, such as an Intel computer running a Windows 2003 server.

To be specific, a router has the following attributes:

- A processor
- An operating system (OS)
- Two or more network interfaces to forward packets through
- A route table indicating which interface the packets should be forwarded to
- Some type of memory to store the OS, route tables, and the configuration information

General-Purpose Computers as Routers

Many server-based OSs can be configured to forward packets between networks. All that is required to allow a Windows 2003 server to perform routing
functions is to install two or more network interface cards (NICs) and configure for packet forwarding. A computer configured with two or more NICs is
considered a **multi-homed** system (or multi-homed computer).

Given that a general purpose OS can assume the functionality of a router,
why would anyone bother to spend the money for a dedicated router? There
are many good reasons to use a dedicated router. Unless you have very simple
requirements, a general-purpose OS just doesn't cut it when it comes to seri-
ous routing. In the case of Microsoft operating systems, a search of Microsoft's
knowledge base reveals a plethora of problems related to multi-homing. In
addition, configurability, flexibility, filtering, security, throughput, and the
ability to run various routing protocols are all issues with multi-homed PCs.

Dedicated Routers

A dedicated router is just that—a computer with one basic function: the forwarding of packets. A dedicated router has all the attributes cited previously:
a processor; an operating system; two or more interfaces; a route table; and
some type of memory to store the OS, route tables and core configuration of
the router. Most router product lines are distinguished by how the aforementioned criteria are incorporated into specific router model.

Processor

Processor type and clock speed vary according to the volume of packets
required to flow through the router in a given period and how much filtering
is performed on those packets. The heavier the workload, the more processing
power is required.

Operating System

At the core of a router is its operating system. Each brand of router runs an OS
proprietary to the vendor. For example, a Cisco router employs the venerable
Cisco IOS (Internetwork Operating System). The Cisco IOS has gone through
a number of versions over the years as features have been added to keep up
with changing network technologies. Although there are various flavors of the
IOS for different router series (2500, 2600, and so on) it is essentially the same
core code. When you have learned how to configure one Cisco router, you
have a handle on configuring *any* Cisco router. It's all about knowing the IOS.

Memory

Routers employ various types of memory for different functions. Table 1-2 illustrates the common memory types.

ROM, Flash, and NVRAM are all *non-volatile* forms of memory. If the router goes down or is powered off, the stored information is retained. RAM memory is *volatile*, but is much faster than non-volatile memory. Information from non-volatile memory is copied to RAM on boot-up to allow faster operation.

Router Interfaces

If routers can't connect to networks, they don't have much value. The number, type, and capabilities of a router's interfaces vary according to a particular product line and model number. However, just about every router you pick up has two traditional categories of routing interfaces: a LAN interface and a WAN interface.

A WAN interface makes possible the connection to a WAN link, such as a modem or a digital line (a T1 or a 56K line for example). The WAN interface on a Cisco router is usually a DB60 female serial port. A DTE/DCE cable[5] is used to connect the WAN interface to a CSU/DSU. DTE stands for Data Terminal Equipment (the router) and DCE stands for Data Circuit-terminating Equipment (the CSU/DSU, Figure 1-4).

A LAN interface connects the router to one or more local networks. The interface takes the physical form of either an RJ-45 jack (100base-T) or a DB-15 female connector. The DB-15 connector was designed to connect to the now-obsolete 10Base-2 networks (coax). Even so, the Cisco 2500 series routers still come equipped with such an interface. If a 2500 series router is to be interfaced to an Ethernet network employing unshielded twisted pair (UTP) wiring, a **transceiver** that converts the DB-15 to an RJ-45 jack is attached to the interface. By the way, the RJ-45 jacks in Figure 1-4 are not LAN connections. Rather, they are used to connect a terminal to the router and program it. The common application to program the router is TELNET.EXE.

Table 1-2 Types of Memory Used in Routers

MEMORY TYPE	TYPICAL USE
ROM	Stores a stripped-down version of the IOS
Flash / (EEPROM)	Stores the operating system
NVRAM	Stores the startup configuration
RAM	Stores the running configuration, route tables, and so on

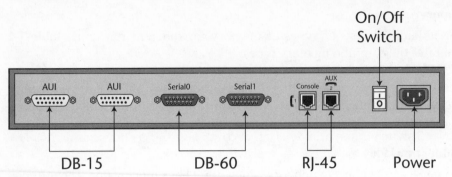

Figure 1-4   Cisco model 2514 displaying (left to right) 2 10Base-T LAN ports and 2 serial WAN ports.

Multi-Purpose Routers

Today's routers have evolved and although you can certainly still purchase a dedicated router, you now have the option of buying a router that has absorbed the functions of other networking devices. One common router hybrid is the layer 3 switch (defined in the next section).

> **EXCEPTION TO THE RULE: NAT**
>
> One exception to the requirement that a router must be used to forward packets between networks would be a network containing a NAT (Network Address Translation) device, which is used to forward packets between two networks.
>
> NAT devices are used to solve the problem of public IP address depletion and are normally used to forward packets from a privately addressed network to a public network. A NAT device exchanges the private source IP address in the header of the packet for a public address, and then forwards the packet to the Internet. Because the network number assigned to the NAT device's private interface must be different from the network number assigned to its public interface, the packet has been effectively routed to a different network. However, *true* routing does not take place because there is no route table on the NAT device and no routing decisions are made. Rather, NAT simply exchanges (translates) one source network number for another. Nonetheless, most consumer networking devices which incorporate NAT (as well as DHCP) are labeled "routers."
>
> Proxy servers and gateways are two other devices that perform IP address substitution and connect two networks together. But as with NAT devices, they do not actually perform routing functions.

Some routers are also capable of handling security functions. The Cisco IOS for example, has native packet filtering capabilities across the product line. Certain routers are also capable of terminating one end of a VPN solution. Still other models have built-in hubs or even built-in switched ports.

Layer 3 Switches

A layer 3 switch is a hybrid device that combines the functions of a switch and a router into one box. With a layer 3 switch, both OSI layer 2 and layer 3 headers can be examined, so a packet can be forwarded either across the local network or to another network. A layer 3 switch with VLAN (virtual LAN) capability allows for a potent one-box solution for most packet-forwarding needs.

CSU/DSUs (TSU)

A Channel Service Unit/Data Service Unit (CSU/DSU, also referred to as a TSU or Terminal Service Unit) is a piece of equipment that sits between the router and a WAN connection such as a T1 line. Although a T1 line is a digital line, the signaling methods used by the phone company are different from digital LAN signaling. The CSU/DSU conditions the signal from the router so that it can be transmitted across the public link. A CSU/DSU on the receiving side converts the signal back to a LAN signal and transmits it to the receiving router[6]. The CSU/DSU, in turn, will typically have an RJ-45 jack that the telco (telephone company) drop plugs into. Table 1-3 summarizes key networking characteristics of the equipment discussed in this section.

Table 1-3 Summary of Packet-Forwarding equipment

HARDWARE	INTRA-NETWORK FORWARDING	INTER-NETWORK FORWARDING	FORMS A COLLISION DOMAIN	FORMS A BROADCAST DOMAIN
Repeater	X			
Hub	X			
Bridge	X		X	
Switch	X		X	
Router		X	X	X
Layer 3 switch	X	X	X	X

TCP/IP Review

What follows is a quick review of TCP/IP networking concepts related to routing. It is by no means a complete primer on IP, but rather is intended to refresh your recollection of IP networking and perhaps fill in some blanks. Having said that, a fairly thorough treatment of classless networking *(subnetting, variable-length subnet masks, supernetting,* and *CIDR)* will be covered, since it is so critical to modern routing. The following topics will be addressed:

- Classful IP addressing
- Classless IP addressing
- Subnetting, variable-length subnet masks (VLSMs), supernetting, and Classless Inter-Domain Routing (CIDR)
- Public and private addressing
- IPv6
- Ports and sockets
- IP protocols related to routing
- TCP/IP utilities related to routing

IP Addressing

An IP address is the number assigned to a host that uniquely identifies the host on both the local network and all IP networks. IP addresses relate to the networking layer (layer 3) of the OSI model. The networking layer handles network addressing and routing of packets, a topic that goes to the heart of this book.

DEFINING A HOST

A host is any device with a network interface assigned an IP address. We often think of a device with an IP address as a workstation or a server but a number of devices—firewalls, printers, NAT devices, and especially routers—have one or more interfaces, each capable of being assigned to an IP address. Even layer 2 switches, which mostly deal with physical (MAC) addresses, may have IP addresses assigned to interfaces for management purposes.

A term sometimes used interchangeably with host is *node*. The two terms are very similar in that they both point to addressable devices connected to a network. However, a host is specifically related to a device with an IP address whereas a node may or may not be configured with an IP address (it might be accessed only by its MAC address or it may also have a differing type of network address such as an IPX address). The term node therefore is more generic than the term host.

IP addresses must be globally unique. No two hosts on any public IP network can have the same address. The only exception to this rule is when the network is isolated from other networks, either because it is a stand-alone network or because the network is *hidden* from other connected networks via a NAT box, gateway, or proxy server. In the latter case, a globally unique IP address is substituted for the host address's sourcing packets bound for another network (as discussed in a subsequent section called "Public versus Private IP Addressing").

In the currently deployed version of IP, IPv4, an IP address is a 32-bit binary number. For ease of readability, it is often expressed in decimal format. To make it even easier to discern an IP address, it is usually represented in *dotted* decimal format, meaning a period is inserted every 8 bits (1 byte). This results in a four-part number expressed in decimal form (see Figure 1-5).

Each of the four portions of the decimal number is an **octet**. This term is derived from the fact that each octet is 8 bits. This means that each octet can vary in value from 0-255, for a total of 256 possibilities ($2^8 = 256$). Which presents the next logical question: How many unique addresses can an IP address represent? Calculating the answer in decimal, you get the following:

```
256*256*256*256 = 4,294,967,296
```

That's over 4 billion possibilities. However, the next thing to understand about an IP address is that it represents not one, but *two* elements. An IP address represents not only a particular host, but also *the network the host is a part of*. The host portion of the address must be unique within a given network, whereas the network portion of the address must be globally unique among all possible connected networks.

Working with Binary Numbers

Not everyone is comfortable with binary numbers. Paradoxically, many nuances of IP addressing, such as subnetting, are more easily understood if the address is expressed in binary rather than decimal. That is why many of the examples in this section will have the address expressed in both decimal and binary forms.

A 32 bit IP address expressed in 3 different formats	
Binary	11001000 11001000 11001000 00000001
Decimal	336,860,601
Dotted Decimal	200.200.200.1

Figure 1-5 IP address notation.

Binary numbers are actually easy to understand because each bit represents only two possibilities: 0 or 1. Therefore, each additional bit doubles the number of possibilities:

```
1 bit  = 2 possibilities    0, 1
2 bits = 4 possibilities    00, 01, 10, 11
3 bits = 8 possibilities    000, 001, 010, 011, 100, 101, 110, 111
4 bits = 16 possibilities   0000, 0001, 0010, 0011, . . . 1111
5 bits = 32 possibilities   00000, 00001, 00010, 00011, . . . 11111
6 bits = 64 possibilities   000000, 000001, 000010, 000011, . . . 111111
7 bits = 128 possibilities  0000000, 0000001, 00000010, . . . 1111111
8 bits = 256 possibilities  00000000, 00000001, 00000010, . . . 11111111
```

That is why an octet (8 bits) represents 256 possible numbers (0–255). 2*2*2*2*2*2*2*2 = 256. A way to express the same thing in less space is 2^8, or 2 raised to the 8th power.

It is not necessary to perform any math by hand when working with IP addresses expressed in binary format. Any calculator that can convert between decimal and binary numbers, like the Windows calculator, will handle it for you. All that is necessary is to switch the calculator to scientific mode. Simply start the calculator program (Start → Programs → Accessories → Calculator), then click View → Scientific.

To convert a decimal number to binary, click the Dec button, type the number, and then click the Bin button. To convert a binary number to decimal, click the Bin button, type the number, and then click the Dec button.

For example, to convert the address the 200.200.200.1 to binary, enter each octet one at a time with the calculator set for Dec and convert to binary. The result should be the 11001000. 11001000. 11001000. 00000001.

Converting from binary to decimal is the same process in reverse. Just be sure to enter the binary numbers 8 bits (1 byte) at a time with the calculator set for Bin and convert to Dec.

You can also easily calculate powers of 2. For example to prove that 2^8 indeed equates to 256, do the following:

1. Be sure calculator is in Dec mode. Type **2**.

2. Click the x^y button once.

3. Type **8** and press Enter.

The result should be 256.

Classful Addressing

The original, and now obsolete, system for denoting the network and host address represented by an IP address was the **classful** system. You will see shortly why the system is no longer used. The classful system mandates three different types (classes) of IP addresses, whereby entire octets are tasked with representing either the network or the host portion of the address. Table 1-4 illustrates classful IP addressing.

Network Numbering

In a classful addressing system, a class A network reserves the *first* octet for network numbering while leaving the remaining three octets for host numbering. A class B address reserves the first *two* octets for network numbering and the remaining two octets for host numbering. A class C address reserves the first *three* octets for network numbers and only one octet for host numbering. How does this all work out? Have a look at Table 1-5.

In the classful system, certain bits in the first octet are "frozen"—they form a set pattern and are never altered. A class A address is defined by the first bit being frozen at 0. Because the network portion of a class A network number is confined to the first octet, this leaves 7 bits that can be manipulated to create network IDs. 2^7 equates to 128 potential class A networks. This isn't very many networks, but with three remaining octets tasked to host numbers, each network has a huge number of potential host addresses.

Class B networks have the first 2 bits of the first octet frozen at 10. Because the first two octets of a class B address form the range of network IDs, 14 bits are available. 2^{14} equates to 16,384 potential class B networks.

Class C networks have the first 3 bits of the first octet frozen at 110. Because the first three octets of a class C address form the range of network IDs, 21 bits are available. 2^{21} equates to 2,097,152 potential class C networks.

In point of fact, not every *potential* network address translates into a valid, usable network address. Certain addresses are considered reserved for other uses, as shown in Table 1-6.

Table 1-4   Classful IP Addressing

ADDRESS CLASS	DIVISION BETWEEN NETWORK AND HOST PORTION OF ADDRESS	EXAMPLES
A	**Network**.host.host.host	**10**.10.10.0
B	**Network.Network**.host.host	**128.50**.0.0
C	**Network.Network.Network**.host	**190.0.0**.0

Table 1-5 Potential Networks in the Classful System

CLASS	FIRST OCTET IN BINARY	FIRST OCTET IN DECIMAL	RANGE OF ADDRESSES	# OF POTENTIAL NETWORKS
A	**0**0000000 to **0**1111111	0 to 127	**0**.0.0.0 to **127**.0.0.0	2^7 or 128
B	**10**000000 to **10**111111	128 to 191	**128.0**.0.0 to **191.255**.0.0	2^{14} or 16,384
C	**110**00000 to **110**11111	192 to 223	**192.0.0**.0 to **223.255.255**.0	2^{21} or 2,097,152
D	**1110**0000 to **1110**1111	224 to 239	Multicast addresses	Multicast addresses
E	**1111**0000 to **1111**1111	240 to 255	Experimental	Experimental

As a general rule, all network bits set to either 0 or 1 (not including frozen bits) create invalid network addresses and explain why most of the addresses shown in Table 1-6 are reserved. Table 1-7 shows the actual number of *usable* networks.

Host Numbering

The number of hosts per network varies according to the network class. Class A networks leave three full octets for the range of host IDs for each network. That's well over 16 million hosts per network!

Class B and C networks leave two octets and one octet, respectively, for host addresses. Table 1-8 illustrates the number of hosts per network for each network class.

Table 1-6 Invalid Network IDs

NETWORK ID	COMMENT
0.0.0.0	First potential class A network address.
127.0.0.0	Last potential class A network address. Used for testing. (Host 127.0.0.1 is for loopback testing.)
128.0.0.0	First potential class B network address.
191.255.0.0	Last potential class B network address.
192.0.0.0	First potential class C network address.
223.255.255.0	Last potential class C network address.
224.0.0.0 and above	Multicast and experimental. Not used for host addressing.

Table 1-7 Usable Network IDs

CLASS	FIRST OCTET IN DECIMAL	RANGE OF ADDRESSES	# OF USABLE NETWORKS
A	1 to 126	1.0.0.0 to **126**.0.0.0	2^7 -2 or 126
B	128 to 191	**128.1**.0.0 to **191.254**.0.0	2^{14} - 2 or 16,382
C	192 to 223	**192.0.1**.0 to **223.255.254**.0	2^{21} -2 or 2,097,150

As with network addresses, not all potential host addresses are valid. The rule is that host addresses of all binary 0s or binary 1s cannot be assigned to a host. A host address of all binary 0s represents the network number itself (the 1.0.0.0), and a host address of all binary 1s represents the broadcast address for the network. So that's two reserved host addresses per network. Table 1-8 accounts for that rule with the formula $2n - 2$ where n = number of host bits.

Enumerating an IP Address

Table 1-9 illustrates the range of host addresses and the broadcast address for each of the three network classes.

Comments on the Classful Addressing Scheme

Obviously, the choice of which address class to use is paramount when you're designing a network under this system. If a class A network is assigned to a company with only 500 hosts, over 16 million addresses are wasted. Because the classful system does not allow organizations to easily share unused host addresses with other organizations, the industry got itself in a jam a few years ago over this exact issue. So many addresses had been wasted that a crisis was inevitable as the Internet took off in the early '90s. This has given rise to a new system for allocating IP addresses on the Internet. This newer *classless* system has become the predominant way of assigning addresses, and is discussed in detail shortly. The classful system is still used in certain circumstances however, and is useful for understanding basic IP addressing.

Table 1-8 Usable Range of Valid Host Addresses for Any Given Network Address

CLASS	HOST ADDRESS RANGE (IN DECIMAL)	HOST ADDRESS RANGE (IN BINARY)	# OF HOSTS PER NETWORK
A	x.0.0.1 to x.255.255.254	x.00000000.00000000.00000001 to x.11111111.11111111.11111110	2^{24} -2 or 16,777,214
B	x.x.0.1 to x.x.255.254	x.x.00000000.00000001 to x.x.11111111.11111110	2^{16} -2 or 65,534
C	x.x.x.1 to x.x.x.254	x.x.x.00000001 to x.x.x.11111110	2^8 -2 or 254

Table 1-9 Enumerating a Sample Class A, B, and C Network

CLASS	EXAMPLE NETWORK	BEGINNING HOST ADDRESS	ENDING HOST ADDRESS	BROADCAST ADDRESS
A	1.0.0.0	1.**0.0.1**	1.**255.255.254**	1.255.255.255
B	128.0.0.0	128.0.**0.1**	128.0.**255.254**	128.0.255.255
C	192.0.0.0	192.0.0.**1**	192.0.0.**254**	192.0.0.255

Public versus Private IP Addressing

As previously discussed, IP addresses used on the Internet must be unique. That requires a type of address known as a *public* IP address. This is simply a range of the IP address space reserved for public use. Isolated networks make use of an area of the IP address range known as *private* addresses. If a privately addressed network ever needs to connect to another network across the Internet, the host initiating the communication must have its private address translated to a public address (usually through NAT).

Public Addressing

In order to insure that every host's IP address is unique, a central assigning authority allocates all addresses that will be used on the Internet. These addresses are known as **public** IP addresses (depicted later in Table 1-10).

NOTE Synonymous terms for public addresses are registered, routable, external, legal, non-reusable, global, and globally unique addresses.

Table 1-10 Public and Private IP Address Range

PUBLIC IP NETWORK ADDRESS RANGE	
Class A	**1**.0.0.0 – **9**.0.0.0 and **11**.0.0.0 – **126**.0.0.0
Class B	**128.0**.0.0 – **172.15**.0.0 and **172.32**.0.0 –**191.255**.0.0
Class C	**192.0.0**.0 – **192.167.255**.0 and **192.169.0**.0 –**223.255.255**.0
PRIVATE IP NETWORK ADDRESS RANGE	
Class A	**10**.0.0.0 (1 network)
Class B	**172.16**.0.0 – **172.31**.0.0 (16 networks)
Class C	**192.168.0**.0 – **192.168.255**.0 (256 networks)

Network portion of address is in **bold**.

WHAT'S AN RFC?

An RFC, Request for Comments, is the method used to define standards for the Internet. An RFC starts life as a public document in *draft* form that is circulated in the Internet community. Each RFC has an assigned number. Once accepted as a standard, the RFC retains the same number and is still called a Request for Comments—just one of those little oddities, like doctors "practicing" medicine.

Private Addressing

RFC 1918 allocates a range of the IP address space for use by private networks. These IP addresses can never be used on the Internet. This action was taken in the mid-1990s to conserve the rapidly depleting number of globally unique IP addresses.

NOTE Synonymous terms for private addresses are non-routable, reserved, internal, local, reusable, illegal, and unregistered.

Because network packets with private addresses are never routed from one domain to another, any number of companies can use the same private addresses. Private IP addresses are free of charge and they can be reused on any number of private networks. Not so with the venerable public range of addresses, which have become rare and expensive.

The implementation of privately addressed networks is what caused the proliferation of proxy servers, NAT boxes, and gateways. These devices substitute a public address for a private address when access to the Internet is required. A small pool of public addresses can server the needs of dozens or even hundreds of privately addressed hosts (see Table 1-10).

The table indicates which range of addresses can be used for private networks. For example, the entire Class A network 10.0.0.0 is available. A Class A network allows for over 16 million hosts (**10**.0.0.1 – **10**.255.255.254). Is that enough addresses for your network? Or, you could subnet the address and create a multitudes of networks.

If you were to instead choose Class B addressing you could select the 172.16.0.0 network, for example, which allows for over 65,000 hosts (**172.16**.0.1 – **172.16**.255.254). Or you could use 172.17.0.0, or 172.18.0.0, or any network number up to 172.31.0.0. Any of those network numbers allows for 65,000+ hosts. Or again, you could subnet and create additional private network numbers.

If you have a smaller network and fewer hosts, you could get by with a private Class C network. For example, the 192.168.0.0 allows for 254 hosts (**192.168.0**.1 – **192.168.0**.254). Most consumer Internet "routers," which incorporate a NAT device for Internet access, default to a class C network (usually 192.168.0.0, 192.168.1.0, or 192.168.2.0).

If you have a routed network, should you employ several private class C addresses or a subnetted private class B address? When making such a decision, recall that one goal in network design is to keep route table entries as small as possible. Another goal is organization of all those addresses. A hierarchical networking scheme with summarized network addresses is the key. This means a private class A or B address may be the preferred choice. Or better yet, make sure you fully understand classless addressing, classless routing, and route summarization before deciding on an addressing scheme for a network. These topics are fully explored throughout this book.

Classless Addressing

With classless addressing, the traditional dividing line between the network and host portion of the address is blurred. While class*ful* addressing draws the dividing line only at octet borders, class*less* addressing draws the network/host line at any bit boundary. This allows for a highly flexible addressing scheme that does not unnecessarily waste IP addresses.

Before getting into the methods of how classless addressing is employed, it is important that you understand how the IP stack running on a host determines the network portion of an IP address. *This is critical in deciding whether a packet needs to be routed to another network.*

Distinguishing the Network ID

How does a host determine which network it is a part of? How does a source host determine the network number of a destination IP address? The traditional method for making that determination was via a technique known as the **First Octet Rule**. However, as you will see, the First Octet Rule only works in a classful environment, not in this modern world of classless addressing. That is why the industry has shifted to using something known as a **subnet mask** and/or **prefix number** to identify the network portion of an IP address. Both methods are explained here.

First Octet Rule

The First Octet Rule was the original mechanism a host employed to determine the address class of an IP address. It was noted earlier that the value of the high order bits (starting left to right) define the address class. It is exactly those bits that the First Octet Rule uses to discern the address class of the source and destination addresses of a packet.

The first octet of the address is examined and the value is used to determine the address class (A, B, or C). Specifically, up to the first four high order bits (left to right) are examined as Table 1-11 indicates.

Table 1-11 First Octet Rule for Address Class

ADDRESS CLASS	BIT PATTERN OF FIRST OCTET
A	00000000 = 0
B	10000000 = 128
C	11000000 = 192
D (multi-casting)	11100000 = 224
E (experimental)	11110000 = 240

Human beings usually recognize address class by memorizing the decimal number 128, which demarcates the beginning of the class B address range (anything under 128 is therefore class A), and the decimal numbers 192 and 223, which demarcate the class C range.

The problem with either system, however, is a built-in assumption that the value of the first octet will always dictate the network number. Unfortunately, with classless addressing redrawing the network/host dividing line *within* an octet as opposed to *between* octets, that assumption is no longer true. The address the 10.4.1.1 typically represented host address the 4.1.1. on network the 10.0.0.0. But with classless addressing, the address the 10.4.1.1 could represent host 1.1 on network the 10.4.0.0 or host .1 on network the 10.4.1.0 (you will see why shortly). The First Octet Rule fails in a classless environment because the IP will fail to understand that a packet with a destination address of say, the 10.4.1.1 may need to be routed to a different network. This is why no modern networking devices use the First Octet Rule for determining the network portion of an address.

Subnet Mask

The contemporary method for determining the network address is the **subnet mask**. A subnet mask does just what it implies: it masks (blocks) out the host portion of the address, thereby revealing just the network number. How that works will be demonstrated shortly. Why is it called a "subnet" mask and not a "network" mask? Actually, sometimes it is called a network mask. It's also referred to as the *net mask*, the *subnet address*, or simply the *mask*.

The subnet mask, like an IP address, is a 32-bit number expressed in dotted decimal format. For classful networks, it takes the form shown in Table 1-12.

NOTE A subnet mask is usually required when you're configuring an IP address on a network interface. Most networking equipment these days utilizes the subnet mask as opposed to the First Octet Rule for determining the network number. Also see the subsequent section on prefix addressing.

Table 1-12 Default Subnet Mask for Classful Networks

ADDRESS CLASS	DEFAULT SUBNET MASK
A	255.0.0.0
B	255.255.0.0
C	255.255.255.0

Figure 1-6 shows a typical IP configuration of a workstation running Windows XP.

IP uses a simple mathematical process, called ANDing, in conjunction with the subnet mask to actually derive the network number from an IP address. ANDing is a boolean logic process that says at least two things must be true before an action is taken. People actually use this type of logic in everyday life: *"If you take the car to work **and** you have time, stop by the store for groceries on your way home."* The recipient of the message will only bring home groceries if he or she has both time *and* a vehicle (*or get groceries regardless, to avoid getting into trouble with his or her mate, but that's a different branch of logic*). It's called boolean logic because a mathematician named George Boole popularized it in the 19th century. In network routing, the boolean logic goes like this: "If the IP address bit is set to 1 and the corresponding subnet mask is set to 1, then the bit is part of the network portion of the address."

Figure 1-6 A default class C subnet mask applied to a class C IP address.

The ANDing process is performed on the IP address and the subnet mask to extract the network number. To understand how this occurs, you need to convert the IP address and subnet mask to binary format. The IP stack performs a comparison of the IP address and the subnet mask, bit by bit, from left to right. The ANDing process is performed on each "bit pair" and a decision is made as to whether the bit is part of the network number or not.

In the following example, the IP address 190.1.1.1 with a mask of the 255.255.255.0 has the ANDing process performed to extract the network address:

```
Address         190        .1         .1         .1
Binary          10111110   00000001   00000001   00000001
                _____   _____   _____   _____
Subnet mask     255        .255       .255       .0
Binary          11111111   11111111   11111111   00000000
                ====================================
ANDing process  10111110   00000001   00000001   00000000
Network ID      190        .1         .1         .0
```

The process follows these steps:

1. IP compares each bit in each octet of the address to the corresponding bit in the subnet mask. To illustrate, the first bit in the 190 octet is 1. This is matched with the first bit in the first 255 octet, which also happens to be 1.

2. For each bit compared, IP says: *"If the source address bit is set to 1 AND the corresponding subnet bit is set to 1, then pass a 1 through. If not, pass a 0."*

3. If either bit is set to 0, the test fails and IP would pass a 0. An example of this is the second bit over. The second bit for the source address is set to 0. The corresponding bit in the subnet mask is set to 1. The test fails because both values are not 1 and IP passes through a 0. It's a very simple rule.

NOTE For some people it's easier to look at it this way: "If the subnet mask bit is set to 1, it passes the corresponding address bit through. If the subnet mask bit is 0, it passes a 0 regardless." The end-result is the same regardless of how you look at it.

4. The process continues until all bits in all octets have been compared. When the resulting number is converted back to decimal, the true network number of the source IP address is revealed.

When making routing decisions, IP performs the ANDing process on both the source and destination addresses, and then compares the results. If both extracted network numbers are the same, the packet is delivered locally. If the results differ, the packet is assumed to be destined for another network, and is routed accordingly. ANDing is the key element of routing decisions in today's classless networking environment and the term will be referred to throughout this guide. Be sure you understand the concept.

Prefix Notation

Prefix notation or *prefix addressing* is simply an alternate method of expressing a network's mask. Prefixes express the address masks in less space. In *prefix notation*, a single number preceded by a "/" is used instead of a 32-bit number. As you may deduce from Table 1-13, prefix notation simply reflects the number of bits turned on in the mask. Notice the default mask in the table expressed in binary form. The first three octets of 255 each represent all binary bits turned on; 24 bits turned on—thus the prefix of /24.

By the same token, a class A mask would be represented as /8 in prefix notation (the 255.0.0.0) and a class B mask would be /16 (the 255.255.0.0). A very simple system. Some operating systems such as Windows XP allow you to enter the network mask as a prefix number in lieu of a subnet mask. Public WAN carriers also commonly use prefix notation. If you are assigned a network number by your ISP, the mask will usually be notated in prefix format.

NOTE Prefix notation is also known as *slash notation, prefix masking, prefix address,* and *prefix routing,* just to name a few.

Classless Addressing and Routing

In discussing classful and classless addressing, we are running smack dab into the main topic of this book: network routing. Not all routing protocols—the protocols that build route tables—support classless addressing. This is because such protocols don't support the use of subnet masks. Without the knowledge of where the network/host dividing line occurs, classful routing protocols are relegated to supporting only classful A, B, and C networks, and even then only for privately addressed networks. Some public class A network IDs have been broken up and distributed to multiple organizations. Classful routing protocols cannot support this classless modification. This topic is discussed in detail in Chapter 4.

Table 1-13   Three Methods for Displaying the Same Class C Subnet Mask

Expressed in decimal	255.255.255.0
Expressed in binary	11111111.11111111.11111111.00000000
Expressed in prefix notation	/24

The Manifestations of Classless Addressing–Subnetting, VLSM, Supernetting, and CIDR

If the concepts of subnetting, VLSMs, supernetting, and CIDR have daunted you in the past, rest easy. They are each just slightly different manifestations of the basic concept of classless IP addressing, which is simply the process of drawing the network/host dividing line at *bit* boundaries as opposed to *octet* boundaries. Drawing the network/host line between any 2 bits breaks all the old rules—something that is always fun to do.

As mentioned earlier, it's important that you understand classless *addressing* in order to understand classless *routing*. To that end, a complete discussion of each of the classless addressing methods is covered here. If you take the time to study the material in the following pages, you will understand subnetting, VLSMs, supernetting, and CIDR like never before.

Let's start with a quick definition of each classless addressing technique, followed by specifics.

Subnetting in Brief

Subnetting is the act of taking a single IP network ID and subdividing it to create two or more network IDs. Subnetting is accomplished by relocating the network/host dividing line to the *right* from its originally assigned position—into the area of the portion of the address representing the host IDs. As the line moves to the right, bit-by-bit, additional network IDs are created as host IDs are sacrificed. That's the trade-off. The further the line is moved to the right, the more networks (subnets) are created and the fewer the number of hosts per network. The "borrowing" of host bits is accomplished by altering the original mask of the network ID. A custom mask is how the ANDing process discerns the subnets created by the bit borrowing process. The subnetting process works the same regardless of whether the original address is classful or classless.

VLSMs in Brief

In standard subnetting, the same subnet mask used to derive the additional subnets is applied to *all* hosts residing on *all* the subnets. With variable-length subnet masks (VLSMs), the subnet mask can be altered (*varied*) again for one or more of the subnets. In effect, this is sub-subnetting. The reason for this apparent insanity is the same as it always is when you're submerged in the world of classless addressing—namely, to provide the utmost in addressing utilization. A standard subnetted class C address may yield say, two subnets with 62 hosts per subnet. But what if one network requires 62 hosts and another network requires say, only two host IDs? In that case, one of the two subnets could itself be subnetted further, creating additional networks with fewer hosts per subnet. One of the two subnets remains the same and keeps the same custom mask, while the other subnet is further subdivided into additional networks with a smaller number of hosts per network and thus a differing mask. That's VLSM in a nutshell.

Supernetting in Brief

Supernetting is simply the reverse of standard subnetting. Instead of moving the network/host dividing line to the *right*—creating *additional* networks with *fewer* hosts per network—the line is moved to the *left*—creating *fewer* networks with a *greater* number of hosts per network. This technique is applied to contiguous blocks of network IDs to create a single network number with the combined total of all host IDs that were originally spread out among several addresses.

CIDR in Brief

Classless Inter-Domain Routing (CIDR) is simply the concept of subnetting/ supernetting and even VLSM techniques applied at the address assignment level, where ISPs and large organizations receive an allotment of addresses. The assigning authority no longer wastes entire classful addresses by handing out say, a class B address with 16,000+ host IDs. Instead, what was a class A, B, or C address is now treated as simply a 32-bit number whose network/host dividing line can be drawn at any point. With CIDR, every public network ID is treated the same, regardless of its previous class distinction. A CIDR address "block" is now assigned with the network/host dividing line determined by the requirements of the organization receiving the address. The organization receives the exact number of addresses it needs—no more, no less.

A pleasant side effect of allocating addresses in this manner allows the minimization of the number of route table entries on Internet routers. Blocks of CIDR assigned addresses can be summarized into a single route table entry, regardless of the number of networks actually assigned. The concept of route summarization goes hand-in-hand with classless addressing techniques. Network summarization is given extensive coverage in Chapter 4 on page 119.

Subnetting in Detail

The basic purpose of subnetting is to derive additional networks from a single network address. Subnetting is accomplished by altering the current subnet mask (prefix number) for the network. The current mask may be a classful A, B, or C mask, or it may be whatever mask was assigned when the address was allocated. Additional networks are created by borrowing bits from the **host** portion of the IP address to create additional network IDs. When a network address is subnetted into multiple networks, the term *subnet* is often used to refer to the additional network addresses created. The result of subnetting is that you gain additional network addresses—at the expense of fewer hosts per network.

Why Subnet?

There are many answers to this question. If the originally assigned network ID is a public address, subnetting may be employed to efficiently allocate this rare and valuable resource. A customer requiring several public network addresses may be able to obtain (for a price) a single address and then subnet it into the required number of networks. In fact, with CIDR addressing, it is fully expected the allocated address will be subnetted.

> **NOTE** Bear in mind that with the popularity of NAT, there is less of a need to subnet public addresses at the organizational level. Just a single or a few public addresses can represent many privately addressed hosts. ISPs, however, routinely subnet their CIDR assigned public addresses to satisfy the demands of their customers.

The other popular reason to subnet (and to variably subnet) is to create a hierarchical addressing scheme for your internetwork. This is true for both public as well as privately addressed networks. In a hierarchically addressed network, blocks of network addresses are allocated in such a manner that a single summarized address can represent many networks. Such an addressing scheme provides several benefits:

- Smaller route tables
- Quicker convergence of route tables
- Less taxing on many different network resources (router CPU and memory, network bandwidth, and so on)
- Much easier to relate an IP address to a specific geographical location and even a specific category of hosts (workstation, printer, router, and so on)

The preceding items will of course make more sense as your knowledge of routing grows. The benefits of summarizing network addresses is a theme this book will frequently return to.

> **NOTE** If there is a single topic in networking technology that most intimidates "beginners," it's the process of subnetting. The following treatment of how to subnet has proven to help time and time again when the author is teaching networking classes.

How to Subnet

You must take the following items into consideration when subnetting:

- Determine the total number of subnets needed. This includes planning for future networks.
- Determine the total number of hosts that each subnet must support now and in the future.
- Define a custom subnet mask that will support the required number of hosts for that subnet.
- Derive the subnet IDs.

- Derive the host IDs for each subnet.
- Derive the broadcast address for each subnet.

You accomplish this process in three steps, as described in this section. The concept of subnetting is far more easily illustrated by looking at the subnet mask in its binary form. Therefore, the examples in this section show the subnet mask in both decimal and binary formats.

Step 1: Create additional network numbers by using a custom subnet mask
This example assumes a company has been assigned the public address range 192.100.50.0 /24. The company wishes to create two smaller subnets connected by a router to reduce broadcast traffic. Figure 1-7 depicts the address as asigned. Note the dividing line separating the network portion of the address from the host portion of the address. This is the default network/host dividing point for a /24 address range.

Borrowing Bits

Creating additional network IDs involves moving the network/host dividing line to the right—into the host portion of the address. In effect, you are removing bits from the host portion of the address and reassigning them for subnet duty. The more bits you borrow, the more subnet IDs you create. *The new subnet IDs are formed strictly from the combinations of the borrowed bits.*

Figure 1-8 shows how 2 bits are borrowed from the host ID. The subnet mask is altered to create the subnets. Let's see how many networks we can create from 2 bits.

The first row shows the original dividing line of the address. In the second row, 2 bits have been borrowed from the fourth octet, moving them into a new field called the **Subnet ID**. In the third row, the borrowed bits have been turned on (set to 1). This is how IP knows the dividing line has been moved to the right. IP (specifically, the ANDing process) always identifies ON bits in the mask (1's) as network addresses and OFF bits in the mask (0's) as host addresses.

Note the Subnet ID field. It's made up solely of the borrowed bits. This "field" is simply there to illustrate the place where the subnet IDs are derived from. IP just sees the address as one long 32-bit binary address.

	1st octet	2nd octet	3rd octet	4th octet
IP address	192	.100	.50	.0
Default subnet mask in decimal	255.	.255	.255	.0
Default subnet mask in binary	11111111	11111111	11111111	00000000
	NETWORK			**HOST**

Figure 1-7   Default network/host dividing line for a /24 address range.

	1st octet	2nd octet	3rd octet	4th octet	
Default mask	11111111	1111111	1111111	00000000	
Borrowing	11111111	1111111	1111111	00	000000
Turn bits on	11111111	1111111	1111111	11	000000
	NETWORK ID			**Subnet ID**	**HOST ID**

Figure 1-8   Borrowing bits redraws the network/host dividing line.

The original network field always remains unchanged, regardless of how many subnets are created. Again, all subnet addresses will be derived from the subnet field. Given that fact, one wonders what use the original network ID has. The 192.100.50.0 will never again represent any *one* network, once the subnetting process has been instituted. However, the 192.100.50.0 can later be used to represent *all* the subnets created from it in the route tables of certain routers. In fact, this is an advantageous thing to do in order to reduce the number of route table entries (also called route summarization or aggregation).

Determining the Custom Subnet Mask

The custom subnet mask is determined by simply converting the modified fourth octet of the mask (which is *always* comprised of 8 bits, regardless of their purpose) back to decimal (see Figure 1-9).

As you can see in the figure, nothing has changed in the first three octets. In the fourth octet, the binary number 11000000 converts to 192. Thus, **255.255.255.192** is the new subnet mask for this network, replacing the default 255.255.255.0 mask. The mask 255.255.255.192 will be used by *all* hosts on *all* subnets of 192.100.50.0. That's standard subnetting. Now you know why it's easier to understand this in binary. It's hard to draw a dividing line on the decimal number 192. But in fact, that octet now partially represents the network ID and partially represents the host IDs. It's weird, but it works. This will be proven in the next step.

	1st octet	2nd octet	3rd octet	4th octet	
From 3rd row of previous table	11111111	11111111	11111111	11	000000
	NETWORK ID			**Subnet ID**	**HOST ID**
Decimal	255	.255	.255	.192	

Figure 1-9   Altered subnet mask converted back to a decimal number reveals a mask of 255.255.255.192.

NOTE You should follow along by performing the conversions yourself. It's very easy. If using Windows, just use the calculator applet in scientific mode (click View → Scientific).

As you can see, the mechanics of creating a custom subnet mask is relatively easy. Just remember that you always borrow from the first octet representing the host portion of the address. For a class C address, that is the fourth octet. For a class B address, you would start borrowing from the third octet, and continue borrowing into the fourth octet if required. For class A addresses, start borrowing from the second octet.

Step 2: Determine the Subnet IDs

Now that the new subnet mask has been determined, the next task is to derive the actual subnet IDs. The total number of subnets created is based on the possible combinations of the borrowed bits. Binary numbering only allows for two possible values for each digit: 0 or 1. In the example with 2 borrowed bits, there are four possible combinations. Both bits can be turned OFF (00), both bits can be turned ON (11), one bit can be OFF and one ON (01), and vice versa (10).

NOTE You can also do the math with the calculator by setting it to binary mode, and then start with 00, add 1, and continuously add 1 to the result (just remember that the calculator won't display leading zeros).

```
00            01            10            11
```

Although four is the maximum number of potential subnets in this example, there is a catch. Subnet addresses of all binary 0s or all binary 1s are reserved addresses and can't normally be used.[7] Therefore, you always lose two potential network IDs when you subnet (and all the host addresses associated with them). So in this example, you are left with two valid network numbers to work with (now you know why you started by borrowing 2 bits and not just 1 bit):

```
00            01            10            11
```

Perform the following steps to determining the subnet IDs:

1. Combine each valid combination of subnet bits with the remaining bits in the octet.

2. Convert the number back to decimal.

3. Append the result to the original network address.

Figure 1-10 illustrates this process.

4th octet			Subnets
Borrowed bits	Remainder of host ID	Combine and convert to decimal	Resulting subnet IDs
~~00~~	~~000000~~	Reserved	~~192.100.50.0~~
01	000000	01000000 = 64	192.100.50.64
10	000000	10000000 = 128	192.100.50.128
~~11~~	~~000000~~	Reserved	~~192.100.50.192~~

Figure 1-10   The process of determining the subnet IDs.

Determining the Subnet IDs

The first column of the table reflects the possible combinations of the 2 bits borrowed from the host portion of the address. The second column simply lists the remaining untouched bits of the host ID. The third column of the table combines the borrowed bits back with the remaining host ID bits and converts the resulting number to decimal. The fourth column reflects the newly created subnet IDs. It takes longer to explain it than to do it.

If you were not familiar with subnetting, you could easily mistake those subnet addresses for host addresses. To the "naked eye" those addresses look like references to host .64 and host .128 on the 192.100.50.0 network. However, they are not *host* addresses anymore. They are *subnet* addresses, otherwise known as *network IDs*. The .64 marks the beginning of the 192.100.50.64 network. The .128 marks the beginning of the 192.100.50.128 network. Network address 192.100.50.0 is now invalid and will never again be used except as previously noted as an optional summary address for routing.

> **NOTE** Remember a cardinal rule of subnetting when converting binary numbers to decimal: Always convert the *entire* octet. Even if bits have been borrowed from an octet to create subnet IDs, you *always* treat the octet as a whole when converting to decimal!

Determining How Many Bits to Borrow

This example arbitrarily borrowed 2 bits and happened to end up with two networks. In reality, you will be trying to create a specific number of subnets. The formula normally used is as follows:

```
2ⁿ - 2, (where n = the number of bits borrowed)
```

For example if you borrowed 3 bits, the formula would be (2^3 - 2 or 2*2*2 - 2), which is 4. Borrowing 3 bits yields six valid subnets.

Step 3: Determine the host IDs and broadcast ID for each subnet

Next, the host IDs belonging to each network are determined. Originally, this class C network number was capable of supporting 254 hosts (190.100.50.1 – 190.100.50.**254**). However, many host addresses are rendered invalid once subnetting occurs, so it's important to understand which host addresses remain and which subnet they belong to.

Begin by ascertaining the total number of host addresses that will be available for each subnet. The range of host addresses available is derived from the remaining bits in the host portion of the address. In this example, 6 bits remain. You can quickly calculate the total number of hosts per subnet with the formula:

```
2ⁿ - 2   (where n = the number of remaining bits)
```

NOTE This is the same formula used to determine the number of valid network numbers for a given subnet mask.

In this case, the formula plays out like this: 2^6 -2 or 2*2*2*2*2*2 - 2 = 62. The reason that 2 is subtracted from the total is because, like a subnet address, a host address of all binary 0s or all binary 1s is reserved. All host bits set to 0 represent the subnet ID itself. All bits set to 1 represent the broadcast address for that particular subnet.

It's quite easy to calculate the host addresses for each subnet. Begin by calculating the first valid host ID for the first network ID. The first host ID is just one number higher than the network number (see Figure 1-11).

Notice that the last host ID has all six host bits turned on except one. If you study the figure for a moment one thing should start to jump out at you. Calculating host IDs is easy. The first ID is just the subnet number plus one, and the last host ID is just two shy of the next subnet, the .128. The broadcast ID is just one short of the next subnet ID. It always works out that way. Now calculate the host IDs for the .128 subnet (see Figure 1-12).

Figure 1-13 summarizes the subnetted network.

192.100.50.64 network				
Host ID	4th octet in binary Subnet ID	Host ID	Convert to decimal	Complete host address
1st host ID	01	000001	.65	192.100.50.65
2nd host ID	01	000010	.66	192.100.50.66
3rd host ID	01	000011	.67	192.100.50.67
4th host ID	01	000100	.68	192.100.50.68
And so on …				
61st host ID	01	111101	.125	192.100.50.125
62nd host ID	01	111110	.126	192.100.50.126
Broadcast ID	01	111111	.127	192.100.50.127

Figure 1-11 Determining the host IDs for the .64 subnet.

192.100.50.128 network				
Host ID	4th octet in binary Subnet ID Host ID		Convert to decimal	Complete host address
1st host ID	01	000001	.129	192.100.50.129
2nd host ID	01	000010	.130	192.100.50.130
3rd host ID	01	000011	.131	192.100.50.131
4th host ID	01	000100	.132	192.100.50.132
And so on ...				
61st host ID	01	111101	.189	192.100.50.189
62nd host ID	01	111110	.190	192.100.50.190
Broadcast ID	01	111111	.191	192.100.50.191

Figure 1-12   Determining the host IDs for the .128 subnet.

Subnetting Summed Up

Here is a summary of the basic steps of subnetting:

- Determine the total number of subnets needed. This includes planning for future networks.

- Determine the total number of hosts that each subnet must support now and in the future.

- Define a custom subnet mask that will support the required number of subnets and hosts per subnet.

- Derive the subnet IDs.

- Derive the host IDs for each subnet.

- Derive the broadcast address for each subnet.

Subnet 1		Subnet 2	
Original network address:	192.100.50.0	Original network address:	192.100.50.0
Custom subnet mask:	255.255.255.192	Custom subnet mask:	255.255.255.192
Subnet address 1:	192.100.50.64	Subnet Address 2:	192.100.50.128
Beginning host address:	192.100.100.65	Beginning host address:	192.100.100.129
Ending host address:	192.100.100.126	Ending host address:	192.100.100.190
Total valid hosts:	62	Total valid hosts:	62
Broadcast address:	192.100.100.127	Broadcast address:	192.100.100.191
The host IDs .1-.63 and .193-.254 are gone. They are rendered invalid because they are now owned by reserved network IDs.			

Figure 1-13   The results of subnetting the 190.100.50.0 with a 255.255.255.192 mask.

The Proof Is in the "ANDing"

If you have any doubts about how the seemingly convoluted process of subnetting works, you can prove that it works beyond the shadow of a doubt by performing the ANDing process.

Here's an example. Host the 190.100.50.65 sends a packet to host the 190.100.50.129:

```
Source address   190        .100       .50        .65
Binary           11000000   01100100   00110010   01000001
                 _____   _____   _____   _____
Subnet mask      255        .255       .255       .192
Binary           11111111   11111111   11111111   11000000
                 =====================================
ANDing process   11000000   01100100   00110010   01000000
Network ID       190        .100       .50        .64


Target address   190        .100       .50        .129
Binary           11000000   01100100   00110010   10000001
                 _____   _____   _____   _____
Subnet mask      255        .255       .255       .192
Binary           11111111   11111111   11111111   11000000
                 =====================================
ANDing process   11000000   01100100   00110010   10000000
Network ID       190        .100       .50        .128
```

Which subnet will IP determine the destination host is on? The destination host belongs to a different network, so the packets must be routed. Remember that the ANDing process masks out the host portion of the address, leaving just the network portion. *Before* subnetting ANDing would have determined that the target host was on the same network. *After* subnetting ANDing shows the target address as being part of a different network.

Subnetting and Routing

Given that the ANDing process of IP will discern that subnets of the 192.150.1.0 now exist, packets destined for a differing subnet must always be routed. Let's underscore that. When you subnet a network, a router *must* be present to forward packets between the subnets.

Variable Length Subnet Masks (VLSMs) in Detail

VLSMs are an extension to subnetting. Put simply, VLSMs allow a subnetted network to be subnetted again . . . and again . . . and again. In the previous section on subnetting, a class C address was subdivided into two networks and both subnets were assigned the *same* subnet mask. All hosts on both subnets used the same mask. This is not mandatory however. In real life scenarios, not all networks require a similar number of hosts for each subnet. This is where VLSMs come in. By varying the subnet mask of one of the subnets a second time (by moving the network/host dividing line further to the right), additional subnets are created, albeit with a smaller number of hosts per network. VLSMs allow for extremely granular control over the number of hosts per subnet. Just bear in mind that for each additional subnet created by a VLSM, a router is required to forward packets to and from the subnet.

As with standard subnetting, the more bits you borrow when varying a subnet mask, the more subnet IDs you create and the fewer hosts per subnet. To illustrate this concept, a class B address will be used as an example. Let's say an ISP has been assigned the class B address 170.1.0.0 /16.[8] The conventional (classful) dividing line between network/host is between the second and third octets (255.255.0.0). It is unlikely the ISP probably has just one customer with a network requiring 65,536 hosts. Rather, the ISP probably has multiple customers with networks requiring far fewer hosts. Therefore, the address will be subnetted.

It is quite common to see class B addresses subnetted with a class C subnet mask (255.255.255.0 or /24). An entire octet is borrowed for subnet IDs, leaving an entire octet for host addresses (see Figure 1-14). This alteration renders 254 subnets, with 254 hosts per subnet ($2^8 - 2$ or $2*2*2*2*2*2*2*2 - 2 = 254$).

Alas, the Internet service provider is not satisfied. The ISP has a large number of point-to-point fractional T1 links connecting to its customer base. These links require only two host addresses per network. There is no way the ISP is going to waste 254 valuable host IDs on each point-to-point network. Variable length subnet masks to the rescue. The ISP can burn just one of its 254 subnets, subdividing it again, thus creating a bunch of sub-subnets. To employ this strategy, the selected subnet will have its mask altered once again to achieve the required result.

Original address: 170.1.0.0/16			
Subnet ID	Subnet Mask in Octet Format	Subnet Mask in Prefix Notation	Host ID range
~~170.1.0.0~~	Reserved		
170.1.1.0	255.255.255.0	/24	170.1.1.1 - 170.1.1.254
170.1.2.0	255.255.255.0	/24	170.1.2.1 - 170.1.2.254
170.1.3.0	255.255.255.0	/24	170.1.3.1 - 170.1.3.254
And so on . . .			
170.1.253.0	255.255.255.0	/24	170.1.253.1 - 170.1.253.254
170.1.254.0	255.255.255.0	/24	170.1.254.1 - 170.1.254.254
~~170.1.255.0~~	Reserved		

Figure 1-14   Standard subnetting of the 170.1.0.0 renders 254 subnets.

NOTE How many additional bits should be borrowed to create the greatest number of subnets possible while providing just two hosts per subnet? . . . (*Jeopardy music plays*) . . . Well, only two *host* bits are required for a two-host subnet ($2^2 - 2 = 2$), therefore six bits can safely be borrowed to create subnet IDs. Borrowing six bits from the fourth octet will render 62 subnets ($2^6 - 2 = 62$). Six borrowed bits also equates to a new subnet mask of 255.255.255.252 (fourth octet: 11111100 = 252). This is the same as a /30 prefix. Let's pick on say, the 24.1.253.0 subnet to perform this diabolical procedure.

Figure 1-15 shows how the subnets of the 170.1.253.0/30 are created.

Note that once a subnet has been further subnetted, all subnets (or sub-sub-nets, if you will) are valid. The rule of no subnets with all 0s or 1s was already obeyed when the original subnets were created. All subnets of a subnet are usable addresses. However, the host addresses of sub-subnets still must obey the rule (no all-binary 0s or 1s in host ID).

The fully enumerated subnet is displayed in Figure 1-16.

To see the big picture, examine the entire assigned address range of the revised allocation for the 170.1.0.0 shown in Figure 1-17.

There is no end to how many times the network can be subdivided. Any other subnet ID could be subdivided just as the 170.1.253.0 just was. Any prefix number higher than /24 could be used depending on how many host IDs per subnet are required. Once sub-subnetted, the subnets could be variably subnetted yet again, as long as bits remain to be borrowed.

Subnet 170.1.253.0 /30			
4th Octet			Subnets
Borrowed Bits	Remainder of Host ID	Combine and Convert to Decimal	Resulting Subnet Addresses
000000	00	00000000 = .0	170.1.253.0
000001	00	00000100 = .4	170.1.253.4
000010	00	00001000 = .8	170.1.253.8
000011	00	00001100 = .12	170.1.253.12
000100	00	00010000 = .16	170.1.253.16
000101	00	00010100 = .20	170.1.253.20
And so on …			
111100	00	11110000 = .240	170.1.253.240
111101	00	11110100 = .244	170.1.253.244
111110	00	11111000 = .248	170.1.253.248
111111	00	11111100 = .252	170.1.253.252

Figure 1-15   Variably subnetting the 170.1.253.0 with a /30 prefix.

170.1.253.0 /30			
Subnet ID	Subnet Mask in Octet Format	Subnet Mask in Prefix Notation	Host ID Range
170.1.253.0	255.255.255.252	/30	170.1.253.1 - 170.1.253.2 (.3 is broadcast ID for subnet)
170.1.253.4	255.255.255.252	/30	170.1.253.5 - 170.1.253.6 (.7 is broadcast ID for subnet)
170.1.253.8	255.255.255.252	/30	170.1.253.9 - 170.1.253.10 (.11 is broadcast ID for subnet)
170.1.253.12	255.255.255.252	/30	170.1.253.13 - 170.1.253.14 (.15 is broadcast ID for subnet)
170.1.253.16	255.255.255.252	/30	170.1.253.17 - 170.1.253.18 (.19 is broadcast ID for subnet)
170.1.253.20	255.255.255.252	/30	170.1.253.21 - 170.1.253.22 (.23 is broadcast ID for subnet)
etc . . .			
170.1.253.244	255.255.255.252	/30	170.1.253.245 - 170.1.253.246 (.247 is broadcast ID for subnet)
170.1.253.248	255.255.255.252	/30	170.1.253.249 - 170.1.253.250 (.251 is broadcast ID for subnet)
170.1.253.252	255.255.255.252	/30	170.1.253.253 - 170.1.253.254 (.255 is broadcast ID for subnet)

Figure 1-16   Enumerating the 170.1.253.0 subnet.

Riding the Hierarchical Highway

As you can start to see, VLSM notation makes it possible to create the aforementioned *hierarchical* structure of network addresses. You can allocate a very few network addresses with a large number of hosts per network to say, one whole division of an organization, or a state, or a branch office, for example. Then, the addresses can be further subnetted to allocate networks to say, a subdivision, a locale, floors of a branch office, and so on. Moreover, the real power of a hierarchical addressing scheme is that if architected carefully, the various subnets can be aggregated together into a very few summary addresses entered in the route tables of the routers. You will really see the power of VLSMs when this topic is covered in Chapter 4. But this same theme is echoed in the subsequent section on CIDR addressing.

Revised allocation for the 170.1.0.0				
Subnet ID	Subnet mask in octet format	Subnet mask in prefix notation	Sub-subnets	Host ID range
~~170.1.0.0~~	Reserved			
170.1.1.0	255.255.255.0	/24		170.1.1.1 - 170.1.1.254
170.1.2.0	255.255.255.0	/24		170.1.2.1 - 170.1.2.254
170.1.3.0	255.255.255.0	/24		170.1.3.1 - 170.1.3.254
And so on . . .				
170.1.253.0	255.255.252.0	/30	170.1.253.0	170.1.253.1 - 170.1.253.2
			170.1.253.4	170.1.253.5 - 170.1.253.6
			170.1.253.8	170.1.253.9 - 170.1.253.10
			170.1.253.12	170.1.253.13 - 170.1.253.14
			170.1.253.16	170.1.253.17 - 170.1.253.18
			170.1.253.20	170.1.253.21 - 170.1.253.22
			And so on . . .	
			170.1.253.244	170.1.253.245 - 170.1.253.246
			170.1.253.248	170.1.253.249 - 170.1.253.250
			170.1.253.252	170.1.253.252 - 170.1.253.254
170.1.254.0	255.255.255.0	/24		170.1.254.1 - 170.1.254.254
~~170.1.255.0~~	Reserved			

Figure 1-17   Variably subnetted network.

Supernetting in Detail

Supernetting is the reverse of subnetting. With supernetting, rather than dividing one network address into multiple subnets, you instead *combine* multiple network addresses into one large network. Why would you want to do that? Take the example of a company needing a single network that can accommodate 1,000 public host addresses. Before the concept of supernetting (and later CIDR), the company had the limited choice of either acquiring a class B network address and wasting more than 65,000 host addresses, or being assigned *four* class C addresses and creating four networks connected by routers. With supernetting, those four class C addresses could be combined into a single network ID by moving the network/host dividing line to the *left* rather than to the right.

Before CIDR addressing was introduced, supernetting obviously had value. CIDR notation negates the need for supernetting public addresses however, because the old class limitations no longer apply. The assigning authority simply allocates an address (even what was once a class C address) with the prefix set to accommodate the number of networks and hosts required by an organization.

CIDR in Detail

Although it is the final classless addressing technique explored here, CIDR (Classless Inter-Domain Routing) is where classless addressing actually starts in today's world. It's only mentioned at the end of the discussion because CIDR embodies the previously mentioned classless addressing methods— with the only exception being that these methods are carried out at the level where Internet addresses are assigned rather than at the organization level. Here's how it works.

The Internet agency responsible for assigning network addresses is called the NIC (Internet Network Information Center) or InterNIC. Traditionally, the InterNIC worked through its subsidy, IANA (Internet Assigned Numbers Authority) to administer the addresses. As the Internet has grown larger and larger, private regional entities have taken on the responsibility of assigning addresses. In America, the local agency allocating network addresses is ARIN (American Registry for Internet Numbers). To avoid confusion, this book just uses the generic term "assigning authority" when referring to the agency that assigns network addresses.

CIDR supports the concept of classless networking between networks, or more accurately between routing domains—thus the moniker *Inter-Domain Routing*. A domain is defined as a network or networks under a single administrative control. For example, CIDR allows organization A and organization B to be assigned classless IP addresses and successfully route packets between the two organizations (domains).

Problems Solved by CIDR

CIDR was created to solve two problems: IP addresses were being handed out in an inefficient, wasteful manner, and the routing tables on the backbone routers were growing frightfully large.

CIDR solves the first problem, wasted address allocation, by employing the same classful rule-breaking method mentioned in this book over and over again—namely the manipulation of the traditional network/host dividing line of an address. In fact, the RFC that specifies CIDR addressing throws out the entire classful addressing architecture. Rather than continue to hand out inefficiently sized class A, B, or C network addresses, CIDR allocates an address or group of addresses sized to fit the actual needs of the requesting organization. No more class A, B, or C addresses!

CIDR addresses the problem of bloated route tables as well. Traditionally, the powerful routers that form the core of the Internet needed to know the route to every possible network. As the Internet has grown, so has the size of the routing tables. This inhibits performance. CIDR deals with this issue by aggregating multiple network addresses into a single entry in the routing table. The process, known as route **aggregation** or route **summarization**, reduces the size and complexity of the routing tables. This concept has been alluded to several times in this chapter and will be fully illustrated in Chapter 4 with several examples. A little more foundational material is required before we can get into the nitty gritty details of summarization, which is why we keep making you wait. For now though, think of an analogy to a housing subdivision that is accessed only from one main road. There are dozens of streets (routes) within the subdivision, but only one way (route) to get to the sub-division itself. Therefore, to get to the subdivision, you need only know the location of the access road. Only upon arriving at the entrance to the subdivision is a more specific map required.

Putting CIDR to Work

Let's be a fly on the wall and track the assignment of a CIDR address from its origination to your friendly neighborhood ISP. This example uses a real public address assigned to fictitious organizations.

Any organization connecting directly to the core of the Internet receives an IP address allocation directly from a previously described assigning authority. Organizations not connecting to the backbone will likely receive an assignment from a directly connected entity that is parceling out ranges of addresses it obtained from the assigning authority. To illustrate how the process works, let's assume an example where a small, local ISP requires about 200 total IP addresses which will be mostly allocated as a number of small, two-host networks for dial-up and leased-line accounts.

This small ISP (MinniMe) is going to receive its address allocation from a medium-sized regional ISP (MiddleMan), which in turn received its allocation from a large ISP (Mammoth) connecting to the Internet core. The large ISP has received its allocation from the assigning authority. We will start at the top of this food chain to see how a CIDR address is efficiently allocated from day one.

Mammoth received an allocation of over 65,000 addresses from the assigning authority. The allocation took the form of 44.0.0.0/16. Before CIDR, this address would have been designated a class A address of over 16 million addresses, and possibly assigned to a single organization where most of the address space would have remained unused. With CIDR notation, the assigning authority allocates just the range of this address space that the customer requires; about 65K addresses.

As you can see from examining Table 1-14, the 44.0.0.0 is used far more efficiently under CIDR. The address, as allocated in the table, satisfies the needs of 256 customers needing a 65K allotment of addresses.

The fun doesn't stop there however. Table 1-15 further illustrates that it is not necessary to apply the same prefix to each portion of the 44.0.0.0.

NOTE The fourth column of the tables in this section on CIDR enumerates the total address space for the given address range rather than the total number of networks and hosts per network. When dealing with CIDR addresses, or any scope of addresses that are subject to varying prefixes, its easier to just refer to the total addressable space, because any subnet within the range is subject to further sub-division.

Of course, varying the mask of a root address smacks of VLSMs (variable-length subnet masks), and indeed the principals of VLSMs are in effect here. Strictly speaking, it's unavoidable. Mammoth is certainly not going to leave its allocation of 44.0.0.0/16 untouched. In order to satisfy the requirements of its customers, the mask of the address will be altered. In this example, Mammoth's customer, MiddleMan, requires about 1,000 addresses for its customers. Therefore, the allocation of Mammoth's 44.0.0.0/16 might look like what is reflected in Table 1-16.

Table 1-14 CIDR Allocation of the 44.0.0.0

ASSIGNMENT	CUSTOMER	ADDRESS RANGE	TOTAL ADDRESSES
44.0.0.0/16	Mammoth	44.0.0.1–44.0.255.254	65,534
44.1.0.0/16	Customer 2	44.1.0.1–44.1.255.254	65,534
44.2.0.0/16	Customer 3	44.2.0.1–44.2.255.254	65,534
And so on . . .			
44.255.0.0/16	Customer 256	44.255.0.1–44.255.255.254	65,534

Table 1-15 CIDR Flexibility in Allocating an Address

ASSIGNMENT	CUSTOMER	ADDRESS RANGE	TOTAL ADDRESSES
44.0.0.0/16	Mammoth	44.0.0.1–44.0.255.254	65,534
44.1.0.0/16	Customer 2	44.1.0.1–44.1.255.254	65,534
44.2.0.0/17	Customer 3	44.2.0.1–44.2.127.254	32,766
44.2.128.0/17	Customer 4	44.2.128.1–44.2.255.254	32,766
44.3.0.0/19	Customer 5	44.3.0.1–44.3.31.254	8,192
44.3.32.0/19	Customer 6	44.3.32.1–44.3.63.254	8,192
44.3.64.0/19	Customer 7	44.3.64.1–44.3.95.254	8,192
And so on . . .			
44.3.224.0/19	Customer x	44.3.224.1–44.3.255.254	8,192
44.4.0.0 /16	Customer y	44.4.0.1–44.4.255.254	65,534
Etc.			

Again, the allocated address can be subdivided into whatever balance of networks/hosts per network is required—within the limits of the total addressable space. Bear in mind that no matter how Mammoth slices up the 44.0.0.0/16, it will only be necessary for routers on the Internet to keep a single entry (44.0.0.0/16) to properly route packets to any of the subnets of this address. Only Mammoth's routers will need to enumerate the subnets in order to deliver packets correctly. This concept will be fully explained in Chapter 4.

Table 1-16 Mammoth's 44.0.0.0/16 Allocation

ASSIGNMENT	CUSTOMER	ADDRESS RANGE	TOTAL ADDRESSES
44.0.4.0/22	MiddleMan	44.0.4.1–44.0.7.254	1,022
44.0.8.0/22	Customer 2	44.0.8.1–44.0.11.254	1,022
44.0.12.0/22	Customer 3	44.0.12.1–44.0.15.254	1,022
44.0.16.0/25	Customer 4	44.0.16.1–44.0.16.127	126
44.0.16.128/25	Customer 5	44.0.16.1–44.0.16.127	126
And so on . . .			
44.0.19.128/25	Customer x	44.0.19.129–44.0.19.254	128
44.0.20.0/22	Customer y	44.0.20.0.1–44.0.23.254	1,022
Etc.			

NOTE If you are daunted by how the range of addresses is determined for a particular prefix, remember that expressing the address in binary will always lend clarity. Take for example the address allocated to MiddleMan, the 44.0.4.0 /22. Use the following sequence to arrive at an understanding of how the address range was derived:

How many addresses required? 1,000

How many bits to allocate? 10 (2^{10} = 1024)

Prefix = 22 (*10 bits remain to satisfy assignment*)

Determine beginning and ending ranges for the 44.0.4.0 /22:

```
assignment          00101100.00000000.000001 | 00.00000000
First address (all assigned bits off - except low order bit ON)
                    11111111.11111111.000001 | 00.00000001
Decimal             44      .0        .4          .1

Last address        all assigned bits on - except low order bit OFF)
                    11111111.11111111.000001 | 11.11111110
Decimal             44      .0        .7          .254
```

The examination of the process in binary form has revealed that the prefix of /22 derives a subnet with the range of the 44.0.4.1 – the 44.0.7.254. The remaining portion of the address is available for allocation elsewhere.

MiddleMan must now allocate an address to the local ISP. MinniMe has requested 200 addresses, so the closest match will be an address space of 8 bits; in other words, a /24 prefix. Table 1-17 elucidates the allocation to MinniMe, along with a few other customers.

Table 1-17   MiddleMan's Allocation of 44.0.4.0/22

ASSIGNMENT	CUSTOMER	ADDRESS RANGE	TOTAL ADDRESSES
44.0.4.0/24	MinniMe	44.0.4.1–44.0.4.254	254
44.0.5.0/24	Customer 2	44.0.5.1–44.0.5.254	254
44.0.5.0/26	Customer 3	44.0.5.1–44.0.5.62	62
44.0.5.64/26	Customer 4	44.0.5.65–44.0.5.126	62
44.0.5.128/26	Customer 5	44.0.5.129–44.0.5.190	62
44.0.5.192/26	Customer 6	44.0.5.193–44.0.5.254	62
44.0.6.0/24	Customer 7	44.0.6.1–44.0.6.254	254
Etc.			

Whoops. If MiddleMan keeps this up, it will soon exhaust its allocation. No problem. MiddleMan can lease additional CIDR blocks from Mammoth if the need arises.

To complete the CIDR example, MinniMe will create a number of small subnets for its subscribers. Table 1-18 reflects a possible allocation.

To sum up, the above examples should demonstrate CIDRs ability to efficiently allocate IP addresses. Furthermore, CIDRs ability to also reduce the size of route tables due to the natural network summarization that takes place with CIDR-assigned address will be reinforced many times throughout this book, especially in Chapter 4.

IPv6 to the Rescue?

CIDR and NAT were created as a solution to the problem of 32-bit network addresses being exhausted. Another solution would be to increase the size of the existing address space beyond 32 bits. That's where the next version of IP, IPv6, comes in. IPv6 purports to ultimately replace the current version of IP, version 4, with a quadrupled address length of 128 bits. It is expected that the industry will slowly migrate to the new version of IP over many years, and that during this transition many IP hosts will run dual IP stacks.

Table 1-18 MinniMe's Allocation of 44.0.4.0/24

ASSIGNMENT	CUSTOMER	ADDRESS RANGE	TOTAL ADDRESSES
44.0.4.0/30	Subscriber 1	44.0.4.1–44.0.4.2	2
44.0.4.4/30	Subscriber 2	44.0.4.5–44.0.4.6	2
44.0.4.8/30	Subscriber 3	44.0.4.9–44.0.4.10	2
44.0.4.12/30	Subscriber 4	44.0.4.13–44.0.4.14	2
44.0.4.16/29	Subscriber 5	44.0.4.17–44.0.4.22	6
44.0.4.24/29	Subscriber 6	44.0.4.25–44.0.4.30	6
44.0.4.32/30	Subscriber 7	44.0.4.33–44.0.4.34	2
And so on . . .			
44.0.4.252/30	Subscriber x	44.0.4.253–44.0.4.254	2
~~44.0.5.0/30*~~	~~Subscriber y~~	~~44.0.5.1–44.0.5.2~~	~~2~~

* Once the address range rolls over to the .5, it is out of range of the allocated CIDR address. Someone else owns the range from there.

IPv6 Reality Check

Here is how things are shaping up for TCP/IP addressing in today's real-world networking environment. Back in the early '90s things were looking very dismal for IPv4. The tremendous popularity of the Internet made it an almost certainty that the inefficient IPv4 address space would be depleted in just a couple of years. That provided the impetus for a new addressing scheme (IPv6). However, the surge in address usage also sparked two important stop-gap measures: CIDR and NAT.

CIDR and NAT have been very successful. With CIDR, allocation of the remaining address space is extremely efficient; even some previously wasted addresses have been reclaimed and then reallocated using CIDR notation. Additionally, NAT has made it possible to use as little as a single public IP address to serve hundreds of hosts. The hosts are addressed with private IP addresses, of which there is no shortage because private addresses can be reused.

Network security comes into play here as well. The security landscape has changed so much in recent years. We're trying to hide our networks from the Internet now. It used to be you had bragging rights if you had enough public addresses to assign one to every workstation. Not anymore. Now the trend is to address hosts with private addresses that hide behind NAT appliances and stateful firewalls. Although IPv6 is slowly permeating into our networks, it is likely to be some time before we all jump on the IPv6 bandwagon.

Ports and Sockets

How does a server know which application or service an incoming IP packet should be directed to? Take a computer running both web server software and FTP software. Such a computer is capable of both serving up web pages as well as transferring files. How does the server know which service the requesting host wants? Do you want a web page or a file? Should I direct you to the web server or the FTP server? On the client side, a user can fire up several web browser windows. How does the system keep track of which page replies should be directed to? The answer is **ports** and **sockets**.

Ports

Ports are values set in a header field of TCP and UDP packets. A port number indicates which application is to be used to process a packet. The receiving computer examines the value of the port field and passes the packet to the application waiting for traffic on that port number.

Port numbers are analogous to apartment numbers. The street address (IP address) of an apartment complex takes you to the correct building, but the apartment number (port) is required to identify the correct location within the building. Take a request for a web page. An incoming packet requesting a web page from xyz.com will contain not only the IP address of the web server; *it will also contain the port number it expects the web server software to be listening on.* How does the packet know which port number to use? That has all been set up in advance. Web servers listen on TCP port 80. Port 80 is one of many so-called "well known" ports. Therefore, if the packet wants to get a web page, it had better request the page on port 80.

When a web server is started up, it immediately begins listening on port 80. When it detects a packet with the port number set to 80, the web server responds by extracting the packet's payload and processing the data. Likewise with an FTP server. An FTP server listens on port 20. It will try to process any packets set to port number 20 (see Table 1-19).

Table 1-19 A Sampling of Popular "Well-Known" Ports

TCP PORTS		UDP PORTS	
20 & 21	FTP (file transfer)	53	DNS
23	Telnet (remote control)	67 & 68	BootP (for DHCP across a router)
25	SMTP (sending email)	69	TFTP (file transfer without verification)
53	DNS (Domain Name System)	119	NNTP (Network News Transfer Protocol)
80	HTTP (web access)	135	RPC (remote procedure call)
110	POP3 (Post Office Protocol 3; retrieving email)	137	NetBIOS name service
135	RPC (Remote Procedure Call)	138	NetBIOS datagram service
139	NetBIOS session service	139	NetBIOS session service
143	IMAP (Internet Message Access Protocol)	143	IMAP (Internet Message Access Protocol)
179	BGP (Border Gateway Protocol)	161–162	SNMP (device management)
194	IRC (Internet Relay Chat)	389	LDAP (Lightweight Directory Access Protocol)
443	SSL (Secure Sockets Layer) HTTPS	443	SSL (Secure Sockets Layer) HTTPS
1863	Windows Messenger	520	RIP routing protocol

(continued)

Table 1-19   *(continued)*

TCP PORTS		UDP PORTS	
3219	Windows Messenger Service	3219	Windows Messenger Service
3389	NetMeeting	3389	NetMeeting
5631–5632	PC Anywhere	5631–5632	PC Anywhere
6891–6900	Windows Messenger file transfer	6970–7170	Real Audio

Ports are numbered from 0–65,535. Port numbers that everyone agrees on are referred to as "well-known." The ports 0–1023 are reserved as well-known ports. They are used by server-based applications. Both the UDP (unreliable) and the TCP (reliable) protocols each have their own range of port numbers numbered 0–65,535.

Sockets

Sockets are easy to understand. A socket is simply the combination of an IP address and a port number. Sockets help identify a specific host, along with the port a particular application is listening on. For example, if the web server for xyz.com is 191.1.1.25, the socket for web traffic on that machine is **191.1.1.25:80** (IP 191.1.1.25 and port 80). Any traffic bound for the web server at xyz.com would have the destination socket **191.1.1.25:80** imbedded in each packet.

> **NOTE** The term "socket" is also used to describe a software abstract in programming, such as BSD Unix *sockets* or Microsoft's *WinSock* programming interface.

Both a source socket and a destination socket are embedded in every packet. The destination socket specifies exactly where the packet is bound for, and the source socket specifies exactly where the packet came from. The source socket is necessary because the server has to direct response packets back to the application on the host that made the request.

You might be wondering which port number the *source* host uses when requesting a web page. Many people would guess port 80. That's actually not correct. Port 80 is reserved only for computers running web **server** software, not web **browser** software. After all, you don't want a host receiving traffic on port 80 if it is not running the software required to process HTTP requests. In fact, clients making requests use any of a series of sequential port numbers between 1024 and 4096. The first port a computer uses upon boot-up is 1024.

The next packet stream will use 1025, then 1026, and so on, up to 4096. Then it rolls over to 1024 again.

> **NOTE** The range of ports used for client requests, server responses, and other functions is not as meticulously followed by everyone in the TCP/IP community as it could be. Like many things, there are always exceptions to the rule, and there is some overlap in the use of port numbers. However the well-known port numbers are pretty universal. Appendix D provides the URL of a site that lists the assignment for all port numbers.

Important Protocols Related to Routing

This section describes the protocols that have special significance for network routing.

TCP and UDP—Layer 4, Transport

The **Transmission Control Protocol** and the **User Datagram Protocol** are the two protocols that facilitate packet delivery. Both protocols handle **end-to-end** (source-to-destination) communications, but only TCP provides guaranteed delivery of packets. TCP is considered a **connection-oriented** protocol. TCP establishes a connection between the source and destination hosts before transferring data packets. UDP is a **connectionless** protocol. UDP does not create an initial connection between the source and destination hosts.

The transport layer is in charge of storing the source and destination port numbers in the layer 4 header. Once the data received from layer 5 has been segmented, a layer 4 header is applied to each segment, which includes the source and destination port numbers. When the segments are passed to layer 3, networking, the source and destination logical addresses (IP addresses) are added, thereby forming the required *sockets*.

UDP Protocol

The UDP protocol is a connectionless protocol. It really does nothing more than store the source and destination port numbers and make a **best effort** (so-called "unreliable") delivery attempt. There is no mechanism to insure the packet is delivered. Any requirement for assured delivery and/or error correction when UDP is used must be handled by the application (application layer 7) and the network technology (data-link layer 2).

So-called unreliable delivery begs the question; Why would you ever send data with a protocol that doesn't follow up on the delivery attempt? A good example of when the UDP protocol is used is for time-sensitive applications such as video or audio transmissions. There is no point in retransmitting a lost packet in real time data streams. Another example is the **Trivial File Transfer**

Protocol (TFTP), which uses UDP. A TFTP program is often used in lieu of a traditional FTP application (which uses TCP) for transferring files when assured delivery is not required. Cisco uses the TFTP protocol to upload the IOS and configuration file to a router. This process often happens over a local network, which is usually a reliable medium. The TFTP application uses checksums for error detection and correction. TCP could be used, but there is far more overhead involved and file transfers would be slower.

UDP is also the protocol used for broadcast packets. Broadcasts are sent to all hosts on a subnet and are usually responded to by one host (if that). It would be pointless to try to assure delivery of all broadcast packets. It's like walking into a bar and shouting out "Is Harry here?" You don't expect every patron to announce that they are not Harry.

TCP Protocol

The TCP protocol on the other hand goes to great lengths to insure packet delivery. This is the protocol of choice when packets *absolutely, positively* have to get there. TCP handles error detection, error correction, packet re-ordering, and flow control.

TCP initially sends a *SYN*[9] (synchronize) packet to the destination host. This is a prerequisite to sending the actual data. A reply from the destination host verifies it is reachable and includes information about how to set up the connection.

The SYN packet is responded to with an **ACK** (acknowledgement) packet. The first SYN and ACK packet contain information the two hosts will use for numbering packets. Each packet in a TCP communication is numbered for tracking purposes. The hosts agree on which number to start with for numbering packets. This number is known as the **sequence number**.

Once the ACK packet is received, the sending host sends one additional packet indicating it has received the reply and has synched to a specific sequence number. This process is analogous to making a phone call where the caller says, "Can you hear me?" and the receiver says, "Yeah. Can you hear me?" and the caller replies, "Yep. I can hear you. Let's talk." This entire setup process is called the *3-way handshake* and is used to initiate every TCP session.

At this point, TCP starts sending data packets. For each packet sent, TCP notes the sequence number and starts a timer. If an ACK for that sequence number is not received before the timer expires, the packet stream will be re-sent.

Flow control is achieved by throttling the number of packets sent. If packets are sent faster than the receiving host can process them, they may be dropped and would have to be re-sent. This slows the communication process. Therefore, only a given number of packets are transmitted before they must be acknowledged. This is known as a **sliding window**. A sliding window is simply a buffer in memory used to store a given number of outbound packets. Once a burst of packets is transmitted, no others are sent until each packet in the burst is acknowledged. Then the window "slides" to the next set of packets waiting in memory and another burst is transmitted. The receiving host can signal the sending host to increase or decrease the size of the sliding window as the session proceeds. The initial size of the sliding window is determined during the 3-way handshake.[10]

IP Protocol—Layer 3, Network

The IP (Internet Protocol) is responsible for logical packet addressing and forwarding datagrams. IP header has fields containing the source and destination IP addresses. IP will determine the "next-hop" of a datagram and forward it to that address. IP is a connectionless protocol. No session is established before exchanging data. IP datagrams are *forwarded and forgotten*. If reliable communications are required, the layer 4 TCP protocol must be invoked by the sending application. In that case, each IP packet will be encapsulated in a TCP header. There's that OSI model at work!

IP Fragmentation

On the sending side, the IP performs fragmentation of outbound datagrams to accommodate the packet size restriction of the underlying layer 2 data-link protocol. On the receiving side, the IP reassembles the datagrams.

IP Error Detection

A TTL (Time to Live) field in the IP header contains a starting value that is decreased at each router the datagram passes through. This causes the datagram to expire after a given number of router hops, preventing errant packets from bouncing around a network in perpetuity. See section 3.1 of RFC 1122 for a nice terse explanation of the IP's job.

ICMP Protocol—Layer 3, Network

The ICMP (Internet Control Message Protocol) is used to communicate error messages when something goes wrong with packet delivery. Since the network layer is where routing occurs, ICMP is a very important protocol to students of routing. In fact, the protocol was primarily developed for signaling an originating host or router that a route has failed. The ICMP also handles status and control messaging regarding routing.

Two important Windows command line utilities that use the ICMP protocol are PING.EXE and TRACERT.EXE. Both utilities are good for troubleshooting failed communications. ICMP also provides error status messages to routers and routing protocols. A header within the IP header carries ICMP data. Here are a few of the more important functions of the ICMP protocol:

- **ICMP echo and echo reply messages:** ICMP is the protocol used in the Windows PING.EXE and TRACERT.EXE utilities, which allows connectivity testing by sending an "echo" message that requires a reply from the destination host. These utilities are discussed later in this chapter.

- **ICMP destination unreachable messages:** If for some reason a destination host cannot be reached, the router that discovers the problem will send back an ICMP destination unreachable message. The message is passed back to the upper layers and the end-user application must handle the error. Depending on how network aware the application is it may do anything from displaying a network error of some kind to simply hanging. The PING.EXE utility displays the errors, as described later in this chapter.

- **ICMP Redirect Message:** Sometimes routers receive packets that have not been routed efficiently. In other words, the receiving router knows a better path to the destination than through itself. In that case, the router can send a redirect message to the source host. The redirect message will include the alternative path suggested by the router. If the receiving host supports ICMP redirects, the host will route packets bound for the same destination through the more efficient path.

When are redirects useful? Most often at the workstation on a network with more than one router. Workstations typically do not have a fully populated route table that allows it to choose the best path to a destination. Rather, workstations typically have a *default gateway*, which is the IP address of just one router. Windows 2003, for example, supports ICMP redirects, so Windows servers can learn better paths to a destination without the need to modify the default route table. Naturally, the server must be multi-homed.

- **ICMP Time Exceeded Message:** Time Exceeded messages are very important in network routing. As mentioned in the discussion of the IP protocol earlier in this chapter, every routed packet has a TTL (Time to Live) field in the IP header. The value of the TTL field is decremented by 1 each time a packet passes through a router. If the TTL field reaches 0, the packet is discarded. The ICMP Time Exceeded message is how the router notifies the sending host that the packet has been discarded. Additionally, a Time Exceeded message is used to report that not all fragments of a fragmented packet arrived at the destination within a reasonable period of time.

DHCP and BOOTP Protocol—Layer 3, Networking

DHCP stands for Dynamic Host Configuration Protocol. DHCP, when configured on a host, allows for automatic assignment of an IP address and subnet mask. DHCP can optionally supply many other IP parameters such as default gateway, DNS addresses, WINS servers, and other items. DHCP is quite helpful in a routing environment because it reduces the chances of misconfiguring critical client information relating to the proper routing of packets (routing begins at the workstation). DHCP also helps conserve precious host addresses because addresses are usually *leased* to the host temporarily. If a host does not renew its lease periodically, it is presumed to be offline, and the address is reclaimed to be reused elsewhere. DHCP relies on DHCP servers responding to requests from hosts for address assignments. Such DHCP servers are configured with a range of addresses available for allocation to the requesting hosts. A DHCP server is also configured with, and supplies the supporting configuration information (subnet mask, default gateway, and so on).

When you're configuring DHCP in a routed environment, it is important to understand that DHCP uses broadcast packets for a portion of its communications, because routers do not pass broadcasts by default. When a host first attempts to contact a DHCP server, it does not know where the server is, so it broadcasts a special packet with request data that a DHCP server will understand and respond to. After a server responds, further communications are unicast. However, a host will also use broadcast packets if it's unable to renew its lease through its current DHCP server. In that case, broadcast packets are again used to locate another DHCP server.

Unless a DCHP server is placed on every subnet containing hosts that require DHCP services, the routers must be configured to pass the DHCP broadcast packets to a subnet containing a DHCP server. To enable this capability, Cisco routers are configured with the `ip helper-address`[11] global configuration command. This command enables pass-through of several types of broadcast messages (BOOTP, DNS, NetBIOS servers, and so on) and must be entered with the proper options for the needs of the system.

Notice the reference to **BOOTP**. BOOTP is the original protocol for auto-assignment of host addresses that DHCP is based on. DHCP is far more flexible than BOOTP and replaced it in principal. However, BOOTP is still the protocol referred to by Cisco routers. That is not a problem, because at the layer 3 routing level, the information the routers care about is the same between BOOTP and DHCP. Both protocols use UDP ports 67 and 68 for DHCP related traffic. The client listens on port 67 and the server listens on port 68. Routers enabled to pass BOOTP broadcasts listen on the same ports to recognize and direct the packets.

NOTE The author is old enough to remember a song by the group Chicago called "Questions 67 & 68." These are rather obscure port numbers and the memory of the song title has helped on certification exams!

Keep in mind that troubleshooting routing problems at the workstation level requires that the workstation's IP stack is configured properly. The Windows-based **IPConfig** command (described soon) is extremely helpful in verifying the IP configuration of a host, and furthermore has command line options to release and renew the DCHP configuration of a host.

Windows-Based TCP/IP Utilities

The following are helpful programs to gather information and troubleshoot routing issues.

PING.EXE

PING.EXE has the following characteristics:

- You use it to check communication link to another host.
- It uses the ICMP protocol.
- Just type **ping** at a command prompt to get help for command line options.

Here are the common command line options:

```
-t (Ping the specified host until stopped. To see statistics and
continue - type Control-Break. To stop - type Control-C)
-n x (count. Where "x" is the number of echo requests to send)
-i x (TTL. Time To Live. Where "x" is the TTL)
-w x (timeout.  Where "x" is the time in milliseconds to wait)
Ex: ping 192.168.1.1 -t  (pings the host continuously)
Ex: ping widgets.com -n 1 (pings the host once)
```

TRACERT.EXE

TRACERT.EXE has the following characteristics:

- You use it to trace which routers a packet travels across to its destination.
- It is an extremely helpful utility for determining where the communication break-down occurs.
- It uses ICMP protocol.
- Just type **tracert** to get help for command line options.

Here are the common command line options:

```
-h (maximum hops. Maximum number of hops to search for target.)
-w (timeout. Wait timeout milliseconds for each reply)
Ex: tracert 10.12.1.4 -h 12
Ex: tracert widgets.com -w 1200
```

ROUTE.EXE

ROUTE.EXE has the following characteristics:

- It displays and optionally alters the route table of a host (not a router).
- Just type **route** to get help for command line options.

Here are the common command line options:

```
-p When used with the ADD command, makes a route persistent.
print         Displays routes onscreen
add           Adds a route
delete        Deletes a route
change        Modifies an existing route
destination   Specifies the host.
mask          Specifies that the next parameter is the 'netmask' value.
netmask       Specifies a subnet mask value for this route entry. If not
              specified, it defaults to 255.255.255.255.
gateway       Specifies gateway.
interface     The interface number for the specified route.
Metric        Specifies the metric, i.e. cost for the destination.

Ex: route ADD 157.0.0.0 MASK 255.0.0.0  157.55.80.1  METRIC 3 IF 2
    destination^          mask^   gateway^                Interface^
Ex: route -p add 192.1.2.0 mask 255.255.255.0
```

IPCONFIG.EXE (98/ Me/NT/2000/XP) and WINIPCFG.EXE (95/98/Me)

IPCONFIG.EXE and WINIPCFG.EXE have the following characteristics:

- They display an array of IP statistics for a computer.
- IPCONFIG/ALL displays many additional configuration options.
- Just type **ipconfig** at a command prompt to get help for command line options.

Here are the common command line options:

```
/all      Display full configuration information
/release  Release the DHCP assigned IP address for the specified adapter
/renew    Renew the DHCP assigned IP address for the specified adapter

Ex: c:>>ipconfig /release
```

TELNET.EXE

TELNET.EXE has the following characteristics:

- You use it to establish a remote control session with another host.
- It is commonly used to configure routers.
- Type **telnet** to run Telnet from the RUN command.

NSLOOKUP.EXE

NSLOOKUP.EXE has the following characteristics:

- It is a utility for managing and checking configuration of DNS servers.
- It tends to be one of the more cantankerous utilities.
- It can be used in command line mode or interactive mode.

This utility is typically used to see resource records on DNS servers. Follow these steps:

1. Start NSLOOKUP. Ignore any messages that might be displayed.
2. Type >ls followed by the domain name you want information on (for example, type **ls widgets.com**).

HOSTNAME.EXE

HOSTNAME.EXE has the following characteristics:

- It returns the host name of a computer.
- No command line options are available.

NETSTAT.EXE

NETSTAT.EXE has the following characteristics:

- It displays the connection status and protocol status.
- It displays the port number used for a TCP/IP connection.
- Just type **netstat /?** to get help for command line options

ARP.EXE

ARP.EXE has the following characteristics:

- It displays and manages local ARP cache.
- Just type **arp** to get help for command line options.

Here are the common, testable command line options:

```
-a or -g (displays current arp table)
-s (adds a permanent entry to route table. Ex: arp -s 192.168.1.24 00-
aa-62-c6-09)
-d (deletes an entry from the arp table. Same syntax as adding a name)
```

Notes

1. The notation that ISO stands for the International Organization for Standardization is not a typo. Rather, it's an artifact of language translation. ISO is based in Switzerland.

2. Computer systems vary in how they represent text and data as a binary code. The letter "A" is represented as 11000001 in ASCII, whereas the same letter in EBCDIC would be represented as 10000001.

3. In common practice, the term "packet" is often used to refer to the DPU of any layer.

4. Routers can be configured to forward broadcast packets in special circumstances, such as for DHCP traffic (see page 62).

5. A DTE/DCE cable is often referred to as a v.35 cable because the two interfaces it connects follow the v.35 standard for high-speed serial communications.

6. CSU/DSUs are seen less often, as the telcos are delivering more and more services with Ethernet interfaces.

7. Cisco routers allow an all-zero network address with the ip subnet-zero global configuration command. This can cause compatibility issues with some networking equipment however, and should be employed with care.

8. It would be unusual for all but the largest ISPs to be assigned an address with so many hosts in today's CIDR base world. See the following section on CIDR.

9. The SYN packet has gained notoriety because it is used to launch Denial of Service (DoS) attacks. In a DoS attack, the sending host floods the target with SYN packets. The target's TCP buffer fills up and it becomes too overwhelmed to respond to inquiries, even valid ones.

10. There are additional timers that fine tune how TCP works, but this is beyond the scope of this review. See Appendix B for recommended reading.

11. The ip helper-address command and its counterpart, the ip forward-protocol command, are beyond the scope of this text. Refer to a Cisco command reference.

Routing Basics

Overview

The purpose of this chapter is to provide foundational information about what routing is and the basics of how it works. Specifics of routing, such as static routing, dynamic routing, and routing protocols are provided in subsequent chapters. The following topics are covered in this chapter:

What Is Routing?

Simply put, routing is the act of forwarding network packets from a source network to a destination network. This is a straightforward concept in principle. In practice, you must take into account a variety of considerations to insure the successful delivery of packets:

- When should you route?
- What is the best route?
- How is the best route determined?
- What if the network topology changes?
- What if there is a network fault?
- What if the destination does not exist?

Routing occurs when a packet must be forwarded off its originating network (determined by the ANDing process covered in Chapter 1). *Any packet with a destination network number that differs from the local network number is, by definition, destined for another network and must therefore be forwarded to the target network.* A router is the designated networking device for forwarding packets between networks. Only a router has the internetwork information and the logic required to make the correct decision about how best to forward the packet.

NOTE As discussed in Chapter 1, NAT devices, gateways, and proxy servers also forward packets between two networks, but such devices lack the routing logic and routing information that routers posses.

Routing Begins at Home—The Workstation's Route Table

The routing process actually starts at the workstation: the local host initiating the communication. If Joe Cool is sending an email to Sally Smart, the determination of whether Sally's workstation is on the same network as Joe's is made at Joe's workstation. These hosts actually have their own route table. If you haven't dealt with routes and routing much, that statement may surprise you. Perhaps you thought that route tables only lived on routers. Not so. For most workstations, however, the route table is very brief. A workstation usually needs only to forward packets bound for another network to its default gateway. Nonetheless, it is helpful to understand the process. Figure 2-1 represents the route table of a typical Windows PC connected to a network. You can see the route table of any Windows-based PC by opening a command prompt and entering c:>**route print**.

The purpose of the local route table is to provide the host with information about how to handle the forwarding of packets exiting the workstation. Every packet has a source and destination address. Once the ANDing process has determined that a packet needs to be routed, the local route table is consulted to determine where to forward the packet. Let's look at the table and try and make sense of it.

Row 1—Default Gateway

```
Network Destination  Netmask  Gateway Address  Interface     Metric
0.0.0.0              0.0.0.0  192.100.100.101  192.100.100.191  1
```

Row 1 defines where to send packets for which there is no specific route. This is known as the **default gateway**, **default route**, or **Gateway of Last Resort**. The first column in row 1 is the network address. This column lists **networks**, as opposed to host addresses (the only exception is the IP address of the local host itself in row 4). Column 1 will always list every possible network the host is aware of. The entry the 0.0.0.0 is a wild card representing *any network not in the list*, and the IP stack uses the information in this row to determine how to forward packets whose destination network is not listed in the table. Most packets bound for another network are sent to the default gateway—a router will have a more robust route table, and so is better equipped to make the best decision about how to reach the destination network.

Network Address = 192.100.100.0
Subnet mask = 255.255.255.0
IP address of local computer = 192.100.100.191
Default Gateway = 192.100.100.101

C:>route print

Active Routes:

	(1) **Network Destination**	(2) **Netmask**	(3) **Gateway Address**	(4) **Interface**	(5) **Metric**	
1	0.0.0.0	0.0.0.0	192.100.100.101	192.100.100.191	1	(Default Gateway address)
2	127.0.0.0	255.0.0.0	127.0.0.1	127.0.0.1	1	(local loopback – tests local TCP/IP stack)
3	192.100.100.0	255.255.255.0	192.100.100.191	192.100.100.191	1	(Local subnet address. Identifies route to local network)
4	192.100.100.191	255.255.255.255	127.0.0.1	127.0.0.1	1	(Network card address. Identifies route to local address)
5	192.100.100.255	255.255.255.255	192.100.100.191	192.100.100.191	1	(Subnet broadcast address)
6	224.0.0.0	224.0.0.0	192.100.100.191	192.100.100.191	1	(Multicast broadcast address. 224 is a class D address)
7	255.255.255.255	255.255.255.255	192.100.100.191	192.100.100.191	1	(Internet broadcast address)

Persistant Routes:
None

(1) Network Destination: The IP address of a host, subnet, network, or Default Gateway.

(2) Netmask: (Subnet mask). Determines what portion of the IP address is the network ID.

(3) Gateway Address The address of a router. Where packets will be forwarded. This will be the Default Gateway address, the local computer's IP address, or a generic loopback address (assuming no static routes have been entered).

(4) Interface: How the packets will leave the local host. This will contain the local host's IP address or the generic loopback address.

(5) Metric The "cost" of the route to the destination network address, usually in terms of time to the destination

Figure 2-1 Display of a Windows-based workstation's route table.

Column 2 defines the network mask, if any, for the network number in column 1. A network mask performs a function similar to a subnet mask. The mask is used to isolate the network portion of the address. Note that it is a 32-bit number broken into four octets, just like a network ID. An entry of 255 allows the corresponding octet in the network ID to be passed through. An entry of 0 blocks the corresponding octet. In the case of a default gateway entry, the mask will usually be the 0.0.0.0. A mask of the 0.0.0.0 effectively means no network number, equating to "any network." This is kind of a weird example. The 0.0.0.0 is a pretty funky mask. More easily understood examples will be shown later.

Column 3 specifies the IP address of the gateway (router). This is the address that the packets are forwarded to.

Column 4 specifies which local interface to forward packets to in order to reach the gateway. In the case of a host with only one network interface card (NIC), this entry is inconsequential. But if the host has two or more NICs installed, this column provides an opportunity to specify which interface the packet should be sent to.

Column 5 indicates the metric. A metric is one way to assign a "cost" to a route. This is not a dollar cost, but rather an indicator of how expensive a route is in terms of time to delivery. For example, let's say that a network has been configured with two separate paths (routes) to a destination network. This is often done for fault tolerance. However, one path may have a T1 connection while the other has a far slower 56K connection. Naturally, you want most of the traffic to go through the path with the T1 link. That is where the metric comes in. *The lower the metric number, the lower the cost of the route.* Therefore, if you assign a metric of 1 to the T1 path and a metric of 2 to the 56K path, the host will choose the T1 path over the 56K path (unless the TI is down, in which case it will fall back to the 56K path).

Row 2—Loopback Address

Network Destination	Netmask	Gateway Address	Interface	Metric
127.0.0.0	255.0.0.0	127.0.0.1	127.0.0.1	1

Row 2 is the loopback address, which is used for testing purposes. The RFCs that specified the assignment of IP addresses reserved the entire the 127.0.0.0 network for testing (too bad). The typical IP address used for loopback testing is the 127.0.0.1. Try pinging the 127.0.0.1 from your command prompt. The results should be similar to the output shown in Figure 2-2.

PING TIP

One way to save time with the `ping` command in Windows is to add the switch −n 1, which will cause the target to be pinged only once, instead of the default 4 times.

Example: `ping −n 1 192.168.1.1`

```
C:>ping 127.0.0.1
Pinging 127.0.0.1 with 32 bytes of data:
Reply from 127.0.0.1: bytes=32 time<10ms TTL=128
Reply from 127.0.0.1: bytes=32 time<10ms TTL=128
Reply from 127.0.0.1: bytes=32 time<10ms TTL=128
Reply from 127.0.0.1: bytes=32 time<10ms TTL=128
Ping statistics for 127.0.0.1:
Packets: Sent = 4, Received = 4, Lost = 0 (0% loss),
Approximate round trip times in milli-seconds: Minimum = 0ms,
Maximum = 0ms, Average = 0ms
```

Figure 2-2   Pinging the loopback address of a host.

Pinging the loopback address is a quick way to test the integrity of the local IP stack. A reply indicates that the stack on the local machine is functioning.

Given what you learned about how to interpret row 1, what do the five columns represent for the loopback test?

- Column 1 represents the loopback network.

- Column 2 is the network mask. A mask of the 255.0.0.0 passes the first octet and blocks the remaining octets, exposing a network address 127.

- In column 3, a gateway address of the 127.0.0.1 is in actuality a *virtual* address that maps to the IP address of the workstation. The IP stack will send test packets to this make-believe address.

- Column 4 indicates to send test packets out the 127.0.0.1, which again is a fictitious gateway address pointing to the local host's IP address.

- The metric in column 5 has little meaning for a loopback, but it shows up with the default value of 1.

Row 3—Local Subnet Address

```
Network Destination Netmask       Gateway Address Interface      Metric
192.100.100.0       255.255.255.0 192.100.100.191 192.100.100.191  1
```

This entry defines the local network or subnet. The term *subnet* does not imply that the network has been subnetted. In this context, it just reflects an individual network—the one that the host is a part of, as shown in column 1. Column 2 reflects whatever subnet mask was entered into the IP configuration of the host, in this case a standard class C network. The Gateway and Interface columns both match the IP address assigned to the host's NIC. This simply identifies the route to this host.

Row 4—IP Address of Host

```
Network Destination Netmask          Gateway Address Interface Metric
192.100.100.191     255.255.255.255  127.0.0.1       127.0.0.1  1
```

To specify the host's actual IP address in the route table, the address is listed in the Network Destination column. A netmask of 255.255.255.255 is necessary to pass all four octets intact and reveal the true host address. The loopback addresses for Gateway Address and Interface are just placeholders that refer to the local IP address.

Rows 5, 6, and 7—Broadcast Information

```
Network Destination Netmask          Gateway Address Interface     Metric
192.100.100.255     255.255.255.255 192.100.100.191 192.100.100.191 1
224.0.0.0           224.0.0.0       192.100.100.191 192.100.100.191 1
255.255.255.255     255.255.255.255 192.100.100.191 192.100.100.191 1
```

A route table needs to reflect how broadcasts are handled. A way to broadcast on the subnet is required, plus a way to broadcast to all hosts, everywhere (scary thought). Also, multicasting is handled here (broadcast to only a subset of hosts).

Row 5 defines how to broadcast on the local subnet. Rather than identifying a single host, it identifies *all* hosts on that subnet. A netmask of the 255.255.255.255 is required to pass the entire address. The host's IP address is used for both the Gateway Address and the Interface.

Row 7 is similar to row 5, so it is explained next. It defines how to broadcast to everybody. Whereas 0.0.0.0 took on the meaning of "any network not in the list," 255.255.255.255 takes on the meaning "*all* hosts on *all* networks." As with the local subnet broadcast entry, a netmask of the 255.255.255.255 allows all bits to be passed through.

Row 6 sets up a multicast entry. The 224 network is reserved specifically for multicasting. Multicasting is used to broadcast to a specific subgroup of hosts. An example of its use would be delivering a pay-per-view seminar across the web. Some routing protocols use multicasting to communicate between routers.

Remember that up until now, no action was required on the administrator's part to populate the workstation's route table except to have specified an IP address, subnet mask, and default gateway address in the IP configuration of the host. The Windows IP stack did the rest. Meaning, you normally don't have to sweat these basic entries. But again, it's helpful to have an understanding of a workstation's route table when it comes time to troubleshoot. In a real life troubleshooting scenario where routing is broken, walking up to a workstation and running the **route print** command gives a quick rundown of the host's IP address, subnet mask, and default gateway, as well as a list of any specific routes that have been configured. Put this command in your troubleshooting arsenal and use it with the **ping.exe** and **tracert.exe** commands covered in Chapter 1. See Chapter 3 for an example of when a workstation's route table might be manually altered.

Anatomy of a Routed Packet

Once a host determines that packets must be routed to another network how does the process actually work? One way to understand routing is to track the journey of a packet from one network to another. We will be a "fly on the wall" as a file transfer is tracked from a host on network A on to a host on network B. Breakout explanations will be provided as the journey progresses.

Track a Packet—Source and Destination on the Same Network

To get warmed up, a packet with the source and destination hosts both residing on the same network will first be tracked. From there, a subsequent example will illustrate how the routing process intervenes when packets must be forwarded off the network to get to reach their destination.

> **NOTE** The following explanation is a micro view of what leads up to the initiation of the routing process. This provides additional details about how TCP/IP and the OSI network models work. Subsequent examples skip this detail.

In this example, someone sitting at computer A is about to copy a file to computer B. Both computers A and B are on network the 160.1.0.0 (class B network). Here is how the file gets transferred (for simplicity sake only a single packet is being tracked; in reality, there would of course be a stream of packets):

1. A user on computer A (the 160.1.0.1) has a drive mapped to Computer B (the 160.1.0.2). The user drags a file in Windows Explorer to a folder on Computer B.

2. Windows Explorer calls on the operating system to initiate a communication session with the destination computer (session layer 5). Microsoft Windows operating systems use the high-level protocol known as the SMB (Server Message Block) protocol to perform many communication tasks. The SMB takes responsibility for setting up the session to transfer the file, but the SMB does not handle the transfer itself. For that job, it calls upon the reliable TCP/IP protocol TCP (layer 4).

3. TCP takes responsibility for insuring the data generated by SMB is sent to the destination intact. The protocol numbers and tracks each packet and signs off on the deal only when ACKs (acknowledgements) of each packet are received from the destination host. TCP, however, has no knowledge of how to initially locate the destination host, so it calls the TCP/IP protocol known as IP (network layer 3).

4. IP adds logical addressing information for both source and destination hosts. The source IP address is known and is added to the IP header of the packet right away. The only thing known about the destination host however is its NetBIOS name (the friendly name of the host). A broadcast packet is sent asking the computer called COMPUTER_B to respond with its IP address. The packet is sent to IP address the 160.1.255.255, the broadcast address for the 160.1.0.0 network. All hosts on the subnet will examine the packet sent to the 160.1.255.255, but only the host named COMPUTER_B will respond with its IP address. The newly learned destination IP address is now added to the IP header of the packet.

5. Now that both the source and destination IP addresses are known, the ANDing process can be used to determine whether or not the destination host is on the same network as the sending host. The subnet mask defined for the source host is applied to both the 160.1.0.1 and the 160.1.0.2 addresses, yielding network numbers the 160.1.0.0 for the source host and 160.1.0.0 for the destination host. A comparison of the two numbers reveals the source and destination host are on the same network. Routing of the packet will not be required.

6. Layer 3 is not done with its work however. Communications do not take place until the MAC address of both hosts is known. MAC addresses are the realm of the data-link protocol (Token Ring, Ethernet, and so on), and since it's the data-link protocol that actually sends the packet, it needs to know the MAC address of the target host. If the target's MAC address is not in the sending host's ARP cache, the ARP protocol is called. ARP sends a broadcast packet to ask for the MAC address of the 160.1.0.2, which replies with its physical (MAC) address. The MAC addresses are passed to the data-link protocol for the local network (layer 2).

VARIATIONS ON A THEME

There are in fact many ways the destination IP address might be learned in step 4. In a Microsoft WINS environment, the address would be retrieved from the WINS database instead of by broadcast. In a pure WIN2K environment sans NetBIOS, the IP address would be looked up via Dynamic DNS. Or, in some cases, the IP address of the destination would already be cached in memory.

7. Armed with the destination's MAC address, the data-link protocol (let's assume Ethernet), vis-à-vis the NIC driver, interfaces with the NIC, which generates the electrical impulses on the network medium, which will be heard by the destination host.

8. The two hosts have now communicated. The initial packet stream will be the 3-way handshake that establishes the session. Then the packets generated by SMB perform the housekeeping required to prepare for the file transfer. Finally, the file transfer will commence.

Track a Packet—Source and Destination on Different Networks—One Router

In this example, someone sitting at computer A is about to copy a file to someone at computer B. Computer A is on network 160.1.0.0 and computer B is on network the 160.2.0.0. The packet has to be routed, as follows:

1. A user on computer A (the 160.1.0.1) has a drive mapped to Computer B (the 160.2.0.1). The user drags a file in Windows Explorer to a folder on computer B.

2. The IP stack on the source host performs the ANDing process on the source and destination IP addresses. The subnet mask defined for the source host is applied to both the 160.1.0.1 and the 160.2.0.1 addresses, yielding network numbers the 160.1.0.0 for the source host and the 160.2.0.0 for the destination host. A comparison of the two numbers reveals that the source and destination hosts are on different networks. The packet must be routed to its destination.

3. Armed with the knowledge that the packet must be routed, the IP stack starts looking for the best route to the target address. The route table on the initiating host is examined. First, an entry with a path to the destination network is searched for. If a path is found, the packets are forwarded to the router specified by the entry[1]. The router must be on the same network as the sending host. This is considered the **next hop** in the packet's path to the destination network.

4. If no path to the destination network is located in the route table of the source host, the IP stack has no choice but to forward the packet to the default gateway. The default gateway is the IP address of a router on the local network that all packets bound for networks not listed in the hosts' route table are forwarded to.

5. The layer 3 ARP protocol is called to derive the MAC address for the 160.1.0.254.

6. As the router receives the packet stream, it has to decide what to do with it. Packet forwarding is kind of like playing Hot Potato. No one wants to hold onto a packet very long. The router first verifies the checksum in the packet (it discards the packet if the checksum is bad). It then applies the rules of any **access lists** that may exist for inbound packets on its receiving interface. (Access lists on a router are similar to firewall rules, where packets are accepted or rejected based on certain criteria applied to the packet.)

7. If the packet is accepted, the router checks its route table for a path to the destination network. In this case, the destination network is directly connected to another interface on the same router. The router then strips off the layer 2 header from the packet. A layer 2 header is media-specific. It is only relevant to the data-link protocol of a specific network. Since the router is about to pass the packet to the interface of a different network, the information is irrelevant. After a check for any access lists on the destination interface, the router checks the data-link protocol of the interface and builds a new layer 2 header, with corresponding source and destination MAC addresses. The source MAC address is the MAC address of the router interface the packet is forwarded *from*, and the target MAC address is the MAC address of the destination host (in this case the target host, but in other cases the MAC address of the next router). The router then decrements the TTL by one, and creates a new checksum. The IP stack running on the router issues an ARP call to IP address the 160.2.0.1, which returns its MAC address. Packet forwarding can be commenced and the game of Hot Potato is over.

TROUBLESHOOTING TIP

One common place to check when network communications break down is the default gateway setting on the sending host. If the specified address is incorrect or missing default routing cannot take place.

It is also common to see problems with the default gateway setting at the destination host. If a destination host has a misconfigured default gateway, packets will reach the host, but replies will not return. This would cause a ping from the source host to the destination host to fail. In this case, the TRACERT.EXE command would show how far the packet got before it encountered trouble.

Workstations tend to rely more on default gateways than routers (known as the Gateway of Last Resort on Cisco routers), but default routing is certainly used on routers, and a router will drop a packet if the destination network is not in the route table and no default gateway has been configured. Moral of the story: Check your default gateways along any portion of the path under your control when troubleshooting failed communications.

THE RETURN PATH

What goes out must come back. How do packets find a return path to the source host? Even in the example of a file transfer, where most packets flow from the source to the destination, packets flow in both directions if for no other reason than to return TCP acknowledgement packets, confirming to the sending host that the packets arrived intact.

In fact, the term "return path" is a misnomer because there is normally no return path per se—no "trail of breadcrumbs" to follow. What was the "destination host" becomes the "source host" and vice versa, and the whole process starts over. The same path determination mechanisms (route tables, default gateways, etc.) are used to forward packets to the initiating host, so packets might very well take a different path on their return trip.

Worth noting in this all-important step is that although the physical MAC addresses change as packets move across networks, the logical addresses (source and destination IP addresses) do *not* change. The logical addresses represent the two endpoints of the communication session and remain the same throughout a packet's journey.

Track a Packet—Source and Destination on Different Networks—Multiple Routers

Let's assume the packet from our last example needed to traverse two routers to reach its destination. This example picks up from when the packet reached the first router:

1. The router has received the packet, but this time after an access list check and the discarding of the layer 2 headers, an examination of the router's route table reveals that the destination network is not directly connected.

NOTE A router's route table is arguably at the heart of any book on routing. At the completion of this example, the focus will shift to the specifics of how route tables work, but for the moment let's simply say that a route to the destination has been determined by performing a lookup on the route table.

The table reveals which router the packet must be forwarded to and which interface the packet must exit this router from in order to reach the next identified router. Therefore, the layer 1 and 2 headers are built for the exit interface's data-link type and the packet stream is forwarded through that interface, after an access list check.

2. Now the process simply repeats itself. When the second router receives the packet everything the first router did is repeated. The layer 2 header

is stripped off, access lists applied to the inbound interface are checked, and a lookup of the route table is performed. If the destination address of the packet matches to a directly connected network, the packet is forwarded out the corresponding interface. Otherwise, the packet is forwarded to the next hop (router) in the path. (By the way, if at any time a router's route table reveals no path to the destination network, a variety of things may occur, depending on how the router is configured. That contingency will be covered shortly.)

Anatomy of a Route Table

Routers depend upon route tables to determine how to route incoming packets. The heart of routing is indeed the route table, so what is required in order to understand route tables? The following topics will introduce you to the workings of route tables:

- How route tables are populated
- How routes are selected—routing metrics and administrative distance
- How routers match destination addresses to a network path
- How packets are handled if a destination network cannot be located

A route table lists every network that a router is aware of. The following figure and table show two route table examples. Figure 2-3 shows the printout of a route table on a Cisco router when the **show ip route** command is executed. Table 2-1 shows a simplified view of the same route table.

```
routerA#show ip route
Codes:   C – connected,  S – static,  I – IGRP,  R – RIP,  M – mobile,  B – BGP
         D – EIGRP,  EX – EIRGP external,  O – OSPF,  IA – OSPF inter area
         N1 – OSPF NSSA external type 1,  N2 – OSPF NSSA external type 2,  E – EGP
         i – IS-IS,  L1 – IS-IS level-1,  L2 – IS-IS level 2,  * - candidate default
         U – per-user static route,  o – ODR
         T – traffic engineered route

Gateway of last resort is not set

O        10.0.0.0 /8 [110/20] via 200.1.1.1, 00:01:30,  Serial0
O        172.16.0.0 /16 [110/15] via 200.1.1.1, 00:01:28,   Serial0
O        192.168.1.0 /24 [110/20] via 200.2.2.2, 00:02:10,  Serial1
         210.1.1.0 /30 is subnetted, 1 subnets
C            210.1.1.4 [0/0] is directly connected, Ethernet0
```

Figure 2-3   Results of the "show ip route" command on a Cisco router.

Table 2-1   Simplified View of the Same Route Table. "AD" is short for Administrative Distance

CODE	NETWORK, MASK	AD/METRIC	NEXT HOP	INTERFACE
O	10.0.0.0 /8	110/20	200.1.1.1	S0
O	172.16.0.0 /16	110/15	200.1.1.1	S0
O	192.168.1.0 /24	110/20	200.2.2.2	S1
C	210.1.1.4 /30	0/0	Directly connected	E0

There are six key elements to each routing entry:

- **Code:** An abbreviation indicating what process discovered the route (see the code explanations in Figure 2-3).

- **Network, Mask:** Indicates the address of the destination network and its subnet mask.

- **Administrative distance/Metric:** Used to select the best route if more than one path to a network exists (covered in the next section).

- **Next hop:** IP address of the next router the packet will be forwarded to (specifically, the address of the interface of the next hop router that shares a network segment with an interface on the source router).

- **Interface:** The interface the packet will be forwarded out of.

Key Concept for Understanding Route Tables

There is something important to understand about route tables that will facilitate your understanding of network routing. Does something seem to be missing from the Table 2-1? Take for example the first route in the list: the 10.0.0.0 network. Notice that the table does not indicate precisely *where* 10.0.0.0 is. The full path to the destination is not indicated. For example, the table does not indicate that to get to the 10.0.0.0 network you must first go through, say, the 63.0.0.0 network, then through the 180.6.0.0 network, and so forth. All the entry tells you about the path to the 10.0.0.0 is that you must forward packets to the 200.1.1.1 via interface S0. The 200.1.1.1 is simply the next hop router. That's it. The router does not worry about how the packet ultimately gets to the 10.0.0.0. It's going to leave that job to the next router down the line. Again, kind of like Hot Potato.

No single route table entry ever reveals the full path to the destination network[2]. The best a routing entry can do is point to the next router along the path. Route tables help packets along their way, one hop at a time. When the packets arrive at the next hop, the process of path determination starts all over again. This may seem like a less-than-efficient process, but it works out well because it provides for great flexibility. There is often more than one path to a destination, and network links and routers can go down. It is impossible for all routers in a system to all have up-to-the-minute information at the same instant. Therefore, a system of recalculating routes after each hop insures more reliable network communications. The obvious conclusion is that every router in an internetwork must have a very good idea about which next hop router will get the packet to its destination most efficiently. This is where dynamic routing comes in (discussed in Chapter 4).

Populating Route Tables

Route tables are populated through one of the following three sources:

- Directly connected networks
- Network paths statically (manually) entered into the route table
- Through one or more dynamic routing protocols

Directly Connected Networks

Any network directly connected to the interface of a router is automatically added to the route table. Whatever IP address and mask were configured for the interface are used to populate the table entry.

Static and Dynamic Routing

Aside from directly connected networks, route tables can only be populated with network paths in one of two ways: the route is manually entered by an administrator, or the router figures out network paths on its own by talking to other routers. A manually entered route is known as a **static route**. On the other hand, **dynamic routes** are routes a router learns from other routers via a routing protocol such as RIP, IGRP, EIGRP, OSPF, or BGP. Routing protocols run as processes on routers. They exchange information about the networks in the system and automatically populate route tables. Static and dynamic routing are important topics and each have their own respective treatments in the following two chapters, respectively. The names of the various routing protocols are listed in Table 2-2.

Table 2-2 Popular Dynamic Routing Protocols

PROTOCOL	PURPOSE
RIP ver 1 (Routing Information Protocol version 1)	Legacy protocol suited for small networks
RIP ver 2 (Routing Information Protocol version 2)	Improvements to RIPv1 to support classless addressing
IGRP (Interior Gateway Routing Protocol)	Legacy Cisco specific protocol to replace RIP
EIGRP (Enhanced Interior Gateway Routing Protocol)	Improved version of IGRP to support classless addressing
OSPF (Open Shortest Path First)	De facto standard for enterprise networks
BGP (Border Gateway Protocol)	De facto standard for exchanging route information between autonomous systems

Routing Metrics

The term *metric* was first introduced when the route table of a local host was explained earlier. Metrics define the *cost* of a route in terms of how long it takes to deliver packets through a particular path. Metrics have special significance for routing protocols. Each routing protocol has its own formula for assigning a metric value to a learned route based on factors such as hop count, bandwidth, reliability of link, and so on. If a routing protocol learns of more than one path to a particular network, it will install the route with the lowest metric into the route table. Depending on the routing protocol, duplicate routes may be kept as backup routes if the primary route fails, or the routing protocol may install multiple routes into the route table and forward packets through all paths to increase throughput.[3]

Administrative Distance

Administrative distance builds on the concept of a metric, but it works as a more global means of route selection and comes into play when *multiple sources* are providing more than one path to a given network. For example, more than one routing protocol can run on a single router. Each routing protocol may learn of the same network, and each protocol will apply its native metrics to determine which path is most efficient to reach the network. But in the end, two different protocols each present a candidate path to the same network for inclusion into the route table. Which route should be installed? An arbitrator is needed to choose between the two candidates. This is where administrative distance comes in. An administrative distance value is assigned to every method for identifying network routes—albeit a directly connected network, a statically entered route, or a route discovered by a routing protocol.

One way to state the differences between metrics and administrative distance is to state that metrics ask the question "Which routes that I know of are the best?" whereas administrative distance asks the question "What source do I believe more?"

As with metrics, the lower the administrative distance value, the better the route. The route with the lowest administrative distance is always installed into the route table. Bear in mind that both metrics and administrative distance can be manipulated by a network engineer (that's you).

The default administrative distances are as follows:

Directly connected interface = 0

Static route = 1

EIGRP (summary routes) = 5

BGP (external) = 20

EIGRP (internal) = 90

IGRP = 100

OSPF = 110

RIP = 120

EIGRP (external) = 170

Internal BGP = 200

Unknown = 255

Note that directly connected routes have the lowest administrative distance, and therefore the highest selection priority. Obviously, if a network is directly connected to a router, there is no need to forward the packet to a different router first. Thus, a directly connected route will always take precedence over any other method of learning about the network. The administrative distance values assigned to the various routing protocols have evolved as routing protocols have evolved. For example, RIP is an older protocol with less robust metrics than OSPF, thus OSPF earns a lower administrative distance value[4]. A router will trust an OSPF learned route over a RIP learned route (assuming both protocols are running on the router). The entries in the above list will make more sense as you complete the subsequent chapters.

Summary

This chapter provided you with insight into why and how packets get routed. Specifically, it covered the following:

- Routing is the process of forwarding packets from one network to another. The ANDing process running on the source host determines if the IP address of a destination packet needs to be routed to another network.

- A variety of devices forward packets from point A to point B (hubs, routers, switches, and firewalls), but only routers have the ability to locate and forward packets to another network.

- One seeming exception to the requirement that routers forward packets between networks is Network Address Translation (NAT). Although NAT forwards packets off the network, it is not true routing because NAT does not incorporate route tables or make decisions about how and where to route packets. Proxy servers and gateways are another exception for the same reason.

- Routing devices must determine valid, economical paths to all destination networks and respond to changing network conditions.

- Route determination begins at the workstation. A workstation's route table usually indicates only the path of a default route, a place where outbound packets with no listed path are sent. However, static routes specifying the path to specific networks can be inserted into a workstation's route table.

- Routers determine the path to a network through the use of routing tables which list known networks. Route tables are populated in one of three ways: directly connected networks are added to the table automatically, routes learned through one or more routing protocols are added automatically, or routes can be manually added as static routes.

- Route tables do not contain the full path that packets will take to reach their destination. Rather, a routing table simply specifies the next router to forward the packet to, pushing the packet closer to its destination. Each router receiving a packet will in turn determine the best path and forward the packet to the next router.

- Routing metrics and administrative distance are the two mechanisms that determine route selection when multiple paths to a destination network exist. Metrics are used to determine the best route learned from a specific source, and are heavily used with dynamic routing protocols. Each routing protocol will choose the best path from among multiple possible paths by picking the route with the lowest metric (cost). Administrative distance is used to choose the best route if the same network is learned from more than one source— the same network may be known through a direct connection, a static entry, or from one or more routing protocols running on the same router.

- Default routes are used to forward packets when no match is found for a packet's destination address in the route table.

It is now time to delve into the specifics of static and dynamic routing—the two principal ways network routes are installed into route tables. Chapter 3 is a short but important chapter on how to configure static routes, and how to know when static routes are required. Chapter 4, in covering routing protocols, not only acts as a springboard for the subsequent chapters on the specific routing protocols, but it covers a broad array of critical routing concepts as well.

Notes

1. If more than one path is found, the route with the lowest metric is chosen and the path is considered to be determined. In either case, packets are then forwarded to the router specified by the entry.

2. Routing protocols *can* be designed to contain the complete path to the destination within the network packet (rather then just the source and destination addresses). In this case, all routing decisions are made at the router sourcing the packet. This is known as **source routing**. Most routing protocols do not incorporate source routing because allowing routing decisions to be made at each router along the path, on-the-fly, provides far more flexibility. Source routing, when it's used, tends to be implemented at the data-link layer. It is also worth noting that some protocols, like OSPF, in certain cases keeps the full path to a destination stored in a special table. However, the route table for OSPF still functions on a hop-by-hop basis.

3. Chapter 4 discusses routing metrics further.

4. The Cisco IOS makes use of the "distance" command to alter the default administrative distance. Default routing metrics can be also altered when entering a static route or when configuring a routing protocol. Specifics are given in the relevant chapters covering routing protocols.

Static Routing

Overview

This chapter explains the various aspects of static routing. Static routing is often used in lieu of, or in conjunction with, dynamic routing protocols. The following topics are covered:

What Is Static Routing?

Static routing was alluded to in Chapter 2. It is the process of manually populating a routing table with routes to a destination network. Static routes can be added to a router, or to any host that uses a routing table, such as a workstation. Aside from directly connected networks, a router's route table can only be populated via static routes (routes added by hand), or via dynamic routing protocols (routes added automatically). The task of manually entering and maintaining static routes on a large network is daunting, if not impossible. Therefore, static routes are used only in special circumstances on such networks.

When to Use Static Routes[1]

The smaller the network and the less often network changes occur that affect routing (routers going up and down, networks being added and removed, network links changing, and so on), the better the chances of successfully using static routes to populate routing tables. Dynamic routing protocols use up network resources to learn where all the networks are (bandwidth, router memory, router CPU time, and so on). Not to dis routing protocols. They perform a critical service and are the only reasonable solution in many environments. But you don't always *have* to deploy a routing protocol. More often though, static routes are used in conjunction with dynamic routing protocols to solve specific problems. Furthermore, static routes can also be employed at workstations in special situations.

Configuring Static Routes on a Router

The following examples will give you an idea of when and how to configure a router for static routes.

Example with a Small Routed Network

Let's say you have set up a network for a company with three branch offices in the city (see Figure 3-1). A public carrier is used to connect the sites. A router is set up at each site. Each router has one LAN interface to connect to the local network and one WAN interface to connect to the public carrier. Redundant links are not used.

This is a pretty small network in terms of routing. For the sake of this conversation, we don't care how many workstations are attached to each network. All that is required is that the three routers have properly populated route tables in order to forward packets to all networks. Networks of this type are often *static* in nature. They don't change all that often in terms of the number of subnets and the network numbering. There is only one path to each subnet. That being the case, static routes could be used here. The risk is that if the network *does* change (say a new router was added), the network administrator must manually change the configuration of each affected router. The risk in this case may be worth taking to negate the overhead used by a routing protocol.

Configuring the Routers

After initial configuration of the routers—*no static routes added and no routing protocols running*—the route table of each router is reflected in Figures 3-2, 3-3, and 3-4.

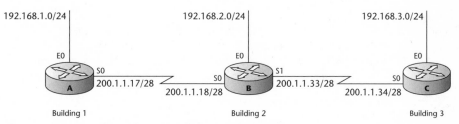

Figure 3-1 A small, stable network that rarely changes.

```
routerA#show ip route
Codes:   C – connected,  S – static,  I – IGRP,  R – RIP,  M – mobile,  B – BGP
         D – EIGRP,  EX – EIRGP external,  O – OSPF,  IA – OSPF inter area
         N1 – OSPF NSSA external type 1,  N2 – OSPF NSSA external type 2,  E – EGP
         i – IS-IS,  L1 – IS-IS level-1,  L2 – IS-IS level 2,  * - candidate default
         U – per-user static route, o – ODR
         T – traffic engineered route

Gateway of last resort is not set

C        192.168.1.0 [0/0] is directly connected, Ethernet0
C        200.1.1.16   [0/0] is directly connected, Serial0
```

Figure 3-2   Results of the **show ip route** command on router A—no static routes yet.

```
routerB#show ip route
Codes:   C – connected,  S – static,  I – IGRP,  R – RIP,  M – mobile,  B – BGP
         D – EIGRP,  EX – EIRGP external,  O – OSPF,  IA – OSPF inter area
         N1 – OSPF NSSA external type 1,  N2 – OSPF NSSA external type 2,  E – EGP
         i – IS-IS,  L1 – IS-IS level-1,  L2 – IS-IS level 2,  * - candidate default
         U – per-user static route, o – ODR
         T – traffic engineered route

Gateway of last resort is not set

C        192.168.2.0 [0/0] is directly connected, Ethernet0
C        200.1.1.16   [0/0] is directly connected, Serial0
C        200.1.1.32   [0/0] is directly connected, Serial1
```

Figure 3-3   Results of the **show ip route** command on router B—no static routes yet.

```
routerC#show ip route
Codes:   C – connected,  S – static,  I – IGRP,  R – RIP,  M – mobile,  B – BGP
         D – EIGRP,  EX – EIRGP external,  O – OSPF,  IA – OSPF inter area
         N1 – OSPF NSSA external type 1,  N2 – OSPF NSSA external type 2,  E – EGP
         i – IS-IS,  L1 – IS-IS level-1,  L2 – IS-IS level 2,  * - candidate default
         U – per-user static route, o – ODR
         T – traffic engineered route

Gateway of last resort is not set

C        192.168.3.0 [0/0] is directly connected, Ethernet0
C        200.1.1.32   [0/0] is directly connected, Serial0
```

Figure 3-4   Results of the **show ip route** command on router C—no static routes yet.

Adding Static Routes to Fully Populate the Route Tables

As you saw in Figure 3-2, router A has no information in its routing table about how to forward packets to either the 192.168.2.0 or the 192.168.3.0 subnets. As it stands right now, if router A received a packet from a host on the 192.168.1.0 bound for say, a host on the 192.168.2.0 network, **it would discard the packet**. Not good. The same is true for routers B and C in that they have no forwarding information about the subnets they are not directly connected to. One way to address this issue is with static routes. The global configuration command **ip route** is used to create static routes on a Cisco router. The command is used here to populate each router's route table with information about how to reach the two other respective networks:

```
routerA#config-term
routerA(config)#ip route 192.168.2.0  255.255.255.0  200.1.1.18 (1)
routerA(config)#ip route 192.168.3.0  255.255.255.0  200.1.1.18 (2)

routerB#config-term
routerB(config)#ip route 192.168.1.0  255.255.255.0  200.1.1.17 (3)
routerB(config)#ip route 192.168.3.0  255.255.255.0  200.1.1.34 (4)

routerC#config-term
routerC(config)#ip route 192.168.1.0  255.255.255.0  200.1.1.33 (5)
routerC(config)#ip route 192.168.2.0  255.255.255.0  200.1.1.33 (6)
```

(1) Adds a static route to the 192.168.2.0.

(2) Adds a static route to the 192.168.3.0.

(3) Adds a static route to the 192.168.1.0.

(4) Adds a static route to the 192.168.3.0.

(5) Adds a static route to the 192.168.1.0.

(6) Adds a static route to the 192.168.2.0.

Now let's have another look at those route tables. Figures 3-5, 3-6, and 3-7 reflect the commands just entered.

NOTE Notice the numbers in brackets [ ]—these represent the administrative distance and metric respectfully. As noted in the administrative distance chart on page 85, directly connected networks have an administrative distance of 0, whereas statically entered routes are 1. You can see that manifested in the route tables.

```
routerA#show ip route
Codes:   C – connected,  S – static,  I – IGRP,  R – RIP,  M – mobile,  B – BGP
         D – EIGRP,  EX – EIRGP external,  O – OSPF,  IA – OSPF inter area
         N1 – OSPF NSSA external type 1,  N2 – OSPF NSSA external type 2,  E – EGP
         i – IS-IS,  L1 – IS-IS level-1,  L2 – IS-IS level 2,  * - candidate default
         U – per-user static route,  o – ODR
         T – traffic engineered route

Gateway of last resort is not set

C          192.168.1.0 [0/0] is directly connected, Ethernet0
C          200.1.1.16  [0/0] is directly connected, Serial0
S          192.168.2.0 [1/0] via 200.1.1.18
S          192.168.3.0 [1/0] via 200.1.1.18
```

Figure 3-5   Router A—static routes added.

Packets can now find their way to any destination on the example network. Pretty straightforward, right? Just keep in mind that we are not necessarily saying this is the *only* way to configure such a network. Rather, it is *one* way. There are other ways the same objective could have been met. One method is to go ahead and implement a dynamic routing protocol, which is covered in the next chapter. Another method is outlined next.

```
routerB#show ip route
Codes:   C – connected,  S – static,  I – IGRP,  R – RIP,  M – mobile,  B – BGP
         D – EIGRP,  EX – EIRGP external,  O – OSPF,  IA – OSPF inter area
         N1 – OSPF NSSA external type 1,  N2 – OSPF NSSA external type 2,  E – EGP
         i – IS-IS,  L1 – IS-IS level-1,  L2 – IS-IS level 2,  * - candidate default
         U – per-user static route,  o – ODR
         T – traffic engineered route

Gateway of last resort is not set

C          192.168.2.0 [0/0] is directly connected, Ethernet0
C          200.1.1.16  [0/0] is directly connected, Serial0
C          200.1.1.32  [0/0] is directly connected, Serial1
S          192.168.1.0 [1/0] via 200.1.1.17
S          192.168.3.0 [1/0] via 200.1.1.34
```

Figure 3-6   Router B—static routes added.

```
routerC#show ip route
Codes:   C – connected,  S – static,  I – IGRP,  R – RIP,  M – mobile,  B – BGP
         D – EIGRP,  EX – EIRGP external,  O – OSPF,  IA – OSPF inter area
         N1 – OSPF NSSA external type 1,  N2 – OSPF NSSA external type 2,  E – EGP
         i – IS-IS,  L1 – IS-IS level-1,  L2 – IS-IS level 2,  * - candidate default
         U – per-user static route,  o – ODR
         T – traffic engineered route

Gateway of last resort is not set

C        192.168.3.0 [0/0] is directly connected, Ethernet0
C        200.1.1.34  [0/0] is directly connected, Serial0
S        192.168.1.0 [1/0] via 200.1.1.33
S        192.168.2.0 [1/0] via 200.1.1.33
```

Figure 3-7   Router C—static routes added.

Static Default Routes

Another way of configuring the example network would have been to institute a **static** *default* **route** on each router. A default route is a way of saying *none of the above*. A static route is a manually entered default route that provides a place to forward packets when there is no match in the route table for the destination address. Unless a path of some type is provided, most routers will drop the packet and return an ICMP *Destination Unreachable* message to the sender.

Default routing actually gets its own special treatment in Chapter 10. Here, a glimpse is given as to how to use default routing with static routes. No routing protocol will be used in the next example, yet the requirement for the administrator to intervene when a change in the network configuration occurs will be diminished.

Cisco routers refer to a default route as a Gateway of Last Resort. In the previous example, no default gateway has been configured on the routers. The statement "**Gateway of last resort is not set**" in the router output reveals this. In the upcoming example, a static default route will be instituted on two of the routers to supply them with a default route.

Refer back to Figure 3-1. Notice that router A and router C have only one interface connecting to other networks. Since there is only one possible interface to forward outbound packets to, why not just set a default gateway instead of adding each individual network to the route table? Then, any packet bound for a network not directly connected will be sent to the Gateway of Last Resort. Here is how the routers would instead be programmed to achieve the desired results:

```
routerA#config-term
routerA(config)#ip route 0.0.0.0  0.0.0.0  200.1.1.18          (1)

routerB#config-term
```

```
routerB(config)#ip route 192.168.1.0   255.255.255.0   200.1.1.18        (2)
routerB(config)#ip route 192.168.3.0   255.255.255.0   200.1.1.18        (3)

routerC#config-term
routerC(config)#ip route 0.0.0.0   0.0.0.0   200.1.1.33                  (4)
```

(1) Set a static default route that points to the next hop router.

(2) Create a static route, same as before.

(3) Create a static route, same as before.

(4) Set a static default route that points to the next hop router.

The route tables in Figures 3-8, 3-9, and 3-10 now reflect that a Gateway of Last Resort exists.

To take as an example a packet sent from the 192.168.1.0 to the 192.168.3.0, router A will forward the packet to its default gateway (the 200.1.1.18) when it can't find a match for the destination network in its route table. Router B *will* find a match and the packet will successfully reach its destination. Note that router A and B use the 0.0.0.0 network to represent the default route.

One advantage to this configuration is that if a fourth router is added downstream of either of the routers configured with a default gateway, fewer routers will need to have their configurations changed. The routers would simply forward packets with destination addresses not matching an entry in the route table to the Gateway of Last Resort. Naturally, attention must be paid in configuring static default routes that packets forwarded to the default gateway will eventually reach their destination. Many more examples of default routing will be presented throughout the book, but the *real* lesson here is that there is often more than one way to configure a routing scheme and one method might work better than another. This gives *you* an opportunity to stand out in your field by thinking through a better solution.

---

routerA#show ip route
Codes: C – connected, S – static, I – IGRP, R – RIP, M – mobile, B – BGP
          D – EIGRP, EX – EIRGP external, O – OSPF, IA – OSPF inter area
          N1 – OSPF NSSA external type 1, N2 – OSPF NSSA external type 2, E – EGP
          i – IS-IS, L1 – IS-IS level-1, L2 – IS-IS level 2, * - candidate default
          U – per-user static route, o – ODR
          T – traffic engineered route

Gateway of last resort is 200.1.1.18 to network 0.0.0.0

C   **192.168.1.0 [0/0] is directly connected, Ethernet0**
C   **200.1.1.16   [0/0] is directly connected, Serial0**

Figure 3-8   Router A now has a populated Gateway of Last Resort.

```
routerB#show ip route
Codes:    C – connected,  S – static,  I – IGRP,  R – RIP,  M – mobile,  B – BGP
          D – EIGRP,  EX – EIRGP external,  O – OSPF,  IA – OSPF inter area
          N1 – OSPF NSSA external type 1,  N2 – OSPF NSSA external type 2,  E – EGP
          i – IS-IS,  L1 – IS-IS level-1,  L2 – IS-IS level 2,  * - candidate default
          U – per-user static route, o – ODR
          T – traffic engineered route

Gateway of last resort is not set

C         192.168.2.0 [0/0] is directly connected, Ethernet0
C         200.1.1.16   [0/0] is directly connected, Serial0
C         200.1.1.32   [0/0] is directly connected, Serial1
S         192.168.1.0 [1/0] via 200.1.1.17
S         192.168.3.0 [1/0] via 200.1.1.34
```

Figure 3-9   Router B still has no default gateway set.

NOTE The static default route technique will not work on router B because router B has *two* interfaces connecting to other networks. Packets from router B bound for the 192.168.1.0 must exit through the S0 interface, whereas packets bound for the 192.168.3.0 must be forwarded through interface S1. In this case, the specific routes must be added to the route tables.

```
routerC#show ip route
Codes:    C – connected,  S – static,  I – IGRP,  R – RIP,  M – mobile,  B – BGP
          D – EIGRP,  EX – EIRGP external,  O – OSPF,  IA – OSPF inter area
          N1 – OSPF NSSA external type 1,  N2 – OSPF NSSA external type 2,  E – EGP
          i – IS-IS,  L1 – IS-IS level-1,  L2 – IS-IS level 2,  * - candidate default
          U – per-user static route, o – ODR
          T – traffic engineered route

Gateway of last resort is 200.1.1.33 to network 0.0.0.0

C         192.168.3.0 [0/0] is directly connected, Ethernet0
C         200.1.1.32   [0/0] is directly connected, Serial0
```

Figure 3-10   Router C now has a populated Gateway of Last Resort.

Static Routes on a Workstation

Although it is rare to alter the route table of a workstation, there are times when routing will be made more efficient by doing so. Figure 3-11 illustrates a small network with two subnets separated by a router. Router A's default configuration lists both the directly connected networks. The workstations all have a standard default gateway pointing to router A. Any packets bound for the corresponding network will first be forwarded to router A, which will perform a lookup on the target network and forward the packets out its opposing interface. This is about as simple as it gets.

In Figure 3-12, a new router has been added to allow access to the Internet. All that's required to provide Internet access to the workstations is to add a default gateway to router A that points to router B (this would be considered a *static* default route since it is manually configured). When a workstation forwards any packet not destined for its local network to its default gateway, router A will receive the packet. If the packet is bound for the other local network, Router A will have a routing entry for the destination address of the packet and forward it out the specified interface. Otherwise router A will forward the packet out its default gateway to router B, which will in turn forward the packet to the Internet.

This new configuration will work fine, but does it optimize routing? Note that the workstations on the 192.168.1.0 have a direct connection to the Internet router, but instead they forward Internet bound packets to router A. This results in one extra hop for Internet bound packets generated from that network.

Routing could be optimized if workstations on the 192.168.1.0 could be told to send packets bound for the 192.168.2.0 to Router A, but to send all other packets to router B. This type of configuration only can occur at the workstation. The default gateway must be re-hypointed from the 192.168.1.254 to the 102.168.3.254. *When there is a router on the network providing access to the Internet, default gateways MUST point the way to that router.* This of course means the default route that previously served to reach the 192.168.2.0 is now defunct (you can only have one default route). The solution is to institute a *static route* at the workstations that specifically lists the path to the 192.168.2.0.

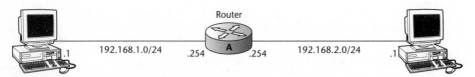

Figure 3-11   Two-network system—workstations use default settings.

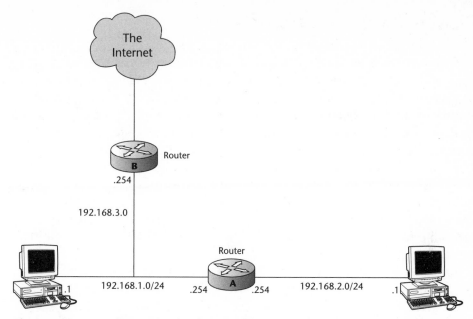

Figure 3-12 Less-than-optimal routing configuration.

Modification of a Windows-based workstation's route table is accomplished with the **route add** command. An example was provided in Chapter 1.

A pleasant side affect of this approach is that if the internal router ever went down Internet access would still be available to the 192.168.1.0. And we all know how important Internet access is!

PLUSES AND MINUSES OF THIS APPROACH

You should be able to see both the advantages and disadvantages to setting a workstation's default gateway to point to the Internet. While modifying the workstation's route table certainly optimizes routing, the downside is that each internal network *must* be listed in the route table of each workstation on 192.168.1.0. Some administrators might balk at this idea, but it all depends on your network and how fast it's growing. With workstation imaging being so prevalent, some would consider the modification of the default route table as simply another of many configuration settings.

Floating Static Routes

A floating static route refers to a static route that may not always be in use—thus it "floats." You may recall from the discussion of administrative distance in Chapter 2 (page 84), that static routes have precedence over dynamically learned routes for installation into the route table. Only directly connected routes have a higher precedence than statically entered routes.

However, administrative distance values can be altered. When a static route is entered it can have its priority altered to a value higher than the native routing protocol in use. In that case, any dynamically learned route to a particular network would be installed in the route table over a static route pointing to the same network. The static route would simply act as backup. If the dynamically learned route was lost the static route would automatically be installed in its place.

To set an administrative distance value other than the default on a Cisco router, simply include the value as follows:

```
ip route 0.0.0.0  0.0.0.0  200.1.1.33 99 (1)
```

(1) Set the administrative distance to 99

In this example, the value of 99 was randomly chosen. In fact, the value only need be one digit higher than the administrative distance value you wish to override. For example, if you're running OSPF, which has an administrative distance value of 110, setting an administrative distance value of 111 on a static route would cause the OSPF route to be installed over the static route, unless the OSPF route was lost, in which case the static route would then be used.

Propagating Static Routes

When dynamic routing is employed, static routes and static default routes can be shared with other routers vis-à-vis routing protocols. Other routers learn about the static routes without having to manually enter the route on each router. The process is referred to as redistribution and is covered in Chapter 10.

Summary

This chapter covered the following:

- Static routes are routes manually added to a routing table.

- Static routes may be suitable for smaller networks without redundant network links.

- Static routes are often employed in conjunction with dynamic routing protocols and as default gateways to solve specific network configuration issues.

- Static routes are configured with the **ip route** command on Cisco routers.

- Static routes have an administrative distance value of 1, which means by default, a static route will always be chosen over a route learned from *any* routing protocol. Only directly connected routes have a higher precedence.

- Floating static routes have had their administrative distance altered to a higher value so that they are only installed in the route table if another route to the same network is lost.

- Cisco provides the ODR (On Demand Routing) facility as an alternative to using static routing.

- Static routes, and static default routes can be propagated throughout the system by way of routing protocols. (See Chapter 10 for details.)

Notes

1. Cisco introduced a facility in later versions of its IOS called On Demand Routing (ODR). ODR reduces the need for static routing, providing a "best-of-both-worlds" solution between static and dynamic routing in very specific cases. ODR is not covered in this book.

Dynamic Routing

Overview

This chapter explains the heady topic of dynamic routing. It is a prelude to the subsequent chapters that cover specific dynamic routing protocols. A number of examples are given that illustrate important routing concepts such as classless routing, route summarization, longest match principal, and so on. The following topics are covered:

KEY TERMS

Interior routing protocols

Exterior routing protocols

Distance vector

Routing by rumor

Link-state

Link-state advertisements

Shortest path first

Topology map

Routing-loops

Metrics

Multipath routing

Load balancing

Hierarchical routing

Classful and classless routing

Classful and classless routing protocols

Summarization

Discontiguous networks

Longest match algorithm

The Need for an Automated Routing Solution

Adding and modifying static routes by hand can get to be anything from monotonous to completely unworkable, depending on the size of a network. On a large, complex network, it is virtually impossible for an administrator to keep the network up via manual manipulation of the route tables. Things change too fast. A single downed router or network link may necessitate dozens or even hundreds of routers to be reconfigured with alternate routes around the failed device. That is where dynamic routing comes in.

The term *dynamic routing* intimates automaticity and flexibility, and indeed those are two of several key features of this routing method. In a dynamic routing environment, routers learn about the condition of the network automatically and modify their respective route tables on-the-fly—without human intervention. Dynamic routing can be deployed on any size network.

What Is a Routing Protocol?

To begin with, a protocol is a set of conventions governing the treatment and especially the formatting of data in an electronic communications system. A routing protocol is a specialized form of a protocol that allows two or more routers to exchange information about the networks they know about. A routing protocol is what enables the concept of dynamic routing. More specifically, a routing protocol is based on an algorithm that runs as a process on the router. An algorithm, on the other hand, is a procedure or formula for solving a problem.

Algorithms used to populate route tables are based on graph theory, which is kind of a "connect-the-dots" approach that applies to connected nodes. Graph theory lends itself quite well to the idea of the node being a router and the network links being the lines that connect the routers. Modern routing protocols are based on early work done by folks like R. Bellman, L.R. Ford, and Edsger Dijkstra. The RIP, IGRP, EIGRP, and BGP protocols use a derivative of the Bellman-Ford Distance Vector algorithm, while OSPF and IS-IS[1] are based on the Dijkstra Shortest Path First algorithm.

A variety of routing protocols have been developed over the years. No single routing protocol is the be-all, do-all, end-all solution (although OSPF has pretty much become the defacto choice for enterprise networks and some ISP networks). Depending on the specific requirements of a network, one protocol may be a better choice then another. It is quite possible that in your entire IT career, you may work with only two or three of these routing protocols. If you work for an ISP, the Border Gateway Protocol (BGP) will be very important. If you are administrating a small- to medium-sized network with a single WAN link to the Internet, you might use RIPv2. On large enterprise networks EIGRP or OSPF is often the preferred protocol.

ROUTING PROTOCOLS VS. ROUTED PROTOCOLS

These are similar terms with very different meanings, which can lead to confusion. *Routing* protocols are protocols that propagate network routing information among routers (OSPF and BGP). Such protocols do not carry user data. *Routed* protocols are layer 3 and layer 4 network protocols that carry user data and are capable of being routed across networks (IPX and TCP/IP). Some network protocols cannot be routed, such as NetBEUI. However, because the industry is quickly converging on IP as the routed protocol of choice, the term "routed protocol" is heard less often.

Considerations for Designing Routing Protocols

When teaching a class, the author often asks students how they would design a solution to a networking problem, prior to discussing what the industry came up with. This helps students better relate to the industry solution and understand the reasoning behind it. Let's apply that approach to the problem of propagating networks among routers.

What are some of the networking issues that must be taken into consideration for a protocol that purports to automatically populate all route tables in the system with accurate, timely information about the system's networks?

At its core, a router running a routing protocol must be able to communicate with other routers. It must be able to tell other routers about the networks it is aware of, and conversely learn about networks other routers are aware of. Therefore, a common language is needed. The language of the routing protocol must have a vocabulary to describe as much about the router, its status, and its routes as needed. That language and vocabulary takes the form of the actual routing protocol itself. Because the language is unique, routers can only exchange information with other routers running the same protocol.[2]

If a routing protocol learns about more than one path to the same network, it must have a means of evaluating which route is best to use. As will be illustrated shortly, a number of factors affect this decision. Off the top of your head, how many factors can you think of that come to bear on choosing the best path to a given network?

A routing protocol must be accommodating to changes in the network. A single downed router or network link can dramatically impact the ability to forward packets to their destination.

If changes in the network demand that all route tables be updated, the delay until this process is completed (known as **convergence**) is extremely important.

One significant problem with routing is the possibility of a **routing-loop** (*often due to slow convergence*). A routing-loop occurs when packets loop endlessly around the network, never reaching their destination. If you think the Internet is slow now, just imagine an ever-growing number of infinitely looping packets congesting it.[3]

The Internet, and many private networks are classlessly addressed (subnetting, VLSM, and CIDR). In order to correctly route packets, the routing protocol must be able to discern that a network is employing classless addressing and be able to forward packets to the correct subnet. In other cases, it is best for the routing protocol to ignore subnets when advertising routes, and summarize a group of addresses as a single route.

Finally, a routing protocol should economize on the use of network bandwidth. Traffic generated by routers talking to each other must be minimized to avoid wasting network bandwidth. The industry, in noting these considerations, has come up with the following terms to describe the characteristics of a routing protocol:

- Robustness
- Optimality
- Flexibility
- Speed of convergence
- Avoidance of routing-loops
- Support for classless addressing
- Simplicity

Each routing protocol's ability to address the aforementioned concerns will be discussed in this chapter as well as the chapters covering the individual protocols.

Metrics of Routing Protocols

As previously discussed, a routing **metric** refers to how a routing protocol decides which route is best if more than one path to a network is discovered. This is also known as the **cost** of the route.

Each route learned by a routing protocol is assigned a metric value. A metric has no meaning if the protocol has discovered only one route to a particular network. But if more than one route is discovered, each router is used to choose the best path. There are a number of factors that the protocol may take into consideration when assigning a metric to a route:

- **Hop count:** Number of routers to traverse in order to reach the destination network.
- **Path length:** A refinement of hop count that allows a more accurate cost to be calculated.
- **Sum of per-link costs**
- **Bandwidth:** Speed of links between routers.
- **Delay:** Time in milliseconds to cross a link.
- **Load:** Congestion on link due to traffic.
- **Reliability:** Based on bit error rates of path.

> ### METRIC VS. COST
>
> Is there a difference between the term *metric* and the term *cost*? If there is, it's minor, as whatever distinction existed between the terms has blurred over the years. Think of "metric" as a generic reference to the concept of a routing protocol choosing one route over another, whereas "cost" is often embodied as a specific value (like "1" or "1784"), and composed of whatever metric criteria the protocol uses: hop count, bandwidth, delay, and so on.
>
> But there are no hard and fast rules for how the terms interrelate. For example, the popular Dijkstra algorithm uses a metric defined as cost, with "cost" not being specified. OSPF, which uses the Dijkstra algorithm, often defines cost as the bandwidth of the network link. Bandwidth is explained in many texts as one of the criteria composing a metric! Go figure.

Not all routing protocols implement each of the aforementioned factors. One reason for the plethora of routing protocols that have been developed, has to with the difference in the metrics each protocol employs. Over the years metrics have improved. Newer routing protocols incorporate these improvements.

Categorizing Dynamic Routing Protocols

Routing protocols are categorized according to the purpose for which they were designed. A good place to begin understanding a routing protocol (and when to employ it) is to understand what networking problem it was designed to solve. There are five different ways routing protocols can be carved up to help understand their intended purpose. Keep in mind that the following descriptions will become clearer as the individual routing protocols are discussed.

Interior versus Exterior Routing Protocols

Interior routing protocols were developed to facilitate routing *within* an **autonomous system**, whereas exterior routing protocols were developed to facilitate routing *between* autonomous systems. An autonomous system (AS) refers to a network under a single administrative control—for example, your organization's network. If you were to one day connect to another organization's network and needed to share routing information, that's where an exterior routing protocol comes in. An exterior routing protocol is tuned for passing routing information *between* autonomous systems. Such a protocol would usually be employed only on each organization's border routers (the router that connects your network to the rest of the world). Any interior routing protocols in use would remain.

Most routing protocols are interior protocols. The only exterior routing protocol in common use is BGP (Border Gateway Protocol). BGP is used extensively in the Internet, tying together thousands of autonomous systems.

Synonymous terms for interior versus exterior protocols are intradomain versus interdomain and intranetwork versus internetwork. You will also see the acronyms IGP (Interior Gateway Protocol) and EGP (Exterior Gateway Protocol). These acronyms refer to interior and exterior routing protocols as a group.

Table 4-1 lists the common routing protocols classified by interior versus exterior.

Distance Vector versus Link-State

One important design aspect of a routing protocol is how the protocol determines the path to networks—which in turn determines the composition of the route table on each router. Routing protocols use either **distance vector** or **link-state** methods (an exception is BGP, which uses a variant of distance vector methods and will be discussed in Chapter 9). Each of these two methods is based on the well-known routing algorithms referred to earlier.

Distance Vector Routing Protocols

Distance vector protocols are based on what is colloquially known as "routing by rumor." Routers running a distance vector protocol don't receive routing information from each router in the system. Rather, a router running a distance vector protocol is told about networks known to other routers by its immediate neighbors. Each router shares routing information with its neighbors in the form of **routing update packets**. The neighboring routers receive these updates, add the information about the newly learned networks to their own route tables, and then send the combined information to *their* neighbors. In this manner, each router in the system eventually learns the path to all networks, but much of the information is secondhand—thus the "routing by rumor" moniker. Figure 4-1 illustrates in basic form how a distance vector protocol communicates.

Table 4-1 Classification of Routing Protocols by Interior versus Exterior

PROTOCOL	INTERIOR/EXTERIOR
RIPv1 (Routing Information Protocol version 1)	Interior
RIPv2 (Routing Information Protocol version 2)	Interior
IGRP (Interior Gateway Routing Protocol)	Interior
EIGRP (Enhanced Interior Gateway Routing Protocol)	Interior
OSPF (Open Shortest Path First)	Interior
BGP (Border Gateway Protocol)	Exterior

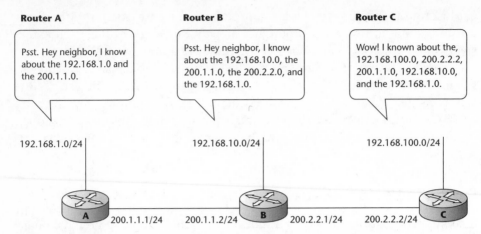

Figure 4-1 Simplified view of distance vector protocol communications.

What information is shared among routers running a distance vector protocol? To begin with, each router informs its neighbors of its directly connected networks. It also includes networks the router has learned of from other neighbors. The routers also share the metric of each network it knows of. The metric a distance vector protocol assigns to a route is a value called **distance**. Traditionally, distance was composed of simply *hop count*—how many routers the packet must hop across to reach its destination. This is true of RIP. If the destination network is three routing hops away, the metric is 3. If the protocol discovered two or more paths to the same network, the route with the lowest hop count would win and be installed in the route table. A distance vector protocol released subsequent to RIP, IGRP, uses *bandwidth* and *delay* to determine the metric value. Although IGRP ignores hop count, it is still considered a distance vector protocol because it behaves in all other respects as a distance vector routing protocol. This point is further illustrated in the following discussion.

Vectors

In a distance vector environment, each router keeps a **vector** for each destination network. A vector is simply a *direction*, taking the form of the next hop router the packet will be forwarded to on the way to its destination. The router stores the IP address of the router that reported the lowest cost path. This router is called the next hop because it is the next location packets will be forwarded to on the way to the destination network.

NOTE Even though IGRP does not employ hop count in its metric, the term "next hop router" applies even to routing protocols that don't employ hop count in ther metric.

Once again, *distance* is derived from the metric of a route; how far it is to the destination network; while *vector* is simply the direction a packet is forwarded as it leaves the router; which interface the packet leaves from. Thus we have the *distance vector* protocol.

More on the Metrics Used by Distance Vector Routing Protocols

As previously mentioned, early distance vector routing protocols such as RIP used hop count as the sole metric for determining the distance to a network. In RIP's mind, the fewer the number of routers the packets need to pass through, the better the route. Hop count as a cost determiner works well on small systems with *similar speed network links*. On such systems, hop count is indeed a good measure of the cost of a path. However, on larger systems, with multiple paths to a destination, and varying bandwidth on network links hop count alone does not always tell the truth about the best path to a network. Figure 4-2 illustrates a problem that arises for distance vector protocols that use only hop count to determine the distance to a network when there are multiple paths to the same network.

After all routers have shared their route tables, but *before* the distance vector protocol has run, router A knows the following (simplified):

I am directly connected to network 1 via Ethernet interface 0.

I am directly connected to subnet 1 via serial interface 0.

I am directly connected to subnet 4 via serial interface 1.

Network 2 is one hop away via serial interface 0.

Network 2 is four hops away via serial interface 1.

Network 3 is two hops away via serial interface 0.

Network 3 is three hops away via serial interface 1.

Network 4 is three hops away via serial interface 0.

Network 4 is two hops away via serial interface 1.

The focus is on getting packets from network 1 to network 4. Router A is aware of two paths to network 4. One path will be *three* hops away out its serial interface 0, the other path *two* hops away out its serial interface 1. Once the distance vector protocol has run, the path through serial interface 1 will be chosen as the best route to network 4 even though the path through Serial 0—with its faster WAN links—is a faster route.

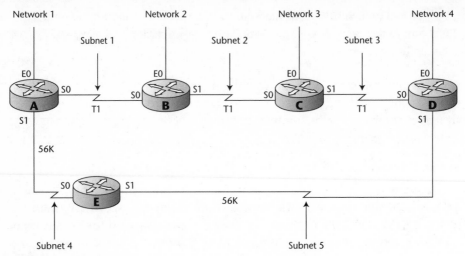

Figure 4-2 Network diagram showing two paths from network 1 to network 4—hop count used as metric.[4]

Table 4-2 shows router A's route table after the distance vector protocol has run (simplified).

As networks started growing in size, the designers of distance vector routing protocols realized the limitations of using hop count for determining path length. IGRP, a proprietary Cisco routing protocol introduced after RIP, use bandwidth (and other factors) to determine the distance to a network. Refer again to Figure 4-2, but this time running a distance vector routing protocol that incorporates bandwidth in determining distance.

After all routers have broadcast their route tables, but *before* the distance vector protocol has run, router A will know the following (simplified):

I am directly connected to network 1 via Ethernet interface 0.

I am directly connected to subnet 1 via serial interface 0.

I am directly connected to subnet 4 via serial interface 1.

Network 2 is reachable through a 1,544 Kbps link via serial interface 0.

Network 2 is reachable through two 56K links and two 1,544 Kbps links via serial interface 1.

Network 3 is reachable through two 1,544 Kbps links via serial interface 0.

Network 3 is reachable through two 56K links and one 1,544 Kbps link via serial interface 1.

Network 4 is reachable through three 1,544 Kbps links via serial interface 0.

Network 4 is reachable through two 56K links via serial interface 1.

Table 4-2   Simplified Route Table for Router A

NETWORK	INTERFACE	DISTANCE
Network 1	E0	Directly connected
Network 2	S0	1
Network 3	S0	2
Network 4	S1	2

When the distance vector algorithm for IGRP is run, the links to the networks will be taken into account and the three-router hop across the T1 links to network 4 will win over the two-router hop across the slower 56K links.

Table 4-3 shows router A's route table after the distance vector protocol has run—bandwidth is used for path determination.

Other Issues with Distance Vector Protocols

Adding metric factors like bandwidth helps distance vector protocols route more efficiently, but they still have their issues. A characteristic that all distance vector routing protocols share is that they are "chatty." Conversations between routers consume network resources. A router running a distance vector protocol defaults to broadcasting its entire route table as often as every 30 seconds out each enabled interface. Route tables can get quite large, and transmitting the entire table that often can significantly impinge on network bandwidth. Chatty protocols also interfere with the ability of the routers to converge due to the delay incurred in sending so many update packets. This issue was addressed with the update to IGRP and EIGRP, which is covered in Chapter 6 and 7.

Distance vector routing protocols also have a tendency to create routing-loops. A routing-loop occurs when two routers point to each other as the path to a network. They end up bouncing packets back and forth to each other instead of delivering the packets to their proper destination. Therefore, distance vector protocols must be engineered with an array of provisions to mitigate the possibility of such loops. A closer look at routing-loops will be pursued when RIP is covered in detail in Chapter 5.

Table 4-3   Simplified Route Table for Router A

NETWORK	INTERFACE	DISTANCE
Network 1	E0	Directly connected
Network 2	S0	1
Network 3	S0	2
Network 4	S0	3

For all the aforementioned reasons, distance vector routing protocols are suitable only for smaller networks.

Link-State Routing Protocols

Link-state-based routing protocols (also known as **shortest path first** protocols) are a step up the routing protocol evolutionary ladder. Link-state protocols are based on the Dijkstra algorithm. Rather than relying on routing information learned through hearsay, link-state routers receive first-hand routing information from each router in the area. The information is transmitted in the form of **Link-State Advertisements,** or LSAs, which are passed from router to router and include information about the state of each router's directly connected links (IP address, speed of link, and so on). Unlike distance vector protocols which only compile lists of networks and the interface to forward packets through in order to reach those networks, link-state protocols allow each router to know how many routers are out there and what networks are connected to each router. Every router ends up with a topology map of the system. Because the routers are only passing information about their own links, rather than the entire routing table, initial convergence is improved. *Furthermore, LSAs are usually only sent when the status of a link changes.* This important feature also improves convergence.[5]

The metric used in link-state protocols is often *bandwidth,* so the network map includes the speed of each network link. With this information, the Dijkstra algorithm is run, the shortest (quickest) path to each network is determined, and the route table is populated. This type of routing protocol is not only a better determiner of the quickest path to a network, it is less prone to routing-loops because with a complete map of the network, routers can't be fooled into advertising routes that lead back through themselves. Figure 4-3 depicts a simplified version of how link-state protocol communicates.

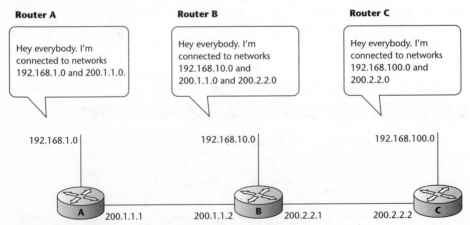

Figure 4-3 Simplified view of link-state protocol communications.

Link-state protocols have other improvements over their distance vector cousins as well. Update packets can be sent as multicasts rather than as broadcasts, thereby relieving the processing load on hosts not acting as routing devices. Some link-state routing protocols can also be configured in a hierarchical fashion. This feature can further reduce unnecessary traffic by confining updates within specific areas of the network. This concept will be illustrated when OSFP is discussed in Chapter 8.

Referring again to Figure 4-2, let's examine what information link-state protocols learn about network routes.

After all routers send their link-state advertisements (LSAs), but *before* the link-state protocol has run, router A (and in fact all routers) will know the following:

Router A is directly connected to network 1 via Ethernet interface 0; the bandwidth is 100 Mbps.

Router A is directly connected to subnet 1 via serial interface 0; the bandwidth is 1544 Kbps.

Router A is directly connected to subnet 4 via serial interface 1; the bandwidth is 56 Kbps

Router B is directly connected to network 2 via Ethernet interface 0; the bandwidth is 100 Mbps

Router B is directly connected to subnet 1 via serial interface 0; the bandwidth is 1544 Kbps.

Router B is directly connected to subnet 2 via serial interface 1; the bandwidth is 1544 Kbps.

Router C is directly connected to network 3 via Ethernet interface 0; the bandwidth is 100 Mbps.

Router C is directly connected to subnet 2 via serial interface 0; the bandwidth is 1544 Kbps.

Router C is directly connected to subnet 3 via serial interface 1; the bandwidth is 1544 Kbps.

Router D is directly connected to network 4 via Ethernet interface 0; the bandwidth is 100 Mbps.

Router D is directly connected to subnet 3 via serial interface 0; the bandwidth is 1544 Kbps.

Router D is directly connected to subnet 5 via serial interface 1; the bandwidth is 56 Kbps.

Router E is directly connected to subnet 4 via serial interface 0; the bandwidth is 56 Kbps.

Router E is directly connected to subnet 5 via serial interface 1; the bandwidth is 56 Kbps.

Router A knows a lot! So does every router in the system. Each router literally has a map of the network topology. They see what you see in the diagram. Each router not only knows how many total routers are in the area, they know which network is connected to which router and the speed of each network link. From this information, the Dijkstra algorithm is run and the route table is built.

As you can see, the key difference with link-state protocols over distance vector protocols is that link-state protocols don't need to be told the distance to a network by another router. Link-state routers make that calculation for themselves because they have enough information to do so.

Summary of Distance Vector versus Link-State Protocols

Now that you have seen examples of how distance vector and link-state protocols work, let's contrast their differences once again. It is said that distance vector protocols carry out "routing by rumor." A router builds its route table based on what another router "whispered in its ear." The router that did the whispering learned most of what it knows in the same manner—from another router. Then, after running the distance vector protocol and populating the route table the entire table is broadcast by each router to its neighbors as often as every 30 seconds. Delays incurred propagating routing information in this manner slows convergence and makes distance vector routing protocols prone to routing-loops. This can severely hamper or even break routing. Therefore, a number of route-loop prevention techniques must be engineered into such protocols.

With link-state protocols, each router speaks only for itself, describing its direct links through advertisements that are relayed to every other router in the area. Once the route table is built, only changes affecting network links need to be propagated.

Although some distance vector protocols include bandwidth information in the metric they are still prone to routing-loops. Link-state protocols reduce the occurrence of routing-loops because each router has a map that keeps it from being fooled into accidentally looping packets. Table 4-4 lists the common routing protocols classified by distance vector versus link-state.

Table 4-4   Classification of Routing Protocols by Distance Vector versus Link-State

PROTOCOL	DISTANCE VECTOR OR LINK-STATE
RIP ver 1 (Routing Information Protocol)	Distance vector
RIP ver 2 (Routing Information Protocol)	Distance vector
IGRP (Interior Gateway Routing Protocol)	Distance vector
EIGRP (Enhanced Interior Gateway Routing Protocol)	Advanced distance vector (hybrid of distance vector and link-state)

Table 4-4 *(continued)*

PROTOCOL	DISTANCE VECTOR OR LINK-STATE
OSPF (Open Shortest Path First)	Link-state
BGP (Border Gateway Protocol)	Path vector (see Chapter 9)

Singlepath versus Multipath

Although any particular routing protocol may become aware of more than one path to a network, not all routing protocols can actually install multiple paths into the route table and route packets through both paths. A **singlepath** protocol must choose the best path from the available paths to a network as the *primary* path (based on the metrics of each route). Only if the primary fails can secondary paths (if any) be used.

On the other hand, **multipath** routing protocols not only choose a primary path to a particular network, but for the purposes of throughput and load balancing, they can route packets via multiple paths (called multiplexing). Multipath routing protocols speed network performance and improve reliability.

Table 4-5 lists the common routing protocols classified by singlepath versus multipath.

Broadcast versus Multicast

Routing protocols differ in how they send update packets to other routers. Certain routing protocols (such as RIP and IGRP) use broadcast packets, which are received by every device on the subnet. More sophisticated protocols use unicast or multicast packets (such as EIGRP, OSPF, and BGP) which are received by only one or a group of devices, respectively.

Table 4-5 Classification of Routing protocols by Singlepath versus Multipath

PROTOCOL	SINGLEPATH VS. MULTIPATH
RIP ver 1 (Routing Information Protocol)	Singlepath[6]
RIP ver 2 (Routing Information Protocol)	Singlepath
IGRP (Interior Gateway Routing Protocol)	Multipath
EIGRP (Enhanced Interior Gateway Routing Protocol)	Multipath
OSPF (Open Shortest Path First)	Multipath
BGP (Border Gateway Protocol)	Singlepath[7]

Flat versus Hierarchical

Most routing protocols are *flat* in nature, meaning routing updates are propagated to all routers throughout the autonomous system (either through distance vector or link-state methods). To minimize the impact of routing updates on network bandwidth, some routing protocols can be configured in a hierarchical manner. Groups of routers within the internetwork can be segregated into **areas** and certain routing updates are confined within an area. Although some routing updates still occur between areas within the internetwork (when a major change occurs that affects the entire internetwork), minor routing updates occur only within an area, reducing overall network traffic as well as the load on the routers.

In short, hierarchical-capable routing protocols give the network administrator an additional tool for managing the resources used by routing advertisements. The design of OSPF provides a splendid example of a well-architected protocol that takes advantage of hierarchical routing structures and will be examined in detail in Chapter 8. Table 4-6 lists the common routing protocols classified by flat versus hierarchical.

Classful versus Classless

Originally, routing protocols were classful in nature, meaning they were designed to operate on networks using classful addressing (class A, B, or C). Classful routing protocols have only limited support for classless addressing, the reason being that such protocols do not include the subnet mask in routing advertisements. The inclusion of the subnet mask is unnecessary in a classful addressing environment because the router receiving an advertisement can make an assumption about the mask in use by simply applying the First Octet Rule to the address. Such assumptions cannot be made in a classless environment however. Therefore, a new strain of routing protocols that include the mask in the advertisement of a network were developed. Such protocols have full support for all classless addressing methods. Table 4-7 lists the common routing protocols classified by classful versus classless.

Table 4-6 Classification of Routing Protocols by Flat versus Hierarchical

PROTOCOL	FLAT VS. HIERARCHICAL
RIP ver 1 (Routing Information Protocol)	Flat
RIP ver 2 (Routing Information Protocol)	Flat
IGRP (Interior Gateway Routing Protocol)	Flat
EIGRP (Enhanced Interior Gateway Routing Protocol)	Flat[8]
OSPF (Open Shortest Path First)	Hierarchical
BGP (Border Gateway Protocol)	Flat

Table 4-7 Classification of Routing Protocols by Classful versus Classless

PROTOCOL	CLASSFUL VS. CLASSLESS
RIP ver 1 (Routing Information Protocol)	Classful
RIP ver 2 (Routing Information Protocol)	Classless
IGRP (Interior Gateway Routing Protocol)	Classful
EIGRP (Enhanced Interior Gateway Routing Protocol)	Classless
OSPF (Open Shortest Path First)	Classless
BGP (Border Gateway Protocol)	Classless (v4)

If you are in a situation where classless addressing methods must be supported by a classful routing protocol, God bless you. Upgrade to a classless protocol.

Route Summarization

In this all-important section of the book, we are taking a broad approach to route summarization. Rather than try and break this topic out and explain summarization in a compartmentalized fashion, it is being treated in-context with the peripheral networking issues surrounding summarization. The following topics are covered in this section:

- Route summarization with interior routing protocols
- Several examples of networking with classless routing protocols
- Reinforcement of classless addressing concepts: subnetting, VLSMs, and CIDR
- Discontiguous networks and the special handling they require
- Longest-match algorithm—how routers actually match a network to a route table entry
- Using summarization in a hierarchical addressing scheme

NOTE You should already be up-to-speed on classless addressing techniques before tackling this section. Classless addressing was covered in detail in Chapter 1 starting on page 32.

Route summarization refers to the concept of reducing the number of entries in route tables while still providing a path to all known networks. One of the unfortunate side affects of creating additional networks via subnetting is that route tables grow in size as they are populated with the paths to all those networks. Every route must be propagated and that takes bandwidth. Also, as route tables get larger, it takes longer for a router to lookup a route. Finally, large route tables require additional router resources such as memory and CPU cycles. Even before classless addressing was introduced, the shear number of classful addresses being assigned, contributed to bloated route tables on the Internet's backbone routers. The additional networks created by classless addressing techniques potentially makes the problem more toxic. The antidote is **route summarization**.

Route summarization, simply stated, allows the propagation of a *single route*, which in fact refers to a path to *multiple* subnets. Summarization reduces the size of route tables because a series of network addresses can be represented as a single *summary* address in the table. This is a critical function in modern networking, so several examples will be presented to illustrate how summarization performs its magic.

Summarization can occur both at the address-assignment level, where the assigning authority allocates IP addresses to ISPs, large organizations, and educational institutions, and at the organization level where smaller organizations receive their address assignments from ISPs.

At the assignment level, summarization takes the form of CIDR addressing, which inherently summarizes a range of allocated addresses into a single address.

At the organizational level, the additional networks created through the use of subnetting and/or VLSMs can be mitigated by configuring route summarization. Here, summarization can best be taken advantage of when the IP addressing scheme has been implemented in a hierarchical fashion.

Finally, the examples will make it clear that route summarization is usually a *good thing*, but there are times when it can break routing. Because summarization is **on by default** in some routing protocols it underscores the need to be familiar with this topic. Table 4-8 lists the common routing protocols classified by summarization capabilities.

Table 4-8 Route Summarization Capabilities

PROTOCOL	SUMMARIZATION
RIPv1 (Routing Information Protocol version 1)	Always summarizes routes at major network boundary (auto-summarization).
IGRP (Interior Gateway Routing Protocol)	Auto-summarization cannot be disabled.
	Never summarizes routes when not crossing a major boundary.

Table 4-8 *(continued)*

PROTOCOL	SUMMARIZATION
RIPv2 (Routing Information Protocol version 2)	Defaults to auto-summarization at major network boundary.
EIGRP (Enhanced Interior Gateway Routing Protocol)	Auto-summarization can be disabled.
	Can be forced to summarize routes even when not crossing a major boundary.
	Summarization can occur at the bit boundary.[9]
OSPF (Open Shortest Path First)	Defaults to summarization off.
	Summarizes routes at area boundaries only.
	Summarization can occur at the bit boundary.
BGP (Border Gateway Protocol)	Defaults to auto-summarization at a major network boundary.
	Can be disabled.

NOTE We're going to be talking about the three common interior classful routing protocols here—RIPv2, EIGRP, and OSPF—even though they are not covered in detail until subsequent chapters. The coverage is mostly conceptual however. Don't worry about the "how to" for now, as that is the easy part, and will be covered in each chapter devoted to these protocols.

Network Example 1

Classfully addressed network

No summarization

Allocated IP addresses: 150.1.0.0/16, 150.2.0.0/16, 150.3.0.0/16

Figure 4-4 portrays a simple, routed network employing pre-CIDR network addresses. Router A connects the departmental networks. Router B is a border (edge) router connecting to the Internet. Router A has sent its route table to router B. Note that the prefix was advertised with the route. Packets from the Internet destined for any of the three networks will be directed to router A. Table 4-9 shows a simplified view of router B's route table.

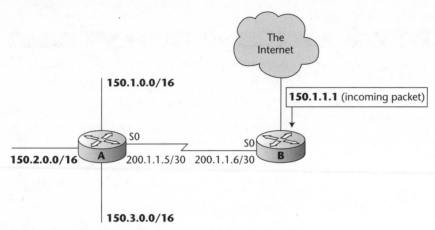

Figure 4-4   Network model for summarization example 1.

In this example, summarization was left at the routing protocol's defaults. RIPv2 and EIGRP will never summarize a classful address and OSPF will never summarize at all until it's told to do so. Router B therefore lists one entry for each of the three networks it learned of.

Tracking an Incoming Packet

An incoming packet with a destination address of 150.1.1.1 arrives at router B. Router B performs a lookup in its route table and finds a route matching the destination address. Figure 4-5 illustrates the action in binary—the best way to view what's really going on when routing decisions are made.

> **NOTE** Normally only the prefix of the address is stored in the route table. The diagram shows the entire 32 bits of the address with the network portion in bold for illustrative purposes only.

Table 4-9   Router B Receiving Three Routes from Router A

ROUTE TABLE FOR ROUTER B (SIMPLIFIED)			
Network	Mask	Next Hop	Interface
150.1.0.0	/16	**200.1.1.5**	S0
150.2.0.0	/16	**200.1.1.5**	S0
150.3.0.0	/16	**200.1.1.5**	S0
200.1.1.4	/30	Directly connected	

Incoming packet (150.1.1.1)
10010110.00000001.00000001.00000001

I'm looking for a match!

Router B's route table in binary	
11001000.00000001.00000001.00000100	(200.1.1.4/30)
10010110.00000011.00000000.00000000	(150.3.0.0 /16)
10010110.00000010.00000000.00000000	(150.2.0.0 /16)
10010110.00000001.00000000.00000000	(150.1.0.0 /16)

(Network portion of address shown in **bold**)

Figure 4-5   An exact match is made with network 150.1.0.0.

How Did That Match Get Made?

Let's take a closer look at exactly how a match is made when a route table look-up is performed. The network mask of a destination address is unknown because the mask is not included in the IP header. Routers use an algorithm known as **longest match** to perform the look-up. A bit-by-bit comparison is performed on the destination address against each route table entry starting with the high-order bits of the destination address and working to the right. The algorithm locates which routing entry *most closely* matches the destination address. More often than not, an *explicit* or exact match is made, meaning only one entry in the route table matches the address. Because table entries only keep the prefix of a network ID, what is considered an explicit match is only in reference to the prefix of the network address.

In example 1, the first three entries in the table fail to make a match, even before the entire network prefix has been compared. The final route table entry, however, does make a match because every bit in the network portion of the entry matches the corresponding number of high-order bits in the destination address of the incoming packet.

EXPLICIT MATCHES ARE NOT ALWAYS MADE

Although explicit matches are often made on a destination address, this is not always the case. Sometimes two or more entries in the table may match the address and in that case the table entry with the greatest number of matching prefix bits is selected—thus the term *longest match*. The ambiguity of multiple route table matches to an address is usually due to the use of variable length subnet masks. Upcoming example 3 demonstrates the longest match principal at work in a VLSM networking model.

Now that the match is made, router B forwards the packet out the interface specified for the 150.1.0.0 network (S0). Router A then delivers the packet to its directly connected interface for the destination address, using the same look-up method.

Network Example 2

Classlessly addressed network

Summarization occurs automatically with certain protocols

Allocated IP address 150.1.0.0/21

Figure 4-6 is the same network from the previous example, except that the organization has been assigned a CIDR address with a /21 prefix. The assigning authority controls the first 21 bits of this address, but the organization can manipulate the remaining 11 bits to tailor whatever number of subnets and hosts per subnet it requires. The address as supplied creates a single network address, 150.1.0.0 /21, with 2,046 hosts ($2^{11} - 2$). Since the organization actually requires several subnets capable of supporting up to 200 hosts per subnet, the prefix is altered to /24. This modification creates the addressing scheme reflected in Table 4-10.

The organization then implements three of the derived subnets on router B's connected networks by configuring the router with the three addresses using the /24 prefix. The specifics of how this is done for each routing protocol will be given in the chapter that covers the protocol.

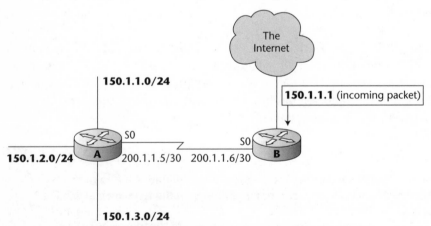

Figure 4-6 Network model for summarization example 2.

Table 4-10   Address Allocation for 150.1.0.0/24

SUBNET ADDRESS	HOST ADDRESSES	BROADCAST ADDRESS
150.1.0.0 /24	150.1.0.1 to 150.1.0.254	150.1.0.255
150.1.1.0 /24	150.1.1.1 to 150.1.1.254	150.1.1.255
150.1.2.0 /24	150.1.2.1 to 150.1.2.254	150.1.2.255
150.1.3.0 /24	150.1.3.1 to 150.1.3.254	150.1.3.255
150.1.4.0 /24	150.1.4.1 to 150.1.4.254	150.1.4.255
150.1.5.0 /24	150.1.5.1 to 150.1.5.254	150.1.5.255
150.1.6.0 /24	150.1.6.1 to 150.1.6.254	150.1.6.255
150.1.7.0 /24	150.1.7.1 to 150.1.7.254	150.1.7.255

Summarization at the Assignment Level

This is the first opportunity to get a look at where route summarization begins—at the assigning level. No other router on the entire Internet, except the routers belonging to this organization, will ever need more than a single route table entry to reach any network in the range of 150.1.0.0 through 150.1.7.0. The address is summarized as route table entry **150.1.0.0/21**, and that is how it will be propagated among Internet routers[10]. Any packet with a destination address falling within the range of the assigned address will be directed to that organization's border router. The individual subnets need not be enumerated until the packets arrive at the border.

Summarization at the Organization Level

Summarization occurs at the organizational level when a router within the autonomous system summarizes a range of networks before advertising them. Table 4-11 illustrates how summarization has occurred on the network in example 2.

Table 4-11   Router B Receiving a Summarized Route from Router A

ROUTE TABLE FOR ROUTER B (SIMPLIFIED)			
Network	Mask	Next Hop	Interface
150.1.0.0	/16	**200.1.1.5**	S0
200.1.1.4	/30	Directly connected	

WHEN DOES AUTO-SUMMARIZATION OCCUR?

RIPv2 and EIGRP have auto-summarization turned ON by default, but summarization only occurs automatically in the following circumstances:

◆ The subnets are using a mask other than the classful mask for that address.

◆ The subnets are being advertised through an interface belonging to a differing major network number.

If both these conditions are true, RIPv2 and EIGRP will auto-summarize subnets to their classful border before advertising them. However, auto-summarization can be turned off for both these protocols.

Router A has advertised a single route representing its three connected networks. It has summarized the three /24 networks to the classful border of /16. This is the default behavior of RIPv2 and EIGRP. These two routing protocols *automatically* summarize routes in certain cases. This behavior is known as **auto-summarization**. OSPF on the other hand, does *not* auto-summarize. Any summarization performed by OSPF must be manually configured. Let's assume for the purpose of this example that OSPF has been configured to summarize router A's subnets in the same manner.

What's Wrong With This Picture?

So, everything is fine and dandy in example 2, right? A very small routing update was sent to router B, which is economizing its own route table by listing a single entry that represents all of router A's subnets. As Figure 4-7 illustrates, an incoming packet will be correctly routed to router A.

In fact, if you try the same thing with any destination address in the range of 150.1.0.1 through 150.1.7.254 router B will make a match and forward the packet to router A.

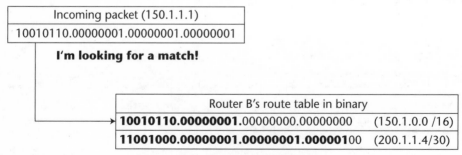

Figure 4-7   Router B makes a match with network 150.1.0.0.

The problem however, is that the summarized address listed in router B's route table covers the entire range of subnets of the 150.1.0.0 /16, *but not all of those subnets are configured on router A.* In fact, the organization does not even own this entire address range. These routes have been over-summarized by router A. Setting aside the fact that router A is listing subnets it does not have routes to, the next example illustrates how deploying additional subnets of the 150.1.0.0 /21 on another router will break routing within the organization.

Network Example 3

Classless addressing

Summarization occurs automatically with certain protocols

Routing fails due to discontiguous network

Allocated IP address 150.1.0.0/21

In Figure 4-8 additional subnets of the 150.1.0.0 /21 have been deployed with the same /24 prefix used on router A. How will these routes be advertised to router B? Table 4-12 shows that router B is having trouble.

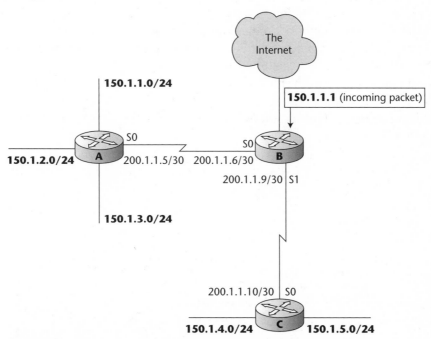

Figure 4-8   Network model for summarization example 3.

Table 4-12   Router A's Attempt to Handle Two Routers Advertising the Same Address

ROUTE TABLE FOR ROUTER B (SIMPLIFIED)			
Network	Mask	Next Hop	Interface
150.1.0.0	/16	**200.1.1.5**	S0
150.1.0.0	/16	**200.1.1.10**	S1
200.1.1.4	/30	Directly connected	
200.1.1.8	/30	Directly connected	

Both routers A and C have advertised the same summarized network to router B. Router B has no way of knowing that certain subnets of the 150.1.0.0 reside on router A, while other subnets of 150.1.0.0 live on router C. Figure 4-9 shows that router B can't properly route an incoming packet bound for any subnet of the 150.1.0.0.

Discontiguous Networks

What has been created here is a **discontiguous network**. A discontiguous network is defined as a major network (a classful network address), being separated by another major network. In the example, the major network 150.1.0.0 is being separated by major network 200.1.1.0. If router B is fooled into thinking that both paths are valid for all subnets of the 150.1.0.0, it will accept the routes and try to load balance between the two paths. Naturally some number of packets will find their destination network and some will not. The symptom of the problem will be an intermittent routing problem and would be difficult to troubleshoot.[11]

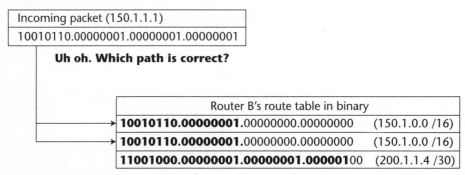

Figure 4-9   A match cannot be made for the incoming packet.

Incorrect summarization has caused a routing failure on this discontiguous network. The network configuration is unworkable. There are three possible remedies:

- Make the network contiguous by not crossing a major network boundary. Auto-summarization does not occur unless a major network number is crossed.

- Disable auto-summarization on RIPv2 or EIGRP. OSPF could get into this jam, but only if it was specifically configured to summarize in this fashion.

- Configure summarization manually.[12]

It's really not necessary to do anything as drastic as renumber the network, as the first solution alludes to. The second solution would solve the problem, but summarization would be lost. Fortunately, modern routing protocols allow summarization to be performed manually—and at any bit boundary. This allows for very flexible route summarization as demonstrated in the next section.

Manual and Bit-Level Summarization

The term **manual summarization** refers to changing the default settings for how a routing protocol handles summarization. As has been demonstrated, auto-summarization behaves in a very restricted manner and has limited usefulness.

When manually configuring summarization, more granular control can be exerted over how the summarization occurs. To begin with, manual summarization allows you to choose which network addresses will be summarized. This can be very helpful, because summarization is not always desirable. Also, manual summarization can be executed at the bit boundary, not just the octet boundary. This feature allows for very fine control over which range of networks are summarized. Indeed, it is the feature that allows for summarization to occur even with discontiguous networks.

Finally, manual summarization is configured at the interface level, so its effects are on a per-interface basis. Not only can the *range* of addresses being summarized be controlled, but *which interfaces* the summary addresses are advertised through can be controlled.

Configuring Bit-Level Summarization

Configuring bit-level summarization is remarkably easy. All that's required is to identify the *common high-order bits* of the subnets you want to summarize. These bits will be masked off:

```
10010110.00000001.00000000.00000000   (150.1.0.0 /24)
10010110.00000001.00000001.00000000   (150.1.1.0 /24)
10010110.00000001.00000010.00000000   (150.1.2.0 /24)
10010110.00000001.00000011.00000000   (150.1.3.0 /24)
```

RIPV2 CONFUSION?

RIPv2, EIGRP, and OSPF all support summarization at the bit boundary. There are texts on routing that dispute this assertion in regards to RIPv2. But in fact, only Cisco's implementation of RIPv2 supports bit level summarization, and only in IOS ver 12.1 or better.

The three networks connected to router A are shown here in binary (also shown is 150.1.0.0 /24, because it falls within the same bit pattern range as the other three subnets). The common bits are shown in bold. There are 22 high-order bits in common among the addresses, thus the prefix /22 (255.255.252.0) is the desired mask. It's that simple. The following is an example of entering the command for EIGRP (RIPv2 uses the same commands, but OSPF uses a different command and syntax):

```
routerA(config)#int serial 0/0
routerA(config-if)#no auto-summary
routerA(config-if)#ip summary-address eigrp 1 150.1.0.0 255.255.252.0[13]
```

Now only the previously specified range of adresses will be advertised! The routes will now be summarized from router A as 150.1.1.0 /22. Note that the commands are entered at the interface level. *Only routes advertised through the specified interface are affected by the summary command.*

Now for router C. The drill is the same. The number of bits common to all subnets of the 150.1.x.x is used as the prefix number for the mask in the **ip summary-address** command:

```
10010110.00000001.00000100.00000000   (150.1.4.0)
10010110.00000001.00000101.00000000   (150.1.5.0)
10010110.00000001.00000110.00000000   (150.1.6.0)
10010110.00000001.00000111.00000000   (150.1.7.0)
```

There are 21 bits in common to the addresses, so the prefix is /21 (255.255.248.0) is used:

```
routerC(config)#interface serial 0/0
routerC(config-if)#no auto-summary
routerC(config-if)#ip summary-address eigrp 1 150.1.4.0 255.255.248.0
```

Note that the address at the beginning of the range is the one specified in the statement. The routes will now be summarized from router B as 150.1.4.0 /21. One notable difference for router C is that the range enclosed by the mask encompasses more than just the two subnets connected to the router. The remaining two subnets are also part of the summarized address because they are within the same unique 3-bit pattern as the other subnets, even though they are not currently in use. This demonstrates that the granularity of control over which networks are summarized extends down to the bit boundary, but no further. If either the 150.1.6.0 or the 150.1.7.0 network is ever used it must be implemented at router C, or downstream of router C. Table 4-13 shows the results on router B.

Note that the route table is now populated in such a manner as to be able to forward packets bound for subnets of the 150.1.0.0 correctly. But don't just take our word for it. Let's prove that this particular brand of madness works by again tracing the path of an incoming packet.

In this case however the diagram for showing the incoming packet making a match to a route table entry has been altered. A more sophisticated diagram is required to reveal a subtle change in how a match is made when bit-level summarization is in use, as follows:

```
10010110.00000001.00000001.00000001    Incoming packet
=====================================================================
                                        Route table
10010110.00000001.000000               150.1.0.0  /22   - Winner!
10010110.00000001.00000                150.1.0.0  /24
11001000.00000001.00000001.00010000    200.1.1.16 /28
11001000.00000001.00000001.00100000    200.1.1.32 /28
```

The Longest Match Algorithm Saves the Day

Up until now *explicit* matches have been made for incoming packets. In previous examples, the entire network prefix of a route table entry matched the high order bits of the destination address. In this case however, the first entry in the route table is declared as the correct path for the packet, even though there are in fact *two* candidates for making a match. Note that the first two entries in the route table make a match. Ambiguity has arisen! This is where the **longest match** algorithm proves its worth. *If the router locates more than one possible match when performing a lookup, the entry with the longest number of matching bits takes precedence.* Indeed, if you refer back to the network diagram, forwarding the packet through the S0 interface routes the packet correctly.

Let's see if a packet bound for a network connected to router C is routed correctly as well.

Table 4-13   Revised Route Table after Fine-Tuning Summarization

ROUTE TABLE FOR ROUTER B (SIMPLIFIED)			
Network	*Mask*	*Next Hop*	*Interface*
150.1.0.0	**/22**	**200.1.1.5**	*S0*
150.1.4.0	**/21**	**200.1.1.10**	*S1*
200.1.1.4	/30	Directly connected	
200.1.1.8	/30	Directly connected	

```
10010110.00000001.00000100.00000001    Incoming packet
==================================================================
                                        Route table
10010110.00000001.000000               150.1.0.0   /22
10010110.00000001.00000                150.1.0.0   /24  - Winner!
11001000.00000001.00000001.00010000    200.1.1.16  /28
11001000.00000001.00000001.00100000    200.1.1.32  /28
```

The correct route is chosen, and the packet is correctly forwarded out of the serial 2 interface to router C.

Network Example 4

Classlessly addressed network with VLSMs

No summarization occurs by default due to contiguous network

Allocated IP address 150.1.0.0/24

Figure 4-10 illustrates a network model that employs VLSMs on router A. In this model, the network also happens to be contiguous, because no major network boundaries are crossed when routers advertise their route. Therefore, RIPv2 and EIGRP won't try to auto-summarize routes. Table 4-14 shows router B's route table before manual summarization is configured.

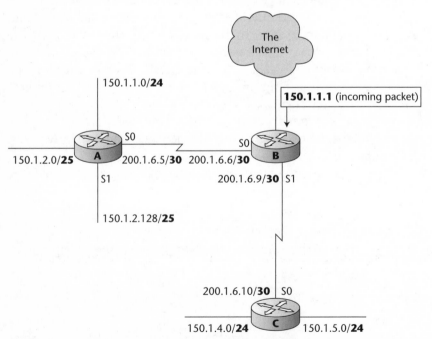

Figure 4-10 Network model for summarization example 4.

Table 4-14 Router B's Route Table Before Summarization

ROUTE TABLE FOR ROUTER B (SIMPLIFIED)			
Network	Mask	Next Hop	Interface
150.1.1.0	/24	150.1.6.5	S0
150.1.2.0	/25	150.1.6.5	S0
150.1.2.128	/25	150.1.6.5	S0
150.1.4.0	/24	150.1.6.5	S1
150.1.5.0	/24	150.1.6.5	S1
150.1.6.4	/30	Directly connected	
150.1.6.8	/30	Directly connected	

The variably subnetted networks connected to router A can easily be summarized using bit-level summarization:

```
10010110.00000001.00000000.00000000   (150.1.0.0 /24)
10010110.00000001.00000001.00000000   (150.1.1.0 /24)
10010110.00000001.00000010.00000000   (150.1.2.0 /25)
10010110.00000001.00000010.10000000   (150.1.2.128 /25)
10010110.00000001.00000011.00000000   (150.1.3.0 /24)
```

As you can see, even with variable subnetting there are 22 high-order bits in common, so the same /22 mask will be used in the summarization command as was used in the previous example. Table 4-15 shows router B's route table after manually summarizing router A's networks.

Table 4-15 Router B's Route Table After Summarization

ROUTE TABLE FOR ROUTER B (SIMPLIFIED)			
Network	Mask	Next Hop	Interface
150.1.1.0	/22	150.1.6.5	S0
150.1.4.0	/24	150.1.6.5	S1
150.1.5.0	/24	150.1.6.5	S1
150.1.6.4	/30	Directly connected)	
150.1.6.8	/30	Directly connected)	

Router C's subnets **cannot** be summarized and this fact has nothing to do with VLSMs. Why? Note that the point-to-point links are employing a subnet ID within the range of subnets that would be summarized at router C, which as demonstrated in the previous example is 150.1.4.0 – 150.1.7.0. Because a subnet within this range is configured on another router, the range is discontiguous and cannot be summarized. Moral of the story: *Plan your network addressing well.*

Summary

As you can see, summarization is a powerful tool for managing routing updates. It must be used with caution though as you need to be aware of when summarization takes place and the range of subnets that are summarized. This chapter covered the following:

- Dynamic routing protocols are used to automatically populate and maintain route tables with the best paths to networks.

- A variety of routing protocols have been developed over the years. As networks have grown in size, routing protocols have evolved to keep up with the demands placed on them.

- Routing metrics help a routing protocol choose the best route when multiple paths to the same network exist.

- Routing protocols are categorized by several criteria:

  - **Interior versus exterior:** Used within an autonomous system or between autonomous systems, respectfully.

  - **Distance vector versus link-state:** Distance vector protocols communicate only with neighboring routers (routing by rumor), whereas link-state protocols build topology maps by talking to all routers in the area.

  - **Singlepath versus multipath:** Multipath protocols can keep more than one path to a network in the route table and optionally load balance among the routes.

  - **Broadcast versus multicast:** Some routing protocols are capable of sending route updates using unicasts and multicasts rather than broadcasts.

  - **Flat versus hierarchical:** Some routing protocols are capable of being configured in a hierarchical architecture to minimize routing updates.

  - **Classful versus classless:** Classful protocols have limited support for classless addressing and no support for VLSMs or discontiguous networks, whereas classless protocols include the subnet mask in routing updates and therefore support VLSMs. Most classless routing protocols even support discontiguous networks via manual summarization at the bit boundary.

- Routes are summarized (aggregated) in order to reduce the number of route table entries.

- Summarization can be employed at both the address assignment level and organization level.

- Auto-summarization is the term used when a routing protocol summarizes routes by default.

- Auto-summarization only occurs when a router advertises a subnet of a major network across a major network boundary.

- RIPv2 and EIGRP *auto-summarize* routes by default when a major network boundary is crossed. Auto-summarization can be disabled. OSPF must be configured to summarize.

- Use of route summarization on discontiguous networks must be employed with extreme caution to avoid dropped routes or incorrectly routed packets.

Notes

1. IS-IS was developed around the time OSPF was, but for several reasons never gained wide acceptance. Therefore, it will not be covered in this book.

2. Chapter 10 describes a facility known as **redistribution**, which allows the routes learned by one routing protocol to be shared with other routing protocols.

3. Chapter 5 describes routing-loops in detail.

4. The terms *network* and *subnet* are being used simply to make it easy to distinguish the networks that contain hosts from the WAN links connecting the routers.

5. OSPF sends infrequent, periodic updates as a backup mechanism to insure that all route tables are synchronized.

6. Cisco's implementation of RIP is multipath in that it incorporates load balancing on multiple paths, but only if each path has the exact same metric value (known as equal cost multipath routing).

7. Some vendor implementations allow for multipath routing.

8. Although EIGRP is not hierarchical in the strictest sense, routing updates can be confined to specific sections of the network in a variety of ways. See the treatment of EIGRP in Chapter 7.

9. RIPv2 only summarizes at the bit boundary with Cisco IOS 12.1 or higher.

10. In fact, the address may be summarized even further for the majority of the Internet, especially if the entire 150.1.0.0 was allocated to a single ISP. This concept was explained in the CIDR section of Chapter 1.

11. In point of fact, the two erroneous entries may or may not show up in the route table, depending on the protocol in use and how it is configured.

12. Another way to deal with the scenario would be to institute static routes to the individual subnets. You could manually configure static routes on the routers that would point to the discontiguous networks. But that is defeating the purpose of dynamic routing, isn't it?

13. The "1" in the command line refers to an autonomous system number identifying which EIGRP process will be affected by the command and has nothing to do with the summary-address command.

CHAPTER

5

RIP

Overview

RIP stands for Routing Information Protocol. It is the oldest interior routing protocol still in common use and it is widely supported. Version 2 supports classlessly addressed networks. It is not suitable for large networks. Table 5-1 shows the basic characteristics of RIP.

Table 5-1   Routing Characteristics of RIP

Metric	Hop count
Interior or Exterior?	Interior
Distance vector or Link-state?	Distance vector
Singlepath or Multipath?	Multipath
Broadcast or Multicast?	RIPv1 = broadcast; RIPv2 = multicast
Flat or Hierarchical?	Flat
Classful or Classless?	RIPv1 = classful; RIPv2 = classless

This chapter covers the following RIP topics:

Advantages of Using RIP

- Supported on the widest variety of networking platforms
- Acceptable for use in smaller networks
- Easy to configure
- Good for networks with few or no redundant paths
- Good for networks with similar speed network links
- May be the only available cross-platform routing protocol supported in certain environments

Disadvantages of Using RIP

- Maximum hop count of 15 hops (can forward packets no more than 16 networks away)
- Prone to routing loops due to slow convergence
- Chatty protocol – sends entire route table periodically

RIP Background

RIP was the first interior routing protocol to achieve widespread use. It is a distance vector protocol suitable for smaller systems without multiple redundant paths to networks. While some would say RIP is more of a *rotting* protocol than a *routing* protocol, it still sees use. Like so many other computer technologies, RIP was created at Xerox PARC (Palo Alto Research Center) in the late 1970s. Although you may have no immediate need to understand distance vector protocols, you should read this chapter because routing loops are covered in the greatest detail here. It's also good to be familiar with RIP because other routing protocols are often compared to RIP when their various features are explained.

RIP is based on the Bellman-Ford algorithm, which it uses to compute the metric for a route. The algorithm uses *hop count* as the metric for stating the cost to a network. Hop count is simply a value that states how many routers (hops) a packet must pass through to arrive at the destination network. RIP cannot take into account variables such as bandwidth, load, reliability, and other factors that can dramatically influence the time required to deliver packets. Given a choice of two possible paths, a distance vector protocol such as RIP will always choose the path with the lowest hop count, even though a path with more hops may be preferable due to say, higher speed network links.[1]

RIP communicates via UDP port 520. RIP has an administrative distance of 120.

RIP Versions

There are two versions of RIP. Version 1 (RIPv1) is a *classful* routing protocol and therefore has only limited support for classless addressing. Classful routing protocols are not considered viable for today's CIDR-based world, so coverage of RIPv1 is limited here. There are very few networking environments that cannot upgrade from a classful routing protocol, and where they are employed it is likely a privately addressed, classfully addressed system behind a NAT box or gateway of some type.

Version 2 of RIP (RIPv2), released in 1993 under RFC 2453, added several enhancements, the most important of which was support for classless addressing through inclusion of the subnet mask in routing advertisements. RIPv2 therefore fully supports CIDR addresses, subnetting, VLSMs, and—with version 12.1 or higher of the Cisco IOS—even discontiguous networks, thanks to the inclusion of bit-level summarization.

RIPv2 Improvements

- Auto-summarization is on by default, but summarization can either be disabled entirely, or manually configured to summarize subnets at any bit boundary.

- Multicasts are used rather than broadcasts to communicate with neighboring routers. RIPv2 routers listen on multicast address 224.0.0.9 for RIPv2 updates. This reduces the processing on network hosts that don't care about RIP traffic (unicasts and multicasts are not processed by other hosts once it is discovered that the MAC address does not match).

- RIPv2 supports simple password **authentication** to verify the genuineness of incoming update packets.

- A field was added to the RIP header that allows a value to be associated with a route known as a **route tag**. Route tags are used with route redistribution, which is covered in Chapter 10.

- The **next hop** field was added in RIPv2 to allow better integration with OSPF networks by potentially reducing the number of hops to an OSPF network. This field potentially avoids routing loops because the receiver can see if its own address is listed as the next hop.

How RIP Works

This section describes the operation of RIPv2.

Advertising Routes

When a router running RIP is first booted, it builds a route table that contains only the directly connected networks and any statically added routes. Once initialized, the router then broadcasts its entire route table to its immediate neighboring routers. In RIP, a neighboring router is any router with an interface sharing a common link with another router. In other words, a router one hop away. By default, the IP implementation of RIP advertises the route table to its neighbors every 30 seconds. A small time variance, sometimes termed "jitter," is introduced so that not all updates are triggered at the exact same instant.

By default, RIP will advertise the entire route table out each interface enabled for RIP. Individual interfaces can be configured to not propagate the route table, yet still advertise the associated network out other interfaces. This prevents advertising routing updates unnecessarily out interfaces with no neighboring router (stub networks that only contain workstations).

Learning Routes

RIP-enabled routers learn about networks from other RIP-enabled routers via the advertisements just described. When a router running RIP learns of a qualifying route to a network from a neighboring router it adds the route to its own route table after first bumping the **hop count** by one. The router then advertises the new route, along with the existing routes it is aware of, to its other neighbors[2] at a predetermined time interval. For example, let's say a router learns about a network x that is two hops away. That router will in effect say to its neighboring routers; "You can get to network x by going through me. Network x is three hops away."

RIP routing updates cascade throughout the autonomous system. After being initialized, every router in the system ultimately learns the path to every network advertised by RIP. When a change to a network link occurs the affected router updates its neighbors, who in turn update their neighbors, and so on. The time it takes for all routers to learn about all routes is referred to as **convergence.** When all route tables have the same information they are considered **converged** or **normalized**.

Even after the route tables have converged, RIP routers continue to broadcast their entire route table every 30 seconds, even if no changes take place. This makes for a chatty protocol. The overall design of RIP (and IGRP) requires a fair amount of bandwidth for router-to-router communications.

Information that RIP Tracks About a Route

RIP stores most of the information about each learned route in the route table. The route table was covered in Chapter 2 on page 81. For convenience, the information is summarized below.

The route table (also known as the forwarding database) contains the following information for each route:

- The address of the destination network (or in some cases an actual host, which is known as **host routing**)
- The subnet mask/prefix number of the destination network
- The administrative distance and metric of the destination network
- The local interface to forward packets out of, in order to reach the next hop
- The address of the next hop to reach the destination network (the receiving interface of the next hop router)
- The timers running for each route

In Figure 5-1, RIP has learned about three routes from its neighbors. Note that the routes all have an administrative distance value of 120, the default value for the RIP protocol. Two of the routes are one hop away and one route is two hops away. The only route timer displayed with the **show ip route** command is the *invalid timer*, which indicates how long since the last update was received for the route. RIP maintains more timers than just the update timer though. (All the timers will be covered shortly.)

NOTE Although the route table reflects the same general information regardless of the routing protocol in use, other protocols store additional routing information in separate databases. RIP itself was enhanced in later versions of the Cisco IOS to store information about advertised routes that were not installed in a separate table.

A Look at How Route Tables Are Populated by RIP

When a router is first booted, it only knows about its directly connected networks (and any static routes), so these will be the only entries in the route table (see Figure 5-2). At this point, a workstation on the 192.168.10.0 network has no chance of reaching the 192.168.20.0 or 192.168.30.0 network (assuming no static default routes have been configured). Note that the metric—which is simply the hop count when you're using RIP—is 0. There are zero hops to directly connected networks.[3]

```
routerA#show ip route
Codes:   C – connected,  S – static,  I – IGRP,  R – RIP,  M – mobile,  B – BGP
         D – EIGRP,  EX – EIRGP external,  O – OSPF,  IA – OSPF inter area
         N1 – OSPF NSSA external type 1,  N2 – OSPF NSSA external type 2,  E – EGP
         i – IS-IS,  L1 – IS-IS level-1,  L2 – IS-IS level 2,  * - candidate default
         U – per-user static route,  o – ODR
         T – traffic engineered route

Gateway of last resort is not set

C        192.168.10.0  /24     [0/0]   is directly connected,  Ethernet0
         200.1.1.0     /30     is subnetted, 2 subnets
C        200.1.1.4             [0/0]   is directly connected,  Serial1
R        200.1.1.8             [120/1] via 200.1.1.6,  00:01:05,  Serial1
R        192.168.20.0 /24      [120/1] via 200.1.1.6,  00:01:05,  Serial1
R        192.168.30.0 /24      [120/2] via 200.1.1.6,  00:01:05,  Serial1
```

Figure 5-1   Route table indicates RIP routes with an "R" preceding the entry.

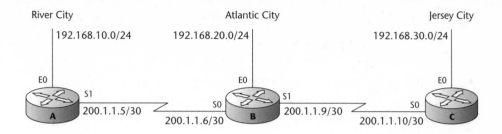

Figure 5-2 caption area:

Route table for router A (simplified)				
network	**mask**	**next hop**	**int**	**a/m**
192.168.10.0	/24	(direct)	E0	0/0
200.1.1.4	/30	(direct)	S1	0/0

Route table for router C (simplified)				
Network	**mask**	**next hop**	**int**	**a/m**
192.168.30.0	/24	(direct)	E0	0/0
200.1.1.8	/30	(direct)	S0	0/0

Route table for router B (simplified)				
Network	**mask**	**next hop**	**int**	**a/m**
192.168.20.0	/24	(direct)	E0	0/0
200.1.1.4	/30	(direct)	S0	0/0
200.1.1.8	/30	(direct)	S1	0/0

State of route tables when routers are first booted
(a/m = administrative distance / metric).

Figure 5-2   Route tables upon boot (no RIP traffic yet).

In Figure 5-3, router B has learned of routes from router A.

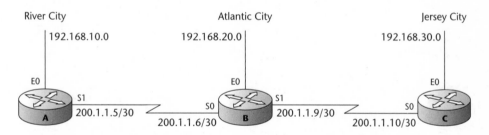

Route table for router A (simplified)				
network	**mask**	**next hop**	**int**	**a/m**
192.168.10.0	/24	(direct)	E0	0/0
200.1.1.4	/30	(direct)	S1	0/0

Route table for router C (simplified)				
Network	**mask**	**next hop**	**int**	**a/m**
192.168.30.0	/24	(direct)	E0	0/0
200.1.1.8	/30	(direct)	S0	0/0

Route table for router B (simplified)				
Network	**mask**	**next hop**	**int**	**a/m**
192.168.20.0	/24	(direct)	E0	0/0
200.1.1.4	/30	(direct)	S0	0/0
200.1.1.8	/30	(direct)	S1	0/0
192.168.10.0/24		**200.1.1.5**	**S0**	**120/1**

Route table B reflects RIP advertisement from A.

Figure 5-3   Route tables after router A advertises its networks to router B.

Note the following:

- Router A sent its route table to router B. Router B has installed router A's networks into its route table (shown in **bold**).

- Router B also bumped the hop count for the learned network by one, resulting in a hop count of 1.

- Router B ignored the advertisement about 200.1.1.4 because it already has an entry for that network with a lower metric.

In Figure 5-4, the network has converged.
Note the following:

- Each router has shared its entire table with its neighbors and the neighbors have done the same down the line. Every router is now aware of every network. The network is converged.

- Router B has acted as a middleman, facilitating router C learning of router A's networks and vice versa. Router A and router C never communicated directly.

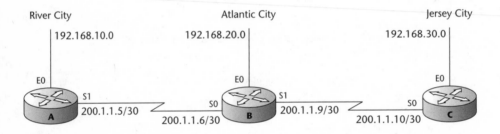

Route table for router A (simplified)

network	mask	next hop	int a/m
192.168.10.0	/24	(direct)	E0 0/0
200.1.1.4	/30	(direct)	S1 0/0
192.168.20.0	**/24**	**200.1.1.6**	**S1 120/1**
192.168.30.0	**/24**	**200.1.1.6**	**S1 120/2**
200.1.1.8	**/30**	**200.1.1.9**	**S1 120/1**

Route table for router C (simplified)

Network	mask	next hop	int a/m
192.168.30.0	/24	(direct)	E0 0/0
200.1.1.8	/30	(direct)	S0 0/0
192.168.10.0	**/24**	**200.1.1.9**	**S0 120/2**
192.168.20.0	**/24**	**200.1.1.9**	**S0 120/1**
200.1.1.4	**/30**	**200.1.1.9**	**S0 120/1**

Route table for router B (simplified)

Network	mask	next hop	int a/m
192.168.20.0	/24	(direct)	E0 0/0
200.1.1.4	/30	(direct)	S0 0/0
200.1.1.8	/30	(direct)	S1 0/0
192.168.10.0	**/24**	**200.1.1.5**	**S0 120/1**
192.168.30.0	**/24**	**200.1.1.10**	**S1 120/1**

Route tables fully populated with RIP learned routes.

Normal text = directly connected networks.
Bold = rip learned routes.

Figure 5-4 Route tables after all routers have advertised their route tables.

RIP's Achilles Heel

The RIP protocol has a major drawback. It's prone to routing loops. A routing loop occurs when a router accepts a route that leads back through itself. This problem in RIP is partly due to slow convergence of the route tables after a change occurs in the network topology and partly because no route-loop detection mechanism is built into RIP. Slow convergence is mostly due to various timers that RIP employs that prevent excess routing update traffic. Until the network converges, some routers may continue to advertise bad routes because they haven't heard the news about the failure. The misleading advertisements propagate to other routers, who tend to trust what they hear from their neighbors. A vicious circle develops.

RIP Timers that Contribute to Slow Convergence

There are a variety of timers that the RIP protocol uses for varying purposes. The timers that influence how quickly RIP converges after a network change are covered here. Other RIP timers will be covered shortly.

Update Timer

The **update timer** dictates the interval of outbound routing updates (advertisements). This is when the entire route table is broadcast out of all interfaces enabled for RIP (the broadcast address is 255.255.255.255). The default setting for the update timer is 30 seconds on Cisco routers.

Invalid and Flush Timers

A RIP-enabled router does not keep RIP learned routes in its route tables indefinitely. It relies on receiving continual updates from its neighboring routers, providing assurance that the networks are still there. If the update for one or more networks stops, RIP assumes something has gone wrong. The last thing a router wants to do is send packets through an invalid route, so two timers are used for every RIP installed route to deal with this issue: an **invalid timer** and a **flush timer**. These timers are both reset each time an update is received for the route.

The invalid timer defines how long to wait for an update before marking the route as invalid in the route table. If no update regarding the route is received before the invalid timer expires, the route is considered dead and is marked as invalid in the route table and advertised with a metric of 16 (unreachable).[4] This is known as **route poisoning**. The route continues to be advertised with the unreachable metric until the flush timer expires. This gives the router time to spread the news about the dead route. When the flush timer expires the route is removed from the route table. The flush timer is always set higher than the invalid timer to allow time for the invalid route to be advertised to the neighbors. The default setting for the invalid timer is 180 seconds (six update periods). The default setting for the flush timer is 240 seconds (60 seconds longer than the invalid timer).

As you can see, even with route poisoning, it takes quite a while to time out a route. The settings on the timers could be lowered, but that would increase the amount of network bandwidth used. So what's a routing protocol to do? RIP is kind of between a rock and a hard spot here, so other means have been developed to speed convergence and prevent routing loops when a change occurs. These techniques will be covered after first explaining how routing loops get started.

How RIP Defends Itself Against the Dreaded Routing Loop

This section illustrates how routing loops get created, how RIP attempts to prevent them from occurring, and how they are stopped if they do occur.

Anatomy of a Routing Loop

Figure 5-5 portrays the beginning of a routing loop. How the loop occurs will be described and then each loop prevention technique will be explained.

A network fault has occurred between routers A and B. Here's what's different about the route tables now:

- The routes to the 200.1.1.4 on routers A and B have been removed from the respective router's route tables. Directly connected networks that fail are removed immediately. (They are shown in the figure in strikeout for illustrative purposes only.)

- Since routers A and B lost a directly connected link, any routes depending on the link are marked invalid and advertised as such (poisoned).

- No change has occurred on router C's route table because C has not yet been made aware of the problem. However, the *invalid* timer on router C is running for the 192.168.10.0 and 192.168.20.0.

How did routers A and B know the link had gone down? Routers use **keep-alive** packets to tell if the links to their directly connected networks are up.[5] The default keep-alive period is 10 seconds. So after a short grace period, both router A and router B detected that the link to the 200.1.1.4 was down and removed the associated network from their respective route tables.

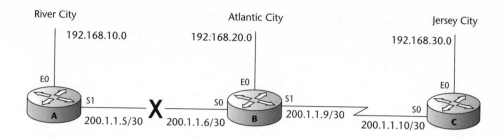

Route table for router A (simplified)				
network	mask	next hop	int	a/m
192.168.10.0	/24	(direct)	E0	0/0
~~200.1.1.4~~	~~/30~~	~~(direct)~~	~~S1~~	~~0/0~~
192.168.20	/24	200.1.1.6	S1	120/1
192.168.30	/24	200.1.1.6	S1	120/2
200.1.1.8	/30	200.1.1.9	S1	120/1

Route table for router C (simplified)				
Network	mask	next hop	int	a/m
192.168.30.0	/24	(direct)	E0	0/0
200.1.1.8	/30	(direct)	S0	0/0
192.168.10.0/24		**200.1.1.9**	**S0**	**120/2**
192.168.20.0/24		**200.1.1.9**	**S0**	**120/1**
200.1.1.4	**/30**	**200.1.1.9**	**S0**	**120/1**

Route table for router B (simplified)				
Network	mask	next hop	int	a/m
192.168.20.0	/24	(direct)	E0	0/0
~~200.1.1.4~~	~~/30~~	~~(direct)~~	~~S0~~	~~0/0~~
200.1.1.8	/30	(direct)	S1	0/0
192.168.10.0	/24	200.1.1.5	S0	120/1
192.168.30.0/24		**200.1.1.10**	**S1**	**120/1**

Ten seconds after WAN link went down.

Normal text = directly connected networks.
Bold = RIP learned routes.
~~Strikeout~~ = removed from table.
Gray = routes marked as invalid.

Figure 5-5 Trouble in River City. The WAN link joining routers A and B went down 10 seconds ago.

Additionally, the RIP-learned routes that depended on the downed link are no longer good, so they are marked invalid immediately without even waiting for the invalid timer to expire. The routes are not removed from the table though. Those entries will be advertised along with the rest of the route table with an unreachable metric of 16 until the flush timer expires.

Meanwhile, router C has no clue what's going on. The RIP learned entries on router C are timing out normally because router C has no knowledge of the downed link at this point. Let's review the timers:

- RIP routers expect to receive routing updates periodically. The default period is 30 seconds.

- A router will wait for six update periods (180 seconds) to get an advertisement from a neighbor about each route in its table and then mark the route as invalid. This is controlled by the *invalid timer*. If the invalid timer expires, the routes will be advertised as unreachable until the *flush timer* expires.

- The flush timer always runs longer than the invalid timer to give the router time to advertise the invalid routes before they are removed from the router's route tables. The flush timer is set to 240 seconds, so the flush timer expires 60 seconds after the invalid timer. Once the flush timer expires the invalid routes are removed and never advertised again. This action has a cascading effect. An invalid and flush timer is running on all routers for each route listed in their tables. As the invalid and flush timers expire, routes are removed from each route table and no longer advertised. Ultimately, every router removes the route and stops advertising the route, and the route tables are considered converged.

So, except for the downed link, everything is OK, right? The invalid and flush timers keep the routers "honest," and after a while router C will dump the dead routes. Right? Wrong. Without additional rules to handle this outage, RIP will get into deep trouble very quickly by creating a routing loop. The problem is with router C which still has an entry in its route table listing routes to the 200.1.1.4 and 192.168.10.0 through router B, which of course are now invalid. Router B has marked the routes invalid but before router B can notify its neighbors in its regular 30 second update, router C sends a periodic update to router B, telling it about the routes that B thought were dead. Router B, *thinking it has a new path to the missing networks*, accepts the updates from router C and increments the metrics for each network by one. This is reflected in Figure 5-6.

Here's what's different about router B's route table now:

- Router B now lists a RIP learned route to the 200.1.1.4 via serial 1 with a metric of 2.

- Router B now lists a RIP learned route to the 192.168.10.0 via serial 1 with a metric of 3.

Here is where things go from bad to worse as a routing loop is inadvertently created. Router B has replaced the invalid routes to the 192.168.10.0 and 200.1.1.4 with routes to the same networks via router C. Router B erroneously thinks the way to these networks is through router C, and router C still thinks the way to the networks is through router B! Without the safeguards in place (which will be discussed in a moment), RIP is too dumb to see what it has done. Every time router B receives a packet bound for the 192.168.10.0 it will forward it to router C. Every time router C receives a packet bound for the 192.168.10.0 it will forward it to router B! The two routers will do nothing except ping-pong the packets back and forth to each other. That's a basic routing loop.

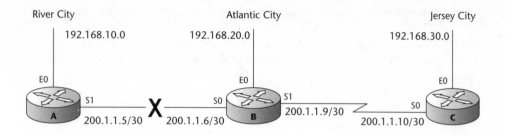

Route table for router A (simplified)				
network	mask	next hop	int	a/m
192.168.10.0	/24	(direct)	E0	0/0
192.168.20	/24	200.1.1.6	S1	120/1
192.168.30	/24	200.1.1.6	S1	120/2
200.1.1.8	/30	200.1.1.9	S1	120/1

Route table for router C (simplified)				
Network	mask	next hop	int	a/m
192.168.30.0	/24	(direct)	E0	0/0
200.1.1.8	/30	(direct)	S0	0/0
192.168.10.0/24		**200.1.1.9**	**S0**	**120/2**
192.168.20.0/24		**200.1.1.9**	**S0**	**120/1**
200.1.1.4	**/30**	**200.1.1.9**	**S0**	**120/1**

Route table for router B (simplified)				
Network	mask	next hop	int	a/m
192.168.20.0	/24	(direct)	E0	0/0
200.1.1.8	/30	(direct)	S1	0/0
192.168.30.0/24		**200.1.1.10**	**S1**	**120/1**
200.1.1.4	*/30*	*200.1.1.8*	*S1*	*120/2*
192.168.10.0	*/24*	*200.1.1.8*	*S1*	*120/3*

30 seconds after WAN link went down.
Router B has been given an invalid path to the 192.168.10.0
and the 200.1.1.4 by router C.

Normal text = directly connected networks
Bold = RIP learned routes
Gray = routes marked as invalid
Italics = RIP learned routes router B just learned about from router C

Figure 5-6 The route tables 30 seconds after the WAN link has gone down (no routing loop safeguards in place).

Measures to Prevent Routing Loops

Several methods of speeding convergence and avoiding routing loops are built into RIP. The following list enumerates the routing loop prevention techniques built into most distance vector routing protocols:

- Maintain only the best route (lowest metric)
- Time out directly connected routes immediately upon failure
- Route poisoning
- Hold-down timer
- Split horizon
- Triggered updates
- Poison reverse
- Maximum hop count (limits the "counting-to-infinity" syndrome to 15 hops)

ROUTING LOOPS OCCUR FOR MANY REASONS

Don't conclude that the scenario being described here is the only way routing loops are created. They can happen for a number of reasons even with routing protocols relatively immune from loops, like EIGRP and OSPF, *if* they are not configured correctly. For example, two trouble spots for routing loops are misconfigured redistribution and incorrectly architected OSPF areas. These issues are discussed in the relevant chapters.

Installing only the routes with the lowest metric not only speeds routing, but since the fewest number of routers are used in the path, there are simply fewer things to go wrong. Routing metrics are a critical function of any routing protocol and will be covered in detail later in the chapter. The concepts of timing out directly connected routes as soon as the keep-alives detect a dead link and poisoning the route were covered earlier in the scenario. Let's turn our attention to the remaining items on the list.

Hold-Down Timer

One mechanism that helps stabilize route tables and avoid looped routes is the **hold-down** timer. The rule for the hold-down timer says this: "Once an entry in a route table is updated (added, changed, or deleted), ignore any updates about the route until the hold-down timer expires." The default value of the hold-down timer for RIP is 180 seconds.

The hold-down timer acts as a buffer when network conditions are changing rapidly. Suppose, for example, the link previously shown in Figure 5-5 was down because of a loose connection. As the connection engages and disengages, the line goes up and down. If it were not for the hold-down timer, a large amount of network traffic would be created as RIP propagates broadcasts saying first that the link is up, then down, then up, and so on. This activity is known as **route flapping**. The hold-down timer will "freeze" the route in its current status in the route table even though RIP advertisements may say the status is otherwise. When the timer expires, the router will start paying attention to updates once again.

The hold-down timer would help in the example under study. It would have probably prevented router B from accepting the faulty routes from router C. Once router B's path to the routes had been altered, the hold-down timer would have prevented router B from accepting the update from router C. That would have given router B time enough to notify router C about the bad routes in its routine 30 second updates.

Split Horizon

While the hold-down timer is helpful, it is by no means a foolproof mechanism for preventing routing loops. Take the advertisement of the 192.168.10.0 for example. Router B originally learned about the the 192.168.10.0 network from router A. Router C learned about the same network from router B. The loop was created because router C kept sending its entire route table to router B, including a claim that router C new how to reach the 192.168.10.0. The inclusion of this network was unnecessary and in fact wrong, because router C had no other path to the 192.168.10.0.

Advertising a route back to the router that told you about the route in the first place is a mistake. What's really needed is a rule that says: *Never advertise a route back through the link you learned the route from*. With this rule, a router would never include a route in an update to a neighbor that had already advertised the route. On the other hand, the router would definitely include the route in advertisements to any other neighbors. Well, they made just such a rule. It's called **split horizon**. Split horizon is a simple loop-prevention technique that would have prevented the routing loop shown in Figure 5-6 from ever occurring. With the split horizon rule in place, router C would not have tried to tell router B about 200.1.1.4 or 192.168.10.0, because router B told it about those routes in the first place.

With split horizon in place router C still thinks it has a path to the 192.168.10.0, but at least it has not tried to convince router B of the same.

Triggered Updates

As things stand right now in the example (previously shown in Figure 5-6), router B will be notifying router C of the invalid routes in the next route update by setting the metric to 16, also known as route poisoning. Route poisoning occurs until the flush timer expires.

SPLIT HORIZON: FRIEND OR FOE?

There are times when split horizon may backfire and prevent propagation of routes on the network. In certain configurations, it is actually necessary for a router to advertise a route back out of the same interface it learned the route on. This happens often with frame-relay networks where multiple logical networks attach to one physical router interface (using sub-interfaces). If the router does not advertise a route learned from one logical network back out the same interface to the other logical networks, the route tables of one or more routers will not be fully populated.

See the command reference later in this chapter for information about how to manually enable and disable split horizon.

To speed convergence, a complementary rule to route poisoning called **triggered updates** (also known as flash updates) makes route poisoning even more efficacious. Router B is not going to wait around for the normal 30-second periodic update period to tell router C about the poisoned route. The triggered updates rule will force router B to trigger a route update immediately (with a small random delay), ignoring the 30-second timer. Triggered updates include only the information about the changed route. Again, convergence is the name of the game, so it's worth creating some traffic to spread this important news.

Triggered updates are so helpful that they are in fact used whenever a change occurs in the network topology.

Poison Reverse

The drive toward rapid convergence does not stop with hold-down timers, route poisoning, split horizon, and triggered updates however. Another rule has been developed called **poison reverse**. The poison reverse rule says that any router that knows of a poisoned route learned through one interface and learns about the same route through another interface, will immediately advertise the route back out of that interface with a metric of 16, thus informing its neighboring router that the route is dead. In effect, this is a temporary suspension of the split horizon rule that helps speed convergence.

By the way, the poison reverse rule is so closely tied with the split horizon rule, the rules are often stated together as "split horizon with poison reverse."

Hop Count

A last-ditch mechanism for preventing routing loops in RIP is to limit the number of times a packet can traverse routers. RIP has a hop count limit of 15, meaning a packet can be forwarded through only 15 routers before it is discarded. Each RIP router receiving a packet increasing the hop count by 1. The fifteenth router receiving the packet will discard it unless it is addressed to a directly connected network.

LIMITING PACKET LIFE AT LAYER 3

While RIP has its own method of limiting the life of a routing packet, there is also a routing protocol-independent means of detecting that a packet has been on a network for too long. It is the TTL (Time to Live) field in the IP header. The TTL field is set to a positive value by the sender, then each router along the way decrements the TTL field by 1. If the value of the TTL field reaches 0, the packet is discarded and the host sends an ICMP message back to the originating host. The TTL is originally set anywhere from 32 to 256, depending on the type of host initiating communications.

Packets bouncing around a network in perpetuity when running a distance vector routing protocol is referred to as **counting to infinity**. RIP sets "infinity" at 15 hops.

Load Balancing

Although there are no provisions for load balancing in the RFC for RIP, Cisco's implementation of IP RIP allows for automatic load balancing across *equal* cost paths (each route to the same network must have the same metric). By default, RIP will keep up to four equal cost paths in the route table and forward traffic through each of them. Two to six equal cost paths may be manually configured.

Default Routing

Default routing is covered in detail in Chapter 10 along with configuration commands. Notations pertaining specifically to RIP are included here.

RIP supports both commands for creating default routes: the **ip route** command and the **ip default-network** command. As a general rule, use the **ip route** command to set a default route on the current router that is **not** to be propagated to other routers, and use the **ip default-network** command to set a default route on the current router that is also propagated as a candidate default route to all other RIP routers in the system.

The **ip route** command creates a static default route that uses a wildcard format of 0.0.0.0 in the statement. When you're using the command specify the IP address of the next hop router interface rather than the local interface name (like "e0") in the statement, or the route may be propagated anyway.

The **ip default-network** command will always propagate a candidate default route, as well as install a default route on the current router. Unlike some other protocols, the network specified in the statement need not be listed on a router to accept the default route, because RIP propagates the default route as network 0.0.0.0.

Use the examples provided in Chapter 10 to configure default routing for RIP.

Redistribution

RIP is capable of including static and externally learned routes in its updates—in other words, redistribution. Chapter 10 provides general information on redistribution. Examples of configuring RIP for redistribution are covered in the following command reference for RIP.

Command Reference—RIP

Figure 5-7 provides a network model for the configuration of RIP. The examples will cover configuring RIP on a Cisco router.

Initial Configuration

An initial configuration of the routers will be performed and the route tables will be shown before the RIP routing protocol is configured.

Configuring the IP Addresses

IP addresses are assigned on a per-interface basis with the **ip address** command, as follows:

```
routerA#configure terminal
routerA(config)#interface fastethernet 0 (1)
routerA(config-if)#ip address 192.168.10.1 255.255.255.0 (2)
routerA(config-if)#exit (3)
routerA(config)#interface serial 1 (4)
routerA(config-if)#ip address 200.1.1.5 255.255.255.252 (5)
routerA(config-if)#exit
routerA(config)#

routerB#configure terminal
routerB(config)#interface fastethernet 0
routerB(config-if)#ip address 192.168.21.0 255.255.255.0
routerB(config-if)#exit
routerB(config)#interface serial 0
routerB(config-if)#ip address 200.1.1.6 255.255.255.252
routerB(config-if)#exit
routerB(config)#interface serial 1
routerB(config-if)#ip address 200.1.1.9 255.255.255.252 (6)
routerB(config-if)#exit
routerB(config)#
routerC#configure terminal
routerC(config)#interface fastethernet 0
routerC(config-if)#ip address 192.168.31.0 255.255.255.0
routerC(config-if)#exit
```

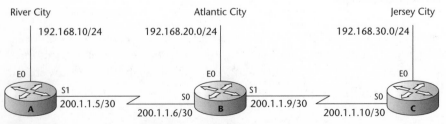

Figure 5-7   Example network for commands.

```
routerC(config)#interface serial 0
routerC(config-if)#ip address 200.1.1.10 255.255.255.252
routerC(config-if)#exit
routerC(config)#
```

(1) Change to interface E0.
(2) Configure the address with a /24 prefix.
(3) Exit interface mode back to global configuration mode.
(4) Change to interface S1.
(5) First subnet of 200.1.1.0 /30.
(6) Second subnet of 200.1.1.0 /30.

Route Tables Before RIP Is Configured

Figures 5-8, 5-9, and 5-10 reflect the state of the route tables before RIP is configured.

```
routerA#show ip route
Codes:   C – connected,  S – static,  I – IGRP,  R – RIP,  M – mobile,  B – BGP
         D – EIGRP,  EX – EIRGP external,  O – OSPF,  IA – OSPF inter area
         N1 – OSPF NSSA external type 1,  N2 – OSPF NSSA external type 2,  E – EGP
         i – IS-IS,  L1 – IS-IS level-1,  L2 – IS-IS level 2,  * - candidate default
         U – per-user static route, o – ODR
         T – traffic engineered route

Gateway of last resort is not set

C        192.168.10.0  /24    [0/0]    is directly connected, Ethernet0
         200.1.1.0     /30    is subnetted, 1 subnets
C           200.1.1.4          [0/0]    is directly connected, Serial1
```

Figure 5-8   Router A – before RIP is configured.

```
routerB#show ip route
Codes:   C – connected,  S – static,  I – IGRP,  R – RIP,  M – mobile,  B – BGP
         D – EIGRP,  EX – EIRGP external,  O – OSPF,  IA – OSPF inter area
         N1 – OSPF NSSA external type 1,  N2 – OSPF NSSA external type 2,  E – EGP
         i – IS-IS,  L1 – IS-IS level-1,  L2 – IS-IS level 2,  * - candidate default
         U – per-user static route, o – ODR
         T – traffic engineered route

Gateway of last resort is not set

C        192.168.20.0  /24    [0/0]    is directly connected, Ethernet0
         200.1.1.0     /30    is subnetted, 2 subnets
C           200.1.1.4          [0/0]    is directly connected, Serial0
C           200.1.1.8          [0/0]    is directly connected, Serial1
```

Figure 5-9   Router B before RIP is configured.

```
routerC#show ip route
Codes:    C – connected,  S – static,  I – IGRP,  R – RIP,  M – mobile,  B – BGP
          D – EIGRP,  EX – EIRGP external,  O – OSPF,  IA – OSPF inter area
          N1 – OSPF NSSA external type 1,  N2 – OSPF NSSA external type 2,  E – EGP
          i – IS-IS,  L1 – IS-IS level-1,  L2 – IS-IS level 2,  * - candidate default
          U – per-user static route, o – ODR
          T – traffic engineered route

Gateway of last resort is not set

C         192.168.30.0  /24      [0/0]     is directly connected,  Ethernet0
          200.1.1.0     /30      is subnetted, 1 subnets
C            200.1.1.8           [0/0]     is directly connected,  Serial0
```

Figure 5-10   Router C before RIP is configured.

Configure RIP

The configuration of RIP is fairly straightforward. The **router rip** command enables RIP on the router—once enabled, it is mostly a matter of specifying which networks to advertise, via the **network x.x.x.x** command, as follows:

```
routerA(config)#router rip (1)
routerA(config-router)#network 192.168.10.0 (2)
routerA(config-router)#network 200.1.1.4 (3)
routerA(config-router)#passive-interface fastethernet 0 (4)
routerA(config-router)#exit
routerA(config)#

routerB#config-term
routerB(config)#router rip
routerB(config-router)#network 192.168.20.0
routerB(config-router)#network 200.1.1.4
routerB(config-router)#network 200.1.1.8
routerB(config-router)#passive-interface fastethernet 0
routerB(config-router)#exit
routerB(config)#

routerC#config-term
routerC(config)#router rip
routerC(config-router)#network 192.168.30.0
routerC(config-router)#network 200.1.1.8
routerC(config-router)#passive-interface fastethernet 0
routerC(config-router)#exit
routerC(config)#
```

(1) Enable RIP on this router (**router no rip** disables RIP).

(2) Include network in RIP advertisements. All interfaces with an address configured within the range of this address will send and receive routing updates.

(3) Include network in RIP advertisements. All interfaces with an address configured within the range of this address will send and receive routing updates.

(4) Suppress routing advertisements on this interface.

Notice that the **network x.x.x.x** command does two things. It both advertises the specified network *and* enables advertising the route through any interfaces configured with an address within range of the specified network. For example, if three subnets of 172.1.0.0 /16 are configured on three separate interfaces of a router, then the statement **network 172.1.0.0** would enable advertising any subnets of 172.1.0.0 through all three interfaces.

The dual behavior of the **network x.x.x.x** command gives rise to the **passive-interface** command. Each router in the example network (shown in Figure 5-11) had to have a **network 192.168.x.0** statement issued in order to advertise the network. However, these are stub networks—there are no neighboring routers on the Ethernet networks—thus, there's no need to advertise the routes through the Ethernet interfaces. The **passive-interface** command suppresses route advertisements through the specified interface, while still allowing the route associated with the interface to be propagated out of any other RIP enabled interfaces.

```
routerA#show ip route
Codes:   C – connected,  S – static,  I – IGRP,  R – RIP,  M – mobile,  B – BGP
         D – EIGRP,  EX – EIRGP external,  O – OSPF,  IA – OSPF inter area
         N1 – OSPF NSSA external type 1,  N2 – OSPF NSSA external type 2,  E – EGP
         i – IS-IS,  L1 – IS-IS level-1,  L2 – IS-IS level 2,  * - candidate default
         U – per-user static route, o – ODR
         T – traffic engineered route

Gateway of last resort is not set

C    192.168.10.0    /24    [0/0]    is directly connected, Ethernet0
     200.1.1.0       /30    is subnetted, 2 subnets
C      200.1.1.4            [0/0]    is directly connected, Serial1
R      200.1.1.8            [120/1]via 200.1.1.6,   00:00:05,   Serial1
R    192.168.20.0    /24    [120/1]via 200.1.1.6,   00:00:05,   Serial1
R    192.168.30.0    /24    [120/2]via 200.1.1.6,   00:00:05,   Serial1
```

Figure 5-11 Router A after RIP is configured.

Route Tables After RIP Is Configured

Figures 5-11, 5-12, and 5-13 show how the route tables look after RIP has been configured and the tables have normalized.

Common RIP Commands

Here are examples of some of the more commonly used commands for configuring RIP.

```
routerB#show ip route
Codes:   C – connected,  S – static,  I – IGRP,  R – RIP,  M – mobile,  B – BGP
         D – EIGRP,  EX – EIRGP external,  O – OSPF,  IA – OSPF inter area
         N1 – OSPF NSSA external type 1,  N2 – OSPF NSSA external type 2,  E – EGP
         i – IS-IS,  L1 – IS-IS level-1,  L2 – IS-IS level 2,  * - candidate default
         U – per-user static route, o – ODR
         T – traffic engineered route

Gateway of last resort is not set

C        192.168.20.0  /24    [0/0]     is directly connected,  Ethernet0
         200.1.1.0     /30    is subnetted, 2 subnets
C           200.1.1.4         [0/0]     is directly connected,  Serial0
C           200.1.1.8         [0/0]     is directly connected,  Serial1
R        192.168.10.0 /24     [120/1]via 200.1.1.5,   00:00:05,    Serial1
R        192.168.30.0 /24     [120/1]via 200.1.1.10,  00:00:05,    Serial1
```

Figure 5-12   Router B after RIP is configured.

```
routerC#show ip route
Codes:   C – connected,  S – static,  I – IGRP,  R – RIP,  M – mobile,  B – BGP
         D – EIGRP,  EX – EIRGP external,  O – OSPF,  IA – OSPF inter area
         N1 – OSPF NSSA external type 1,  N2 – OSPF NSSA external type 2,  E – EGP
         i – IS-IS,  L1 – IS-IS level-1,  L2 – IS-IS level 2,  * - candidate default
         U – per-user static route, o – ODR
         T – traffic engineered route

Gateway of last resort is not set

C        192.168.30.0  /24    [0/0]     is directly connected,  Ethernet0
         200.1.1.0     /30    is subnetted, 2 subnets
C           200.1.1.8         [0/0]     is directly connected,  Serial0
R           200.1.1.4         [120/1]via 200.1.1.9,   00:00:05,    Serial0
R        192.168.20.0 /24     [120/1]via 200.1.1.9,   00:00:05,    Serial0
R        192.168.10.0 /24     [120/2]via 200.1.1.9,   00:00:05,    Serial0
```

Figure 5-13   Router C after RIP is configured.

Setting the RIP Version

RIP defaults to sending version 1 updates and receiving version 1 or version 2 updates. The statement **version 2** forces RIP to send and receive version 2 updates exclusively. This is a global command that affects all interfaces. Executing the **version 2** command on **every** RIP router is all that is necessary to enable RIPv2 and thus enjoy all its benefits such as classless addressing support. Here's how:

```
routerX(config)#router rip
routerX(config-router)#version x (1)
```

where:

(1) x = 1 or 2

In the rare case where more granular control is required, the RIP version can be set at the interface level. Since routers configured for version 2 of RIP ignore RIP version 1 updates, a specific interface could be set to accept version 1 advertisements if say, one router was still using RIPv1. Here's how:

```
routerX(config)#int e0

routerX(config-if)#ip rip send version 1

routerX(config-if)#ip rip receive version 1
```

If need be, the interface level RIP commands could be used to advertise and/or receive both versions of RIP updates, like this:

```
routerX(config)#int e1

routerX(config-if)#ip rip send version 1 2

routerX(config-if)#ip rip receive version 1 2
```

Displaying the RIP Version

```
routerX(config)#show ip protocols
```

Changing Default Timers

Most RIP timers can be altered from their default settings. Care should be taken when changing a timer, and it is best to match any changes on all RIP routers in the system.

The format of command is as follows:

```
routerX(config-router)#timers basic update invalid holddown flush x (1)
```

where:

(1) x = number of seconds

For example:

```
routerX(config)#router rip
```

```
routerX(config-router)#timers basic 60 180 180 240 (2)
```

where:

(2) doubles the length of time between routing updates from 30 to 60 seconds and maintains all other timers at default.

Load Balancing—Changing the Default Number of Multiple Paths

The Cisco implementation of RIP defaults to load balancing up to four equal cost paths. This can be altered with the following command:

```
RouterX(config)#router rip
```

```
RouterX(config-router)#Maximum-paths x (1)
```

where:

(1) x = (1-6)

Enabling and Disabling Split Horizon

Split horizon is on by default for most configurations, but may be off by default on serial interfaces and/or sub-interfaces. You can check the status of split horizon on a particular interface with the **show ip interface x** command. For example, to see the status of split horizon on serial 0, execute the following:

```
routerX(config)#show ip interface s 0
```

Scan the output for the statement "Split horizon is enabled" or "Split horizon is disabled." Split horizon can be forcibly enabled or disabled on an interface level with the following command:

```
routerX(config-if)#{no} ip split-horizon
```

Configuring Summarization

Auto-summarization is on by default for both RIPv1 and RIPv2 when advertising a route across a major network boundary. This behavior cannot be altered for RIPv1. Auto-summarization can be disabled for RIPv, and can optionally be configured to summarize at any bit boundary. (Summarization was covered in Chapter 4.) Here is an example of the command syntax for RIP:

```
routerX(config)#interface s0

routerX(config-if)#no auto-summary (1)

routerX(config-if)#ip summary-address rip 192.168.1.0 255.255.255.0 (2)
```

where:
(1) disables auto-summarization on specified interface only.
(2) summarizes advertised subnets of the 192.168.1.0 on this interface to a class C boundary.

Configuring for the IP Classless Feature

The **ip classless** command is explained in Chapter 10. This command should be executed if default routing is configured. The command to enable classless routing is the same for all routing protocols:

```
routerX(config)#router rip
routerX(config-router)#ip classless
```

As of Cisco IOS 12.1, classless routing is enabled by default.

Redistribution

The general principals of redistribution are covered in Chapter 10. Listed here is a sample configuration of redistributing IRGP routes into RIP (redistribution is OFF by default in RIP):

```
routerX(config)#router rip

routerX(config-router)#redistribute igrp 100 tag 1

routerX(config-router)#default-metric 10
```

The key to including external routes in RIP is to get the metric right. RIP can only deal with a metric in the range of 1–15. The metrics of other routing protocols have significantly larger values. Values larger than 15 are treated as unreachable networks in RIP.

The **redistribute igrp 100 tag 1** statement causes IGRP update packets to be injected into the RIP process. An assumption is made that IGRP is running on the same router. RIP will include any IGRP-learned networks with its regular updates. All IGRP routes will be tagged with the number 1. This allows other routers to identify the IGRP injected routes if need be. The **default-metric 10** statement applies a metric of 10 to all injected routes. This is mandatory because IGRP metrics make no sense to RIP. The number "10" in this case is arbitrary. The IGRP-learned networks are not necessarily 10 hops away, but that does not prevent the delivery of packets. To mitigate the possibility of a routing loop, use a metric value greater than the metric of any IGRP routes that RIP is also aware of. In other words, if both IGRP and RIP are aware of a route to 172.1.0.0, then RIP will become aware of the route again when the IGRP routes are redistributed into RIP. The external route should be set to a metric less than the current metric RIP has for the route it learned from another RIP router. This will force RIP to choose the routes it learned directly over the external IGRP routes.

Alternative Method of Applying a Metric to Redistributed Routes

The **redistribute** command provides an option for applying a metric to just the IGRP injected routes, as follows:

```
routerX(config)#router rip
routerX(config-router)#redistribute igrp 100 tag 1 metric 10
```

These statements have the same effect as the previous example, except that they apply only to IGRP-injected routes, whereas the default-metric statement in the previous example applies to any protocol being redistributed into RIP. This provides for more granular control over the redistribution process.

Redistributing Static Routes

Static routes configured on a RIP router can be included in routing updates. The following command causes all static routes to be included in updates on the router it is executed on:

```
routerX(config)#router rip
routerX(config-router)#redistribute static
```

Be advised that static *default* routes are configured slightly different (see Chapters 3 and 10).

Filtering Redistributed Routes with a Distribution List

Although distribution lists and access lists are not covered in this book, an example of how they are pertinent to redistribution is given here. The following statements prevent any subnets of 190.100.100 from being redistributed from IGRP into RIP:

```
routerX(config)#access-list 1 deny 190.100.100.0 0.0.0.255
routerX(config)#router igrp 100
routerX(config-router)#distribute-list 1 out
routerX(config-router)#exit
routerX(config)#router rip
routerX(config-router)#redistribute igrp 100
```

A distribution list allows you to control which external routes the native routing process learns about. An access list must be created that specifies which networks will be permitted or denied. In this example, the **access-list** statement denies any subnets of the 192.100.100.0. Until the access list is applied somewhere, the distribution list is meaningless. The **router igrp 100** statement accesses the IGRP routing process. Then the access list is applied to outgoing routing updates in the form of an outbound distribution list with the statement **distribute-list 1 out**. IGRP will now be prevented from advertising this network from this router. Finally, the **redistribute igrp 100** statement injects IGRP updates into RIP (minus network 190.100.100.0).

Be advised that this example prevents IGRP from advertising the 190.100.100.0 network to anybody, not just RIP. However, this does not prevent other IGRP processes on other routers to propagate the network throughout the IGRP system.

Show Commands for RIP

Here are a few of the common commands for displaying the state of a RIP router.

Showing the Configuration

The following command shows all routing protocols, RIP timers, filters, redistribution, version, and summarization status:

```
routerA#Show ip protocols
```

Showing the RIP Database

The following command shows all information learned from updates, before the algorithm is run to populate route tables:

```
routerA#show ip rip database
```

Showing the Route Table

The following shows static, directly connected, and RIP learned routes:

```
routerA#show ip route (shows all routes)

routerA#show ip route xxx.xxx.xxx.xxx (1)
```

where:

(1)   shows all Routes.

(2)   shows more detail for a single route.

Troubleshooting Commands

If you get into trouble, these commands can help get you out.

Showing RIP Updates

The **debug ip rip** command shows the actual routing updates. This is a great way to get a sense of how RIP communicates with routers and is indispensable when things aren't going right. Care should be taken with this command however, as it consumes router resources.

Activating Debugging

Use the following command to activate debugging:

```
routerA#debug ip rip
```

Showing Debug Status

Use the following command to show the debugging status:

```
routerA#show debug
```

Stopping Debugging

Use the following command to stop debugging:

```
routerA#undebug all
```

Notes

1. This characteristic was illustrated in Chapter 4, in the section on distance vector routing protocols, page 109.

2. The term "neighbor" has various meanings, depending on the specific routing protocol. EIGRP and OSPF require an initial exchange between routers to establish a neighbor relationship and share route tables. RIP, however, rather blindly broadcasts updates without prior knowledge of who may be out there. Every RIP router sharing a network link on an interface enabled for RIP is automatically considered a neighbor.

3. The command reference later in this chapter lists the configuration commands and actual router output for this model.

4. RIP cannot forward packets more than 15 hops away, therefore advertising a route with a metric of 16 is telling other routers the route cannot be used.

5. Routers can also detect the loss of a carrier on some types of WAN links, which is an even faster indication that the link has gone down.

Overview

IGRP stands for Interior Gateway Routing Protocol. It is one of the early replacements for RIP that eliminated the hop count limitation and used more robust metrics. It provides the same limited support for classlessly addressed networks as RIP. It is a Cisco-proprietary protocol. In its time, IGRP provided a good solution, but now it should be replaced by the classless protocols EIGRP or OSPF. Table 6-1 shows the basic characteristics of IGRP.

Table 6-1 Routing Characteristics of IGRP

Metric	Bandwidth + delay
Interior or Exterior?	Interior
Distance vector or Link-state?	Distance vector
Singlepath or Multipath?	Multipath
Broadcast or Multicast?	Broadcast and unicast
Flat or Hierarchical?	Flat
Classful or Classless?	Classful

This chapter covers the following IGRP topics:

Advantages of Using IGRP

- Acceptable for use in smaller, classfully addressed networks
- Easy to configure
- Good for networks with few redundant paths
- Good for networks with varying speed WAN links
- Better metrics than RIP
- No hop count limitation
- Can unicast route table
- Composite metric composed of more than hop count

Disadvantages to Using IGRP

- Proprietary to Cisco IOS—must employ all Cisco routers to avoid having to run multiple routing protocols
- Prone to routing loops due to slow convergence

- Chatty protocol—sends entire route table periodically
- Has limited support for classlessly addressed networks

IGRP Background

IGRP is a proprietary classful routing protocol developed by Cisco to replace RIPv1. It was released in 1986. IGRP runs only on Cisco routers. IGRP attempted to overcome RIPv's limitations such as using hop count for the metric and transmitting the route table every 30 seconds. IGRP is considered a distance vector protocol for use within autonomous systems (as is RIP).

Rather than hop count, IGRP uses the *bandwidth* of the link and *delay* of the link to calculate the metric. Additionally, an administrator can add *load* of the link and *reliability* of the link to the metric (these terms were defined in Chapter 4 on page 107).

IGRP can even be optionally configured for hop count and MTU (Maximum Transmission Unit), but these factors are not incorporated into the metric. Hop count is used only to set a limit on *counting to infinity* problems. The hop count can be manually configured for up to 255 hops—the default is 100 hops. The MTU is a setting identifying the maximum MTU that can be handled by any networking device in the system. It is desirable to set an MTU no larger than the *smallest* MTU of any link on the network. This prevents routing update packets from being fragmented and thus improves throughput.

IGRP has more in common with RIPv1 than any other routing protocol. It is therefore recommend that you read Chapter 5 even if you have no intention of working with that protocol. Chapter 5 goes into detail about how distance vector protocols propagate routes and how routing loops are handled. Table 6-2 illustrates the difference between IGRP and RIP.

Table 6-2 IGRP versus RIP Comparison Chart

FEATURE	RIPV1	RIPV2	IGRP
Broadcasts entire table	Yes	Yes	Yes
Hop count for metric	Yes	Yes	No
Supports subnet masks	No	Yes	No
Equal-cost multipath routing	Yes	Yes	Yes
Unequal-cost multipath routing	No	No	Yes

Because IGRP is a classful routing protocol, it does not support subnet masks, so it cannot fully support classless addressing. IGRP can support unequal-cost multipath routing. It was noted in Chapter 5 that only the Cisco implementation of RIP supports multipath routing. But even then, only *equal*-cost multipath routing is supported in RIP—meaning multiple paths to the same destination can be shared for load balancing only if the metric is the same for each path. With IGRP's *unequal*-cost multipath routing capability, multiple paths to the same destination will be installed in the route table even if the metrics are not all the same value.

How IGRP Works

IGRP behaves much like RIP when it comes to learning and propagating routes. IGRP transmits the entire route table periodically to neighboring routers. As with RIP, routes are learned from neighboring routers, who in turn share routes they have learned from their neighbors (routing by rumor). By default, IGRP uses broadcasts to propagate routing update packets, but like RIPv2, the protocol can be configured to send unicast updates (see the command reference at the end of the chapter).

IGRP Timers

IGRP has timers similar to RIP that control route propagation and limit routing loops. However, as Table 6-3 illustrates, the values for these timers are quite different for IGRP.

Table 6-3 Comparison Chart of RIP versus IGRP Timers

TIMER	RIP	IGRP
Update timer	30	**90**
Invalid timer	180	**270**
Flush timer	240	**630**
Hold-down timer	180	**280**

As you can see, IGRP is not nearly as chatty as RIP. Saving network bandwidth is a good thing. But what keeps IGRP from slipping in the convergence department? IGRP implements **flash updates**. When a router learns of a change to a route (link down, new route, different metric for an existing route, and so on), it immediately sends an update to its neighbors. Flash updates are similar to RIP's triggered updates. In earlier releases of the Cisco IOS, IGRP's flash updates were triggered by a wider variety of events than RIP, but RIP convergence has been improved in later releases of the IOS.

Split Horizon

As with RIP, IGRP usually does not advertise a route back through the same interface the route learned. However, the same cautions regarding Frame Relay apply here, namely that split horizon may need to be disabled on Frame Relay sub-interfaces.

Poison Reverse

This feature works the same as with RIP.

IGRP Metrics

IGRP calculates a metric for a route differently than RIP. Stated in its simplest form, with default values, the formula for the algorithm is shown in Figure 6-1

This formula reduces to a single value based on the assignments for bandwidth and delay shown in Table 6-4.

Table 6-4   Assignments for Bandwidth and Delay Metrics

LINK TYPE	BANDWIDTH (IN KBPS)	DELAY (IN MICRO-SECONDS)
Ethernet	10,000	1000
Fast Ethernet	100,000	100
Gigabit Ethernet	1,000,000	10
FDDI	100,000	100
Token Ring (16 Mbps)	16,000	630
T1	1544	20,000

The values from the table are manipulated to render the actual metric. Let's take the example of a route passing through two WAN links: one link is FDDI and one link is T1. The algorithm first divides 10,000,000 by the **slowest link in the path,** then adds the result to the **sum** of the delay values for each link, and divides by 10. The slowest link in this example is the T1 link, so the formula looks as the one shown in Figure 6-2.

Bandwidth + Delay

Figure 6-1   Basic formula for metric calculation in IGRP.

$$(10,000,000 / \text{Bandwidth}) + ((\text{sum of delays}) /10)$$
$$(10,000,000/1,544) + ((20,000+100) /10)$$
$$6477 + 2,010$$
$$8487$$

Figure 6-2 Calculating the metric.

The metric yielded is 8487[1]. This number can be compared to IGRP metrics derived from other routes to the same destination. The path with the lowest number will be chosen by IGRP as the best route. Note that delay values include *outbound* interfaces only.

Bandwidth and delay metrics can be modified from their default values if required. These factors can be adjusted on Cisco routers with the **metric weight** command. The metric formula is adjusted to accommodate these optional weighting factors as reflected in Figure 6-3.

The variables k1 and k3 are set to 1 by default, so they normally have no effect (1 x a number = that number). But if the settings are altered, they affect the metric as shown in the figure.

If desired, the factors *load* and *reliability* can be added to weigh the metric, but most deployments do not do so. When used, the formula is now fully expressed in Figure 6-4.

The additional variables k2, k4, and k5 have been added. They all have a default value of 0, so unless they are altered, they have no impact on the formula.

Note that the IGRP algorithm is not as adept at automatically picking the best route as it would seem from all the factors that contribute to the composite metric. All metric factors except reliability and load are static values, and reliability and load metrics are not active by default. Furthermore, you must have a very good handle on your network traffic before going here and futzing with these settings. Cisco recommends leaving the values at their default, which means you are dealing with a protocol that, in the end, uses the formula as first expressed (Bandwidth + Delay).

$$(k1 \times (10,000,000 / \text{Bandwidth})) + (k3 \times (\text{sum of delays} /10))$$

Figure 6-3 IGRP metric formula with optional weighting factors.

$$((k1 \times (10,000,000 / \text{Bandwidth})) + ((k2 \times \text{Bandwidth}) /$$
$$(256-\text{load})) + ((k3 \times (\text{sum of delays} /10)) \times (k5 / (\text{reliability} + k4))$$

Figure 6-4 Complete rendering of the IGRP metric formula.

> **NOTE** Since bandwidth is a core part of IGRP's metric, it is important that you manually set the bandwidth on all serial interfaces. The router may not detect the true bandwidth of the link. For example, if a Cisco router does not detect the link speed on a serial interface it will assume a bandwidth of 1.544 Kbps. If the link is faster or slower, setting the true bandwidth will result in more accurate routing decisions (see command reference at the end of this section).

Autonomous Numbers

Unlike RIP, IGRP (and EIGRP) can run multiple instances of its routing process on a single router. An instance of IGRP is identified by an **autonomous system number** associated with the routing protocol when it is enabled. Multiple instances of IGRP are isolated from each other. Each instance sends and receives separate updates and builds separate route tables. You could, for example, run two instances of IGRP on one router if there are two autonomous systems under separate administrative control that need to share routing information.

Load Balancing in IGRP

The IGRP routing protocol goes a step further than RIP by supporting not only equal, but *unequal* multipath routing. With equal multipath routing, IGRP will load balance by sending an equal number of packets through each of up to six parallel (redundant) routes that can reach the same destination network. Each route must have the same metric—that is what defines equal cost load balancing. Equal multipath routing for up to four routes is on by default[2].

IGRP also supports unequal multipath routing by load balancing traffic across up to six redundant paths with *varying* metrics. The route with the lowest cost is selected as **primary**, with the other redundant routes acting as failover routes and/or for load balancing. When performing unequal multipath routing IGRP will allocate a percentage of packets based on the metric of the route. Routes with lower metrics (faster links) will receive a proportionally greater number of packets than routes to the same destination with higher metrics.

Unequal multipath routing is OFF by default. To activate the feature, the **variance** IGRP subcommand must be used. Figure 6-5 portrays a network example to illustrate how the variance feature works.

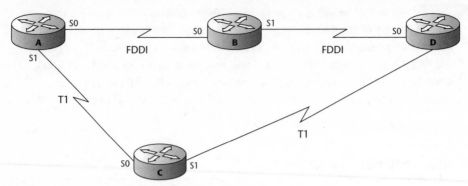

Figure 6-5 Network with varying routing metrics.

Router A has a 100 Mbps path to router D through the FDDI link. Router A also has a 1.544 Mbps path to router D through the T1 link. The metric for the path to router D via the FDDI link is 120 and via the T1 link is 10477. By dividing the larger metric by the smaller metric, the multiple between the two values can be determined as 87.3 (10477/120). So the metric 10477 is **87.3** times larger then the metric 120. That number will be needed in a moment.

Until the variance command is issued, router A will use router B to get to router D exclusively, since the metrics of the two paths are dissimilar. In order to activate the other path, the metric of the path through router C must be a *lower effective metric* then through router B. This is where the variance command comes in. A variance must be entered that is greater than the multiple between the larger and smaller metric. A variance of 88 will do the trick. After configuring the variance, the two paths will now be active. The faster link will carry 88 percent more packets than the slower link. (See the previous discussion about flow-based splitting. See the command reference for the exact commands.)

Default Routing

Default routing is covered in Chapter 10. Differences pertaining specifically to IGRP are noted here.

IGRP does not support the **ip route** command (**ip route 0.0.0.0 0.0.0.0 x.x.x.x**) for configuring default routing because the protocol does not understand the 0.0.0.0 network. Instead, the **ip default-network** command must be used. Unlike RIP, all routers must list the network specified in the **ip default-network** statement, or the default route will not be accepted.

Redistribution

IGRP is capable of including static and externally learned routes in its updates (redistribution). The general principals of redistribution are covered in Chapter 10. Redistribution is OFF by default in IGRP, with one exception: IGRP and EIGRP, which have similar metrics, automatically distribute routes to each other when both routing protocols are running on the same router and both protocols are using the same autonomous system number. The one dissimilarity between the protocols, the metric multiplier of 256, is automatically adjusted when routes are redistributed. It is clear that EIGRP, IGRP's successor, was engineered to make an easy upgrade from IGRP.

Route Summarization in IGRP

IGRP, being a classful routing protocol, can only summarize to a classful border. Furthermore, summarization cannot be forcibly enabled or disabled. Routes will be auto-summarized to the classful border whenever the address is advertised across a major network number.

Command Reference—IGRP

Figure 6-6 provides a network model for the configuration of IGRP. The examples will cover configuring IGRP on a Cisco router.

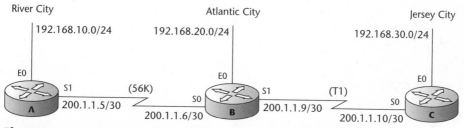

Figure 6-6 Example network for commands.

Initial Configuration

An initial configuration of the routers will be performed, and the route tables will be shown before the IGRP routing protocol is configured.

Configuring the IP Addresses

```
routerA#configure terminal
routerA(config)#interface fastethernet 0 (1)
routerA(config-if)#ip address 192.168.10.0 255.255.255.0 (2)
routerA(config-if)#exit (3)
routerA(config)#interface serial 1 (4)
routerA(config-if)#ip address 200.1.1.5 255.255.255.252 (5)
routerA(config-if)#bandwidth 56 (6)
routerA(config-if)#exit
routerA(config)#

routerB#configure terminal
routerB(config)#interface fastethernet 0
routerB(config-if)#ip address 192.168.20.0 255.255.255.0
routerB(config-if)#exit
routerB(config)#interface serial 0
routerB(config-if)#ip address 200.1.1.6 255.255.255.252 (7)
routerB(config-if)#bandwidth 56
routerB(config-if)#exit
routerB(config)#interface serial 1
routerB(config-if)#ip address 200.1.1.9 255.255.255.252 (8)
routerB(config-if)#bandwidth 1544
routerB(config-if)#exit
routerB(config)#

routerC#configure terminal
routerC(config)#interface fastethernet 0
routerC(config-if)#ip address 192.168.30.0 255.255.255.0
routerC(config-if)#exit
routerC(config)#interface serial 0
routerC(config-if)#ip address 200.1.1.10 255.255.255.252
routerC(config-if)#bandwidth 1544
routerC(config-if)#exit
routerC(config)#
```

(1) changes to interface E0.

(2) configures the address with a /24 prefix.

(3) exits interface mode back to global config mode.

(4) changes to interface S1.

(5) configures the address with a /30 prefix.

(6) sets the bandwidth to match the link speed.

(7) is the first possible subnet of the 200.1.1.0 /30.

(8) is the next possible subnet of the 200.1.1.0 /30.

Route Tables Before IGRP Is Configured

Figures 6-7, 6-8, and 6-9 reflect the state of the route tables before IGRP is configured.

```
routerA#show ip route
Codes:   C – connected,  S – static,  I – IGRP,  R – RIP,  M – mobile,  B – BGP
         D – EIGRP,  EX – EIRGP external,  O – OSPF,  IA – OSPF inter area
         N1 – OSPF NSSA external type 1,  N2 – OSPF NSSA external type 2,  E – EGP
         i – IS-IS,  L1 – IS-IS level-1,  L2 – IS-IS level 2,  * - candidate default
         U – per-user static route, o – ODR
         T – traffic engineered route

Gateway of last resort is not set

C        192.168.10.0  /24     [0/0]     is directly connected,  Ethernet0
         200.1.1.0     /30     is subnetted, 1 subnets
C            200.1.1.4         [0/0]     is directly connected,  Serial1
```

Figure 6-7   Router A – before IGRP is configured.

```
routerB#show ip route
Codes:   C – connected,  S – static,  I – IGRP,  R – RIP,  M – mobile,  B – BGP
         D – EIGRP,  EX – EIRGP external,  O – OSPF,  IA – OSPF inter area
         N1 – OSPF NSSA external type 1,  N2 – OSPF NSSA external type 2,  E – EGP
         i – IS-IS,  L1 – IS-IS level-1,  L2 – IS-IS level 2,  * - candidate default
         U – per-user static route, o – ODR
         T – traffic engineered route

Gateway of last resort is not set

C        192.168.20.0  /24     [0/0]     is directly connected,  Ethernet0
         200.1.1.0     /30     is subnetted, 2 subnets
C            200.1.1.4         [0/0]     is directly connected,  Serial0
C            200.1.1.8         [0/0]     is directly connected,  Serial1
```

Figure 6-8   Router B – before IGRP is configured.

```
routerC#show ip route
Codes:   C – connected,  S – static,  I – IGRP,  R – RIP,  M – mobile,  B – BGP
         D – EIGRP,  EX – EIRGP external,  O – OSPF,  IA – OSPF inter area
         N1 – OSPF NSSA external type 1,  N2 – OSPF NSSA external type 2,  E – EGP
         i – IS-IS,  L1 – IS-IS level-1,  L2 – IS-IS level 2,  * - candidate default
         U – per-user static route, o – ODR
         T – traffic engineered route

Gateway of last resort is not set

C        192.168.30.0  /24     [0/0]     is directly connected,  Ethernet0
         200.1.1.0     /30     is subnetted, 1 subnets
C            200.1.1.8          [0/0]     is directly connected,  Serial0
```

Figure 6-9   Router C – before IGRP is configured.

Configuring IGRP

```
routerA(config)#router igrp 100 (1)
routerA(config-router)#network 192.168.10.0 (2)
routerA(config-router)#network 200.1.1.4 (3)
routerA(config-router)#passive-interface fastethernet 0 (4)
routerA(config-router)#exit

routerB#config-term
routerB(config)#router igrp 100
routerB(config-router)#network 192.168.20.0
routerB(config-router)#network 200.1.1.4
routerB(config-router)#network 200.1.1.8
routerB(config-router)#passive-interface fastethernet 0
routerB(config-router)#exit
routerB(config)#

routerC#config-term
routerC(config)#router igrp 100
routerC(config-router)#network 192.168.30.0
routerC(config-router)#network 200.1.1.8
routerC(config-router)#passive-interface fastethernet 0
routerC(config-router)#exit
routerC(config)#
```

(1) enables IGRP on this router with an AS number of 100.

(2) and (3) include network in IGRP advertisements. All interfaces with an address configured within the range of this address will send and receive routing updates.

(4) suppresses routing advertisements on this interface.

One of the key differences configuring IGRP versus RIP is the inclusion of an autonomous system (AS) number. This is due to the capability of IGRP to run multiple instances of the routing protocol on one router. If more than one instance of IGRP is activated on a router, the AS number will isolate all IGRP activity within each AS number. Separate route tables will be built and updates will be confined within the AS.

Route Tables After IGRP Is Configured

Figures 6-10, 6-11, and 6-12 show how the route tables look after IGRP has been configured and the tables have normalized.

```
routeA#show ip route
Codes:   C – connected,  S – static,  I – IGRP,  R – RIP,  M – mobile,  B – BGP
         D – EIGRP,  EX – EIRGP external,  O – OSPF,  IA – OSPF inter area
         N1 – OSPF NSSA external type 1,  N2 – OSPF NSSA external type 2,  E – EGP
         i – IS-IS,  L1 – IS-IS level-1,  L2 – IS-IS level 2,  * - candidate default
         U – per-user static route,  o – ODR
         T – traffic engineered route

Gateway of last resort is not set

C    192.168.10.0   /24  [0/0] is directly connected,  Ethernet0
     200.1.10            /30 is subnetted, 2 subnets
C       200.1.1.4          [0/0] is directly connected,  Serial1
I       200.1.1.8          [100/1]  via 200.1.1.6,  00:00:05,  Serial1
I    192.168.20.0  /24  [100/1]  via 200.1.1.6,  00:00:05,  Serial1
I    192.168.30.0  /24  [100/2]  via 200.1.1.6,  00:00:05,  Serial1
```

Figure 6-10   Router A after IGRP is configured.

```
routerB#show ip route
Codes:   C – connected,  S – static,  I – IGRP,  R – RIP,  M – mobile,  B – BGP
         D – EIGRP,  EX – EIRGP external,  O – OSPF,  IA – OSPF inter area
         N1 – OSPF NSSA external type 1,  N2 – OSPF NSSA external type 2,  E – EGP
         i – IS-IS,  L1 – IS-IS level-1,  L2 – IS-IS level 2,  * - candidate default
         U – per-user static route,  o – ODR
         T – traffic engineered route

Gateway of last resort is not set

C        192.168.20.0  /24     [0/0]    is directly connected,  Ethernet0
         200.1.1.0     /30     is subnetted, 2 subnets
C           200.1.1.4          [0/0]    is directly connected,  Serial0
C           200.1.1.8          [0/0]    is directly connected,  Serial1
I        192.168.10.0  /24 [100/1]via 200.1.1.5,   00:00:05,    Serial1
I        192.168.30.0  /24 [100/1]via 200.1.1.10,  00:00:05,    Serial1
```

Figure 6-11   Router B after IGRP is configured.

```
routerC#show ip route
Codes:   C – connected,  S – static,  I – IGRP,  R – RIP,  M – mobile,  B – BGP
         D – EIGRP,  EX – EIRGP external,  O – OSPF,  IA – OSPF inter area
         N1 – OSPF NSSA external type 1,  N2 – OSPF NSSA external type 2,  E – EGP
         i – IS-IS,  L1 – IS-IS level-1,  L2 – IS-IS level 2,  * - candidate default
         U – per-user static route,  o – ODR
         T – traffic engineered route

Gateway of last resort is not set

C        192.168.30.0  /24     [0/0]    is directly connected,  Ethernet0
         200.1.1.0     /30     is subnetted, 2 subnets
C           200.1.1.8          [0/0]    is directly connected,  Serial0
I           200.1.1.4      [100/1]via 200.1.1.9,   00:00:05,   Serial0
I        192.168.20.0  /24 [100/1]via 200.1.1.9,   00:00:05,   Serial0
I        192.168.10.0  /24 [100/2]via 200.1.1.9,   00:00:05,   Serial0
```

Figure 6-12   Router C after IGRP is configured.

Common IGRP Commands

Here are examples of some of the more commonly used commands for configuring IGRP.

Changing Default Timers

Most IGRP timers can be altered from their default settings. Care should be taken when changing a timer and it is best to match any changes on all IGRP routers in the system.

The format of the command is as follows:

```
routerX(config)#router igrp
routerX(config-router)#timers basic update invalid holddown flush x (1)
```

where:

   (1) x = number of seconds

For example:

```
routerX(config)#router igrp
routerX(config-router)#timers basic 180 270 280 630 (2)
```

where:

   (2) doubles the length of time between routing updates from 90 to 180 seconds and maintains all other timers at default.

Load Balancing—Changing the Default Number of Multiple Paths

IGRP defaults to load balancing up to four equal cost paths. This can be altered with the following command:

```
routerX#config term
routerX(config)#router igrp
routerX(config-router)#maximum-paths x (1)
```

where:

   (1) x = (1-6)

Load Balancing—Configuring Unequal Multipath Routing

Unequal multipath routing is configured by issuing the **variance** command, which encompasses the range of metrics on the paths to be included for load balancing the traffic to a specific network. The method for determining the variance value was shown earlier. Here are the commands to configure a variance of 88 from the example:

```
routerX#config term
routerX(config)#router igrp 100
routerX(config-router)#variance 88
routerX(config-router)#exit
```

Configuring K Values for Metric Manipulation

```
routerX(config)#router igrp 100
routerX(config-router)#metric weights 0 1 1 1 1 1 (1)
```

where:

(1) shows default K values being assigned.

Enabling or Disabling Split Horizon

Split horizon is on by default for most configurations, but may be off by default on serial interfaces and/or sub-interfaces. You can check the status of split horizon on a particular interface with the **show ip interface** *x* statement. For example, to see if split horizon is enabled on serial 0, execute the following:

```
routerX(config)#int s0
routerX(config-if)#show ip interface s0
```

Scan the output for the statement "Split horizon is enabled" or "Split horizon is disabled." Split horizon can be forcibly enabled or disabled on an interface level with the following command:

```
routerX(config-if)#{no} ip split-horizon
```

Show Commands for IGRP

Here are a few of the common commands for displaying the state of a IGRP router.

Showing Configuration

The following command shows all routing protocols, IGRP timers, filters, redistribution, and summarization status:

```
routerA#Show ip protocols
```

Showing the Route Table

The following command shows static, external, directly connected, and IGRP-learned routes:

```
routerX#show ip route (shows all routes)
routerX#show ip route x.x.x.x (more detail for a single route)
```

Troubleshooting Commands

If you get into trouble, these commands can help get you out.

Showing IGRP Events

Use the following command to show IGRP events:

```
routerX#debug ip eigrp events (use sparingly - consumes resources)
```

Showing Debug Status

Use the following command to show the debugging status:

```
routerX#show debug
```

Canceling the Debug

Use the following command to cancel the debugging process:

```
routerX#undebug all
```

Notes

1. Note that in the formula 10,000,000 is divided by the bandwidth in order to generate an inverse number scaled by a factor of 10^e 10. The delay value is divided by 10 to convert microseconds to milliseconds.

2. Regardless of the routing protocol employing equal cost load balancing, traffic is not always split perfectly across the multiple paths. For example, some router vendors will direct all traffic for a particular TCP session along a single path—otherwise performance might actually be degraded.

Overview

EIGRP stands for Enhanced Interior Gateway Routing Protocol. It is a contemporary, widely implemented routing protocol with full support for classlessly addressed networks. Table 7-1 shows the basic characteristics of EIGRP.

Table 7-1 Routing Characteristics of EIGRP

Metric	Bandwidth + delay
Interior or Exterior?	Interior
Distance vector or Link-state?	Hybrid
Singlepath or Multipath?	Multipath
Broadcast or Multicast?	Multicast and unicast
Flat or Hierarchical?	Flat
Classful or Classless?	Classless

This chapter covers the following EIGRP topics:

Advantages of Using EIGRP

- Classless protocol—full support for classless addressing
- Scalable protocol—can be used on large networks
- Supports multiple networking protocols—single routing protocol solution for IP, IPX, and Appletalk
- Optimized for minimum bandwidth use
- No hop count limitation
- Fast convergence
- Guaranteed loop-free routes
- Equal and unequal cost multipath routing
- Summarization configurable at the bit boundary

- Similar metrics to IGRP—simplifies migrating from IGRP to EIGRP
- Communication among routers sent via unicasts and multicasts
- Optional authentication of routing packets (MD5 encryption with IOS 11.3 and higher)

Disadvantages of Using EIGRP

- Proprietary to Cisco IOS—must employ all Cisco routers to avoid having to run multiple interior routing protocols
- Flat protocol—cannot be configured into areas as OSPF can (this can be mitigated to some degree by running multiple instances of EIGRP)

EIGRP Background

EIGRP was released in the early 1990s by Cisco Systems, subsequent to releasing IGRP. EIGRP was developed to address problems inherent to distance vector routing protocols such as RIP and IGRP. Like IGRP, EIGRP is proprietary to Cisco and is only available on Cisco routers. EIGRP has similarities to IGRP only in that it uses a very similar metric. Cisco calls EIGRP an *advanced distance vector routing protocol* because EIGRP is actually a hybrid of distance vector and link-state technologies—incorporating features of each design. EIGRP is a classless routing protocol and therefore fully supports CIDR notation, subnetting, VLSMs, and even discontiguous networks. EIGRP and OSPF are the two widely accepted interior IP routing protocols for large networks.

EIGRP Terminology

There are a number of terms associated with the operation of EIGRP and its routing engine, DUAL. One potential roadblock to understanding the protocol is that its associated terminology is not always intuitive. For example, the currently installed route in the route table is known as the *successor*. Another example is when a path to a network is no longer functioning, the route becomes *active*. There are good reasons for the use of these terms, but they tend to be counterintuitive until fully understood. The core terms will be introduced now so that you will have some familiarity with them when you encounter them later.

Neighbor

The term *neighbor* has a more specific meaning with EIGRP than with RIP and IGRP. Any router sharing a network link with another router is *potentially* a neighbor. But to actually qualify as a neighbor, routers sharing a network link must meet certain criteria and establish a **neighbor relationship** before exchanging routing information.

Neighbor Discovery and Recovery

These terms specify the process of establishing and tearing down neighbor relationships. Establishing, maintaining, terminating, and re-establishing neighbor relationships are based on the exchange of **Hello packets** in a timely manner. Neighbor relationships are critical to EIGRP because without them routers don't exchange routing information.

Packet Types

There are five types of packets used in EIGRP[1]:

- **Hello packets:** Exchanged between routers and used to discover and maintain neighbors.
- **Update packets:** This is the main packet type used to exchange routing information. The data stored in the topology table (defined shortly) is what is passed in an update packet. Update packets are sent initially when a neighbor relationship is established and then periodically when there is a change in the status of a link that affects routing.
- **Query packets:** Initiated by a router to its neighbors when it loses a route. The query packet asks if the neighbor knows of a path to the lost route.
- **Reply packets:** Used to respond to a query.
- **ACK packet:** A Hello packet with no data; used to acknowledge packets sent with the Reliable Transport Protocol (RTP).

Hold-Time

This is the time interval to wait for receiving Hello packets from an established neighbor. Hello packets must be periodically exchanged between neighboring routers. If a router stops receiving either Hello packets or any other type of EIGRP packets the hold-time timer expires and the neighbor relationship terminates. The router must then find new routes to networks that were previously reachable through the non-responsive neighbor.

Neighbor Table

This is a separate table used to maintain the list of known neighbors.

Topology Table

This is a separate table that lists all qualified routes. (Qualified routes are known as **feasible successors**.)

Route Table

Also known as a **forwarding table**, this is a separate table that lists the actual routes used to forward packets. The route table is built from the topology table.

Reliable Transport Protocol (RTP)

EIRGP has its own mechanism for reliable delivery of packets, when required. RTP is used in lieu of TCP.

Retransmission Timeout (RTO)

This timer establishes how long a router should wait for acknowledgements to packets sent with RTP protocol.

Smooth Round Trip Time (SRRT)

This timer establishes the average time a router waits for acknowledgements to packets sent with RTP protocol. It is used to calculate the Retransmission Timeout (RTO).

Reported Distance (RD)

This is also known as **advertised distance** (**AD**). When advertising a route, this is the metric of the route from the reporting neighbor to the destination network.

Feasible Distance (FD)

This is the overall metric from the current router to the destination network. It includes the metric of the current router to the reporting router, added to the reported distance value received from the reporting router.

Feasibility Condition (FC)

This is a route whose *reported distance* to a network is less than the *feasible distance* of the current route installed in the route table. Such a route has met the "feasibility condition" and is either installed into the route table or kept as a standby route.

Successor

The route with the lowest metric to a destination network (lowest feasible distance) is known as a *successor* and is installed in the route table. (There can be more than one successor route if multipathing is enabled.)

Feasible Successor (FS)

A route that meets the feasibility condition, but is being kept as a backup route (because a route with a lower metric that met the feasibility condition was installed instead), is referred to as a *feasible successor*. Feasible successors are maintained in the topology table and installed in the route table if the successor route fails.

Diffusing Update ALgorithm (DUAL)

DUAL is the algorithm that EIGRP uses to perform its route calculations. Because EIGRP is basically a distance vector routing protocol, it's prone to routing-loops. DUAL assures "100 percent loop-free routes at every instant" by performing a feasibility test on advertised routes before installing them. This will be explained in detail later.

Some rather complex calculations must be performed by DUAL to assure loop-free routes. This tends to shift resource demands away from network bandwidth and onto a router's CPU and memory. To mitigate this factor, DUAL distributes the processing among routers using *diffused computations* (the traffic of course uses bandwidth). Later examples will demonstrate how DUAL behaves in this regard.

DUAL Finite State Machine

A *finite state machine* is a computer model that defines specific (finite) states, within which, specific input and/or actions occur, and where specific conditions are met to transition from one state to another. DUAL is built on such a model.

Passive and Active Route States

The normal condition of an operational route is known as **passive**. At this time, the router is not seeking to replace a lost route (no diffusing computations are being generated). When the router becomes aware that a route in the route table has become invalid, DUAL is run on the topology table, and a feasible successor is searched for. If no feasible successor is found, the route goes into **active** state, and DUAL initiates a diffusing computation by sending query packets to other routers in an attempt to find a replacement path to the network.

Stuck in Active (SIA)

If replies to queries regarding an active route are not received in a timely manner, the route is considered **stuck in active.**

How EIGRP Works

EIGRP shares similar metrics with its predecessor, IGRP, and it uses distance vector methods of sharing routing information, but its architecture is different in most other ways. The following sections describe the behavior of Cisco's flagship interior routing protocol.

EIGRP Architecture

EIGRP has a clever design for speeding convergence, eliminating routing-loops, and minimizing the use of network bandwidth and router resources. Although an EIGRP router does not transmit a router's links and its state (as OSPF does), it makes the best of the information it does learn from its neighbors. EIGRP keeps all information about qualified routes—routes that meet what is known as a **feasibility condition**—in a topology table. A feasibility condition is a means test (issued by DUAL) to insure a route is loop-free. Only routes meeting the feasibility condition are accepted. Once the topology table is populated, DUAL selects routes from the topology table for installation into the route table, based upon the metric values of the routes.

Routing updates are sent only when a router detects a change for a network it is aware of. When a route fails, a replacement route can often be found *locally* in the router's topology table. EIGRP inter-router communications are kept to a minimum this way. When a replacement route cannot be located locally, the router proactively interrogates its neighbors to see if they are aware of a replacement route.

Small **Hello packets** are exchanged between routers to establish and maintain neighbor relationships. Failure to receive Hello packets in a timely manner gives routers early notification when another router (or link to a router) has failed, so that action can be taken to find alternative paths around the failure. *On a stable network, Hello packets are the only traffic generated by EIGRP.*

The proprietary Reliable Transport Protocol (RTP) also speeds convergence by creating time frames for responses to updates and queries. RTP allows for assured updates (each routing update is acknowledged), which mitigates the need to transmit the entire route table periodically.

Finally, the fact that EIGRP supports multiple routed protocols potentially makes it a single routing protocol solution (EIGRP can ride on IP, IPX, and Appletalk/RTMP packets, thus providing routes to IP networks, NetWare networks, and Appletalk networks).

Now let's take a look at what makes all this wonderfulness possible.

How EIGRP Addresses Distance Vector Protocol Issues

Although EIGRP incorporates features of both distance vector and link-state routing protocols in its architecture, EIGRP is primarily a distance vector protocol. As with RIP and IGRP, EIGRP learns about routes from neighbors advertising a distance to the route (*routing by rumor*). The designers of the protocol, however, in order to speed convergence and eliminate the propensity toward routing-loops, made key changes to the traditional distance vector architecture by borrowing a few tricks from its link-state brethren.

To begin with, EIGRP does not periodically transmit the entire route table to its neighbors. In fact, the only time the entire route table is ever transmitted is when two routers initially exchange their routing information upon forming a neighbor relationship. After that, only incremental changes regarding affected routes are transmitted. This greatly reduces the bandwidth consumed by routing updates and is similar to the approach taken by link-state protocols.

Also, recall that traditional distance vector routing protocols have fairly high settings on the timers that time out routes. Lower settings on these timers improves convergence time but increases bandwidth usage. But in the case of EIGRP, the significant amount of bandwidth saved by not periodically transmitting the entire route table allows the protocol to spend a little bandwidth by timing out routes more quickly. This is another feature attributed to link-state protocols and helps EIGRP achieve the goal of quicker convergence when a change occurs.

To achieve the goal of eliminating routing-loops, EIGRP dropped the traditional Ford-Bellman algorithm in favor of an algorithm that takes a radically different approach to avoiding loops. Although certain traditional distance vector-loop avoidance mechanisms such as split-horizon and route poisoning are still employed, EIGRP relies on the **Diffusing Update ALgorithm** (DUAL) to guarantee loop-free routes. Through rigid inspection of candidate routes, a topology table that lists backups to routes already installed in the route table, and a procedure for interrogating other routers to find lost routes to a network, DUAL not only furthers the cause of quick convergence, the algorithm promises "100 percent loop-free routes at every instant."

Core Communications—Packet Types, Timers, Multicasts, and RTP

Unlike RIP and IGRP, which simply accept any routes they hear of from other routers, EIGRP only considers routes learned from routers known to it. Because EIGRP does not blindly broadcast routing updates, a method is needed to discover other routers sharing the same network links and to establish **neighbor relationships**[2] with them. Neighbors are discovered through the multicasting of **Hello packets** that are heard by other EIGRP routers sharing the same network link.

Hello packets contain the IP address of the interface of the sending router. They are transmitted periodically. On high-speed links (greater than T1 speeds), Hellos are sent every 5 seconds, whereas low-speed links (T1 speeds or less) send Hellos every 60 seconds. Hello packets are multicast on address 224.0.0.10. Using multicasts as opposed to broadcasts keeps other network devices from having to waste resources to see if the packet is intended for them. An interruption of the stream of Hello packets alerts a router to the possible loss of a neighbor (and of course the loss of all routes through that neighbor).

A *hold-time* timer is used by EIGRP to maintain neighbor relationships. This timer tracks expected Hello packets from established neighbors. By default, the hold-time is three times the Hello interval (either 15 or 180 seconds). Each reception of a Hello packet resets the timer.[3] If the hold-time timer expires, the neighbor is presumed to be dead and the relationship is terminated. A new path must be found for any routes that forwarded packets through the defunct neighbor as the next hop to the destination network.

Routing updates are sent in *update packets*. Updates are sent when the neighbor relationship is first established and later when a change occurs that affects routing.

Routers sometimes make inquiries to other routers when trying to reestablish a lost route. Such inquiries are in the form of *query packets* and the replies are in the form of *reply packets*. This behavior is pivotal to the operation of EIGRP and DUAL. Not all advertised routes are accepted by an EIGRP router. Routes that don't meet a *feasibility condition* are rejected and not installed into the topology table.[4] Under certain conditions, queries will be made to see if other routers know of the rejected routes.

EIGRP has the capability to use reliable communication when necessary. It has its own reliable protocol, the Reliable Transport Protocol (RTP). RTP allows for assured delivery of packets in proper sequence. The choice of whether to use reliable communication is more a function of the network type than of the nature of the communication. RTP, therefore, may be utilized for any packet type (Hello packets, update packets, and so on). An ACK packet (which is simply an empty Hello packet except for a sequence number) is used to acknowledge an RTP packet.

Two timers in addition to the hold-time timer are used with EIGRP. A *smooth round trip time* (SRRT) timer is used to establish the average amount of time for RTP packets to be acknowledged. That information is used by the *retransmission timeout (RTO)* timer to inform the router when an RTP packet has not been acknowledged in a reasonable time frame.

EIGRP Tables

At the core of EIGRP are the tables maintained by the protocol on each router. EIGRP maintains three separate tables that facilitate the learning, use, and maintenance of routes to networks.

Neighbor Table

The neighbor table is the first table built when an EIGRP router is powered up. The neighbor table lists all known neighbors the router is aware of.

Hello packets are used to establish and maintain neighbors. When a router first receives a Hello packet it responds with an update packet listing its directly connected networks. The neighbor receiving the route update reciprocates with its directly connected routes.

The following information is tracked in the neighbor table:

- The IP address of the neighbor
- The interface the neighbor was learned through
- The hold-time for the neighbor—a timer that tracks the reception of Hello packets
- The uptime for the neighbor—how long the neighbor relationship has existed
- The number of Hello packets in the queue, which can be used to spot network congestion
- If the RTP has been used to transmit a Hello packet:
  - Smooth Round Trip timer (SRRT)
  - Retransmission (RTO)
  - A queue indicating the number of reliably sent packets waiting a reply
  - The sequence number of the last acknowledged packet

Topology Table

The topology table contains all qualified routes to networks; routes that have met the so-called feasibility condition. Initially the topology table contains only the router's directly connected networks. As routing updates arrive from established neighbors, routes that meet the feasibility condition are added to the topology table. In essence, when routers send update packets to their neighbors they are exchanging the contents of their topology tables.

The topology table is an example of how EIGRP differs from other distance vector routing protocols. RIP, for example, selects the best route it hears of (the lowest metric) and discards information about other routes to the same destination. If RIP loses the path to the route it selected as the best, it must first time out the route, and then wait for a routing update from a neighbor, in hopes of finding a new path to the network. EIGRP dramatically improves convergence by keeping track of every known route that meets the feasibility condition. When a fault occurs, EIGRP can often converge instantly if a backup route is located in its topology table.

The topology table keeps track of the following information for each route:

- The minimum bandwidth of all links to the destination network
- Total delay (the sum of all delays on all outgoing router interfaces along the path to the destination network)
- Path reliability (a dynamically assigned value of the overall reliability of the path—not used in metric by default)
- Path loading (a dynamically assigned value of the current load on the path—not used in metric by default)
- The minimum MTU (The routers will not use an MTU larger than the minimum specified size. This prevents fragmentation of update packets and further speeds convergence.)

LONG LIVE RIP?

We don't want to paint too bleak a picture of traditional distance vector protocols. Keep in mind that the Cisco implementation of RIP and IGRP will install up to six equal cost routes in the route table. And IGRP will even keep up to six unequal cost routes if the variance command is issued.

Six redundant paths may seem like a lot, but on larger networks, it is not unusual to have even more than six paths to the same network. That is where EIGRP starts to show off its scalability features by keeping *all* qualifying routes in the topology table.

Even so, Cisco continues to improve its legacy routing protocols. As of IOS versions 12.0T and 12.1, RIP maintains a database of learned routes that it can quickly install in the route table if needed.

- The reported distance of the route
- The feasible distance of the route
- The route source (static, internal, external, and so on)
- The IP address of the destination network

Route Table

The route table, as with any other routing protocol, contains the actual routes used to forward traffic. (See command reference at the end of the chapter for the forms of the **show ip route** command that shows EIGRP specific data.)

Remember that we are still discussing EIGRP architecture. A later example will show the actual population of these tables, and the actual router output for each table will be explained at that time.

EIGRP Metrics

EIGRP metrics are almost the same as the metrics for IGRP, which in its simplest form, is minimum bandwidth + the sum of delays (see Table 7-2). The only difference in EIGRP is that the metric is scaled up by multiplying it by 256. This is done simply to add granularity to the metric. However, unlike IGRP, a route's metrics are first applied to qualify it for inclusion into the topology table (example to follow). Later, the metrics are applied again when the route is considered for installation into routing table.

NOT ALL TOPOLOGY TABLES ARE CREATED EQUAL

EIGRP has a topology table. Pure link-state routing protocols such as OSPF have topology tables. Are they both the same? A comparison of EIGRP's and OSPF's topology tables, described in this chapter and the next, will reveal that the answer to this question is a resounding *"No."*

OSPF builds its topology table through each router reporting its directly connected networks. The topology table in OSPF is a composite listing of all those routers and their attached links. This gives OSPF an actual map of the network topology (which is how OSPF avoids the bad routing information that leads to routing-loops).

The topology table in EIGRP is quite different. It is not a map. It is mostly a listing of distances and vectors, and metrics of qualified routes that are available to be installed into the route table if the installed route fails. So even though it's called a "topology table," don't assume that EIGRP routers end up with a topology map of the network in the way that link-state protocols like OSPF do.

Table 7-2 Assignments for Bandwidth and Delay Values (Same as IGRP)

LINK TYPE	BANDWIDTH (IN KBPS)	DELAY (IN MICRO-SECONDS)
Ethernet	10,000	1000
Fast Ethernet	100,000	100
Gigabit Ethernet	1,000,000	10
FDDI	100,000	100
Token Ring (16 Mbps)	16,000	630
T1	1544	20,000

Take the example of a route passing through two WAN links; one link is FDDI and one link is T1. The algorithm first divides 10,000,000 by the **slowest link in the path,** then adds the result to the sum of the delay values for each link, and divides by 10 (to convert microseconds to milliseconds). The result is then multiplied by 256. The slowest link in this example is the T1 link, so the formula looks like what is portrayed in Figure 7-1.

As with IGRP, other metrics such as load and reliability can be added by manipulating the K values. The procedures are shown in Chapter 6 on page 172, however Cisco recommends that the default metric be used.

Calculating a Route's Metric

When a route is learned from a neighbor, it includes the metric the neighbor had calculated for the route using the formula shown in Figure 7-1. The value is the distance from the neighbor to the destination network. The router learning of the route refers to this value as the *reported distance* (also known as the *advertised distance*). The router must then calculate a second metric that includes the overall distance from itself to the destination network. This is known as the *feasible distance*.

$$((10,000,000 / Bandwidth) + ((sum of delays) /10)) *256$$
$$((10,000,000/1,544) + ((20,000+100) /10)) *256$$
$$(6,477 + 2,010) * 256$$
$$8,487 * 256$$
$$2,172,591$$

Figure 7-1 Calculating a metric in EIGRP.

Populating the Topology Table and Route Table

The initial population of a route into the topology and route tables is quite different from subsequent additions of routes already installed. When a neighbor advertises a route to a network that the receiving router does **not** already have an entry for, the route is immediately added without question to both the topology and route tables. Any route installed into the route table is referred to as the **successor**. Successors are used to forward packets.

> **NOTE** The term "successor" may seem counterintuitive because it portends that the specified route would take over in case the primary route fails. Rather, the successor route *is* the primary route. The term refers to the fact that the entry in the table specifies the next "successive" router in the path.

Once a successor for a route has initially been chosen, additional routes to the same network must qualify for inclusion into both the topology table and the route table, by passing a *feasibility condition* test issued by DUAL, to be sure the route is not looped. We're fully into algorithm country now and the DUAL evaluates newly learned routes with the following basic equation:

```
reported distance < feasible distance
```

If the advertised route's *reported distance* is less than the *feasible distance* of the successor, the route has met a *feasibility condition*. It qualifies! The route is guaranteed to be loop-free. The route will either be kept in the topology table as a *feasible successor*—meaning it is a backup route if the successor fails, or if the route's *feasible* distance is less than the feasible distance of the successor route, it will replace the successor.[5]

OK. What exactly does that mean? How does the fact that the reported distance being less than the feasible distance guarantee the route is not looped? Quite simply, any advertised route that has a larger reported metric value than the metric of the route currently in use, might possibly include the current router in the path; otherwise known as a *routing-loop*. On the other hand, if the metric from the reporting neighbor to the destination network is *less* then the metric from the current router to the destination network, the current router could not possibly be included in the advertised route—the route is guaranteed not to be looped.

WHY ISN'T THE FEASIBILITY TEST APPLIED TO THE FIRST ROUTE INSTALLED

If a router does not already have an entry for a route to a particular network, it can't have been advertising the route. If the router has not been advertising the route, there is little chance that it will learn of a route to the network that leads back through itself.

The best way to understand this concept is by demonstrating it. An example will first be used to describe the neighbor, topology, and route tables of a converged network, followed by a series of examples illustrating how DUAL evaluates newly learned routes.

Example 1—A Closer Look at the Neighbor, Topology, and Route Tables

In the Figure 7-2, router A has only one neighbor: router B. This is reflected in the neighbor table, which shows router B's interface address of 200.1.1.6 (Figure 7-3). It should not be difficult to extrapolate that router B's and router C's neighbor table would respectively show two entries (A and C), and one entry (B).

Working from left to right, the neighbor table shows the following:

- **H** is a value indicating the order neighbors were learned in.
- **Address** is the IP address of the neighbor's interface.
- **Interface** is the local interface the neighbor was learned through.
- **Hold** is the all-important hold-time timer. The hold-time timer determines how long the router should wait to receive the next Hello packet from the neighbor. Since EIGRP does not implement periodic routing updates, it cannot timeout routes as pure distance vector protocols do. Instead, EIGRP times out *neighbors*. When neighbors send Hello packets, a value for the hold-time is included. The receiving router resets the hold-time to that value. If the timer expires before receiving another Hello packet, EIGRP considers the neighbor (and the routes through it) dead. The expired neighbor is removed from the neighbor table, the associated routes are removed from the route table, and a routing update regarding any dead routes is sent to any other neighbors known to the router. The router then starts the process of discovering new paths for the lost routes.[6] By default, the hold-time is three times the Hello interval (5 seconds on low bandwidth networks and 60 seconds on high bandwidth networks), but this value can be altered (see the command reference at the end of the chapter). Because the value of the EIGRP hold-time is so much shorter than typical distance vector timers, the protocol times out routes much faster and convergence is improved.
- **Uptime** is the amount of time the neighbor relationship has existed.
- **SRRT** is the smooth round trip time. It indicates the average time it takes a packet to be sent and acknowledged when the RTP is used.
- **RTO** is the roundtrip timeout. This timer establishes how long the router will wait for the acknowledgement of a packet sent with RTP. The value of this timer is based on the SRRT.

- **Q** is the number of packets sent with RTP that are waiting acknowledgement. A growing Q value indicates trouble on the network.

- **SEQ NUM** indicates the sequence number of the last received Update, Query, or Reply packet. The RTP tracks the numbers to insure proper sequencing of received packets.

Now the topology table will be examined. The topology table in Figure 7-4 shows three networks. Note that each entry is prefaced with a *P*, indicating the route is in a passive state, meaning the router believes it has at least one stable route to the network.

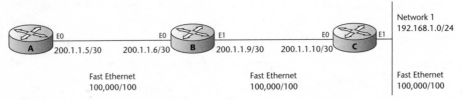

Figure 7-2 Network model for initial population of topology and route tables.

---

routerA#show ip eigrp neighbors
IP-EIGRP neighbors for process 1

H	Address	Interface	Hold (sec)	Uptime	SRTT (ms)	RTO	Q Cnt	Seq Num
0	200.1.1.6	et0	12	00:10:01	10	300	0	123

Figure 7-3 Output from router A when executing the **show ip eigrp neighbors** command.

---

routerA#show ip eigrp topology
IP-EIGRP Topology Table for process 1

Codes: P – Passive, A – Active, U – Update, Q – Query, R – Reply, r – reply status

P   200.1.1.4/30, 1 successors, FD is 28,160
        via Connected, Ethernet0

P   200.1.1.8/30, 1 successors, FD is 30,720
        via 200.1.1.6 (30,720/28,160) , Ethernet0

P   192.168.1.0/24, 1 successors, FD is 33,280
        via 200.1.1.6 (33,280/30,720) , Ethernet0

Figure 7-4 Output from router A when executing the **show ip eigrp topology** command.

For each entry, the destination network is first listed, followed by the number of successor routes (the number of routes installed in the route table), followed by the feasible distance (the metric from router A to the destination network).

The second and any additional lines of the entry display all feasible successors for the route. These are routes that have met the feasibility condition (*reported distance < the feasible distance of the current successor*). Each entry indicates that either the route is directly connected or the next hop interface is displayed. If the route is not directly connected, the feasible distance and reported distance are shown respectively in (). Finally, the local interface that packets will exit from on their way to the destination network is displayed.

Let's review the math for the metrics shown in Table 7-5. From router A's perspective, the reported distance for each route is shown is Figure 7-5.

Finally, let's examine the route table (Figure 7-6).

1. 200.1.1.4 directly connected = 28,160 $((10{,}000{,}000/\underline{100{,}000}) + (\underline{100}/10))*256$
   minimum bandwidth ↑   total delay ↑

2. 200.1.1.8 via router B = 30,720 $((10{,}000{,}000/\underline{100{,}000}) + (\underline{100+100}/10))*256$
   minimum bandwidth ↑   total delay ↑

3. 192.168.1.0 via router B and C = 33,280 $((10{,}000{,}000/\underline{100{,}000}) + (\underline{100+100+100}/10))*256$
   minimum bandwidth ↑   total delay ↑

Figure 7-5 Metric calculations for example ! routes.

```
routerA#show ip route
Codes:   C – connected,  S – static,  I – IGRP,  R – RIP,  M – mobile,  B – BGP
         D – EIGRP,  EX – EIRGP external,  O – OSPF,  IA – OSPF inter area
         N1 – OSPF NSSA external type 1,  N2 – OSPF NSSA external type 2,  E – EGP
         i – IS-IS,  L1 – IS-IS level-1,  L2 – IS-IS level 2,  * - candidate default
         U – per-user static route, o – ODR
         T – traffic engineered route

Gateway of last resort is not set

      200.1.1.4 is subnetted, 2 subnets
C        200.1.1.4    [0/0] is directly connected, Serial0
D        200.1.1.8    [90/30720] via 200.1.1.6, 00:10:01, Serial0
D        192.168.1.0  [90/33280] via 200.1.1.6, 00:10:01, Serial0
```

Figure 7-6 Results of the **show ip route** command on router A.

Again, the two learned routes were installed without question because there were no pre-existing routes to those networks. The next example demonstrates what will happen when a second route to 192.168.1.0 is discovered.

Example 2—DUAL Evaluates a Newly Learned Route

The revised network model in Figure 7-7 reveals a new path to 192.168.1.0.

Router D has just come online. There is now a redundant path from router A to 192.168.1.0. Let's see how this change in the network will be handled. The neighbor, topology, and route tables will be examined again. Figure 7-8 reflects that router A and router D share a common network and have therefore exchanged Hello packets, establishing a neighbor relationship.

Figure 7-9, however, shows that the topology table is unchanged. Where is the new route? DUAL has rejected the route through router D as a suitable path to 192.168.1.0 because the route did not meet the feasibility condition. DUAL only accepts newly learned routes if the reported distance is less than the feasible distance of the current successor. The feasible distance of the current route to 192.168.1.0 is **30,720**. The reported distance of the newly discovered route is **284,160**: ((10,000,000/10,000) + (100 + 1,000 /10)) * 256. The route doesn't qualify.

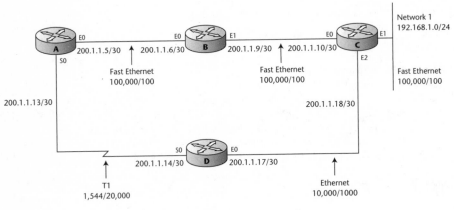

Figure 7-7 A new router has been added to the network.

```
routerA#show ip eigrp neighbors
IP-EIGRP neighbors for process 1
```

H	Address	Interface	Hold (sec)	Uptime	SRTT (ms)	RTO	Q Cnt	Seq Num
0	200.1.1.6	et0	12	00:10:01	10	200	0	123
1	200.1.1.14	Se0	10	00:01:01	30	300	0	101

Figure 7-8 Router D shows up as a new entry in the neighbor table.

```
routerA#show ip eigrp topology
IP-EIGRP Topology Table for process 1

Codes: P – Passive,  A – Active,  U – Update,  Q – Query,  R – Reply,  r – reply status

P     200.1.1.4/30,  1 successors, FD is 28,160
          via Connected, Ethernet0

P     200.1.1.8/30,  1 successors, FD is 30,720
          via 200.1.1.6 (30,720/28,160)

P     192.168.1.0/24,  1 successors, FD is 33,280
          via 200.1.1.6 (33,280/30,720)
```

Figure 7-9 The topology table is unchanged despite the new path to the 192.168.1.0 via router D.

Translated into English, DUAL is saying:

Dear advertised route,
*The distance you are reporting from yourself to the network you are advertising **must** be less than the distance I currently have from myself to the same network. Otherwise, we can't have a relationship, at least right now.*
Love,
DUAL

Why is DUAL so finicky? Remember that a reported distance for a route larger than the current feasible distance for a route to the same network flags the proposed route as *possibly* looped. But if you consider what comprises the default metric in EIGRP—bandwidth and delay—an advertised route with a metric larger than the current feasible distance is entirely possible, depending on the speed of the links. In the case of example 2, the route is valid—it's just that the path through the T1 links dramatically raised its metric. But DUAL takes a very conservative stance on the matter. Indeed, a route that is loop-free, and has simply committed the sin of having a larger metric, may be barred (at least initially) from the topology and route tables. In the next example, DUAL will be forced to reconsider the rejected route for admission into the route table.

Example 3—Installing a Previously Rejected Route

In Figure 7-10, the successor for 192.168.1.0 has failed. Let's see how the failure is handled by router A and what action is taken to find a new route.

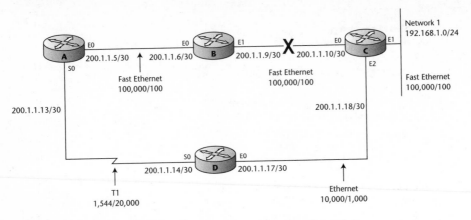

Figure 7-10   The successor for the 192.168.1.0 has failed.

After about 15 seconds, router B's hold-time timer expires waiting for Hello packets from router C. Among several actions that router B will take, it will poison the route to the 192.168.1.0 by sending an update packet to router A with the hop count set to infinity.[7]

Upon receiving the update regarding the failed route, router A will immediately remove the route to the 192.168.1.0 from the route table. Router A then uses a *local* computation to examine its topology table for a feasible successor. Finding no feasible successors to promote to successor, DUAL changes the state of the route from **passive** ("I can handle this myself") to **active** ("I need help finding a path to the network"). *A route becomes active when a router has exhausted the possibility of locating a replacement route locally and must turn to its neighbors.*

In active mode, DUAL commences a *diffusing* computation whereby it will query its neighbors for a path to the lost network (the idea of having other routers spend CPU time helping to find a replacement route is where the *diffuse* comes from in **Diffusing Update ALgorithm**). Up until now, only *Hello* packets and *update* packets have been sent between neighbors. Now a *query* packet is sent to neighbors asking if they have a route to the 192.168.1.0. Query packets are always sent with the RTP protocol because replies to the query are required, and therefore time-sensitive.

Router D receives the query from router A. Router D has one successor to the 192.168.1.0. It has no feasible successors, because the path to the 192.168.1.0 through router A and B did not meet the feasibility condition. Router D replies to the query with the information about the successor route, including its reported distance of 284,160.

Router A receives the update, and because there is no current successor to compare to, it immediately installs the route in the topology table and route table. Router A now has a successor route to the 192.168.1.0.

Stuck in Active (SIA) Routes

If router D had found no path to the 192.168.1.0, it too would have initiated a diffusing query to its neighbors. Every neighbor that receives a query either responds immediately with a path to the requested network or in turn sends queries to *its* neighbors before replying. Every router must ultimately reply to a query however, even if it takes time to hear back from the neighbors it queried, some of whom have queried *their* neighbors for a path, and so on. At the end of the query process either a new path to the network has been discovered—in which case the route returns to passive state—or it is determined by all routers in the **query range** that there is no path to the network and the route is dropped.[8]

But a query can only go on for so long. For each router that initiates a query, a **Stuck in Active (SIA)** timer begins to run. If the timer expires, the route is considered SIA. An SIA route is trouble for a network and should rarely occur in a well designed, well maintained system. If a router does not receive a reply to its query, unnecessary network delays may be occurring. The problem of course needs to be tracked down and corrected. The issue may stem from the way EIGRP has been implemented, network design issues, or simply a temporary outage.

If an SIA event is due to the configuration of EIGRP, it is likely the range of the query is too broad for the network in question. In other words, the query is being relayed through too many routers, delaying the reply. Only routers that are likely to have a path to the network in question should be queried.

Query ranges are bounded by the following:

- The edge of network is reached

- A distribution list forcibly limits the query range

- A route summarization boundary is reached, whereby queries do not extend to routers that have received only a summary address for the network in question

- Queries do not extend beyond the autonomous number of the EIGRP process for the router that generated the query

As you can see, there are a number of methods for restricting the range of a query. Depending on the network configuration, one or more of the aforementioned methods will provide an appropriate solution.

On the other hand, if the issue is with the network itself, the source of the problem could be anything from congestion on one or more links to temporary outages. Anything that delays general network traffic could be the cause of an SIA route.

The default setting for the SIA timer is 3 minutes. This can be altered with the **timers active-time** command (see the command reference at the end of this chapter).

DUAL Prevents a Routing-Loop

In example 2, a perfectly valid route from router A through router D was initially rejected for not meeting the feasibility condition. In this example, DUAL will catch a looped route red-handed and prevent it from being installed.

Example 4—Preventing a Routing-Loop

Normal Operation of This Network

This example focuses on routers B and D. One thing that needs to be avoided in this model (see Figure 7-11) is having any router accept a path to the 192.168.1.0 that leads through router D. Router A has a much better path to the destination network directly through router B. And if router B were to forward all packets bound for the destination network through router D, the packets would never reach the 192.168.1.0 because there would be a routing-loop.

First, the metrics for the routes will be calculated and then the routing-loop scenario will be described. Table 7-3 shows the metrics for the routes.

Table 7-3 Route Metrics from Each Router in Example 4 to 192.168.1.0

PATH	REPORTED DISTANCE	FEASIBLE DISTANCE
C → 192.168.1.0	n/a	28,160
B → 192.168.1.0 via C	28,160	30,720
A → 192.168.1.0 via B and C	28,160	33,280
D → 192.168.1.0 via B and C	281,600	286,720

Creation of a Routing-Loop

Let's say router B sends update packets to its neighbors advertising a route to the 192.168.1.0 through router C. Router A and router D learn about the route. Focus on router D. Router D now wants to tell its neighbors about the route. Router D will advertise the route to router A, but router A will likely already know about the route from router B and reject the offering from router D because the reported distance from router D of 286,720 is not less than router A's current feasible distance of 33,280 to the same network through B.[9]

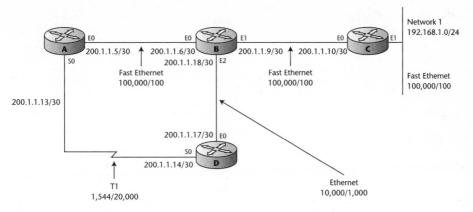

Figure 7-11   Network model prone to incurring a routing-loop.

Would router D try to advertise the route back to B? Normally no, thanks to the split-horizon rule, but there are some scenarios where it would, which is one reason DUAL is around. DUAL does not assume split-horizon is always active.

One possible issue related to split-horizon is that it may have been disabled. Split-horizon can either be manually disabled, or in the case of certain point-to-point or multi-point configurations with sub-interfaces configured, split-horizon would be off by default. In such cases, router D would go ahead and advertise the network back to router B. DUAL would show its stuff here by rejecting the route—the reported distance of 286,720 would not be less than router B's feasible distance of 30,720 to the same network. In this case, the suspicion raised by a higher reported metric would be justified.

Another factor that could cause router D to advertise the 192.168.1.0 to router B is if a network problem had prevented router D from learning about the 192.168.1.0 from router B in the first place. Remember that EIGRP does not periodically advertise all networks in routing updates. Only changes to routes are advertised. If a network problem had prevented router D from receiving the update packet regarding the 192.168.1.0 from router B, it would likely advertise the route to router B after it learned it from A, thus potentially creating a routing-loop. Again, DUAL would put a stop to such nonsense. *A looped route will always have a larger reported distance than the receiving router's current feasible distance to the network, because the route includes a path through the router receiving the advertisement.* This is how DUAL achieves 100 percent loop-free routes.

Load Balancing

EIGRP handles both equal and unequal cost load balancing in the same manner as IGRP. The command reference at the end of this chapter has a brief example. Refer to Chapter 6, page 173, for details.

Default Routing

Default routing is covered in Chapter 10. Differences pertaining specifically to IGRP are noted here.

EIGRP supports both forms of configuring default routing via the **ip route** and **ip default-network** commands.

Redistribution

EIGRP is capable of including static and externally learned routes in its updates, via redistribution. The general principals of redistribution are covered in Chapter 10. Redistribution is OFF by default in EIGRP with one exception. EIGRP and IGRP, which have similar metrics, automatically distribute routes to each other when both routing protocols are running on the same router—and both protocols are using the same autonomous system number. The one dissimilarity between the protocols, the metric multiplier of 256, is automatically adjusted when routes are redistributed.

Route Summarization

EIGRP excels at route summarization by not only allowing the disabling of auto-summarization and configuration of manual summarization, but summarization can be performed at any bit boundary—the key to support for discontiguous networks. The topic of summarization is covered in detail in Chapter 4.

Command Reference—EIGRP

Figure 7-12 provides a network model for the configuration of EIGRP. The examples will cover configuring EIGRP on a Cisco router.

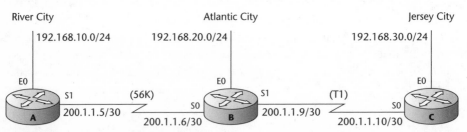

Figure 7-12 Example network for commands.

Initial Configuration

An initial configuration of the routers will be performed, and the route tables
will be shown before the EIGRP routing protocol is configured.

Configuring the IP Addresses

```
routerA#configure terminal
routerA(config)#interface fastethernet 0 (1)
routerA(config-if)#ip address 192.168.10.0 255.255.255.0 (2)
routerA(config-if)#exit (3)
routerA(config)#interface serial 1 (4)
routerA(config-if)#ip address 200.1.1.4 255.255.255.252 (5)
routerA(config-if)#bandwidth 56 (6)
routerA(config-if)#exit
routerA(config)#

routerB#configure terminal
routerB(config)#interface fastethernet 0
routerB(config-if)#ip address 192.168.20.0 255.255.255.0
routerB(config-if)#exit
routerB(config)#interface serial 0
routerB(config-if)#ip address 200.1.1.4 255.255.255.252 (7)
routerB(config-if)#bandwidth 56
routerB(config-if)#exit
routerB(config)#interface serial 1
routerB(config-if)#ip address 200.1.1.8 255.255.255.252 (8)
routerB(config-if)#bandwidth 1544
routerB(config-if)#exit
routerB(config)#

routerC#configure terminal
routerC(config)#interface fastethernet 0
routerC(config-if)#ip address 192.168.30.0 255.255.255.0
routerC(config-if)#exit
routerC(config)#interface serial 0
routerC(config-if)#ip address 200.1.1.8 255.255.255.252
routerC(config-if)#bandwidth 1544
routerC(config-if)#exit
routerC(config)#
```

(1) changes to interface E0.

(2) configures the address with a /24 prefix.

(3) exits interface mode back to global config mode.

(4) changes to interface S1.

(5) configures the address with a /30 prefix.

(6) sets the bandwidth to the actual speed of the interface.

(7) is the first possible subnet of the 200.1.1.0 /30.

(8) is the next possible subnet of the 200.1.1.0 /30.

Route Tables Before EIGRP Is Configured

Figures 7-13, 7-14, and 7-15 reflect the state of the route tables before EIGRP is configured.

```
routerA#show ip route
Codes:  C – connected,  S – static,  I – IGRP,  R – RIP,  M – mobile,  B – BGP
        D – EIGRP,  EX – EIRGP external,  O – OSPF,  IA – OSPF inter area
        N1 – OSPF NSSA external type 1,  N2 – OSPF NSSA external type 2,  E – EGP
        i – IS-IS,  L1 – IS-IS level-1,  L2 – IS-IS level 2,  * - candidate default
        U – per-user static route, o – ODR
        T – traffic engineered route

Gateway of last resort is not set

C       192.168.10.0  /24  [0/0]  is directly connected,  Ethernet0
        200.1.1.0       /30  is subnetted, 1 subnets
C            200.1.1.4      [0/0]  is directly connected,  Serial1
```

Figure 7-13   Router A – before EIGRP is configured.

```
routerB#show ip route
Codes:  C – connected,  S – static,  I – IGRP,  R – RIP,  M – mobile,  B – BGP
        D – EIGRP,  EX – EIRGP external,  O – OSPF,  IA – OSPF inter area
        N1 – OSPF NSSA external type 1,  N2 – OSPF NSSA external type 2,  E – EGP
        i – IS-IS,  L1 – IS-IS level-1,  L2 – IS-IS level 2,  * - candidate default
        U – per-user static route, o – ODR
        T – traffic engineered route

Gateway of last resort is not set

C       192.168.20.0  /24  [0/0]  is directly connected,  Ethernet0
        200.1.1.0       /30  is subnetted, 2 subnets
C            200.1.1.4      [0/0]  is directly connected,  Serial0
C            200.1.1.8      [0/0]  is directly connected,  Serial1
```

Figure 7-14   Router B – before EIGRP is configured.

```
routerC#show ip route
Codes:  C – connected,  S – static,  I – IGRP,  R – RIP,  M – mobile,  B – BGP
        D – EIGRP,  EX – EIRGP external,  O – OSPF,  IA – OSPF inter area
        N1 – OSPF NSSA external type 1,  N2 – OSPF NSSA external type 2,  E – EGP
        i – IS-IS,  L1 – IS-IS level-1,  L2 – IS-IS level 2,  * - candidate default
        U – per-user static route,  o – ODR
        T – traffic engineered route

Gateway of last resort is not set

C       192.168.30.0   /24  [0/0]  is directly connected,  Ethernet0
        200.1.1.0      /30  is subnetted, 1 subnets
C          200.1.1.8        [0/0]  is directly connected,  Serial0
```

Figure 7-15   Router C – before EIGRP is configured.

Configuring EIGRP

```
routerA(config)#router eigrp 100 (1)
routerA(config-router)#network 192.168.10.0 (2)
routerA(config-router)#network 200.1.1.4 (3)
routerA(config-router)#passive-interface fastethernet 0 (4)
routerA(config-router)#exit


routerB#config-term
routerB(config)#router eigrp 100
routerB(config-router)#network 192.168.20.0
routerB(config-router)#network 200.1.1.4
routerB(config-router)#network 200.1.1.8
routerB(config-router)#passive-interface fastethernet 0
routerB(config-router)#exit
routerB(config)#int s1
routerB(config-if)#bandwidth 56
routerB(config-if)#exit
routerB(config)#


routerC#config-term
routerC(config)#router iegrp 100
routerC(config-router)#network 192.168.30.0
routerC(config-router)#network 200.1.1.8
routerC(config-router)#passive-interface fastethernet 0
routerC(config-router)#exit
routerC(config)#
```

(1) enables EIGRP on this router with an AS number of 100 (**router no eigrp** disables EIGRP).

(2) includes the network in EIGRP advertisements. All interfaces with an address configured within the range of this address will send and receive routing updates.

(3) includes the network in EIGRP advertisements. All interfaces with an address configured within the range of this address will send and receive routing updates.

(4) suppresses Hello packets on this interface.

Route Tables After EIGRP Is Configured

Figures 7-16, 7-17, and 7-18 show how the route tables look after IGRP has been configured and the tables have normalized.

```
routerA#show ip route
Codes:   C – connected,  S – static,  I – IGRP,  R – RIP,  M – mobile,  B – BGP
         D – EIGRP,  EX – EIRGP external,  O – OSPF,  IA – OSPF inter area
         N1 – OSPF NSSA external type 1,  N2 – OSPF NSSA external type 2,  E – EGP
         i – IS-IS,  L1 – IS-IS level-1,  L2 – IS-IS level 2,  * - candidate default
         U – per-user static route, o – ODR
         T – traffic engineered route

Gateway of last resort is not set

C    192.168.10.0  /24  [0/0]    is directly connected, Ethernet0
     200.1.1.0      /30   is subnetted, 2 subnets
C        200.1.1.4        [0/0]    is directly connected, Serial1
D        200.1.1.8        [90/1]  via 200.1.1.6,  00:00:05,  Serial1
D    192.168.20.0  /24  [90/1]  via 200.1.1.6,  00:00:05,  Serial1
D    192.168.30.0  /24  [90/2]  via 200.1.1.6,  00:00:05,  Serial1
```

Figure 7-16 Router A after EIGRP is configured.

```
routerB#show ip route
Codes:   C – connected,  S – static,  I – IGRP,  R – RIP,  M – mobile,  B – BGP
         D – EIGRP,  EX – EIRGP external,  O – OSPF,  IA – OSPF inter area
         N1 – OSPF NSSA external type 1,  N2 – OSPF NSSA external type 2,  E – EGP
         i – IS-IS,  L1 – IS-IS level-1,  L2 – IS-IS level 2,  * - candidate default
         U – per-user static route, o – ODR
         T – traffic engineered route

Gateway of last resort is not set

C    192.168.20.0  /24   [0/0]      is directly connected,  Ethernet0
     200.1.1.0     /30   is subnetted, 2 subnets
C       200.1.1.4        [0/0]      is directly connected,  Serial0
C       200.1.1.8        [0/0]      is directly connected,  Serial1
D    192.168.10.0 /24 [90/1]  via 200.1.1.5,    00:00:05,  Serial1
D    192.168.30.0 /24 [90/1]  via 200.1.1.10, 00:00:05,  Serial1
```

Figure 7-17   Router B – after EIGRP is configured.

```
routerC#show ip route
Codes:   C – connected,  S – static,  I – IGRP,  R – RIP,  M – mobile,  B – BGP
         D – EIGRP,  EX – EIRGP external,  O – OSPF,  IA – OSPF inter area
         N1 – OSPF NSSA external type 1,  N2 – OSPF NSSA external type 2,  E – EGP
         i – IS-IS,  L1 – IS-IS level-1,  L2 – IS-IS level 2,  * - candidate default
         U – per-user static route, o – ODR
         T – traffic engineered route

Gateway of last resort is not set

C    192.168.30.0  /24   [0/0]      is directly connected,  Ethernet0
     200.1.1.0     /30   is subnetted, 2 subnets
C       200.1.1.8        [0/0]      is directly connected,  Serial0
D       200.1.1.4        [90/1]  via 200.1.1.9,    00:00:05,  Serial0
D    192.168.20.0 /24 [90/1]  via 200.1.1.9,    00:00:05,  Serial0
D    192.168.10.0 /24 [90/2]  via 200.1.1.9,    00:00:05,  Serial0
```

Figure 7-18   Router C – after EIGRP is configured.

Common EIGRP Commands

Here are examples of some of the more commonly used commands for configuring EIGRP.

Load Balancing—Changing the Default Number of Multiple Paths

EIGRP defaults to load balancing up to four equal cost paths. This can be altered with the following command:

```
routerX#config term
routerX(config)#router eigrp
routerX(config-router)#maximum-paths x (1)
```

where:

(1) x = (1-6)

Load Balancing—Configuring Unequal Multipath Routing

Unequal multipath routing is configured by issuing the variance command, which encompasses the range of metrics on the paths to be included for load balancing the traffic to a specific network. The method for determining the variance value was shown on page 173. Here are the commands to configure a variance of 88 from the example:

```
routerX#config term
routerX(config)#router iegrp 100
routerX(config-router)#variance 88
routerX(config-router)#exit
```

Configuring K Values for Metric Manipulation

Cisco does not recommend altering K values. However, in a white paper on EIGRP, Cisco recommends that if K values must be altered, you should manipulate the delay value rather then the bandwidth value to avoid routing-loops:

```
routerX(config)#router eigrp 100
routerX(config-router)#metric weights 0 1 1 1 1 1 (1)
```

where:

(1) shows default K values being assigned.

Enabling and Disabling Split Horizon

Split horizon is on by default for most configurations, but may be off by default on serial interfaces and/or sub-interfaces. You can check the status of split horizon on a particular interface with the **show ip interface x** command. For example, to see if split horizon is enabled on serial 0, execute the following:

```
routerX(config)#int s0
routerX(config-if)#show ip interface s0
```

Scan the output for the statement "Split horizon is enabled" or "Split horizon is disabled." Split horizon can be forcibly enabled or disabled on an interface level with the following command:

```
routerX(config-if)#{no} ip split-horizon
```

Configuring Summarization

Auto-summarization is ON by default. Configuration commands for disabling auto-summarization and/or configuring manual summarization are given in Chapter 4, starting on page 130. As with IGRP, manual summarization is configured at the interface level. The following example summarizes address range 150.1.0.0–150.1.4.0 as 150.1.0.0:

```
routerX(config)#int serial 0/0
routerX(config-router)#no auto-summary
routerX(config-if)#ip summary-address eigrp 1 150.1.1.0 255.255.252.0
```

Configuring for IP Classless Feature

The **ip classless** command is explained in Chapter 10. The command should be executed if default routing is configured. The command to enable classless routing is the same for all routing protocols:

```
routerX(config)#router eigrp
routerX(config-router)#ip classless
```

As of Cisco IOS 12.1, classless routing is enabled by default.

Inhibiting Hello Packets from Being Sent Out a Specific Interface

When a network is added to EIGRP with the **network** *x.x.x.x* command, EIGRP will send Hello packets out all interfaces with addresses configured within the range of the specified address. If one or more of these interfaces are stub networks (no other router on the link), Hello packets will be sent out unnecessarily. The **passive-interface** command prevents the Hello packets from being sent out the interface specified in the command:

```
routerA(config-router)#passive-interface ethernet 0 (1)
routerA(config-router)#exit
routerA(config)#
```

where:

(1) disables sending routing updates through this interface.

Changing the Hello Interval for Outgoing Hello Packets

```
routerX(config)#router eigrp
routerX(config-router)#ip Hello-interval eigrp x
```

The default Hello interval is 5 seconds for bandwidth links greater than T1. Less than T1 default interval is 60 seconds. The hold-time timer must be altered if the Hello interval is altered to maintain a 3:1 ratio of hold-time to Hello interval.

Changing the Hold-Time Timer for Timing Out Neighbors

```
routerX(config)#router eigrp
routerX(config-router)#ip hold-time eigrp x
```

Changing the Maximum Amount of Bandwidth Used by EIGRP Packets

```
routerX(config)#router eigrp

routerX(config-router)#ip bandwidth-percent eigrp x (1)
```

(1) The default bandwidth usage by EIGRP is 50 percent.

Changing How Long EIGRP Waits for a Reply to a Query Packet

```
routerX(config)#router eigrp
routerX(config-router)#timers active-time x (1)
```

(1) The default timeout is 3 minutes in later IOS releases.

Show Commands for EIGRP

Here are a few of the common commands for displaying the state of an EIGRP router.

Showing the Configuration

The following command shows all routing protocols, EIGRP timers, filters, redistribution, version, and summarization status:

```
routerX#show ip protocols
```

Showing the Route Table

The following command shows static, external, directly connected, and EIGRP-learned routes:

```
routerX#show ip route (shows all routes)
routerX#show ip route x.x.x.x (more detail for a single route)
```

Showing the Neighbor Table

The following command shows the neighbor table:

```
routerX#show ip eirgp neighbor
```

Showing the Topology Table

The following command shows the topology table:

```
routerX#show ip eirgp topology
```

Troubleshooting Commands

If you get into trouble, these commands can help get you out.

Tracking EIGRP Packets

Use the following command to track EIGRP packets:

```
routerX#(un) debug eigrp packets (1)
```

where:

(1) The command **debug eigrp packets** is used to see options for filtering out specific packet types.

Tracking EIGRP Packets to and from All Neighbors

Use the following command to track EIGRP packets to and from all neighbors:

```
routerX#(un) debug eigrp packets
routerX#(un) debug eigrp neighbor
```

Tracking EIGRP Packets to and from One Neighbor

Use the following command to track EIGRP packets to and from just one neighbor:

```
routerX#(un) debug eigrp packets

routerX#(un) debug eigrp neighbor as-number interface-addresss-of-neighbor (1)
```

where:

(1) restricts the debug command to EIGRP packets concerning the specified neighbor.

Showing the Debug Status

Use the following command to show the debugging status:

```
routerX#show debug
```

Canceling the Debug

Use the following command to cancel the debugging process:

```
routerX#undebug all
```

Notes

1. Technically there are six packet types. The sixth packet type relates to Novell IPX, which is not covered here.

2. To be recognized as neighbors, routers sharing the same link must be configured with the same autonomous system (AS) number, and their configured timer settings must be identical.

3. Later versions of the IOS reset the hold-time timer upon receipt of any type of EIGRP packet from a neighbor.

4. Routes not meeting the feasibility condition are actually installed into the topology table, but they are hidden. This improves performance if the route is later accepted.

5. Up to six routes to the same network can be installed into the route table if their metric is equal. Additionally, EIGRP, like IGRP, supports unequal-cost multipath routing through the use of the **variance** command. The **variance** command was explained on page 173.

6. The receipt of any EIGRP packet resets the hold-time timer in later IOS versions.

7. Although hop count is not used in a route's metric, there is a field for hop count in the packet structure of update packets.

8. If the route is dropped, once the broken link is repaired, routers B and C will "discover" the route and the route will again be propagated throughout the network.

CHAPTER 8

Overview

OSPF (Open Shortest Path First) is the defacto open standard routing protocol for large networks. Table 8-1 shows the basic characteristics of OSPF.

Table 8-1   Routing Characteristics of OSPF

Metric	Cost
Interior or Exterior?	Interior
Distance vector or Link-state?	Link-state
Singlepath or Multipath?	Multipath
Broadcast or Multicast?	Multicast
Flat or Hierarchical?	Hierarchical
Classful or Classless?	Classless

This chapter covers the following OSPF topics:

Advantages of Using OSPF

- Widely supported open standard—runs on most platforms
- Classless protocol—full support for classless addressing and therefore classless routing
- Scalable protocol—can be used on very large networks
- Extensible—periodically updated via RFCs to keep pace with evolution of the Internet
- Highly configurable to manage bandwidth utilized by routing protocol traffic
- No hop count limitation
- Fast convergence with small routing updates

- Not prone to routing loops
- Routing traffic sent via multicasts
- Optional authentication of routing packets—prevents rogue routers from advertising unauthorized routes

Disadvantages of Using OSPF

- Perceived as relatively complex to configure (not necessarily true)
- Runs over IP only
- Does not support unequal cost multipath routing (can be mitigated through metric manipulation)
- Summarizes routes at area borders only
- May require renumbering of network in order to obtain desired summarization of routes

OSPF Background

OSPF, like IGRP and EIGRP, was developed to overcome the shortfalls of RIP. RIP's relatively slow convergence, tendency to create routing loops, 15 hop count limitation, and RIPv1's lack of support for CIDR made it untenable for larger networks. Most of the development of routing protocols designed to replace RIP was done in the late '80s and early '90s. Although RIPv2 and IGRP improved somewhat on RIPv1, large networks (over 50 routers for example) needed a more scalable solution for propagating and maintaining routes. While Cisco was developing its proprietary EIGRP protocol, an open standards committee (the IETF) developed OSPF. OSPF is mostly used on enterprise networks and some ISP backbones.[1]

Both EIGRP and OSPF are suitable for large networks but each protocol approaches the problem of large-scale routing differently. EIGRP is a distance vector protocol that uses some link-state methods and makes use of the Diffusing Update Algorithm (DUAL) to learn and maintain routes, whereas OSPF employs strictly link-state methods and uses the Shortest Path First (SPF) algorithm to learn and maintain its routes. (Chapter 4 explains how distance vector and link-state routing protocols function.)

Explaining OSPF

OSPF has a lot of terminology associated with it. Routing terminology is not always intuitive, and the resulting "terminology fog" can often be a hindrance rather than a facilitator to learning any technology. It would be a shame for this to happen with OSPF, because although the protocol has a reputation for being complex, it is in fact an efficient, elegant solution for populating route tables with optimal paths to networks. Every feature built in to OSPF is there for a good reason and the more you understand the *why* behind the architecture of OSPF, the easier the protocol itself is to understand.

It's easy to get into a chicken-or-egg thing when explaining OSPF, so after a short introduction designed to give you an idea of how OSPF works and the vision behind its architecture, OSPF terminology will be explained in brief. From there, two passes will be made through the core material. In Part 1, the building blocks of OSPF will be explained. You will learn about the different network types the protocol runs on and the various elements of OSPF that come into play in different network configurations. OSPF operation in both single and multiple area configurations will be covered. In Part 2, all of the building blocks will be tied together, providing specific examples of how to implement OSPF in various network configurations. A command reference with several example models follow. Although this approach gives rise to a certain amount of redundancy, you *want* a little repetition with OSPF.

Introduction to OSPF

OSPF has evolved into the industry standard for larger networks requiring an interior routing protocol, partially because it is built on open standards. OSPF fully supports classless addressing and thus it supports subnetting, variable subnetting (VLSMs), and CIDR. Unlike EIGRP, OSPF supports only one routed protocol—IP. OSPF was designed from the beginning as an Internet routing protocol. OSPF has specific extensions for dealing with routes learned from the pervasive routing protocol for handling interdomain routing on the Internet: BGP.

Inherent to the design of OSPF is its ability to support a hierarchical routing environment. An OSPF autonomous system can be divided into multiple **areas** that share a controlled amount of routing information across their borders.

This approach has many advantages, among them a significant reduction in the amount of network bandwidth consumed by routing updates. OSPF areas are arranged into a two-level hierarchy whereby one or more areas attach to a central backbone area.

NOTE It should be underscored that the term *hierarchy* does not imply that areas occur within areas, within areas, and so on. Rather, it is a hub and spoke design; an approach that mitigates the possibility of routing loops.

This hierarchical approach to managing routing updates goes hand-in-hand with a hierarchical IP addressing scheme. OSPF is very strict about where route summarization takes place. It therefore relies on a well-architected addressing scheme—more so than any other interior routing protocol. Although OSPF has a reputation for being difficult to configure, the real art to deploying the protocol is in proper planning and design. You need to understand your network well and have it properly addressed for an optimal implementation.

OSPF is a highly configurable routing protocol with a number of design elements that enable precise control over its operation. *Much of the flexibility of OSPF has to do with minimizing network traffic generated from routers talking to one another.* While the myriad number of configuration options may seem a bit daunting at first, the payoff is in having a reliable network that is not bogged down with routing updates clogging its pipes. Moreover, most OSPF parameters can normally be left at the default settings.

How OSPF Works

This section is an overview of how OSPF functions. Details regarding these concepts will be forthcoming in subsequent sections. The idea here is to give you a big picture of how this routing protocol works. The *devil in the details* will come later.

Initial Startup

OSPF initializes by first building neighbor relationships with routers sharing a common network link. This is the same as with EIGRP. But that is where the analogy ends. Unlike EIGRP, OSPF shares routing information only with *certain* neighbors. The neighbor relationship with a router must be upgraded to a status known as **adjacent** before the exchange of routing information actually takes place. This is one of many techniques employed to minimize routing traffic. Also, OSPF, being a true link-state routing protocol, only shares information about *network links*, not routes, with adjacent neighbors. Put another way, rather than tell a neighboring router about all the networks it is aware of, and how far away they are—as distance vector protocols do—an OSPF router simply reports a variety of information about its own directly connected networks (its links). This link-state information is relayed to all routers in an area, allowing each router to build a map of the local network topology when the Shortest Path First (SPF) algorithm is run.

Link-state information is stored in a database known, amazingly enough, as the **link-state database**. Every router maintains its own link-state database. When the network is converged, all routers in an area have the exact same link-state database. As mentioned earlier, the link-state database is built by each router advertising its links to adjacent neighboring routers, which in turn forward the information to their adjacent neighboring routers. These advertisements are called Link-State Advertisements or **LSA**s. The initial synchronization of each router's link-state database is done through an efficient process whereby a subset of each LSA is sent to the adjacent router. The receiving router can request more information on each LSA as needed. Ultimately, each router in an area becomes adjacent to at least one other router in the area, and therefore every router receives the LSAs it needs to fully populate its link-state database, run the SPF algorithm, and populate its route table. LSAs are usually multicast to minimize the impact on non-interested hosts.

The process of forwarding LSAs to all routers is known as known as **flooding**, a somewhat misleading term that portends that the router sourcing the LSAs will somehow deluge the other routers with update packets. In fact, flooding simply refers to getting a copy of the LSAs to all adjacent neighbors. The process itself is quite orderly: the source router simply forwards LSAs to its adjacent neighbors, who add the received LSAs to their local link-state database, and forward the LSA to their adjacent neighbors, and so on.[2] So in a way, OSPF propagates routing information in a manner similar to a distance vector protocol, except that the information is different—*router IDs* and the *state of their directly connected networks*, as opposed to *network destinations* and *their distance* (OSPF routers never transmit their route tables). The propagation of LSAs even follows the *split-horizon* rule of not advertising routing information (in this case, LSAs) out the interface it was received on.

Running SPF

Once every router has a fully populated link-state database, the SPF algorithm is run on each router to populate its route table. SPF first creates a **shortest path tree** with the local router at the root of the tree. Performing this task on all routers gives each router in the area a view of the network from its own perspective. Once the tree is built, a map of the area exists. The shortest path to each network in the tree is calculated and the route table is populated. The metric used by OSPF to determine the shortest path is *cost*, with cost being unspecified by the RFC for OSPF. A popular implementation of OSPF is the Cisco IOS, which defines cost as simply the bandwidth of the link. The speed of a link is converted to a value ranging from 1 to 65535. The higher the bandwidth, the lower the number. The exact formula will be shown when OSPF metrics are covered on page 284. Figure 8-1 illustrates the network model used for building the shortest path tree.

Figure 8-2 shows a simplified view of the link-state database on router A before the SPF algorithm is run.

When the link-state database is complete, the SPF algorithm builds the shortest path tree. Figure 8-3 shows router A's tree.

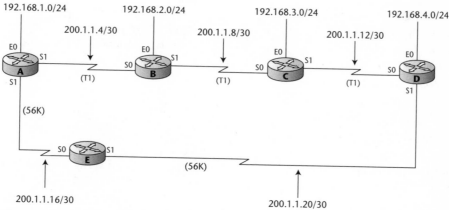

Figure 8-1 Network diagram for the OSPF example.

Router A is directly connected to network 192.168.1.0. The mask is /24. The bandwidth is 100mbp/s
Router A is directly connected to network 200.1.1.4.   The mask is /30. The bandwidth is 1.544mbp/s
Router A is directly connected to network 200.1.1.16.   The mask is /30. The bandwidth is 56kbp/s
Router B is directly connected to network 192.168.2.0. The mask is /24. The bandwidth is 100mbp/s
Router B is directly connected to network 200.1.1.4.   The mask is /30. The bandwidth is 1.544mbp/s
Router B is directly connected to network 200.1.1.8.   The mask is /30. The bandwidth is 1.544mbp/s
Router C is directly connected to network 192.168.3.0. The mask is /24. The bandwidth is 100mbp/s
Router C is directly connected to network 200.1.1.8.   The mask is /30. The bandwidth is 1.544mbp/s
Router C is directly connected to network 200.1.1.12.   The mask is /30. The bandwidth is 1.544mbp/s
Router D is directly connected to network 192.168.4.0. The mask is /24. The bandwidth is 100mbp/s
Router D is directly connected to network 200.1.1.12.   The mask is /30. The bandwidth is 1.544mbp/s
Router D is directly connected to network 200.1.1.20.   The mask is /30. The bandwidth is 56kbp/s
Router E is directly connected to network 200.1.1.16.   The mask is /30. The bandwidth is 56kbp/s
Router E is directly connected to network 200.1.1.20.   The mask is /30. The bandwidth is 56kbp/s

Figure 8-2 Simplified view of the link-state database before SPF is run.

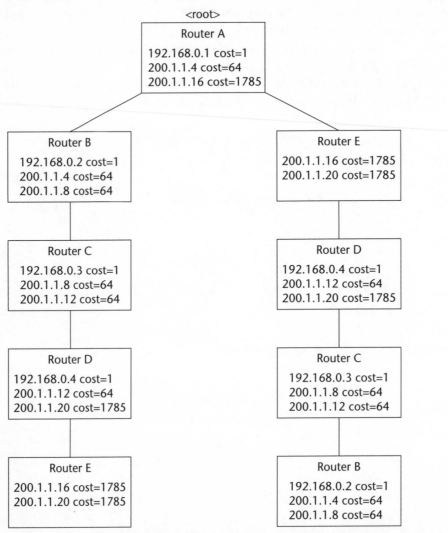

Figure 8-3 Simplified view of the shortest path tree created by the SPF algorithm.

   The SPF tree gives you an idea of how the network is viewed by router A. For example, router A can see that there are two paths to the 192.168.0.4/24 subnet attached to router D. One path is via router E and the other is via routers B and C. The bandwidth of the links have been converted to a cost value so SPF can easily determine which path is better. It is now a straightforward process of calculating the shortest path to each network and populating the route table as shown in Figure 8-4.

   In the case of the path to the 192.168.0.4, the route through routers B and C was chosen as the shortest (quickest) path and installed into the route table. The path through the T1 links is far quicker than the path through the 56K links, even though a greater number of routers are traversed. A more complete form of this process will be illustrated after additional fundamentals of OSPF have been covered. Figure 8-5 summarizes the steps required to initialize OSPF and commence routing.

```
routerA#show ip route
Codes:   C – connected,  S – static,  I – IGRP,  R – RIP,  M – mobile,  B – BGP
         D – EIGRP,  EX – EIRGP external,  O – OSPF,  IA – OSPF inter area
         N1 – OSPF NSSA external type 1,  N2 – OSPF NSSA external type 2,  E – EGP
         i – IS-IS,  L1 – IS-IS level-1,  L2 – IS-IS level 2,  * - candidate default
         U – per-user static route,  o – ODR
         T – traffic engineered route

Gateway of last resort is not set

C     192.168.1.0 /24 is directly connected, Ethernet0
      200.1.1.0 /30 is subnetted, 5 subnets
C        200.1.1.4 is directly connected, Serial0
C        200.1.1.16 is directly connected, Serial1
O        200.1.1.8 [110/128] via 200.1.1.6, 00:00:10, Serial0
O        200.1.1.12 [110/192] via 200.1.1.6, 00:00:10, Serial0
O        200.1.1.20 [110/256] via 200.1.1.6, 00:00:10, Serial0
O     192.168.2.0 [110/74] via 200.1.1.6, 00:00:12, Serial0
O     192.168.3.0 [110/138] via 200.1.1.6, 00:00:12, Serial0
O     192.168.4.0 [110/202] via 200.1.1.6, 00:00:12, Serial0
```

Figure 8-4 Results of the **show ip route** command on router A after the route table is populated from the SPF algorithm.

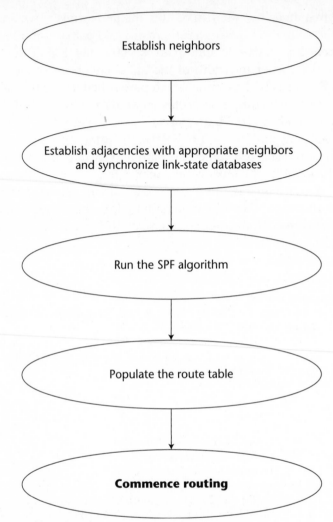

Figure 8-5 Summary of steps to initiate routing in an OSPF area.

Maintaining Routes

Once every router achieves a complete link-state database, runs the SPF algorithm, and populates the route table, OSPF generates minimal network traffic. Hello packets are sent periodically between neighboring routers to keep the neighbor relationship alive (usually every 10 seconds). Additionally, a router's link-state database is re-flooded every 30 minutes. Even though LSAs are sent reliably with OSPF's proprietary mechanism for assured delivery, they are re-sent periodically to be absolutely sure every router has a synchronized link-state database. An accurate link-state database is critical to the proper functioning of the SPF algorithm. If for some reason a router's link-state data-base becomes corrupt, this periodic flooding of LSAs insures that any issues regarding the integrity of the database will be short-lived.

Network Failures

If a router or network link fails, the failure is detected through the loss of layer 2 data-link keep-alive packets. This will normally occur even before the loss of Hello packets from an established neighbor is detected. In either case, the router noticing the failure, after timing out the link and/or neighbor, will notify adjacent neighbors that a change has occurred in the state of the link. This information is propagated like any other update: an LSA is flooded throughout the area. As each router receives the LSA, it updates its link-state database, runs the SPF algorithm, and modifies the route table as needed. This process happens fast, because the link is timed out quickly and the update packet is small and confined within an area, giving OSPF the reputation for quick convergence.

OSPF Areas

A fundamental design aspect of OSPF is that the autonomous system running the protocol can be divided into multiple areas. What exactly does that mean? Quite simply, this is one of OSPF's many methods for controlling the traffic generated by routing updates (LSAs).

The type of LSA discussed so far, the one used within an area, carries enough detailed information about routers and their links to build the topol-ogy map required by SPF. But this process takes up router resources and band-width. As networks grow to incorporate multiple buildings, multiple cities, or even multiple continents, the need for every router to have a detailed map of the entire system is lessened. Why is that? Keep in mind that the SPF algorithm only wants all that topology detail to choose the optimal path to a network. On larger networks, not every router needs detailed information about every net-work to choose the best path. This concept gave birth to the OSPF *area*. Areas share routing information with each other, but only routes and their metrics—not topology information. Figure 8-6 illustrates this principal.

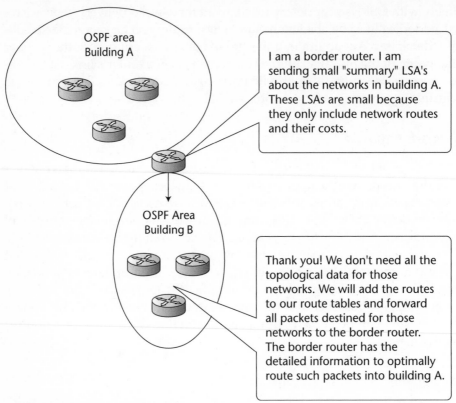

Figure 8-6 This network model makes a case for not propagating detailed route information between buildings.

The networks in building A are separated from the networks in building B by a single router bordering the buildings. Why should the routers in building A need to know the path to each network in building B, when that task could be handed off to the router bordering the two areas? After all, any packet bound for building B will be sent to the border router anyway in this particular model. Therefore, only **summary** LSAs, listing minimal network information will be exchanged between buildings.

Even in cases where there are two or more routers redundantly bridging locations, only the routers bordering the locations need full information for determining the best path to a network in the corresponding location. All that the routers within an area require for optimal forwarding of packets bound for other areas is the best border router to send the packets to. In OSPF, a border router is a part of the area, so it's naturally part of the topology map of each area. Forwarding packets to the border router is therefore always optimal.

An additional benefit of dividing a system into areas is that routes learned from another area are not required to have the SPF algorithm run on them.

After all, there is no topology information to act on. Rather, the route is considered for inclusion into the route table based simply on its metric. Obviously, this method saves on the processing power required to run the SPF algorithm. The fewer the SPF calculations, the faster routing commences. Areas are a win-win feature of OSPF, provided care is taken that optimal routing is not impinged.

Finally, the bandwidth savings of summary LSAs sent between areas is further leveraged when route summarization is introduced. Aggregating many subnets into a single network ID means fewer summary LSAs are required to describe the networks within an area. Summary LSAs and route summarization go hand-in-hand because with OSPF summarization only occurs at the border of an area (as it should). In other words, summarization is more an integral part of OSPF than with other routing protocols. The same can be said of default routing, which OSPF also tasks border routers to handle. Route summarization and default routing are not an after thought with OSPF. They need to be considered as part of the overall design of the implementation process. It is said that in real estate, it's all about location, location, location. In OSPF, it's all about planning, planning, planning. Understand the concept of areas and you are well on your way to successfully implementing a well-architected OSPF system.

OSPF Terminology

Like EIGRP, OSPF has an abundant amount of terminology. Therefore, a first pass will be made through the terms surrounding OSPF in order to familiarize you with them and gain some perspective. These terms will be further defined as needed later. This section can also serve later as an OSPF glossary of terms.

Important Networking Terminology

OSPF behaves differently on differing network types. Some network types require special configuration. It is therefore important to be aware of the characteristics of certain network types and that in some cases special configuration may be required, especially on networks that don't support multicasting. Here are the key network types:

- **Point-to-point:** Only connects two devices—typically a serial link, with one router on each end. Broadcasts and multicasts are supported.

- **Broadcast, multi-access:** A LAN, such as Ethernet, Token Ring, or FDDI. Usually includes two or more routers attached to the same network segment. Broadcasts and multicasts are supported.

- **Non-broadcast, multi-access (NBMA):** Physically a point-to-point connection that may reach multiple destinations through a WAN cloud — Frame Relay, ATM, SMDS, or X.25. Broadcasts and multicasts may not be supported. Additional configuration may be required to facilitate OSPF routing.

- **Point-to-multipoint:** A single physical interface with multiple logical sub-interfaces, connecting multiple destinations through a WAN cloud — Frame Relay, ATM, SMDS, or X.25. Broadcasts and multicasts may not be supported.

- **Demand circuits:** Such "dial-on-demand" networks inhibit the periodic routing traffic generated by OSPF and require special consideration.

Important OSPF Terminology

The remainder of this section lists most common OSPF terminology.

OSPF Tables and Databases

OSPF uses three main tables and databases[3]:

- **Neighbor table:** Contains the list of all known routing neighbors and various information regarding the neighbors.

- **Link-state database (also known as a topology database):** Contains all links (networks) in the area and their states. When first initialized, a router is only aware of its directly connected links. As new links are learned from neighboring routers the link-state database grows, exposing the topology of the network.

- **Route table (also known as a forwarding database):** Contains the routes used to forward traffic. It is populated from the link-state database after the SPF algorithm has run.

Hello Packets

This is one of five packet types unique to OSPF. Hello packets are sent out all OSPF enabled interfaces of a router running the OSPF process. They are used to identify neighboring routers with at least one interface on the same subnet. Hello packets are multicast to multicast address 224.0.0.5 (known as All-SPFRouters). Hello packets also act as keep-alives between neighboring routers.

Neighbor

Routers sharing a common network link and exchanging Hello packets become neighbors. Certain OSPF configuration parameters on each router interface must match for two routers to become neighbors.

Adjacency

An adjacency is a status established between neighboring routers to enable actual routing information to be exchanged (link-state databases are shared). This additional relationship between routers helps minimize the amount of traffic generated by routing updates.

Designated Router and Backup Designated Router

On broadcast, multi-access media, a single router is designated to send routing updates (LSAs) to all other routers. Routers sharing the same segment (subnet) become adjacent only with the Designated Router (DR) and Backup Designated Router (BDR), and share their link-state database only with the DR and BDR. This is done by transmitting the link-state information to multicast address 224.0.0.6 (AllDRouters). The DR then transmits the completed link-state database to all routers on the subnet. Subsequent updates regarding links are handled in the same manner.

The BDR takes over if the DR goes down. The routers on the segment elect the DR and BDR.

DRother

DRother defines all routers sharing the segment that are not the DR or BDR. This is terminology in keeping with describing *all* OSPF routers, regardless of whether they are DRs or not (AllSPFRouters), and describing DRs just designated and BDRs (AllDRouters).

Hello Protocol

The Hello protocol uses Hello packets to establish neighbors and adjacencies, and handles the election of the DR and BDR.

Router Priority

Router priority, which can be manually configured, dictates which routers are eligible to become DR and BDR. The higher the router priority the more likely a router will win an election to become DR or BDR.

Router ID

The router ID uniquely identifies each OSPF router. The highest IP address on the router becomes the router ID. If a loopback address has been configured, it becomes the router ID regardless of numerical precedence.

Router States

OSPF, like other routing protocols such as EIGRP and BGP, uses a finite state machine.[4] OSPF routers transition through various *states* as neighbor and adjacency relationships are formed with other routers.

Down State

This is one of three states used to form a neighbor relationship between two routers. The down state is the initial state when the router is initialized. The router is sending Hello packets but has not received a reply from any potential neighbors.

Init State

The init state occurs when router X receives a Hello packet from router Y, but the packet does not yet contain router X's Router ID. This is also known as a **1-way state**.

2-Way State

This is the third and final state for establishing a neighbor relationship. It occurs when router X receives a Hello packet from router Y, and the packet contains router X's router ID. At this point, a neighbor relationship has been established. This is also the starting point for establishing adjacencies between routers.

Attempt State

This state only applies to network types with manually configured neighbors (for example, non-broadcast, multi-access networks). If a router loses contact with an established neighbor (loss of Hello packets), it will enter the attempt state. In the attempt state, periodic Hello packets are sent at the poll-interval (defaults to 120 seconds) rather than the Hello-interval (defaults to 60 seconds on NBMA networks). This reduced rate conserves bandwidth but still allows the neighbor relationship to be re-established.

Exstart State

In this state, link-state databases are exchanged between pairs of adjacent routers. The router with the highest interface address becomes the **master** and will initiate the exchange (if a DR exists, it always becomes a master). The other router becomes the **slave**.

Exchange State

The router designated **master** begins sending **DataBase Description** (DBD) packets, which describe an LSA, to the **slave**. Upon completion, the slave reciprocates to the master.

Loading State

This state is only entered when a router must request, or is waiting for, additional information from another router after the initial exchange of database description packets.

Full State

When a router's link-state database is fully synchronized, it is in the full state. Upon reaching this state, the Shortest Path First (SPF) algorithm is run on the link-state database (topology table), the route table is built, and the routing of network packets commences.

Flooding

This term is used to describe the transmission of routing update packets throughout an area. Routing updates are multicast and relayed by each adjacent router throughout the area so that all adjacent routers in the area receive the update. Flooding is done reliably, with an acknowledgement received for each LSA sent.

Areas

An area in OSPF is a logical grouping of routers that share the exact same link-state database. Areas are one of several mechanisms for controlling the resources consumed by routing updates. It is not necessary for all routers in an autonomous system to receive detailed link-state information from all other routers in the system, and areas provide a means to limit such traffic. OSPF allows for several types of areas, depending on the network configuration.

Backbone Area

This is the only mandatory area in an OSPF network. The backbone area is always designated area 0 (or 0.0.0.0.). There can be one, and only one area 0. Normally, all other areas connect to area 0 and pass routing traffic bound for other areas through area 0. As with all area types, link-state advertisements are summarized before being advertised to other areas.

Standard Areas

A standard area is similar to the backbone area in terms of the amount of routing information circulated. Full routing information is shared between a standard area and area 0 (but not topology information). A standard area is often distinguished by the fact that it has multiple gateways (internal and/or external) that connect to area 0 and possibly connects directly to other autonomous systems.

Stub Areas

Stub areas generally have only one or a small number of gateways connecting their networks to area 0. Stub areas usually have no direct connection to other autonomous systems except through the backbone (area 0). Because of this, certain types of routing information can be summarized at the border, and bandwidth can be saved. Two stub area types are specified in the RFC for OSPF, with a third type proprietary to Cisco routers.

Stub Area

Stub areas (also referred to as *standard stub areas*) receive only a subset of routing information from area 0. External routes (routes outside the OSPF system) are not propagated into a stub area. Instead, a default route is injected. All traffic bound for destinations outside the system use the default route that points to a router bordering the stub area and area 0.

Totally Stubby Areas

This is a vendor-specific implementation (Cisco) not specified by the RFCs covering OSPF. A totally stubby area takes the concept of a standard stub area one step further by propagating only a default route into the totally stubby area. Not only are external routes represented as a default route, but inter-area routes (routes from other OSPF areas within the system) are as well. This is a resource-saving measure when a stub area is connected to the backbone through only a single router. The routers within the area are populated with only intra-area routes, and simply forward all inter-area and external traffic to a default route pointing to a border router. As is the case with any stub area, the border router has a more complete route table and carries out optimal routing from there.

Not-So-Stubby Areas (NSSA)

This area type allows for routers within the stub area to connect directly to other autonomous systems. In this case, external routes learned from such directly connected routers can be propagated throughout the NSSA, so routers within the area can access external networks without going through the backbone. Many other options for handling the external routes learned by the NSSA are available as well.

Partitioned Area

A partitioned area is not an area type. A partitioned area occurs when a failed link causes one or more routers within an area to lose communication with one or more routers within the same area.

Isolated Area

An isolated area occurs when one or more routers within an area are unable to find a path to the backbone.

Virtual Links

Ideally, all OSPF areas should connect to area 0 directly. Virtual links allow an area to instead connect to area 0 via another area. Virtual links can also be used to repair a partitioned area until the links come back up.

Transit Area

This is not a specific area type, but rather a characteristic of the area when configured to participate in a virtual link, in which case traffic just passes through the area on the way to another area (as defined in the RFC specifying the operation of OSPF). In other contexts, the backbone area can be thought of as a transit area since in normal operation traffic passes from one area to another area via area 0, without a virtual link.

Router Types

Router types go hand-in-hand with area types and are matched to the role they play within the area.

Internal Router

An internal router has all interfaces contained within a single area and does not connect to any other areas.

Area Border Router (ABR)

An ABR connects at least two areas. It maintains a separate link-state database for each area it connects to. Link-state summarization and route summarization occur at border routers.

Backbone Router

This is a router that has at least one interface in area 0. A backbone router that also has an interface in another area is also considered an ABR.

Autonomous System Boundary Router (ASBR)

An ASBR has at least one interface connecting to another autonomous system (or redistributes a static route). It is through ASBRs that external routes are learned and redistributed into the OSPF system.

OSPF Packet Types

OSPF packets are used for router-to-router communication in an OSPF system. Five types of packets are commonly used (not to be confused with the 11 types of link-state advertisement packets).

Hello Packet—Type 1 OSPF Packet

As described earlier, this packet type builds and maintains neighbor relationships.

Database Description Packet—Type 2 OSPF Packet

This packet type is circulated when two routers are initially exchanging their link-state databases. It contains enough information to identify an LSA, but does not hold the actual link information.

Link-State Request (LSR)—Type 3 OSPF Packet

This packet type is used to request complete information about a link learned from another router. If the receiving router does not already have the complete LSA, or if the current LSA has an older time stamp than the LSA advertised by the database description packet, an LSR is sent to the advertising router asking that the complete LSA be sent.

Link-State Update (LSUs)—Type 4 OSPF Packet

Link-state update packets are used to send any of 11 types of Link-State Advertisements (LSAs). LSAs are used by a router to transmit pieces of its link-state database. Only the six commonly used LSA types are described in this book.[5]

Router LSA—Type 1
This packet type is generated by all routers. It describes the routers' links and their states. The router LSA is flooded to all adjacent neighbors within an area on multicast address 224.0.0.5.

Network LSA—Type 2
This is generated only by DRs. This type of LSA describes the number of routers attached to the subnet the DR serves and also contains the subnet mask for the subnet.

Summary LSA (or Network Summary LSA)—Type 3
Summary LSAs are generated only by Area Border Routers (ABR). They are used to summarize the network links for the area, and contain only a subset of the information that LSA type 1 packets carry. These summary LSAs are transmitted from non-zero areas into area 0, which in turn propagates the collective summary information to all other areas.

ASBR Summary LSA—Type 4

ASBR summary LSAs are generated only by Area Border Routers (ABR). They are similar to type 3 LSAs except that the packet advertises an Autonomous System Boundary Router (ASBR) rather than a network.

External LSA (or Autonomous System External LSA)—Type 5

These LSAs are generated only by Autonomous System Boundary Routers (ASBR). They are used to advertise routes learned from outside the OSPF autonomous system (external routes). They can optionally advertise a default route in lieu of advertising each external route and can also perform route summarization on external routes.

NSSA External LSA—Type 7

This LSA is generated **only** by Autonomous System Boundary Routers within a not-so-stubby area. This special LSA type is similar to a type 5 LSA, except that the routers in the NSSA area, which don't listen to type 5 LSAs, will process type 7 LSAs, allowing the routers to learn of external networks from a locally attached ASBR.

Link-State Acknowledgement–Type 5 OSPF Packet

Link-state advertisements sent in response to a link-state request are sent reliably with the OSPF Hello protocol. The link-state acknowledgement packet acknowledges receipt of an OSPF packet.

Segment

The term "segment" has a flexible definition in general networking. In discussions of OSPF, a segment usually refers to a multi-access network identified by a unique IP network number.

External Route Type-1 (E1) and Type-2 (E2)

This has to do with how a metric is calculated for an external route. Type-1 routes include both the cost of the externally learned route (assigned at the ASBR), plus the cost of forwarding the packet from an internal router to the ASBR. Type-2 routes include only the cost of the route assigned at the ASBR.

OSPF Timers

OSPF does not employ the timers associated with distance vector protocols, but the protocol does use a number of timers related to neighbor maintenance, link-state updates, and route flapping. Some of the more commonly referenced timers are listed here. See the current OSPF RFC (2328) for a complete list.

Hello-Interval

This timer specifies how often a router sends a Hello packet. The default period is 10 seconds on broadcast multi-access networks and 60 seconds on non-broadcast, multi-access networks. The Hello interval value is included in a router's Hello packet. *This timer must be set to the same value on routers that want to become neighbors.*

RouterDeadInterval

Hello packets include a value for a field called RouterDeadInterval, which specifies how long a router should wait to receive a Hello packet from an established neighbor. If continuous Hello packets are not received, the neighbor relationship is terminated. The default value of RouterDeadInterval is 4 times the Hello interval. *The value of RouterDeadInterval must be set the same for two routers to become neighbors.*

SPF Hold-Time

This specifies how long a router should wait after calculating the route table before it will calculate the route table again. This prevents overloading router resources due to route flapping (a route constantly going up and down). The default value for the SPF hold-time is 10 seconds.

LsAge and MaxAge Timers

After routers become adjacent, each router transmits an LSA every 30 minutes for every entry in its link-state database. This is done to be absolutely sure that all routers in an area have identical link-state databases. A field for each LSA known as **LsAge** tracks the age of an LSA. When LsAge reaches an age of 30 minutes, the LSA is refreshed and flooded again. If somehow an LSA reaches an age of 1 hour (known as **MaxAge**), it's deemed invalid and is flushed from the database.

Poll-Interval

Applies only to non-broadcast network types. Specifies how often a router should poll (send a Hello packet to) a neighbor that has transitioned from a status of at least 2-way to a status of *attempt*. The default poll-interval is 120 seconds. This is used to reduce network traffic generated by Hello packets while attempting to reestablish a lost neighbor relationship.

LSA Retransmit-Interval

LSAs sent in response to a link-state request are sent reliably. If an acknowledgement for the packet is not received, the LSA is retransmitted. The LSA retransmit-interval specifies how often the LSA is retransmitted. When LSAs are retransmitted, they are sent unicast to the host that has not acknowledged the transmission.

Wait Timer

This timer applies only to network types that elect a DR and BDR. It specifies how long a router should wait to see a DR and BDR listed in a neighbor's Hello packet before forcing an election of a DR or BDR. It defaults to the same value as the *RouterDeadInterval* timer.

InfTransDelay or Transmit Delay

The age of LSAs are tracked so that routers can discern which LSAs have newer information if the router receives multiple LSAs regarding the same link. The transmit delay timer assists this process by incrementing the age of an LSA as it exits an interface. It is an estimate of the amount of time it takes the LSA to traverse the link connected to the interface (LSAs also age while held in each router's database). The default setting for the *InfTransDelay* timer is 1 second.

RxmtInterval

This is the amount of time a router waits before retransmitting a database description packet. It relates to the synchronizing of link-state databases.

Watch Out for the "Type" Trap

Many OSPF features are categorized by "type." Don't get confused over these various terms. They are summarized here to help you keep them straight. All types are described in detail later in the chapter. With that said, here is a brief description of the OSPF feature types:

- **Media and network types:** OSPF behaves differently on different network types. It distinguishes among five types of networks: broadcast/multi-access; non-broadcast/multi-access (NBMA); point-to-point; point-to-multipoint; demand circuits.

- **Database types:** OSPF tracks routing information in three types of databases (tables): neighbor table, which tracks known routing neighbors; link-state database, which tracks network links; and route table, which maintains the list of active routes.

- **OSPF packet types:** Five different packet types are used for varying purposes with one of the types handling Hellos between neighbors, and the other four having to do with sharing link-state data. The five types are: Hello packets; Database Description packets; Link-State Request packets; Link-State Update packets (with 11 sub-types); Link State Acknowledgement packets.

- **LSU/LSA packet types:** There are a total of 11 types (subtypes if you will) of Link-State Update (LSU) packets, all which take the form of Link State Advertisements (LSAs). Only six of these types are in common use: router LSAs; network LSAs; summary LSAs; ABR summary LSAs; external LSAs; and not-so-stubby external LSAs. LSAs are carried in type 4 OSPF packets.

- **Area types:** OSPF defines four different area types, which are used mainly to minimize routing traffic. The four area types accommodate the varying amount of routing information an area requires depending on its connectivity to other areas. The types are: backbone area, standard area, stub area, and not-so-stubby area. Cisco defines a fifth type, the totally stubby area.

- **Router types:** Router types are categorized according to the function they perform. They are: internal router, Area Border Router (ABR), backbone router, Autonomous System Boundary Router (ASBR).

- **Destination types** (sometimes called **route types**): A destination type simply denotes whether the IP address of a route refers to an actual network or a router. This information is used by the SPF algorithm for determining the shortest path to each network.

- **Link types:** OSPF likes to know what an advertised link is connecting to, i.e. another router, a stub network, and so on. Four different types of links are recognized. They are identified and described on page 267.

- **Path types:** OSPF distinguishes among six different path types, which are displayed in the route table adjacent to the routing entry descriptions: intra-area (O), inter-area (IA), external type 1 (E1) or type 2 (E2) paths, and NSSA type 1 (N1) or type 2 (N2). Intra-area routing is routing within an area, whereas inter-area routing is routing between areas. The two types of external routes, E1 and E2, refer to external networks and were defined earlier in this section. Finally, NSSA path types refer to external networks learned by not-so-stubby areas. The corresponding NSSA E1 and E2 types are defined the same as external E1 and E2 types. Figure 8-7 shows these path types in the router output.

```
routerA#show ip route
Codes:   C – connected, S – static, I – IGRP, R – RIP, M – mobile, B – BGP
         D – EIGRP, EX – EIRGP external, O – OSPF, IA – OSPF inter area
         N1 – OSPF NSSA external type1, N2 – OSPF NSSA external type 2,
         E1 – OSPF external type 1, E2 – OSPF external type 2, E – EGP
         i – IS-IS, L1 – IS-IS level-1, L2 – IS-IS level 2, * - candidate default
         U – per-user static route, o – ODR
         T – traffic engineered route

Gateway of last resort is not set

     192.168.1.0 is subnetted, 3 subnets
C        192.168.1.0      is directly connected,   serial0
C        192.168.4.0      is directly connected,   Ethernet0
O        192.168.8.0/30   [110/40] via 192.168.4.1, 00:00:38, Ethernet0
O E1     170.2.2.4/30     [110/90] via 192.168.1.1, 00:00:30, Serial0
O E2     170.2.2.8/30     [110/90] via 192.168.1.1, 00:00:30, Serial0
O IA     192.168.12.0/30  [110/220] via 192.168.4.1, 00:00:38, Ethernet0
```

Figure 8-7 The various types of OSPF path types are indicated in the output of a route table.

OSPF Operation, Part 1: The Building Blocks

With an overview of OSPF, and a first look at OSPF terminology under your belt, we now approach the intimate operation of the protocol. The first order of business is to examine the network types that OSPF runs on and how the protocol behaves on different types of networks. Then the actual operation of OSPF in a single area configuration will be covered, followed by operation in a multiple area environment. As has been the convention throughout the discussion of routing protocols, most of the actual configuration commands and the associated router outputs will be listed at the end of the chapter.

OSPF and Network Types

OSPF cares about what type of network it runs on for two primary reasons. For one thing, OSPF uses multicasts to communicate routing information among routers. A key distinction regarding various network types is whether broadcasts and its variant, multicasts, are supported. Some types of networks support only unicast traffic. This is often true for certain multi-access WAN based architectures that operate through a WAN "cloud," otherwise known as an NBMA (Non-Broadcast, multi-Access) network. Since OSPF uses multicasting by default, special configuration is required when running on non-broadcast media. For example, routing neighbors may need to be manually configured, because they won't discover each other automatically.

Second, OSPF cares whether the network type is multi-access or not. This second consideration is strictly for running the OSPF protocol efficiently. On a multi-access network, the possibility exists for many routers to have an interface sharing a single network segment (subnet). In that case, rather than have every router forward its link-state database to every other router on the segment, it's mathematically more economical to elect a single router to receive all LSAs from all attached routers, and then transmit the completed link-state database back to all attached routers. The router chosen to act as the reception point for the segment's router LSAs is known as the Designated Router (DR). The DR has a deputy known as the Backup Designated Router (BDR). The BDR takes over if the DR fails. When a DR and BDR are elected, all routers on the segment form an adjacency with the DR and the BDR and forward their link-state databases to the DR and BDR. The DR then forwards the completed link-state database back to each router on the segment. The greater the number of routers sharing the segment, the more efficient this method is. Point-to-point networks on the other hand, only have two routers on a segment, so a DR is not required.

For the DR concept to work, the DR and BDR must have *direct* access to each router on the segment. It is by design that the DR and BDR be able to transmit link-state information directly. The routing data cannot be passed indirectly to the target routers through another router. This is not a problem on *broadcast* based multi-access media such as Ethernet or Token Ring. But care must be taken when a designated router is elected in a *non-broadcast*, multi-access environment (NBMA) like some Frame Relay or ATM implementations. Why? As the examples that follow illustrate, a DR or BDR may or may not have direct access to all routers on the subnet, due to the underlying WAN topology. If the network is not configured in a manner that allows for a DR and BDR to directly reach every router on the segment, it may be wiser to not use a DR/BDR configuration and pay the price of incurring a bit more routing traffic.

Network Types

Four unique network types (data-link media) exist from OSPF's point of view, with additional variants for one of the types. In many cases, OSPF will automatically detect the network type and configure itself accordingly. At other times, the network type must be set manually with the **ip ospf network** command.[6]

Broadcast, Multi-access Networks

This refers to a LAN, such as Ethernet, Token Ring, or FDDI; may include multiple routers attached to the same network segment; broadcasts and multicasts are supported. Figure 8-8 denotes a broadcast, multi-access network. This type of network will elect a DR and a BDR.

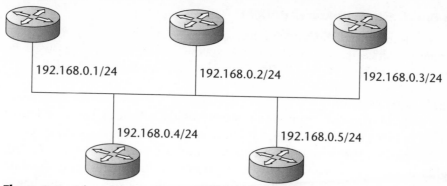

Figure 8-8 A broadcast, multi-access network. A DR will handle synchronizing the link-state databases.

This very common type of network will be automatically detected by OSPF as **broadcast**. Neighbor relationships will be automatically formed, and a DR and aBDR will be elected. Adjacencies will be formed between the DR and BDR and all other routers on the segment.

Point-to-Point

In this case, there are only two devices on the subnet (see Figure 8-9). These devices are typically a serial link with PPP or HDLC encapsulation and one router on each end of the link. Broadcasts and multicasts are supported. No DR will be elected.

Point-to-point networks are a common WAN type used for serial links and will run over media such as a fractional T1 line. Such a network type will have one router attached to each end of the line. OSPF will recognize this network type as **point-to-point**, and because this network type supports broadcasts, a neighbor relationship between the two routers will be automatically formed. Since there are only two routers on this type of network, no DR or BDR will be elected. Instead, the two routers will form a neighborhood relationship, immediately upgrade it to adjacent, and multicast their link-state databases to each other on multicast address 224.0.0.5 (AllSPFRouters). Multicasts are used in lieu of unicasts to allow for the possibility of unnumbered links, where the address of each router's interface used for the point-to-point network may not be known.

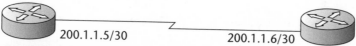

Figure 8-9 A point-to-point network. No DR is required.

Non-Broadcast, Multi-Access (NBMA)

This is a multi-access WAN technology that may or may not support broadcasts and multicasts, depending on the specific configuration. It is used by Frame Relay, ATM, X.25, and SMDS. Three variants are described below.

NBMA, Fully Meshed

When a non-broadcast, multi-access data-link architecture such as Frame Relay is in use, OSPF will default to the **non-broadcast** network type, which requires special configuration. If broadcasts and multicasts are not supported, neighbors will have to be manually configured with the **neighbor** command. It may be possible to configure the underlining data-link service to simulate a broadcast network. If so, you can force OSPF to see the network type as broadcast by using the **ip ospf network** command with the **broadcast** keyword. The simulation is carried out by replicating LSAs for each router sharing the network segment. In this configuration, OSPF will behave very much like a broadcast, multi-access network. A DR or BDR will be elected, and only one subnet will be burned. However, this model will only work properly if the network is fully meshed; meaning every router has a direct link to every other router through the WAN cloud as depicted in Figure 8-10.

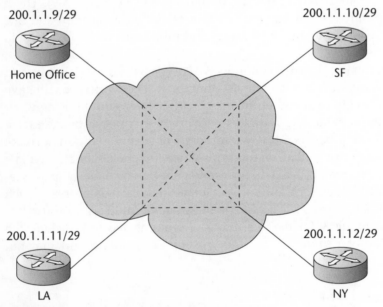

200.1.1.9/29

200.1.1.10/29

Home Office

SF

200.1.1.11/29

200.1.1.12/29

LA

NY

Figure 8-10 Fully meshed Frame Relay network. Permanent virtual circuits connect every router to every other router.

NBMA, Point-to-Point Sub-interface Configuration

Fully meshed networks are expensive. Is there anyway to run OSPF in a WAN cloud without purchasing all those WAN links? Some router vendors allow for multiple **logical sub-interfaces** to be configured on a single physical serial interface. This allows the *logical* topology of the network to differ from the *physical* topology. One of the two common ways to take advantage of this feature is to create point-to-point sub-interfaces when initially configuring the router interfaces. In such a model, one router acts as a hub in a hub-and-spoke topology. A separate sub-interface is configured on the hub router for each router it connects to through the WAN cloud. This results in separate subnet IDs for each sub-interface (see Figure 8-11). OSPF will recognize the network type as **point-to-point**. If the media does not support broadcasts/multicasts, neighbors may need to be manually configured.

There are several caveats to this model. No DR or BDR is elected because it is a point-to-point configuration. This means less efficient utilization of the protocol. Also, a subnet address is burned for each point-to-point sub-interface. Keep in mind that these are usually public IP addresses, which may not come cheap (this issue can be mitigated however, through the use of VLSMs and/or unnumbered links). Finally, if the underlying data-link service is unreliable, routing can easily break. Check out the next variation.

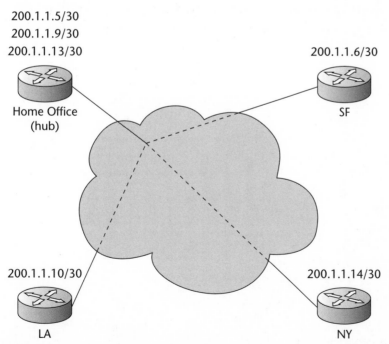

Figure 8-11   Point-to-point sub-interfaces used in a partial mesh Frame Relay network in a hub-spoke topology; burns one subnet ID for each link.

NBMA, Point-to-Multipoint Sub-interface Configuration

Rather than configure point-to-point sub-interfaces, point-to-**multi**point sub-interfaces can be configured, and in fact is the recommended method for partially meshed networks (see Figure 8-12). Like the previous point-to-point configuration, this version may produce additional routing traffic because no DR or BDR is elected, but the point-to-multipoint model is more reliable than the point-to-point model. Another advantage with point-to-multipoint links is that a single subnet ID is used for all sub-interfaces.

In the point-to-multipoint configuration, OSPF must have the network type manually configured as **point-to-multi-point** by issuing the **ip ospf network** command. If the layer 2 media does not support multicasts, the optional keyword **non-broadcast** must also be used in the statement. In that case, neighbors will need to be configured manually with the **neighbor** command.

Demand Circuits

A demand circuit (also known as a dial-on-demand circuit) is unique in that the link is only established when there is a need to send traffic. Quite often, the customer pays a metered rate for the service. The more it is used, the more it costs. ISDN is an example of this technology. The issue with demand circuits and routing protocols is that the routing protocol will "wake up" the line just to send periodic routing updates. In the case of OSPF, periodic routing traffic occurs with Hello packets (sent as a keep-alive feature to be sure the link is up) and with summary LSAs (sent every 30 minutes even if no change has occurred).

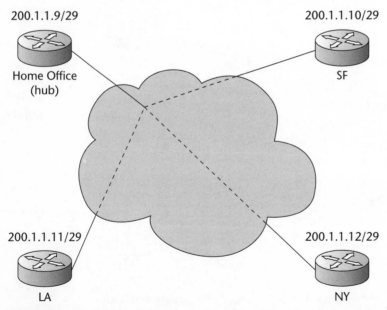

Figure 8-12 Point-to-multipoint sub-interfaces are the recommended configuration for partial mesh Frame Relay networks.

To accommodate the concern of excess costs due to periodic routing traffic, version 11.2 of the Cisco IOS introduced the interface-level command **ip ospf demand-circuit** that will suppress this periodic maintenance traffic. Once the command has been issued and the network has converged, both periodic Hello packets and periodic LSAs are suppressed. Only an actual change on the network affecting routing will trigger OSPF packets to be sent over the interface.

> **NOTE** One other so-called network type recognized by OSPF is the *virtual link*, which is actually an OSPF configuration related to areas that run on top of the underlying data-link layer, and uses the *area virtual link* command rather than the *ip ospf network* command. Virtual links are therefore discussed separately.

OSPF Areas

The concept of OSPF areas was discussed in the introduction to this section. The main reason to carve an OSPF autonomous system into areas is to manage the amount of routing information carried on the network. Most routing information is carried in link-state advertisements (LSAs). Routers advertise detailed information about a network link within an LSA packet. It is the sharing of these LSAs that allows every router to become aware of every network link and build its own topology table. The type of LSA that performs this work is known as a **Router LSA**. On larger networks, the kind of detail carried in a Router LSA is simply not required by all routers. Bandwidth can be saved if more distant routers receive only the amount of routing information required to perform optimal routing. OSPF accommodates this need with a special type of LSA that contains a subset of the data stored in a normal LSA. Areas can also provide a layer of security because the internal area topology is not distributed outside of the area The demarcation between groups of routers that circulate router LSAs is the OSPF area border.

Knowing when to configure an OSPF system into multiple areas, and an explanation of the special LSA types that circulate between areas, will be covered shortly. But first, the operation of OSPF in a single area will be covered.

OSPF Operation in a Single Area

With a background in OSPF terminology and OSPF network types, and a brief introduction to OSPF areas behind you, the operation of OSPF in a single area will now be covered. A look at how neighbor relationships and adjacencies are formed will be rendered, followed by an examination of how routing information is shared among routers. The following concepts and terms will be covered:

- Router ID
- Hello protocol
- Neighbors
- Neighbor table
- Topology table
- Adjacencies
- Router states for establishing neighbor relationships
- Router states for establishing adjacencies
- Master and slave router relationships
- Database description packets
- OSPF packet types
- Link-State Advertisement types related to a single area
- Link-State Request packets
- Link-State Acknowledgement packets
- Link-State Retransmission List
- LSA retransmit-interval timer
- Designated Router and Backup Designated Router
- Router priority

Two network examples will be used to illustrate OSPF operation in a single area: one model requiring a DR and a model not requiring a DR.

Example 1—Single Area. Point-to-Point Model. No Designated Router

Figure 8-13 illustrates a simple point-to-point network. No DR is required.

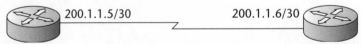

Figure 8-13 Network example #1—point-to-point network, no DR required.

Here is a mostly plain English explanation of the steps to initialize OSPF on this network (afterwards, the nitty-gritty details will be delved into):

1. Upon power-up or reinitialization, OSPF will initialize itself on all enabled interfaces.

2. Neighboring routers must discover each other. This occurs by the **Hello protocol** multicasting **Hello packets** to address 224.0.0.5 (All-SPFRouters) out all enabled interfaces. Routers are identified uniquely by a **router ID**, which is either the highest IP address from an interface or the address assigned to a loopback interface, if configured.

3. Upon reception of Hello packets, each router will form a **neighbor relationship** with the router it received the Hello packet from if certain criteria are met. Neighbor information is stored in the **neighbor table**. Link-state databases are not shared between neighbors. The neighbor relationship must be upgraded to the status of **adjacent** for that to occur. It's kind of like if you're neighbors you just date, but an adjacency is like getting married and producing offspring. Since this is a point-to-point network no DR will be elected, so in this case, neighbor relationships are immediately upgraded to an **adjacency**.

4. The key aspect to forming an adjacency is the sharing of the **link-state databases** (topology tables). To carry this out, the router with the highest IP address becomes the **master** and starts the exchange by sending **database description packets** (DDPs) to the **slave** router, which in turn sends DDPs to the master.

5. Database description packets contain only a subset of the actual link-state information. This is yet another bandwidth saving measure not to be confused with the subset of link data sent between areas. In this case, a DDP contains a **link ID**—a unique ID assigned to every LSA—along with some information that identifies the LSA's age. If the receiving router finds that it does not have a link-state entry referenced by a particular database description packet, or if the received information about an entry is newer, the receiving router sends back a **Link-State Request** packet for the complete entry, which the other router will respond to by sending a **Link-State Advertisement** (LSA) with the complete information for the link. Upon reception of LSAs, the packets are acknowledged with **Link-State Acknowledgement** packets. When the link-state databases on each router are fully synchronized, the adjacency is complete.

6. Once each router has a complete link-state database, the SPF algorithm is run and the **route table** is populated.

Now let's look under the hood at how this all happens.

Hello Protocol and Hello Packets

The Hello protocol is responsible for transmitting Hello packets. Hello packets are transmitted periodically. They are used to establish and maintain neighbor relationships and for electing a DR and a BDR. Hello packets are OSPF type 1 packets. (Table 8-2 at the end of this section shows the critical fields of a Hello packet.)

Becoming Neighbors

Neighbor relationships must be established between all routers with an interface that shares a common network link. Several parameters—stored in the Hello packet—must be identical for two routers to become neighbors. The parameters are as follows:

Network mask—*net mask of the sending router*

Area ID—*area ID of the sending interface*

Hello interval—*how often Hello packets are transmitted*

Dead interval—*how long to wait for Hello packets before terminating neighbor*

Authentication type and password—*optional*

Stub area flag—*specifies the type of stub area, if applicable*

Be advised that if you alter the Hello interval and/or dead intervals, you must change the setting on all routers sharing the link, or neighbor relationships will not be established. If neighbors are not being established, review the list to be sure all parameters match. Naturally, not all items on the checklist have been covered yet.

Becoming neighbors requires bidirectional communication between routers. The routers transition through three distinct states to become neighbors:

1. **Down state**

   The down state is the initial state when a router is first powered up or when the OSPF process is reinitialized. In this state, the router sends Hello packets out all OSPF-enabled interfaces on multicast address 224.0.0.5 (AllSPFRouters). For clarity, let's call this router router A. In this state, the neighbor list field is empty.

2. **Init state**

   Before router A can send a Hello packet to router B, router A receives a Hello packet from router B (see Figure 8-14). Router A does not see its own router ID listed in the neighbor list field of the packet because router B has not received any Hello packets from router A, but router A now knows there is another router out there and transitions to the init state (also known as a 1-way state).

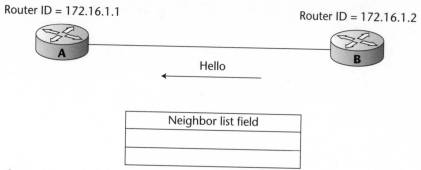

Figure 8-14 Router A enters init state upon reception of a Hello packet.

Now in the init state, router A adds router B's router ID to the neighbor list field for all subsequent outbound Hello packets, and sends a populated Hello packet to router B, as shown in Figure 8-15.

3. **2-way state**

In Figure 8-16, router A receives a Hello packet from router B with router A's router ID listed in the neighbor list field. Both routers are now listed in the neighbor list field of the Hello packets. This indicates that bidirectional communication has been established—the neighbor relationship has been established.

NOTE On network types with manually configured neighbors (for example non-broadcast, multi-access networks), an additional state is possible. If a router loses contact with an established neighbor (via loss of Hello packets), the router will enter the attempt state. In the attempt state, periodic Hellos are sent at the *poll-interval* (defaults to 120 seconds on NBMA) rather than the Hello-interval (defaults to 60 seconds on NBMA). This reduced rate conserves bandwidth but still allows the neighbor relationship to be re-established.

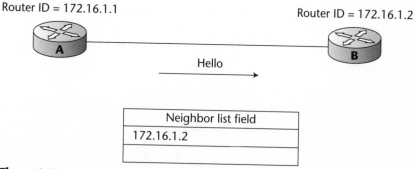

Figure 8-15 Router A populates a Hello packet with its router ID.

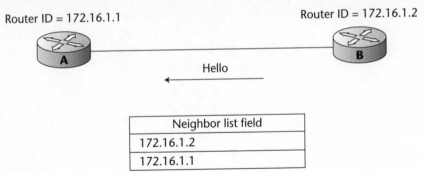

Figure 8-16   Receiving a Hello packet listing a router's own router ID triggers a transition to the 2-way state.

Establishing an Adjacency

Routers that will become adjacent to one another continue communicating after the neighbor relationship has been established. The routers transition through the following four additional states to establish the adjacency, whereby they share (synchronize) their link-state databases. In this example of a point-to-point network, the two neighboring routers will immediately establish an adjacency.

1. **Exstart state**

   In exstart state, the routers determine which one will share its link-state database first. Link-state databases are exchanged via the aforementioned **database description packets** (**DDPs**). With no DR present, the router that goes first is strictly arbitrary and is determined by router ID. The router with the highest router ID becomes the **master**, while the other router becomes the **slave** (also known as primary and secondary). This is determined by each router sending a single DDP to its adjacent neighbor. The packet contains no link-state data, but simply includes the local router ID and a sequence number.

   The router with the higher Router ID becomes the master and sends a populated DDP to the slave, using the same sequence number for the first packet. The slave expects the first DDP to have the agreed upon sequence number.

2. **Exchange state**

   Now that the master and slave roles are agreed upon, and a beginning sequence number is set, the master sends the first DDP, and the slave responds with a populated DDP describing its link-state database. The DDP sent by the slave uses the same sequence number as the master. The exchange state has commenced.

Once the master receives the slave's first populated DDP, the master bumps the sequence number and sends the next DDP. Only one DDP is outstanding at a time. Only the master can retransmit a DDP. It waits a period of time set by the **RxmtInterval** timer before ever retransmitting a DDP. The slave does not need a retransmit capability, because the master receiving a DDP from the slave proves the slave received the master's DDP. If the master does not receive a DDP from the slave within the timeout period, the master retransmits the same DDP using the same sequence number. Only upon receipt of a DDP from the slave is the next DDP sent by the master.

The process of exchanging DDPs continues until both routers have exchanged the contents of their link-state databases.

The database description packets sent between routers contain a subset of a single link-state entry, specifically, the LSA header, which contains the link-state ID. The packet also contains general identification information and other fields (see Tables 8-3 and 8-4).

The receiving router uses the link-state ID, the age, and the sequence number to determine if it already has current information for this link. If the receiving router does not already have a matching link-state ID, or if the DDP contains a more recent version of an existing link-state ID, then the router will generate a **link-state Request** requesting a **link-state Update** (LSU). The request may be for one or more LSAs.

An LSU packet is the carrier for Link-State Advertisements, of which there are 11 possible types. In the case of this database synchronization, where an LSR has requested an LSU for details on one or more links, a router LSA (Type 1) will be sent. Router LSAs contain the core information of a link and are the primary means of synchronizing link-state databases within an area. (The pertinent fields of the OSPF packets discussed in this section are listed at the end of this section in Tables 8-2 through 8-8).

NOTE This is a good place to slow down and do a quick review, because LSAs are where the rubber meets the road in OSPF. LSUs carry LSAs. LSAs carry link-state information. Within an area, type 1 (router) LSAs are used to share link-state database entries with adjacent neighboring routers. Type 1 LSAs are sent in response to a link-state request, which was generated when the router receiving a DDP determined that it had missing or outdated information for one or more links. Type 1 (router) LSAs are also sent by each router every 30 minutes to insure the link-state databases remain synched.

3. **Loading state**

    The loading state is not always required. It is entered only if there is still business to do after all DDPs have been sent. There are two reasons for this.

    If any Link-State Requests were generated (due to receiving a DDP that required a complete LSA), and the corresponding LSAs have not been received by the time the DDPs have been sent, the routers will enter the loading state.

    Second, LSAs are sent reliably using the proprietary assured delivery mechanism built into OSPF. They are acknowledged with **LSA** packets. Transmitted LSAs are queued in a **Link-State Retransmission List**. The LSA is retransmitted if the *LSA retransmit-interval timer* expires. Unacknowledged LSAs will transition the router's state to **loading**. Only after any requested LSAs are acknowledged, does the router transition out of this state.

4. **Full state**

    The full state is entered when the adjacent routers' link-state databases are fully synchronized. LSAs have been received for all generated LSRs, and each LSA has been acknowledged. When the full state is reached, the SPF algorithm is run and the route table is populated. Routing can now commence.[7]

Example 2—Single Area. Broadcast Multi-access Model

In this example, a DR handles the propagation of the link-state database.

Designated Router and Backup Designated Router

Figure 8-17 depicts a broadcast, multi-access network such as an Ethernet network. When one or more multi-access networks exist within an area, not all neighboring routers will form adjacencies. For such network types, it makes more sense to designate a single router to receive all the link-state advertisements from each router on the segment and then have the DR transmit the collective link-state database back to each router. It has been demonstrated mathematically that this method results in less network traffic. Thus, you have the DR and its side-kick, the BDR, which has no duties except to take over if the DR fails. When a DR and a BDR are elected, routers on the segment will only form adjacencies with the DR/BDR. *Broadcast*, multi-access networks like Ethernet, Token Ring, and FDDI will always elect a DR and a BDR. *Non-broadcast*, multi-access networks may or may not elect a DR and a BDR, depending on how they are configured (see the earlier discussion of network architectures on page 245).

HOW ARE DOWNED LINKS ADVERTISED?

If a router needs to invalidate an existing LSA, say because the link associated to the LSA goes down, the router will generate a fresh LSA with the LsAGE field set to MaxAge, which is 1 hour. The LSA will be flooded, and upon receipt, the LSA will be purged from the link-state database of all routers in the area. Each router will then run SPF and update their route tables as needed. This procedure is referred to as *premature aging* in the RFC for OSPF.

The designers of OSPF, having determined that a Designated Router was a good thing, had to work out some basic logistics like: Who gets to be the Designated Router? How is every router informed of who the Designated Router is? What happens if the Designated Router goes down?

To begin with, every router sharing the link needs to be uniquely identified. This is easy because each OSPF router has the aforementioned router ID. The DR is chosen through an election process. Each router is configured with a priority number referred to as the **router priority**. The default router priority is 1. The priority can be manually set from 0–254. The higher the number, the greater the priority. A priority of 0 means the router is ineligible to participate in elections.

Hello packets carry the information about the DR and BDR. There is a field for the DR, the BDR, and the router priority for each router (shown in Table 8-2 at the end of this section). If the DR field is set to 0.0.0.0, an election is held. The router with the highest priority becomes the DR, and the router with the next highest priority becomes the BDR. In case of a tie, the router with the highest router ID wins. If the DR goes down, the BDR is promoted to DR and an election is held for a new BDR.[8]

The election of a DR and a BDR occurs after the neighbor relationships have been established. Recall from the previous example that this is signified by the 2-way state being entered. The election is held after the 2-way state is reached, but before the exstart state is entered.

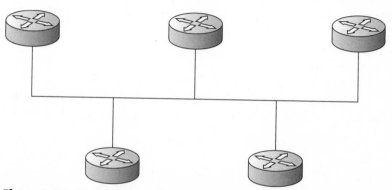

Figure 8-17   Network example #2—multi-access network. A DR will be elected.

CONTROLLING WHICH ROUTER IS ELECTED DR AND/OR BDR

The DR and BDR do more work than other routers on the segment. Therefore, you may want to control which routers take on the task of assimilating and transmitting the link-state database. One may assume from the discussion so far that simply setting the router priority of the two routers that are intended to be the DR and BDR higher than the other routers on the segment would do the job. That step will help, but be advised that if the routers that are elected DR and BDR are not online when the election is held, they will *not* get elected when they do come online. The first router with a priority of any value other than 0 to come online becomes the DR. The only thing that can be done in this case would be to force an election by temporarily taking the current DR and BDR offline (the BDR must go offline because it will immediately be promoted to DR when the DR goes down). Not an ideal solution, so naturally you want to be sure these routers are online when the network is first brought up. Of course, routers that should never be elected DR or BDR can have their priority set to 0.

Propagation of the Link-State Databases in a Designated Router Environment
In a DR environment, routers sharing the multi-access link are classified with three designations: **AllSPFRouters**, which represents every router attached to the segment; **AllDRouters**, which represent the DR and BDR; and **DRothers**, which represents any router that is not a DR or BDR. Figure 8-18 depicts this relationship.

After the election of the DR and BDR, each DRothers router transitions to exstart state and forms an adjacency with AllDRouters. The DRother routers become slaves, with the DR and BDR acting as masters. From here, the process of completing the adjacency is the same as described in the previous section for point-to-point links. Figure 8-19 depicts the adjacencies formed on a multi-access network.

The DR also takes responsibility for advertising the existence of all routers attached to the multi-access network segment. This is done with an LSU carrying a type 2 (network) LSA, and is flooded to every router in the area. A network LSA contains the router IDs of all adjacent routers (shown in Table 8-7 at the end of this section).

Maintaining the Link-State Database
Regardless of whether a DR is in use or not, the link-state database for every router is maintained by flooding LSAs when a change to a network link occurs. Dropped links, added links, links transitioning from up to down or

WHY ARE TYPE 2 (NETWORK LSAS) REQUIRED?

The answer lies in the same reasoning that spawned the idea of the DR in the first place—namely the mitigation of unnecessary routing traffic. SPF wants to know how every router links to every other router in an area to accurately build the area's topology map. Normally a router will generate an LSA that identifies the router on the other end of each link (excluding stub networks of course). On a multi-access segment however, such reporting will cause a number of redundant LSAs to be generated. Since the DR is fully aware of which routers share the common link, it is in a position to report the router relationships without the redundancy.

vice versa, and a change in the metric value of a link all require each router in the area to be notified. The router sourcing the change of a link's state will flood the area with a type 1 (router) LSA that describes just the changed link.

Regardless of any changes to links, each LSA in a link-state database is reflooded by the router the link is connected to (known as the originating router) every 30 minutes. This insures the integrity of the database on each router.

Breakdown of the OSPF Packets That Circulate Within an Area

Initializing OSPF in an area requires the following packet types:

- Type 1 (Hello) OSPF packets (see Table 8-2)
- Type 2 (Database Description) OSPF packets (see Table 8-3)
- Type 3 (Link-State Request or LSR) OSPF packets (see Table 8-5)
- Type 4 (Link-State Update or LSU) OSPF packets that in turn carry the following:
  - *Type 1 (router) Link-State Advertisements (see Table 8-6)*
  - *Type 2 (network) Link-State Advertisements (see Table 8-7)*
- Type 5 (Link State Acknowledgement) OSPF packets (see Table 8-8)

The format of these packet types is described in Tables 8-2 through 8-8. Bear in mind that these are partial listings. See the appendix for a source of the complete packet format of all OSPF packet types.

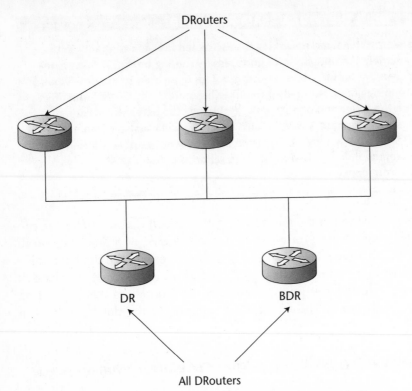

DRouters

DR

BDR

All DRouters

Figure 8-18 Router designations for synchronizing link-state databases on a multi-access network.

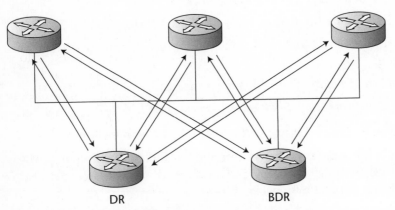

DR

BDR

Figure 8-19 Adjacencies formed on a multi-access network.

Table 8-2   Abbreviated Listing of a Type 1 (Hello) OSPF Packet

PACKET FIELD	DESCRIPTION
IP Header	Identifies payload as an OSPF packet by specifying protocol #89.
OSPF Header	Identifies 1 of 5 types of OSPF packets. This is a type 1 (Hello) OSPF packet.
Router ID	Router ID of the source router.
Area ID	Area ID of the source router.
Network Mask	Network/subnet mask of interface sourcing Hello packet.
Hello Interval	Defines how often the Hello packet is sent.
Router Priority	Used for the election of a DR and BDR.
RouterDeadInterval	Defines how long to wait before declaring that a neighbor is down.
Designated Router	IP address of the DR, if elected.
Backup Designated Router	IP address of the BDR, if elected.
Neighbor List	Lists the interface IP address of a neighbor. This field is repeated for each valid neighbor.
Options	Defines the capabilities of the router sourcing the Hello packet.

Some of these Hello packet fields require further explanation:

- **IP Header:** All OSPF packets are encapsulated in an IP header. The OSPF protocol uses its own registered IP number 89. OSPF packets do not use UDP or TCP.

- **OSPF Header:** All OSPF packets have an OSPF header that indicates the type of OSPF packet.

- **Router ID:** A Router ID is an IP address forced unique by using an interface address configured on the router. The highest address is used, unless a loopback interface is configured, in which case the address of the loopback is used, regardless of whether it is the highest address or not.

- **Area ID:** This is the area ID configured for the interface sending the Hello packet. Bear in mind that a router may have interfaces in more than one area, such as with Area Border Routers (ABRs).

- **Network Mask:** The subnet mask of the local interface transmitting the Hello packet.

- **Hello Interval:** The Hello packet will include the value set for the Hello interval, which determines how often Hello packets are sent, along with

the dead interval, which establishes how long a router will wait for a periodic Hello packet before declaring a neighbor dead. The default values for
these timers is 10 seconds for Hello packets (30 seconds on NBMA media),
and 40 seconds for the dead interval (120 seconds on NBMA media).

- **Router Priority:** Determines the likelihood of a router being elected as
  the DR or BDR. The default value is 1. The higher the value, the more
  likely the router will be elected. A value of 0 removes the router from
  contention as a DR or BDR.

- **RouterDeadInterval:** This timer determines how long to wait if the
  stream of periodic Hello packets that maintain the neighbor relationship is discontinued. The default is 4 times the Hello interval. If the
  timer expires, the neighbor relationship is terminated.

- **Designated Router:** This field will be filled in when a DR has been
  elected. It indicates the presence of a DR (no need for an election) and
  allows the router to unicast packets to the DR. A value of 0.0.0.0 indicates there is no DR. This forces an election.

- **Backup Designated Router:** Same as for Designated Router.

- **Neighbor List:** When a router receives a Hello packet from another
  router, the receiving router will add its own router ID to the Hello packets it sources. When the corresponding router receives these Hello packets, it recognizes itself in the packets and commences the steps required
  to establish a neighbor relationship. Once the neighbor relationship is
  established, the interface address of the neighbor is added to the neighbor field.

- **Options:** This field describes a router's capabilities from the perspective of how it will behave in an OSPF routing domain. The Options
  field is present in three different OSPF packet types, so it makes more
  sense to describe it in a separate section (see page 300).

Table 8-3 Abbreviated Listing of an OSPF Type 2 (Database Description) Packet

DDP FIELD	DESCRIPTION
IP Header	Identifies payload as an OSPF packet by specifying protocol #89.
OSPF Header	Identifies 1 of 5 types of OSPF packets. This is a type 2 (Database Description) OSPF packet.
Router ID	The router the packet came from.
Area ID	Must match the area ID of the recipient router.

Table 8-3   *(continued)*

DDP FIELD	DESCRIPTION
Database Description Sequence Number	Used to order DD packets.
LSA Header	The LSA header information (detailed in Table 8-4).

Table 8-4   Abbreviated Listing of an LSA Header

LSA HEADER FIELD	DESCRIPTION
Age	The number of seconds since the LSA was created by the originating router.
Link-State ID	Varies according to LSA type.
Advertising Router	The router the link is actually connected to.
Sequence Number	Incremented each time the LSA is transmitted.
LS Type	LSA type (specifies 1 of 11 LSA types).

Table 8-5   Abbreviated Listing of a Type 3 (Link-State Request) OSPF Packet

LSA TYPE 3 PACKET FIELD	DESCRIPTION	NOTE
IP Header	Identifies payload as an OSPF packet by specifying protocol #89.	
OSPF Header	Identifies 1 of 5 types of OSPF packets. This is a type 3 (LSR) OSPF packet.	
Router ID	Router ID of router sourcing request.	
Area ID	Area ID of router sourcing request.	
Link-State Type	Identifies which type of LSA is being requested (of 11 types).	Repeated for each link being requested.
Link-State ID	Varies according to the link-state type. See Table 8-6.	Repeated for each link being requested.
Advertising Router	The router that originated the LSA.	Repeated for each link being requested.

Table 8-6 Abbreviated Listing of an LSA Type 1 (Router) Packet

LSA TYPE 1 PACKET FIELD	DESCRIPTION	NOTE
IP Header	Identifies payload as an OSPF packet by specifying protocol #89.	
OSPF Header	Identifies 1 of 5 types of OSPF packets. This is a type 4 (LSU) OSPF packet.	
LSA Header	Identifies 1 of 11 LSA types. This is a type 1 (router) LSA.	
Age	The number of seconds since the LSA was created by the originating router.	
Options	Any option bits are set here.	
Link-State ID	ID of the router that originated the LSA.	
Advertising Router	The router the link is connected to.	
Sequence Number	Incremented each time the LSA is originated.	
E-Bit	If set to 1, this identifies the originating router as an ASBR.	
B-Bit	If set to 1, this identifies the originating router as an ABR.	
Number of Links	The number of LSAs in this packet.	
Link Type	Specifies one of four types of links: 1: Point-to-point connection to another router 2: Link-to-transit network 3: Link-to-stub network 4: Virtual link	Repeated for each link in packet.
Link ID	Varies according to link type: Link type 1: Neighboring router's router ID Link type 2: IP address of the DR's sending interface Link type 3: IP address of the subnet Link type 4: Same as type 1	Repeated for each link in packet.
Link Data	Varies according to Link Type: Link type 1: The originating router's interface address Link type 2: Same as type 1 Link type 3: Subnet mask Link type 4: Same as type 1	Repeated for each link in packet.

Table 8-6   *(continued)*

LSA TYPE 1 PACKET FIELD	DESCRIPTION	NOTE
Metric	Cost of the link.	Repeated for each link in packet.

Some LSA type 1 packet fields in Table 8-6 require further explanation:

- **Age and Sequence Number:** OSPF uses the Age field and the Sequence Number field (along with the checksum field, which is not shown) to determine if an LSA is newer then one a router may already have for the same link. A newer LSA replaces an existing LSA.

- **Link Type, Link ID, and Link Data:** OSPF wants to know the type of network being advertised in the LSA. This information is mainly used by the SPF algorithm for building the route table. Link type 1 refers to a pair of routers on a point-to-point link. Link type 2 refers to a multi-access network with a DR. A type 3 link is simply a stub network—no other routers share the link. Link type 4 refers to the special case of a virtual link. The value of the Link ID and Link Data fields vary according to the link type. For example if the link type is 1, OSPF wants identifying information about the neighboring router, as indicated in the table. For the multi-access network specified by link type 2, OSPF wants identifying information about the DR. For the stub networks specified by link type 3, there is no router information required. Rather, this is where the net mask for stub networks is collected. All this data assists SPF in determining the shortest path to all networks.

Table 8-7   Abbreviated Listing of an LSA Type 2 (Network) Packet

LSA TYPE 2 PACKET FIELD	DESCRIPTION	NOTE
IP Header	Identifies payload as an OSPF packet by specifying protocol #89.	
OSPF Header	Identifies 1 of 5 types of OSPF packets. This is a type 4 (LSU) OSPF packet.	
LSA Header	Identifies 1 of 11 LSA types. This is a type 2 (network) LSA.	
Age	The number of seconds since the LSA was created by the originating router.	
Sequence Number	Used to identify age of packet.	

(continued)

Table 8-7 *(continued)*

LSA TYPE 2 PACKET FIELD	DESCRIPTION	NOTE
Link-State ID	Interface address of the advertising DR.	
Advertising Router	Router ID of the advertising router.	
Network Mask	Mask of the multi-access network.	
Attached Router	Router ID of a router on the multi-access network.	This field is repeated for each attached router.

Table 8-8 Abbreviated Listing of a Type 5 (Link-State Acknowledgement) OSPF Packet

LSA TYPE 5 PACKET FIELD	DESCRIPTION
IP Header	Identifies payload as an OSPF packet by specifying protocol #89.
OSPF Header	Identifies 1 of 5 types of OSPF packets. This is a type 5 (link-state acknowledgement) OSPF packet.
Router ID	Router ID of the router sourcing acknowledgement.
Area ID	Area ID of the router sourcing acknowledgement.
LSA Headers	Includes only the headers of the LSAs being acknowledged.

NOTE The fields of the various OSPF packet types can appear a bit daunting at first. For example, the Link-State ID is not only an IP address, it can refer to a DR, the interface of a neighbor, a network address, or another entity, depending on the link type. Exploring packet formats places you deep in the bowels of the protocol. We will not endeavor here to explain each field of each packet type in detail, but instead note that the data in these packets is primarily used to identify the state of links, help in link-state database synchronization, and build an area's topology table.

Single Area Review

An area is a logical grouping of routers with identical link-state databases. Adjacencies are created between neighboring routers for the purpose of synchronizing the link-state databases of each router in the area. Every router must form an adjacency with at least one other router. In the case of multi-access networks, a DR is elected to propagate the link-state database for the segment.

OSPF Operation in a Multiple-Area System

This section describes the operation of OSPF in a multiple-area configuration. It builds on the previous section, which explained the operation of OSPF in a single area. Each area in a multiple-area system initializes routing as previously described. What is added to the mix is how **inter-area** communications are handled, and what the characteristics of different area types are.

The first order of business in discussing multiple areas is to understand when it is necessary to create multi-area OSPF systems in the first place.

To Area or Not to Area

When should an OSPF system be subdivided into areas and how many areas should it have? What's the magic formula? Well, like many things in life, there are no hard and fast rules for answering these questions. General guidelines for when to create multiple areas fall into the range of autonomous systems with 30 to 200 routers—a very wide-ranging value! In smaller, simpler OSPF networks, you can get away with a single area configuration. Medium- and large-sized networks usually should take advantage of the multiple-area architecture of OSPF. Here are some of the factors that dictate when to configure for multiple areas:

- Available network bandwidth for routing information
- Number of links in the autonomous system
- Available router memory
- Available router CPU cycles
- The desire to summarize routes
- Failed routes are advertised only within the area
- Subnets IDs can be hidden within an area and remain unknown outside the area
- Political, administrative, and security concerns

Processing routing information takes up memory and CPU cycles on a router. The more time a router spends processing routing information, the less time it has for forwarding data packets. As an OSPF network grows larger, the number of links increase, and the link-state database therefore grows in size, as does the route table. The more links there are in a system, the greater the chance of a link changing its state (going up or down, metric changing, and so on), which results in more routing traffic and a heavier load on routers as they re-compute the route table. As the load on routers and network links gets heavier, a point is reached where it becomes clear that subdividing the system into multiple areas (or adding another area to an existing multiple area system) is required. Routes to networks learned from other areas require less processing. This saves on router resources. Furthermore, routes learned from other areas are advertised with far less information. This reduces packet size and saves on bandwidth.

Something else to be aware of in multiple-area configurations is that when routers learn of a route to a network residing in another area, *they do not run the SPF algorithm on the route*. Such routes are simply evaluated for inclusion into the route table based on their metrics. The reason for this is that routes learned from other areas within the system don't include all the topology information that links learned within the area do. Only *networks* and their *metrics* are advertised between areas.

But wait. What kind of heresy is this? If only networks are advertised between areas, and not the routers they are connected to, how can the topology map be built by SPF? Isn't that the key to how OSPF works— knowing the location of all routers in the system? Isn't this what guarantees fast, efficient, loop-free routing?

Indeed, managing network resources by excluding some networks from the SPF algorithm appears at first to be a bit of a tradeoff. Advertising only routes and their metrics is kind of like – dare we say – *routing by rumor*. It is, but the designers of OSPF took all this into account. There are specific restrictions as to how the hierarchy of areas can be configured. Having all non-zero areas connect to area 0 helps prevent a router learning of a route that leads back through itself, also known as a routing-loop.

Another factor that affects the need for multiple areas is route summarization. In OSPF, route summarization takes place only at the border between areas. Summarization leverages the concept of small packets passing between areas by causing fewer of those packets to be generated, thanks to a fewer number of networks being advertised. Summarizing routes is another factor to consider when planning where to place areas boundaries. You may even want to employ multiple areas on smaller networks in order to enjoy the benefits of route summarization.

The number of areas to implement may even be affected by political considerations. A manager might have two squabbling network administrators and choose to put the administrators in charge of their own respective "areas." A silly concept perhaps, but you know how silly real life can be sometimes. In another vein, a paranoid (perhaps with good reason) manager might wish to take advantage of the fact that packet authentication can be set at an area's border, preventing unauthorized routes from being advertised into the area. Because many IT professionals take a *layered* approach to security, this feature might be worth considering.

Finally, whether you are growing a newer network or changing routing protocols on an existing system, it is important to benchmark your system. This means making baseline measurements of system performance before, during, and after OSPF is introduced. Bandwidth usage should be monitored as well as key router metrics like memory and CPU usage. Proper benchmarking helps provides core information for determining how many areas are ultimately required.

Multiple Areas Mean Multiple Area Types, LSA Types, and Router Types

The network configuration within an area determines the amount and type of routing information that needs to be shared with the area. Toward that end, OSPF discerns among four different types of areas as described later.[9] Area types are simply another means of managing routing traffic. To handle the specific routing information required by different area types, additional types of LSAs are brought to bear. The single-area configuration presented earlier introduced two types of LSAs: type 1 (router) LSAs, which flood the network links throughout the area; and type 2 (network) LSAs, which flood the area with a listing of each router connected to a multi-access network. Those two LSAs are used for *intra*-area routing. Four additional types of LSAs will be introduced that are used for *inter*-area and external routing, which totals six common LSA types in use out of 11 total types specified in the RFCs for OSPF.

When an OSPF autonomous system is broken into multiple areas, the routers within each area take on varying roles. A router with all interfaces within a single area handles routing differently than a router that straddles two areas (by having an interface configured for each area). Therefore, OSPF discerns between a total of four types of routers, based on their location within an area.

Area types, *LSA types*, and *router types* are integral components to multiple-area routing. As stated in the introduction to this section, these building blocks will be explained in sequence in this treatment, and then used in practical examples in the subsequent section, "OSPF Operation, Part 2: Tying It All Together."

Area Types

As mentioned previously, there are four RFC sanctioned area types that OSPF uses to route traffic. They are as follows:

- Backbone area
- Standard area
- Stub Area (2)

Backbone Area

The backbone area—also referred to as area 0 or 0.0.0.0, since that must be its numeric designation—is mandatory when more than one area exists.[10] The backbone area acts as a sort of hub which all inter-area network traffic passes through. Each non-zero area connects to the backbone area.[11] Traffic passing from a network in area 1 to a network in area 2, for example, uses the backbone area as a transit area. It is not necessary for area 1 and area 2 to be directly connected, nor should it be.

NOTE Area IDs are 32-bit numbers and can be expressed as a single number or in dotted decimal format like an IP address. Therefore, area "0" and area "0.0.0.0" are equivalent.

Use of the backbone area creates a two-level hierarchy scheme, thus OSPF's designation as a hierarchical protocol. Here again you can see the need for a well-planned implementation of OSPF. By designing all areas to connect through a single area 0, an efficient, logical network design is achieved. It should be noted that because of this design, the network engineer should be aware that some or all routers in area 0 need to be configured to accommodate the extra transit traffic it must handle.

Figure 8-20 shows one possible multi-area configuration. Notice that geographically dispersed networks are configured into separate areas. An assumption is made here that much of the network traffic is contained within a single building or surrounding buildings (departments are often grouped together geographically). Inter-area traffic is therefore kept to a minimum. The FDDI backbone is accessed primarily for Internet access and when access to networks in other areas is required.

Figure 8-21 illustrates a slightly different configuration. Here the areas are connected via a public carrier and are very geographically dispersed. However, in spite of the distances involved, the autonomous system can still be architected to connect areas 1, 2, and 3 to the backbone area. Notice that area 0 can be configured with networks that contain hosts. It is not relegated to serving only transient traffic. Note also that in this model each area has its own connection to the Internet. The significance of whether an area directly connects to external networks will be accounted for as we explore the other area types.

> **NOTE** Area 0 is automatically recognized by OSPF as the backbone area simply by designating its numeric assignment 0 or 0.0.0.0 when configuring OSPF (see the command reference).

Standard Area

A standard area (also known as a normal area) is characterized by the following criteria:

- Advertises summaries of its network links to backbone area 0
- Accepts summaries of network links from area 0, which comprise links within area 0, as well as summarized network links area 0 has learned of from other areas
- Accepts redistributed (externally learned) routes
- Can optionally accept a default route representing redistributed routes

Figure 8-22 illustrates a standard area. Standard areas receive the most routing information of any non-zero area type. The main characteristic of a standard area is that it can receive individual routes to both inter-area and external locations. Optionally, a standard area may receive a default route representing external routes. All other area types receive less routing information, mainly having to do with external routes.

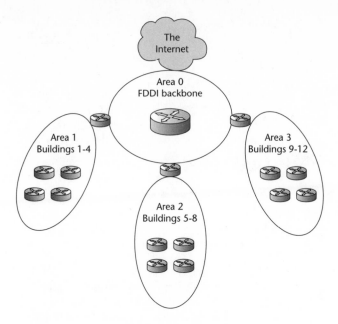

Figure 8-20 Multiple OSPF areas. This model has no hosts in area 0.

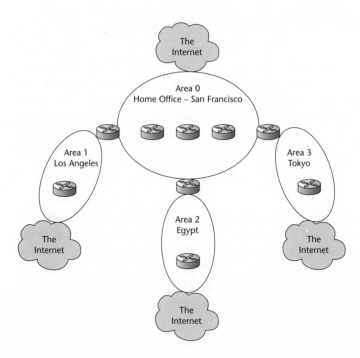

Figure 8-21 Multiple OSPF areas. Area 0 contains hosts in this example.

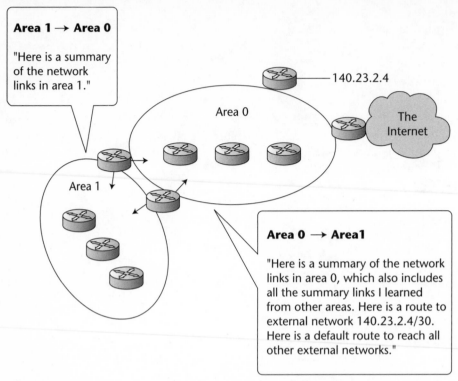

Figure 8-22   Example of a standard area with two connections to area 0.

Standard areas are often used when the area has redundant connections to area 0 and/or when the area's routers connect to external networks without going through the backbone. With multiple paths to choose from for inter-area and/or external routing, having the maximum amount of routing information may improve routing decisions. A standard area is also the only area type that can be used as a transit area for a virtual link connecting a non-zero area to the backbone.

Stub Area

Stub areas accept less routing information than standard areas. A group of routers are normally configured into a stub area when there is only a single connection to the backbone, therefore requiring less detailed routing information (although there are exceptions as noted later). There are two flavors of stub areas specified by the RFC for OSPF, with a third type incorporated by certain routing vendors such as Cisco. These various stub area types are characterized by the type of routing information they send and receive. They are stub, totally stubby, and not-so-stubby.

Stub Area

A stub area (also known as a standard stub area) is the same as a standard area except that it does not accept any information about external routes (see Figure 8-23). Rather than learn about routes to external networks, a stub area will simply accept a **default route** that will lead to a router that has more detailed information about how to reach external networks. This is a logical choice if the area has no internal routers connecting to external networks and only has a single connection to area 0. Why populate the route tables with listings of external networks if there is only one possible routing decision? A stub area is characterized by the following criteria:

- Advertises summaries of its network links to backbone area 0
- Accepts summaries of network links from area 0, which comprise links within area 0, as well as summarized network links area 0 has learned of from other areas
- Accepts a default route leading to external networks

Totally Stubby Area

A totally stubby area takes the concept of a (standard) stub area one step further as shown in Figure 8-24. Instead of just pumping a default route for external networks into the stub area, a totally stubby area receives a default route for *all* traffic bound for destinations outside the area. The RFCs for OSPF do not specify a totally stubby area, but Cisco's implementation of OSPF accommodates this area type. Totally stubby areas accept no routing information other than a single default route. This is a reasonable solution in a Cisco-only shop, where access to all routes outside the area is through a single border router connecting to area 0. A totally stubby area is characterized by the following criteria:

- Advertises summaries of its network links to backbone area 0
- Accepts a default route leading to all networks outside the area

Not-So-Stubby Area (NSSA)

A not-so-stubby area goes the opposite direction from the totally stubby area. This area type is slightly *less* restrictive than a stub area. An NSSA breaks the rules for stub areas by allowing a connection to one or more external networks from within the stub area. An example of the need for an NSSA area would be a branch office that directly connects to another AS, such as an EIGRP system, as shown in Figure 8-25. By configuring the area as NSSA, the networks from the EIGRP domain could be propagated to all routers within the stub area. The special LSAs that carry external routes and circulate only within an NSSA area can even be translated into the external LSAs used by other areas and advertised to area 0. The NSSA is also a good solution for a branch office with its own Internet connection. Don't forget that a rule of thumb for area types is to propagate the least amount of information into an area that still allows for *optimal* routing. The NSSA area type is a viable option when an area only requires the amount of routing information provided to a stub configuration—but hey, it needs an ASBR too. An NSSA is characterized by the following criteria:

- Advertises summaries of its network links to backbone area 0
- Accepts summaries of network links from area 0, which comprise links within area 0 as well as summarized network links area 0 has learned of from other areas
- Accepts a default route from area 0 leading to external networks
- Learns of external networks from a router within the NSSA
- Optionally advertises external networks learned from within the area to area 0

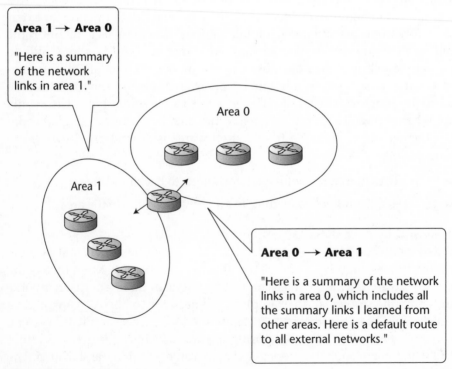

Figure 8-23   Example of a stub area.

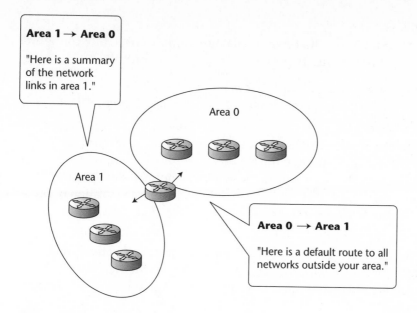

Figure 8-24   Example of a totally stubby area.

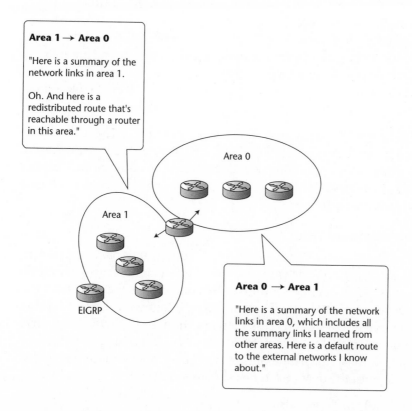

Figure 8-25   Example of a not-so-stubby area.

Router Types

There are four unique roles that routers play in multiple area OSPF configurations, resulting in four router types recognized by the protocol:

- **Internal router:** Has all its interfaces within a single area. The exception is area 0 which has a separate router type designation. *Internal routers maintain a single link-state database for one area.*

- **Area Border Router (ABRs):** Play a very important role in multiple-area systems. They straddle the two areas, bridging them with one interface connected to one area and another interface connected to another area. ABRs is where link-state database summarization occurs, as well as route summarization. *ABRs maintain a link-state database for each connected area.*

- **Backbone router:** A router with at least one interface in area 0. If all interfaces of the router are in area 0, the router is still designated a backbone router, not an internal router, although in common use either term may be used.

- **Autonomous System Boundary Router (ASBR):** A router with at least one interface connecting to a network outside the OSPF autonomous system. ASBRs are responsible for injecting (redistributing) external routes into the OSPF domain. ASBRs may run both OSPF and the native routing protocol of the external system, or in lieu of running another protocol, they may simply be populated with static routes to external destinations. Good design practice suggests that the ASBR be placed in area 0, which all inter-area traffic normally flows through.

Notice in Figure 8-26 that some routers have multiple roles. This drives home the point that router types are *interface*-based as opposed to *router*-based. For example, the router connecting area 1 to area 0 is both an area border router (ABR), since it bridges two areas, and a backbone router, since it has at least one interface in area 0.

Link-State Advertisement Types

In the previous discussion of single area OSPF configurations, two different LSA types were introduced which are carried in Link-State Update (LSU) packets: type 1 (router) LSAs operates within an area and carries the detailed information of a router's link-state database, and type 2 (network) LSAs advertise the routers connected to a multi-access network through the area. LSUs carry four additional common LSA types to handle the advertising of inter-area routes. For completeness, the listing of LSA types from the previous discussion will be repeated, with the new LSA types shown in **bold**:

- Type 1 (Hello) OSPF packets
- Type 2 (Database Description) OSPF packets

- Type 3 (Link-State Request or LSR) OSPF packets
- Type 4 (Link-State Update or LSU) OSPF packets that in turn carry;
  - Type 1 (router) Link-State Advertisements
  - Type 2 (network) Link-State Advertisements
  - **Type 3 (summary) Link-State Advertisements**
  - **Type 4 (ASBR summary) Link-State Advertisements**
  - **Type 5 (external) Link-State Advertisements**
  - **Type 7 (not-so-stubby area external) LSA**
- Type 5 (Link-State Acknowledgement) OSPF packets

Type 3 (Summary) LSA

Summary LSAs are the principle way network links are advertised to other areas. This is where the promise of reduced routing traffic is fulfilled, because only a subset of the information about a network's links that circulate *within* the area is advertised *outside* the area.

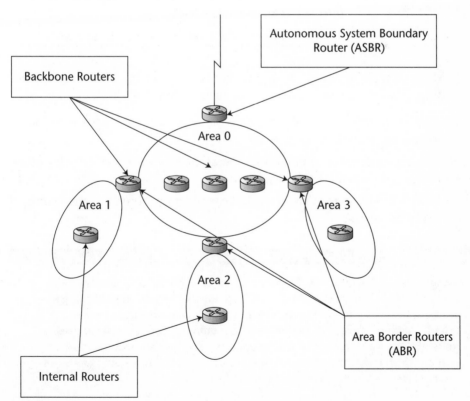

Figure 8-26   OSPF router types. One router can assume multiple roles.

Recall that an intra-area type 2 (router) LSA includes a number of items about a link, including the type of link (point-to-point versus stub network), a link ID, the originating router's interface address, the age of each link, metric, and so on. A type 3 (summary) LSA on the other hand includes only the minimum data needed to identify the route. Table 8-9 illustrates a summary LSA.

Table 8-9   Abbreviated Listing of an LSA Type 3 (Summary) Packet

LSA TYPE 3 PACKET FIELD	DESCRIPTION
IP Header	Identifies payload as an OSPF packet by specifying protocol #89.
OSPF Header	Identifies 1 of 5 types of OSPF packets. This is a type 4 (Link-State Update) OSPF packet.
LSA Header	Identifies 1 of 11 LSA types. This is a type 3 (summary) LSA.
Link-State ID	Network/subnet address being advertised.
Advertising Router	The ABR sourcing the advertisement.
Network Mask	The mask of the network/subnet.
Metric	Cost of the route from the ABR to the advertised network.

Additionally, a summary LSA is not necessarily transmitted for each corresponding network link being advertised. Here's why:

- If redundant paths to the same network exist, only the route with the lowest metric will be advertised.

- If route summarization is configured at the border router, only the summarized network ID will be advertised.

- LSA type 3 packets are also used to carry default routes, representing many networks.

SUMMARY LSA'S VS. ROUTE SUMMARIZATION

Be sure you understand the difference between *summary LSAs* and *route summarization*. Summary LSAs are an OSPF mechanism for advertising an area's networks to another area, whereas route summarization is a more broadly defined process of summarizing a number of contiguously addressed network IDs as a single route. OSPF supports route summarization at the area border, which results in a reduced number of summary LSAs being produced— fewer networks to advertise means fewer type 3 LSAs.

After an area has advertised summary LSAs into area 0, they are flooded throughout the backbone. The ABRs in area 0 then flood the LSAs into all other areas, making everyone aware of the routes. Routers receiving these LSAs do not run the SPF algorithm on the learned networks. As previously mentioned, the routes are simply added to the route table (or not) based on their metric.

Type 4—Autonomous System Boundary Router (ASBR) LSA

The ASBR summary LSA is quite similar to the type 3 (summary) LSA. It also is generated by Area Border Routers and advertised into area 0 and standard areas, but not into any form of stub area. In fact, the type 4 LSA uses the same packet format as the type 3 LSA. The type 4 LSA however, advertises ASBR *routers*, not networks. The advertisement helps routers populate their route tables with optimum paths to external networks. Table 8-10 shows the packet structure of a type 4 LSA.

Table 8-10   Abbreviated Listing of an LSA Type 4 (ASBR) Packet

LSA TYPE 4 PACKET FIELD	DESCRIPTION
IP Header	Identifies payload as an OSPF packet by specifying protocol #89.
OSPF Header	Identifies 1 of 5 types of OSPF packets. This is a type 4 (Link-State Update) OSPF packet.
LSA Header	Identifies 1 of 11 LSA types. This is a type 4 (summary) LSA.
Link-State ID	The router ID of the router being advertised.
Advertising Router	The ABR sourcing the advertisement.
Network Mask	Always set to 0.0.0.0.
Metric	Cost of the route from the ABR of the area to the advertised ASBR.

Type 5—Autonomous System External LSA

If type 4 LSAs only advertise the location of Autonomous System Boundary Routers, how do the external routes learned by ASBRs get propagated? This is handled by type 5 LSAs, which are generated at the ASBRs. In the case of an ASBR attached to area 0, the external routes learned by the ASBR are flooded throughout the backbone via type 5 LSAs. These LSAs are then advertised into standard areas through the ABR, but not into stub areas, which instead receive a default route pointing to the stub area's border router. Table 8-11 shows the packet structure of a type 5 LSA.

Table 8-11   Abbreviated Listing of an LSA Type 5 (AS External) Packet

LSA TYPE 5 PACKET FIELD	DESCRIPTION
IP Header	Identifies payload as an OSPF packet by specifying protocol #89.
OSPF Header	Identifies 1 of 5 types of OSPF packets. This is a type 4 (Link-State Update) OSPF packet.
LSA Header	Identifies 1 of 11 LSA types. This is a type 5 (external) LSA.
Link-State ID	IP network number of external route.
Advertising Router	ASBR advertising the external route.
Network Mask	Network mask of external route.
E-bit	A bit that when set to 0 sets the type of metric to type 1, external path. When set to 1, this sets the type of metric to type 2, external path.
Metric	Cost of route as set at the ASBR.
Forwarding Address	IP address packets bound for the advertised network should be forwarded to.

In a type 5 LSA packet, the link ID is the external route being advertised. As you can see, the mask of the network is advertised as well. To advertise a default route, both fields are set to 0.0.0.0.

The E-bit indicates whether the external path type is type 1 or type 2, which affects how the metric for the route is calculated. Type 2 external paths (the default) only use the metric calculated for the route by the ASBR that learned it—in other words, the cost of the route from the ASBR to the external network. That means all routers in the entire OSPF use the same metric for the route. Type 2 paths are used when the metric to the external network is heavily weighted over the internal cost to reach the ASBR.

Type 1 external paths, on the other hand, include the cost from the sourcing router to the ASBR, *plus* the cost from the ASBR to the external network. This means that the metric will vary for each router within the OSPF autonomous system. The availability of the optional type 1 external path is for flexibility. In certain configurations, the internal cost of the path to the external network will have a bearing on routing decisions if there are multiple paths to the same external network. In that case, the administrator has the option to include the internal cost by configuring the path as external type 1.

Type 7—Not-So-Stubby Area (NSSA) External LSA

Recall that NSSAs are stub areas that allow for an ASBR within the area. The traditional LSA type to propagate external routes is the type 5 (external) LSA. However, the routers in a stub area block type 5 LSAs. Enter the type 7

LSA, which circulates only in not-so-stubby areas, bringing its router's news of external networks available through the locally attached ASBR.

In the event it is desired to share the routes learned by the NSSA ASBR, the type 7 LSAs can be converted to type 5 LSAs at the Area Border Router and advertised into other areas. In fact, this is the default setting. However, this behavior can be inhibited (see the command reference). Table 8-12 dissects the type 7 LSA packet.

Table 8-12   Abbreviated Listing of an LSA Type 7 (NSSA External) Packet

LSA TYPE 7 PACKET FIELD	DESCRIPTION
IP Header	Identifies payload as an OSPF packet by specifying protocol #89.
OSPF Header	Identifies 1 of 5 types of OSPF packets. This is a type 4 (Link-State Update) OSPF packet.
LSA Header	Identifies 1 of 11 LSA types. This is a type 7 (external) LSA.
Link-State ID	IP network number of external route.
Advertising Router	ASBR advertising the external route.
Network Mask	Network mask of external route.
Forwarding Address	ASBR ID.
Metric	Cost of the route; varies according to whether E-bit is set to external type 1 or external type 2.

Summary of Area Types, Router Types, and LSA Types

As you can see from this discussion of area types, router types, and LSA types, these building blocks of OSPF all come together to populate the route table of each router in the autonomous system with accurate, appropriate information about the location of networks within and without the system. But how do you wrap all those extraneous pieces of information into a cohesive, integrated body of practical knowledge that cannot only quiet your mind from attempting to track all that minutiae, but be applied to real world scenarios? That is what "OSPF Operation, Part 2: Tying It All Together" is designed to do. Before that however, we need to wrap up this section with a discussion of OSPF metrics, route table population, route summarization, and some particulars on redistribution and default routing.

OSPF Metrics and Population of Route Tables

In the previous sections that discussed the flooding of LSAs and the synchronization of an area's link-state database, reference was made to the running of the SPF algorithm and population of the route tables. The operation of the Shortest Path First (SPF) algorithm was described on page 286, but little has been said about OSPF metrics and how a route table is actually populated. The SPF algorithm will be revisited here, along with a closer look at route table population now that you have developed some background with the protocol.

Overview

For the sake of perspective, it's worth noting that with distance vector routing protocols, once a router has learned of a route to a network and derived that it has the lowest metric, the route is installed into the route table. OSPF, however, requires an additional step because it does not yet *know* the shortest path to each network. Unlike distance vector routing protocols, which transmit distance information with the route update, OSPF has to come up with the "distance" to each network on its own. This of course is where the Shortest Path First (SPF) algorithm comes in. SPF actually does its work in several phases. It creates the all-important topology map (the shortest path tree), laying out in its mind the location of each router in the area and the networks attached to it. This process is performed in several iterations. For example, the location of the area's routers are mapped out and then the stub networks are added to the tree.

When the tree is complete, the algorithm calculates the shortest, loop-free, path to each network. To accomplish this, SPF calculates each route's complete metric.

At some point, inter-area routes and external routes are added to the tree so that all known networks can be evaluated for inclusion into the route table. As with any routing protocol, the path to each network with the lowest metric is then installed. Redundant routes to the same network may be installed as well, because OSPF is capable of equal cost multi-path routing.

OSPF Metrics

In OSPF, the metric is based on "cost," which in the case of the popular Cisco IOS, is simply the bandwidth of the link. Specifically, cost in the Cisco implementation of OSPF is derived by the formula shown in Figure 8-27.

$$10^8/BW$$

Figure 8-27   Formula for the OSPF metric when the bandwidth is used as the cost.

For example, the bandwidth of Fast Ethernet is 100,000,000 bits per second, so the formula reduces as shown in Figure 8-28.

Table 8-13 shows the cost for some common network transmission speeds.

Table 8-13   OSPF Costs Assigned to Various Media

NETWORK TYPE AND SPEED	COST
Giga Ethernet (1,000,000,000/bps)	.1
Fast Ethernet (100,000,000/bps)	1
FDDI (100,000,000/bps)	1
Ethernet (10,000,000/bps)	10
16M Token Ring (1000/bps)	6
4M Token Ring (1000/bps)	25
T1 (1.544/Mbps)	64
DSO (64/Kbps)	1562
56K (56/Kbps)	1785

There's one "gotcha." Note that the cost of gigabit Ethernet is .1. When OSPF was first implemented, such speeds did not exist. The Cisco IOS, for example, did not recognize a cost less than 1. Starting with Cisco IOS version 11.2, the **auto-cost reference-bandwidth** command was introduced, which allows the formula constant to be altered from 100 to say, 1000, for example. The constant is in million bits per second (bps), so 1000 alters the constant to 1gig/s (see the command reference).

Set the Proper Bandwidth on an Interface

It is important to set the correct bandwidth on serial interfaces when you're running routing protocols that incorporate bandwidth into their metric. As of Cisco IOS version 10.3, the speed of a serial interface is auto-detected and the cost of the link is automatically set. If necessary, the bandwidth of the link can be manually configured with the interface configuration mode **bandwidth** command.

$$100,000,000 / 100,000,000$$
$$1/1$$
$$cost = 1$$

Figure 8-28   Calculating the metric for a Fast Ethernet link.

Altering the Default Metrics of a Route

The **auto-cost reference-bandwidth** and **bandwidth** commands are used to insure the cost of a link is set correctly. However, the cost of a link can be overridden if need be. There are enough various commands in the Cisco IOS affecting routing metrics to warrant listing them all in one place to put them into perspective. Here they are:

- **ip ospf cost:** Used to assign a specific cost to an interface. Can be used in lieu of the **bandwidth** command to override the default cost OSPF automatically applies to an interface. Either command will get the job done, but **ip ospf cost** is more direct, because you simply specify the cost in the command line, rather than specifying a bandwidth value that gets *converted* into a cost value.

- **area default-cost:** Used to alter the metric of a summary route advertised by an **ABR** into a stub area.

- **default-metric:** Used to globally set a default metric for redistributed routes. See Chapter 10 and the redistribution section in this chapter (page 294).

- **redistribute:** with optional keyword **metric x:** Used to alter the metric of a specific external route advertised by an **ASBR** into an OSPF system.

- **default-information originate:** with optional keyword **metric x:** Used to alter the metric of a default route advertised by an **ASBR** into the OSPF system.

As you can see, many of the commands that influence a route's metric relate to redistribution and default routing, and are therefore covered in Chapter 10. A subsequent section in this chapter entitled "Default Routing in OSPF" covers the use of these commands as does the command reference at the end of the chapter.

Running the SPF Algorithm

Figure 8-29 depicts an OSPF network. The SPF algorithm is about to run on router A. Note the following:

- Assume all LAN links are Fast Ethernet (cost = 1).

- Area 1 is advertising a single route—172.16.100.0/20 to area 0. This area's networks have been summarized at the ABR. The /20 prefix includes the range of subnets 172.16.100.0 through 172.16.112.0.

- The ASBR attached to area 0 is advertising an external route into area 0.

- From router A's perspective, there are two paths to reach networks in area 1.

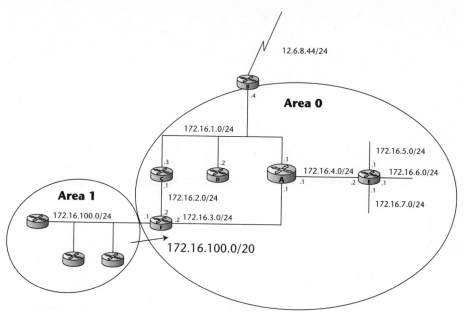

Figure 8-29   Example network for running SPF and building the route table.

Figure 8-30 shows the link-state database on router A before SPF has run (simplified).

Notice the absence of the 172.16.100.0 and 12.6.8.44 networks in the list. The SPF algorithm is initially run only on the link-state database. The inter-area and external routes are included in the tree later as candidates for inclusion in the routing table.

Running SPF

Now the SPF algorithm runs. When it completes all its iterations the resulting shortest path tree is as shown in Figure 8-31.

Router ID 172.16.5.1	(router A) is connected to network 172.16.1.0/24.	The bandwidth is 100mbp/s
Router ID 172.16.5.1	(router A) is connected to network 172.16.3.0/24.	The bandwidth is 100mbp/s
Router ID 172.16.5.1	(router A) is connected to network 172.16.4.0/24.	The bandwidth is 100mbp/s
Router ID 172.16.1.4	(router B) is connected to network 172.16.1.0/24.	The bandwidth is 100mbp/s
Router ID 172.16.2.1	(router C) is connected to network 172.16.1.0/24.	The bandwidth is 100mbp/s
Router ID 172.16.2.1	(router C) is connected to network 172.16.2.0/24.	The bandwidth is 100mbp/s
Router ID 172.16.1.2	(router D) is connected to network 172.16.1.0/24.	The bandwidth is 100mbp/s
Router ID 172.16.7.1	(router E) is connected to network 172.16.4.0/24.	The bandwidth is 100mbp/s
Router ID 172.16.7.1	(router E) is connected to network 172.16.5.0/24.	The bandwidth is 100mbp/s
Router ID 172.16.7.1	(router E) is connected to network172.16.6.0/24.	The bandwidth is 100mbp/s
Router ID 172.16.7.1	(router E) is connected to network 172.16.7.0/24.	The bandwidth is 100mbp/s
Router ID 172.16.100.1	(router F) is connected to network 172.16.2.0/24.	The bandwidth is 100mbp/s
Router ID 172.16.100.1	(router F) is connected to network 172.16.3.0/24.	The bandwidth is 100mbp/s
Router ID 172.16.100.1	(router F) is connected to network 172.16.100.0/20.	The bandwidth is 100mbp/s

Figure 8-30   Router A's link-state database.

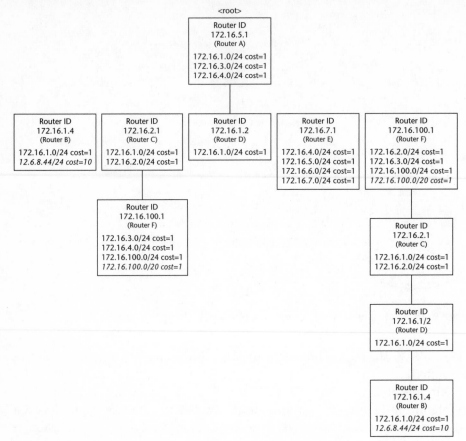

Figure 8-31   Shortest path tree created by the SPF algorithm.

NOTE The inter-area and external networks are now shown, along with their accompanying metrics. They will be included as each route is evaluated for inclusion into the route table. Bear in mind that we are presenting a somewhat simplified view of the SPF process. Detailed information on the SPF algorithm is found in RFC 2328.

Populating the Route Table

With knowledge of every advertised network, the route table can now be built. Populating the route table of OSPF learned routes is similar to how route tables are populated by any routing protocol: by evaluating each route's metric. OSPF adds a couple of twists however. Before a route's *metric* is considered, routes are first categorized according to their sources. For example, OSPF will always give preference to a route learned from within the area as opposed to learned from another area, regardless of the metric. The following subsections explain how it breaks down.

Path Type

Recall that there are six path types reflected in the route table: **Intra-area**, **Inter-Area**, **E1 External**, **E2 External**, **N1 NSSA External**, and **N2 NSSA External**. The first two path types simply denote routes learned internally to the OSPF system. The other four path types all denote externally learned routes. The E1 External/N1 NSSA External path type refers to a route whose metric is made up of both the cost assigned to the external route at the ASBR that learned of the route, *plus* the cost of forwarding the packet between an internal router and the ASBR. The E2 External/N2 NSSA External path type refers to a route whose metric is composed solely of the cost assigned at the ASBR.

NOTE The NSSA path types mimic the two external types, except the designation refers to external routes learned specifically from NSSA areas. An area will have either external routes or NSSA external routes to evaluate, but never both, because NSSA external routes are only found in NSSA areas, and NSSA areas never learn of other external routes directly. Any NSSA external routes advertised into other areas are advertised as external path types, because the type 7 (NSSA) LSA is converted to a type 5 (external) LSA.

Intra-area routes have precedence over any other way a route was learned. Why route a packet out of the area to reach a destination network within the area? Inter-area routes have the next highest priority. This is based on the axiom, "Why trust a route learned from a foreign source over the same route learned of within the OSPF system?"

Path types E1 External and E1 NSSA External have the next order of precedence. These path types are given more weight than their E2 counterparts because the metric includes the internal cost as well as the cost assigned at the system border. In cases where an OSPF system has multiple ASBRs, the composite metric may render more optimal routing.

Destination Type

OSPF also distinguishes between routes to *networks* and routes to *other routers*. Link-state information about the location of ABRs and ASBRs is included in the initial SPF calculation, but only routes to networks are considered at this point.

Installing the Routes

Once the preferred routes have been ranked by path type, the routes are then installed based on the lowest metric. When multiple equal cost routes are installed, OSPF will load-balance among them.

The rubber hits the road in Figure 8-32 as the route table output from router A shows the results of all the work performed by SPF.

```
routerA#show ip route
Codes:   C – connected,  S – static,  I – IGRP,  R – RIP,  M – mobile,  B – BGP
         D – EIGRP,  EX – EIRGP external,  O – OSPF,  IA – OSPF inter area
         N1 – OSPF NSSA external type 1,  N2 – OSPF NSSA external type 2,
         E1 – OSPF external type 1,  E2 – OSPF external type 2,  E – EGP
         i – IS-IS,  L1 – IS-IS level-1,  L2 – IS-IS level 2,  * - candidate default
         U – per-user static route,  o – ODR
         T – traffic engineered route

Gateway of last resort is not set

       172.16.0.0 is variably subnetted, 8 subnets
C         172.16.1.0/24      [0/0] is directly connected, Ethernet0
C         172.16.3.0/24      [0/0] is directly connected, Ethernet2
C         172.16.4.0/24      [0/0] is directly connected, Ethernet1
O         172.16.2.0/24      [110/2] via 172.16.1.3,00:00:30, Ethernet0
O         172.16.2.0/24      [110/2] via 172.16.3.2,00:00:33, Ethemet2
O         172.16.5.0/24      [110/2] via 172.16.4.2,00:00:10, Ethernet1
O         172.16.6.0/24      [110/2] via 172.16.4.2,00:00:10, Ethernet1
O         172.16.7.0/24      [110/2] via 172.16.4.2,00:00:10, Ethemet1
O IA      172.16.100.0/20    [110/2] via 172.16.3.2,00:00:42, Ethernet2
O E2      12.6.8.44/24       [110/10] via 172.16.1.4, 00:00:55, Ethernet0
```

Figure 8-32 Route table output after SPF runs and populates the table.

Let's walk through the entries, to be sure it's clear what's there, and why it's there. The first three route table entries reflect router A's three directly connected networks, thus they are denoted with a C code. The next two entries coded O for OSPF intra-area routes are two equal-cost paths to the 172.16.2.0/24. OSPF will forward roughly equal portions of traffic bound for that network through both links. Note that the metric for both routes is 2, because SPF summed the cost of the links to the network at each outbound interface.

The .5, .6, and .7 intra-area networks are then listed, all with a metric of 2, again reflecting the sum of two links, which were assigned a cost of 1 based on the interface bandwidth.

The 172.16.100.0/20 network shows up in the route table with an intra-area code because the route was learned from a border router with an interface into area 1. The 172.16.100.0 network is of course a summary route, representing the condensed subnet IDs in area 1. Not only does this configuration reduce the number of entries in the route table, all subnets in area 1 were advertised into area 0 with a single, small summary LSA. This is a sign of a wellarchitected OSPF system. The metric of 2 is a sum of the metric advertised by the ABR (router F) plus the cost of the link between router F and router A (the default cost applied to an inter-area summary route is 1).

Finally, the route to the 12.6.8.44 is indicated with the E2 code, indicating its metric is composed simply of the cost assigned to the route at the ASBR (router B). The metric would have been 11 rather than 10 if the path type had been set to E1.

Route Summarization in OSPF

Route summarization is another tool for minimizing the impact of routing updates on the network. The benefits of route summarization were discussed in detail in Chapter 4 beginning on page 119. It is suggested you review that section if you are not up to speed on this topic. The following information is specific to route summarization in OSPF.

Summarizing Inter-Area Networks

OSPF summarizes inter-area networks only at the border of an area. By summarizing network IDs at ABRs, fewer type 3 (summary) LSAs need be created and propagated into other areas.

Although summarized LSAs occur naturally at the area border, summarized routes don't. Routes both within the autonomous system as well as external routes can be summarized, but you must tell OSPF to do so. For Cisco routers, route summarization for *inter-area* networks occurs at **Area Border Routers** (**ABRs**) and is configured at the ABR with the **area-range** command. Route Summarization for *external* networks occurs at **Autonomous System Boundary Routers** (**ASBRs**) and is instead configured at the ASBR with the **summary-address** command. Usage examples of these commands are found in the command reference.

Inter-area networks may be summarized as they are advertised into area 0. Likewise, area 0's networks may be summarized into non-zero areas.[12] It makes sense to do both, but you can perform such summarization only if your network has been addressed with summarization in mind. IP addresses must be assigned in contiguous blocks within an area to take full advantage of summarization. Figure 8-33 illustrates an example of an autonomous system that has been architected for summarization. The non-zero areas are advertising their networks to area 0. Because route summarization has been enabled, only a single network address is being advertised from each area. OSPF, being a fully classless routing protocol, can summarize routes at any bit border.

In Figure 8-34, as area 0 becomes aware of the networks in non-zero areas, it advertises the networks to all other areas in type 3 (summary) LSAs. Since area 0's ABRs have also been configured for route summarization, area 0's own subnets are summarized as well. Note that a maximum of three networks are ever advertised across an area boundary, even though up to 64 or more subnets may exist in the system. Also note that OSPF employs a split-horizon style rule by not advertising a network back to the area it learned the network from.

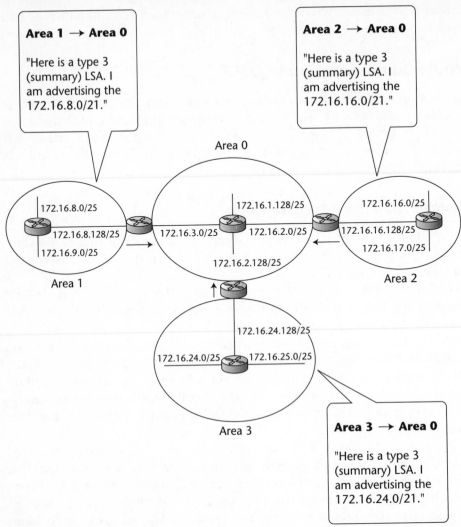

Figure 8-33 Route summarization in an OSPF system—what non-zero areas advertise to area 0.

Summarizing External Networks

Summarization of externally learned networks is configured at the ASBR. Because ASBRs advertise external routes in type 5 (external) LSAs, summarization results in fewer of these type 5 packets being generated. There are two caveats. Rather than summarize external networks, ASBRs can instead be configured to inject a default route into the OSPF autonomous system representing the router's external networks (a default route of course being the ultimate in summarization). In that case, routers within the system simply use the default route to reach external destinations. See the following section on default routing to develop an understanding of when this approach is practical.

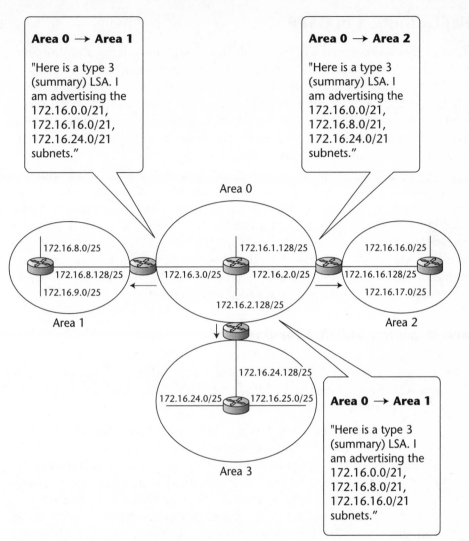

Figure 8-34   Route summarization in an OSPF system—what area 0 advertises to non-zero areas.

Second, to advertise an external route, summarized or not, you must redistribute it. Be aware that when you redistribute external routes, the key word **subnets** must be used with the **redistribute** command, or only classful networks will be advertised. We mention this here because leaving off the **subnets** keyword is not the same as route summarization. Without the subnets keyword, subnets are *dropped* rather than summarized to a classful boundary and advertised. Some treatments of OSPF state that summarization is *on* by default for external routes, when in fact the text is referring to the fact that leaving out the optional keyword **subnets** results in only classful addresses being redistributed. The resulting dropping of routes is not route summarization!

Redistribution in OSPF

Redistribution is covered in Chapter 10. The reason for talking about redistribution in the last chapter of the book is certainly not because the topic has the least importance, but rather because it makes more sense to explore redistribution after the routing protocols themselves have been covered. What is covered in this short section are some caveats regarding redistribution as it applies to OSPF. Naturally, this material will make more sense if you go through the general treatment of redistribution first.

There are special considerations for redistribution with OSPF. As a reminder, redistribution is the process of advertising networks into the autonomous system that were not learned by the native routing protocol. These may be routes learned through another routing protocol, static routes, and even directly connected networks on interfaces not enabled for OSPF. OSPF routers, as with any routing protocol, won't automatically advertise networks that haven't been learned through the OSPF process. Such routes need to be brought into the fold, so to speak. The act of doing that is called *redistribution*.

Redistribution Specifics for OSPF

- The **redistribute** router configuration command is used to advertise non-OSPF routes into an OSPF system. This is the same as with any interior routing protocol.

- The **default-information originate** router configuration command is a special form of the redistribute command used to advertise a **default route** into the OSPF system, in lieu of advertising individual or summarized external routes. The command is entered on a router whose route table is populated with the external routes, causing the default route to be advertised. For routing to be successful, it is mandatory that the router configured with the **default-information originate** command also have a static default route configured. Therefore, the **ip route** command is also used to create the default route (see the command reference for details).

- Redistribution of non-OSPF routes occurs at ASBRs only. Executing the **redistribute** or **default-information originate** command is, in fact, what makes a router an ASBR (along with any other roles it plays).

- Redistributed routes may be propagated throughout the autonomous system in one of three ways:

  1. On a one-for-one basis using the **redistribute** command. Each externally learned network is advertised into the OSPF system.[13]

  2. The external networks also can be summarized before being advertised using a form of the **redistribute** command. Summarization can occur at any bit border.[14]

3. A default route may be propagated that represents the route to the *external networks using the aforementioned* **default-information originate** command.

■ Redistribution can occur between two OSPF systems. OSPF is configured with a process ID, and two completely separate OSPF autonomous systems, with differing process IDs, can redistribute routes to each other.

■ By default, only major network numbers are redistributed: the 170.1.0.0/16 is redistributed, but the 170.1.1.0/24 is not. In order to redistribute subnets of major networks, the **subnets** keyword must be included in the redistribute command.

Assigning a Metric to Redistributed Routes

If left at the defaults, OSPF will advertise redistributed routes with a metric of 20. This behavior can be altered with the same generic commands mentioned in Chapter 10. The **default metric** command can alter the metric OSPF applies to all redistributed routes. Likewise, a metric can be set for a particular route at the time the **redistribute** command is executed, thereby overriding any other metric setting. Finally, a default route generated with the **default-information originate** command can also have a metric applied when the command is executed, again, overriding any default metric.

Default Routing in OSPF

The topic of default routing, like redistribution, is covered in Chapter 10, because the information is easier to digest when you already know a few things about the routing protocol you are interested working with. So, as with redistribution, it's worthwhile studying the general treatment of default routing in Chapter 10, and then come back here and read about the OSPF specifics of default routing.

Default routing has several unique properties when applied to OSPF. Let's briefly summarize them, and then get into the details:

■ Default routes can only be originated on ABRs and ASBRs.

■ Default routes are automatically generated by OSPF for stub areas at the ABR.

■ Static default routes may be created with the **ip route** command, but the **default-information originate** command must also be used to actually advertise (redistribute) the default route to other routers.

DANGER WILL ROBINSON

We repeat the warning from the redistribution section: Redistribution is an advanced topic, and you should review additional material on the subject before messing with it. If redistribution is not deployed properly, suboptimal routing and/or routing loops will occur.

Only ABRs and ASBRs Originate Default Routes

In OSPF, all routes *within an area* are populated into the route table via type 1 (router) LSAs. Therefore, a default route pointing to a network within the area is unnecessary. Therefore, the use of default routing in OSPF is generally to provide a default path *out of the area*, which may be a default route to other networks within the autonomous system and/or to external networks. Therefore, only ABRs and ASBRs originate default routes. (Is that enough *therefores* for you?)

When ASBRs advertise a default route, the route is carried in a type 5 (external) LSA. When ABRs generate a default route into a stub area, the route is instead carried in the same type 3 (summary) LSAs that carry inter-area routes, since stub areas do not accept type 5 (external) LSAs.

OSPF Handles Some Aspects of Default Routing Automatically

The fact is, there may be less of a need to manually configure default routing in OSPF than with other routing protocols. The reason is simple; areas of the network that require a default route can often be configured as some form of stub area, in which case default routes are automatically generated and propagated. Recall that stub and NSSA area types have a default route injected into the area that represents the path to any external network, and totally stubby areas are given a default route that represents the path to *any* network (both inter-area and external). In either case, OSPF automatically injects the default route into the stub area at the ABR without further configuration. After all, summarizing routes external to the area is what the "stub" in stub areas is all about (a default route is a summary route taken to its logical conclusion).

Default Routes for Non-Stub Areas

If there is a need to represent external networks to non-stub areas as a default route (area 0 and/or a standard area), what better place to do so than at the router responsible for redistributing external networks into the OSPF autonomous system—the ASBR. As was pointed out in the previous section on redistribution, a default route is one of three ways to redistribute external routes into an OSPF domain. In certain circumstances, a default route is a preferable solution to advertising a bunch of external networks to the non-stub areas. The question is, as it always is with default routing: Can it be employed without impacting *optimal* routing? In the case of a system with a single ASBR, the answer is usually yes. Externally bound packets would have no other routing choice except to exit through the sole ASBR.

Even if multiple ASBRs are employed, default routing may still be a viable option. If all ASBRs are the same distance to the same set of networks, each ASBR could be configured to propagate a default route rather then redistribute the external routes. Default routes are advertised with a metric, just like any other route, so each router throughout the system would choose the closest ASBR based on the advertised metric for each candidate default route.

Manually Configuring Default Routing

To create a default route in OSPF you use the **ip route** global configuration command. However, even though this command, properly formatted, is enough to propagate a default route in other routing protocols (or in some cases the **redistribute static** command is required), OSPF requires an extra step to have the default route advertised. The **default-information originate** command discussed in the previous section on redistribution must be employed. The **default-information originate** command is used because it forces the router to take on the role of ASBR, and because it provides more configuration options than the **redistribute static** command. The options are as follows:

- Set the metric
- Set the path type (External type 1 or External type 2)
- Set the IS-IS level
- Force the route to remain advertised even if the route is flapping
- Advertise the default route into other routing protocols
- Add a route map

DEFAULT ROUTING AND REDISTRIBUTION GO HAND-IN-HAND

Notice how closely default routing is tied to redistribution. In and of itself, the act of configuring a default route on a single router is performed without any routing protocol. However, if you want that default route to be made available to other routers—you don't want to run around and hand configure the default route on every affected router—then a routing protocol is mandatory, and now we're talkin' redistribution. Therefore, to fully understand default routing means knowing a thing or two about redistribution. This point is underscored in OSPF, which because of its area-based architecture, more closely integrates redistribution and default routing than other interior routing protocols.

Setting the Metric

The **default-information originate** command has an option for manually setting the cost (metric) of a default route. In an OSPF system configured to generate only one default route, the metric has little meaning because any router hearing of only a single default route will accept it. In cases where a router may hear of more than one default route, having the ability to set the metric of the default routes provides the administrator with a means to weigh each redistributed default route so that a router choosing from among multiple candidate default routes will choose the one that provides the optimal path to the destination networks. The default metric is 20.

Setting the Path Type

Here again is an aforementioned tool for fine-tuning how routers will choose from among multiple candidate default routes. Like externally learned routes, default routes can be redistributed as either external type 1 or external type 2 path types. Recall that type 2 external routes include only the cost assigned to the route at the point of redistribution. In that case, the route is advertised to all routers in the OSPF system with the exact same metric. Type 1 routes however, also include the metric from the point of origin (an ABR or ASBR) to the router the default route is advertised to.

The other options of the **default-information originate** command mostly have to do with interaction with other routing protocols and are considered advanced topics that will not be covered in this book. However, the sample configurations in the command reference will cover both inter-area and external default routing scenarios.

Partitioned Areas

When one or more routers within an area lose connectivity to any other router in the area, that area is considered *partitioned*. The severity of a partitioned area depends on whether it is the backbone area (area 0) or a non-zero area.

Partitioning of non-zero areas will not break routing as long as every router can still reach an ABR. OSPF will automatically treat the partitioned area as *two separate areas*. Routing packets between the two disjoined sections of the area will continue by forwarding packets to the backbone and then back into the other partitioned section of the area.

Partitioning of area 0 is more problematic. Because inter-area traffic passes through area 0, a downed link can break routing, as shown in Figure 8-35.

The chances of an area becoming partitioned are mitigated through the use of redundant links. As you can see, area 0 needs redundancy if the system is to be reliable. One option if an area does become partitioned; it can be temporarily repaired through the use of Virtual Links, which are discussed next.

ARE VIRTUAL LINKS GOOD THINGS OR BAD THINGS?

Some texts tend to criticize the idea of using virtual links in an OSPF system. Virtual links are sometimes characterized as something of a fall-back position for a less then ideally architected system. In the example under study, virtual links were definitely a "plan B" when a link went down. But can virtual links be included in a straight-out implementation of OSPF? The designers of OSPF seemed to think so. The RFC for OSPF treats virtual links as a capable tool for dealing with the realities of real world networks. It is sometimes difficult to impossible to physically connect each non-zero area to area 0. That's where a virtual link can help.

Keep in mind that what you are doing with a virtual link is essentially tunneling data through the transit area. Although the area being linked to the backbone through the transit area does not *physically* connect to the backbone, it is *logically* connected and therefore the two-level hierarchical mantra of OSPF design remains intact.

Having said that, configuration of virtual links should be well thought out and employed with care. There are a few limitations. Virtual links are therefore considered an advanced topic and will not be covered further in this book. The appendix will refer you to recommended places to obtain more information.

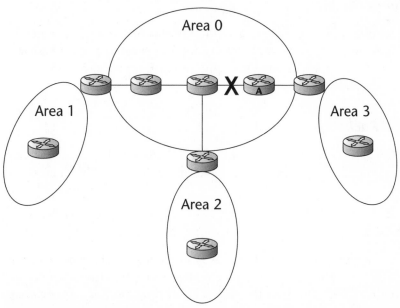

Figure 8-35 A failed link in area 0 has cut area 3 off from area 2, area 1, and part of the backbone.

Virtual Links

Virtual links allow a non-zero area to connect to the backbone via another area. The problem just illustrated in Figure 8-35, where the backbone became partitioned, could be solved if area 3 could connect to the backbone through area 2. In this case, area 2 would be considered a **transit area** for the virtual link.

Conversely, a virtual link can help in the same example by making the backbone contiguous. The networks connected to router A are unreachable through the backbone, but not through area 3. A virtual link could be configured from the backbone through area 2 and area 3 to make the backbone contiguous again.

Options Field

The options field describes a router's capabilities. The field is present in three OSPF packet types: Hello packets, database description packets, and all LSA packets. The value of various bits set in the options field determines how a router will behave in an OSPF routing domain. Some of the more important options bits are described next.

E-bit (Hello Packets)

This option bit defines whether or not a router is part of a stub area. When set to 0, it indicates the router is part of a stub area. If it is set to 1, the router will not accept type 5 (external) LSAs. The value of the E-bit must match for two routers to become neighbors.

N-bit (Hello Packets)

This option bit defines the router as part of an NSSA area. If it is set to 1, the router will send and receive type 7 (NSSA external) LSAs. If the N-bit is set, the E-bit must be 0.

P-bit (NSSA LSAs)

When this option bit is set to 1, it tells the ABR of a not-so-stubby area to translate type 7 (NSSA external) LSAs to type 5 (external) LSAs. This is how routes learned through ASBRs attached to NSSAs are propagated into other areas. The default is to translate the LSAs and advertise the NSSA learned routes.

DC-bit (Hello and LSA Packets)

This is set when a router supports OSPF over demand circuits.

M-bit (Database Description Packets)

This is used to control the flow of database description packets in the exstart state when synchronizing link-state databases.

OSPF Operation, Part 2: Tying It All Together

At this point, you have a grasp of the building blocks of the OSPF protocol. You have been exposed to the protocol's terminology and have seen how area types, router types, and LSA types relate to each other and how they facilitate single and multiple area routing. You have also seen how OSPF metrics work, how route tables are populated, how OSPF summarizes routes, and how redistribution and default routing are handled by the protocol.

Here, a series of examples will be presented that reinforce all those OSPF concepts and solidify your understanding of how the protocol can be put to use in real world scenarios. Following this section is the command reference, which will give you the *how-to* portion of configuring OSPF. A series of examples demonstrating the Cisco IOS commands for implementing a variety of OSPF configurations will be presented.

Designing OSPF Networks

When designing an OSPF network, don't worry about things like choosing which router types and LSA types will be used. You're not going be saying; "Gee, which LSA types do I want to run on my network?" The LSA type used is a function of the router type of a particular interface. Meanwhile, the router type is a function of the area type and the router's position in the area.

A better question with a hierarchical protocol like OSPF is; "How much routing information do I need to propagate to each router in the system to enable optimal routing, and how should the areas be configured to make that so?" Out of that strategic query flows tactical questions like the following: What is the minimum amount of routing information that needs to propagate both within and between the various areas of the network while maintaining optimal routing? Where are my redundant links and how can I best configure OSPF to take advantage of them to avoid partitioned areas, especially through the backbone? Where are the narrow pipes where routing information *must* be minimalized? Where are my stub networks? How many external routes must I propagate throughout the system? Where can I get away with using default routes? How much of an impact by the OSPF routing protocol can various routers handle? Where are the most heavily trafficked areas of the network?

Ultimately, you are deciding how many areas are right for your system and what type they should be. The earlier discussion entitled "To Area or Not to Area" on page 269 should help. Keep in mind that you can alter the area configuration at a later date. If you find that routers and/or links are becoming overwhelmed with route calculations and/or routing traffic, you can split the area. Conversely, areas that turn out to have available overhead for LSA type 1 and type 2 traffic can be reconfigured to join another area. A significant factor lies in whether you are growing a relatively small network, or migrating a larger, mature network away from another routing protocol. Either way, **benchmarking** is indispensable for spotting issues as you implement OSPF. You should know ahead of time what the load on network links, router interfaces, router memory, and related items currently is. Then take periodic readings as you make changes. Be smart. Stay a step ahead of trouble.

When you have an idea of how many areas you need, you then want to determine what *kind* of areas they will be. Here is where we will get into some examples that will clarify the purpose and role of each area type.

Backbone Area

If you're implementing a multiple area system, it's a no-brainer that you will have a backbone area, because you have to. But how big will it be? How many routers will it encompass? Bearing in mind the considerations just mentioned for the size of an area, think about three other factors:

- Consider how all other areas will connect to area 0.
- Consider that all inter-area traffic must pass through area 0.
- Consider placing all or most all ASBRs in area 0—a good central location.

All non-zero areas must connect to area 0. That's the rule; even if the connections are through a virtual link. So area 0 should include the routers that will act as ABRs to straddle into each non-zero area.

Because best practice specifies that traffic passing from one non-zero area to another non-zero area will transit through the backbone area, area 0 must have routers with sufficient CPU and memory to handle both inter-area traffic as well as transient intra-area traffic. Naturally you want to have supersized and/or redundant network links in the backbone as well.

All else being equal, it may be smart to place your ASBRs in area 0, simply because it provides a central location to be reached by the non-zero areas. Of course, external traffic entering and exiting through area 0 must also be considered. Other locations for ASBRs are standard areas and not-so-stubby areas. Figure 8-36 depicts a properly designed area configuration.

The backbone area, like all area types, floods type 1 (router) LSA and type 2 (network) LSA packets within the area. Type 4 (ASBR summary) LSAs, and type 5 (external) LSAs also circulate in area 0, carrying information on external routes, as well as propagating default routes. And of course, area 0 carries transit inter-area traffic.

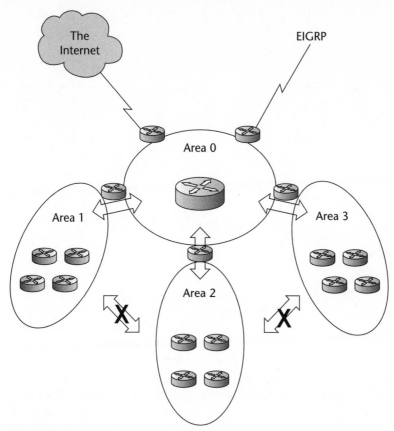

Figure 8-36   In a properly architected system, all inter-area traffic flows through backbone area 0.

Standard Area

Standard areas absorb the most routing information of any non-zero area type. All three intra-area LSA types—type 3 (summary) LSAs, type 4 (ASBR summary) LSAs, and type 5 (external) LSAs—are accepted. Therefore, routers in standard areas learn about all networks within the autonomous system, the location of all ASBRs, and the external routes distributed by ASBRs—or simply a default route representing the non-OSPF routes, depending on how the ASBRs are configured.

A standard area is appropriate when there are multiple paths leading out of the area, and granular routing data is required for both intra-area and external routes in order to make optimal routing decisions. Furthermore, a standard area can contain an ASBR for cases when it is best to have external routes injected directly into a non-zero area, rather than have the external routes be accessed through area 0. Figure 8-37 depicts a typical standard area.

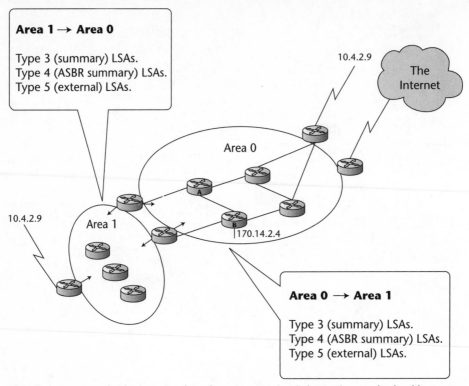

Figure 8-37 Standard areas circulate the same routing information as the backbone area.

Let's assume in the diagram that all links in area 0 have the same bandwidth. Note that there are multiple paths from area 1 to both inter-area and external networks.

In terms of inter-area routing from area 1 to area 0, the path to the 170.14.2.4 in area 0 has a differing metric through router B than through A. Depending on the network configuration within area 1, some routers may have an optimal path through router B, while others may reach the 170.14.2.4 quicker through router A. It is therefore wise to have both ABRs advertise the 170.14.2.4 into area 1. Standard areas allow type 3 (summary) LSAs, so each router in area 1 will have the detailed information they need about how best to reach the 170.14.2.4.

Likewise with external routes. There are two paths to the 10.4.2.9. To provide area 1 with access to the 10.4.2.9 through area 0, area 1 must receive an advertisement for the network. It won't due to simply have the ABRs inject a default route that points to the ASBR connected to the 10.4.2.9, even if it is to be used as a backup if the route to the 10.4.2.9 in area 1 goes down. Why? The ASBR connected to the Internet needs to supply the default route in order to give all networks access to the Internet. The default route propagated by the ABRs connecting to area 1 must point to the Internet ASBR. The route to the 10.4.2.9 must be specifically advertised.

Because standard areas let type 4 (ASBR summary) and type 5 (external) LSAs in, the routers in area 1 can learn about the additional ASBR in area 0 and learn of a path to 10.4.2.9 through it. The route with the shortest path, based on its accumulative metric, will be installed into the route table and optimal routing will ensue. In the event the installed route becomes invalid, the alternate path to 10.4.2.9 will be installed.

Stub Area

Stub areas are more restrictive than standard areas because they don't allow type 4 (ASBR summary) or type 5 (external) LSAs. A stub area can't contain an ASBR because type 4 and type 5 LSAs are literally ignored by routers configured to be a part of a stub area.[15] Such routers accept only types 1, 2, and 3 LSAs. In this case, the only way to propagate external networks into the stub area is with a default route injected at the ABR. Because type 3 (summary) LSAs are allowed into the area, the default route is contained in that LSA type. The default route simply forwards packets to the ABR, which will either itself have a default route pointing to external networks, or its route table will be populated with external routes, depending on how redistribution has been configured at area 0's ASBRs. Figure 8-38 depicts how LSAs circulate in a stub area.

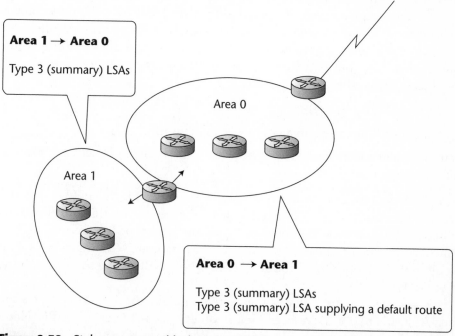

Figure 8-38 Stub area routers block type 4 (ASBR summary) and type 5 (external) LSAs. A default route is injected for external networks.

Stub areas were originally designed for routers with limited resources, particularly memory. If such routers can be located where a default route can represent the path to many networks—preferably optimal paths—stub areas make sense. In fact, any area of the network where optimal routing can ensue when external routes are represented by a default route, are worthy of consideration as a stub area.

Totally Stubby Area

Once you start pondering the stub area in Figure 8-38, it inevitably occurs to you that the default route injected by the ABR could be used as a path for *all* traffic exiting area 1—both external as well as all inter-area traffic. Cisco had the same thought and came up with the totally stubby area, which does just that. The ABR of an area configured as totally stubby will advertise only a default route into the area. All traffic bound for networks outside the area will use the default route.

The model in Figure 8-38 is a great candidate for a totally stubby area because it has a single connection to the backbone. There is simply no need to supply the area with anything but a default route.

The real question if you are a Cisco shop is: How do you know whether to configure an area as stub or totally stubby? For the answer to that question, we present the network model in Figure 8-39.

A stub area is not necessarily restricted to having only a single connection to the backbone. Always remember that the rule of thumb for choosing the area type is to configure as restrictive an area as possible that doesn't inhibit optimal routing. Let's put that rule to work in this example. Note the following about the OSPF system in Figure 8-39:

- There is only one ASBR.
- Each ABR has an equivalent metric to the ASBR.
- The metric from each ABR to any particular network in area 1 is likely to vary.

A totally stubby area would not be the best choice for this network model because the two ABRs don't have the same metrics for reaching destinations within area 0. You *want* the detail provided by those type 3 (summary) LSAs. However, the area need not be configured as standard. Configuring as stub would not sacrifice optimal routing because both ABRs have the same metric to the ASBR.

However, let's assume that some routers in area 1 have a differing cost to each ABR. It's best to have each area 1 router choose the closest ABR. Not a problem. This will happen automatically. With the area configured as a stub, each ABR will advertise a candidate default route. The metric for each route will be the cost of the route from the area 1 router receiving the advertisement to the ABR, which will vary from router to router. Every area 1 router will receive two advertisements for a default route, one from each ABR. The candidate default route with the lowest metric will be chosen. Optimal routing will take place.[16]

Not-So-Stubby Area

Not-so-stubby areas (NSSAs) are the newest area type, introduced to OSPF in 1994 via RFC 1587. It allows the normal rule of "no ASBR in a stub area" to be broken.

Sometimes the network configuration of a group of routers reveals that optimal routing can still occur if the area is configured as stub . . . but . . . you want to have a router within the area connect to one or more external networks. That of course is a no-no with stub and totally stubby areas—the routers will simply ignore the type 5 (external) LSAs generated by an attached ASBR. This situation comes up often with remote locations that have a local Internet connection or connect to another autonomous system for example. You want to benefit from the reduced routing traffic enjoyed by a stub area, but you need an ASBR in the area.

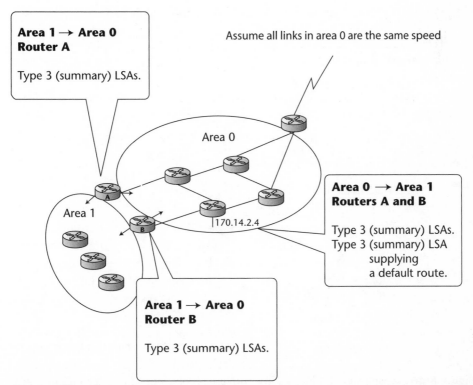

Figure 8-39   Stub areas can have more than one connection to the backbone area.

> ### ONLY THE AREA BORDER ROUTER NEED BE CISCO
>
> **If you are attracted to the idea of a totally stubby area, but are not a fully Cisco shop, bear in mind that only the ABR needs to be a Cisco router. In that case, the routers within the area would be configured as stub (an RFC-sanctioned area type), while only the ABR would be configured as totally stubby. This strategy is easy to understand because the only difference between stub areas and totally stubby areas is with how wide a range of networks are summarized as a default route—and this distinction is only implemented at the ABR. The routers within the area configured simply as stub don't care if they don't receive inter-area routes. (It's not like they're going to revolt or anything.)**

Enter the not-so-stubby area. Like a stub area, an NSSA area allows only type 3 (summary) LSAs into the area, and represents external networks as a default route injected by the ABR. However, unlike stub and totally stubby areas, external routes from a *locally connected* ASBR can be propagated into the area. In this case, the ASBR is configured as NSSA, and special type 7 (NSSA External) LSAs are circulated just within the area.

The routers in the NSSA can either populate their route tables with paths to specific external networks learned by the NSSA ASBR, or the NSSA ASBR can simply inject a default route.[17] Figure 8-40 illustrates an NSSA configuration.

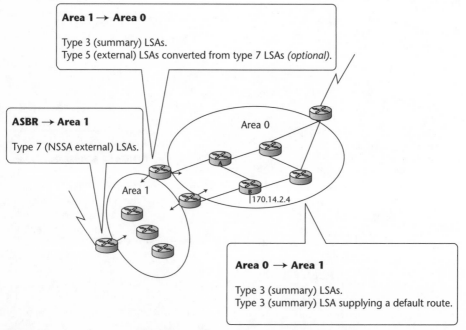

Figure 8-40   Having an ASBR located in a stub area is only possible with an NSSA type.

Propagating an NSSA's External Routes to the Backbone

Type 7 LSAs can never cross an area border. Non-NSSAs areas simply don't understand them. But the ABRs of an NSSA will convert the type 7 (NSSA External) LSAs into type 5 (external) LSAs and advertise the routes into the backbone. In fact, this is the default setting. There are a number of additional configuration options for this very flexible area type that are summarized in the command reference.

Command Reference

This command reference includes not only the specific router commands used to configure OSPF, but narration explaining many of the commands is also provided. A single area network model will be presented first with just the minimum commands required to run OSPF. Then a multi-area model will be configured, again with just the bare bones commands needed to get OSPF up and running. From there, additional OSPF commands will be presented that apply to both single and multi-area configurations.

Single Area Model

Figure 8-41 depicts the network model used for the single area configuration commands.

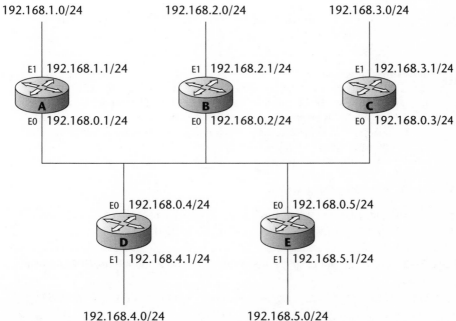

Figure 8-41   Single area model—broadcast, multi-access network.

Initial Configuration—No Routing Protocol Yet

```
routerA#configure terminal
routerA(config)#interface fastethernet 0 (1)
routerA(config-if)#ip address 192.168.0.0 255.255.255.0 (2)
routerA(config-if)#exit (3)
routerA(config)#interface fastethernet 1 (4)
routerA(config-if)#ip address 200.1.1.4 255.255.255.252 (5)
routerA(config-if)#exit
routerA(config)#
```

(1) changes to interface E0.

(2) configures the address for the multi-access network with a /24 prefix.

(3) exits interface mode back to global configuration mode.

(4) changes to interface E1.

(5) configures the address for the stub network with a /24 prefix.

Notes:

- The configuration is the same for routers B-E with obvious adjustments.

- There is no need to set interface speed because LAN interfaces auto-detect correct link speed.

Router Output After Initial Configuration

Figure 8-42 shows how the route tables look before OSPF is configured.

```
routerA#show ip route
Codes:   C – connected,  S – static,  I – IGRP,  R – RIP,  M – mobile,  B – BGP
         D – EIGRP,  EX – EIRGP external,  O – OSPF,  IA – OSPF inter area
         N1 – OSPF NSSA external type 1,  N2 – OSPF NSSA external type 2,  E – EGP
         i – IS-IS,  L1 – IS-IS level-1,  L2 – IS-IS level 2,  * - candidate default
         U – per-user static route, o – ODR
         T – traffic engineered route

Gateway of last resort is not set

C        192.168.1.0   /24 is directly connected, Ethernet1
C        192.168.0.0   /24 is directly connected, Ethernet0
```

Figure 8-42   Router output of single area multi-access network before OSPF is configured.

Configure OSPF (Single Area)

```
routerA(config)#router ospf 1
routerA(config-router)#network 192.168.0.0 0.0.0.255 area 0
routerA(config-router)#network 192.168.1.0 0.0.0.255 area 0

routerB(config)#router ospf 3
routerB(config-router)#network 192.168.0.0  0.0.255.255 area 0

routerC(config)#router ospf 5
routerC(config-router)#network 0.0.0.0  255.255.255.255 area 0

routerD(config)#router ospf 5
routerD(config-router)#network 0.0.0.0  255.255.255.255 area 0

routerE(config)#router ospf 1
routerE(config-router)#network 0.0.0.0  255.255.255.255 area 0
```

Explanation (Single Area)

The OSPF process ID and the **network** command require explanation.

The *router ospf 1* Statement

Unlike IGRP and EIGRP, which use an *autonomous system number*, OSPF uses a *process ID* that simply allows for more than one instance of OSPF to run on a router.[18] The process ID has significance only at the router it is used on, so another router in the same area or system can use a differing process ID. OSPF doesn't care. Differing process IDs are used in the example to illustrate this point.

The *network* Statement

The **network** command is used very differently for OSPF than for other interior routing protocols. Protocols such as EIGRP use only a classful address as the argument to the network command. Any interfaces configured with a subnet within the range of the specified address are automatically enabled for the routing protocol. Remember though that in OSPF, a router can be a member of more than one area within the system. The network command not only enables OSPF on an interface, but it also assigns the interface to an area. For that reason, a more granular method of specifying which interfaces will be assigned to which areas is required.

To accomplish this, OSPF uses an address coupled with an **inverse mask** to define the range of addresses that will determine whether an interface is enabled for OSPF or not, and if so, what area it will join. In effect, 0 bits in the mask dictate that an *exact match* must be made between the respective portion of the interface address and the corresponding portion of the address specified in the network statement. Conversely, 1 bit in the mask simply passes through any value in the corresponding address, thus you will often see the moniker "don't care bits" used to describe 1 bits.[19]

Referring to Figure 8-41, router A had the OSPF process enabled on interface E0 by constructing the first network command to force a specific match on the accompanying address. Notice in the first network statement that the network portion of the address has to have an exact match. In fact, the command syntax is so specific the command had to be issued twice—once for each of the two networks. For the first statement, only the address 192.168.0.x would match. Indeed, when the address on interface E0 is compared to the statement, OSPF is enabled on that interface, the interface is added to area 0, and the 192.168.0.0 network will be advertised. Likewise with the second statement in which the 192.168.1.0 is added to area 0 and advertised.

Because both networks are being added to the same area, it was not necessary to construct such a narrow match that two statements were required. It is simply used to illustrate how the command syntax works. With router B, a shortcut was taken. Because the first two octets of the mask are set to 0, the first two octets of an interface address must match. However, because the second two octets of the mask are set to 255 (all "don't care bits"), the second two octets of the interface address will make a match, regardless of their value. Thus in one statement, both the 192.168.0.0 and 192.168.1.0 are enabled for OSPF on the corresponding interfaces. In this more encompassing version of the network command, any 192.168.x.x subnet would be added to area 0.

With routers C, D, and E, the broadest possible form of the network command was executed. A mask of all "don't care bits" means any interface address will match the statement. Thus, any active interface with an IP address will be made part of area 0 and the corresponding network will be advertised. This is just fine and dandy, as long as there are no router interfaces that need to participate in a different area. Because this is a single area configuration model, all the routers are internal OSPF routers, and the statement can be used without a problem.

Router Output After OSPF Configuration (Single Area)

In Figure 8-43, four additional networks have been discovered by the OSPF process and added to the route table. Because this is a broadcast, multi-access network, the neighbor table will be examined to see who got elected as the Designated Router (see Figure 8-44).

Because the default router priority has not been altered, all routers have a priority of 1 for being elected DR or BDR. Therefore, the DR or BDR will be elected on the basis of the highest router ID (assuming all routers came online at the same time). The highest router ID is based on the highest IP address of any configured interface because no loopback address has been set. The other neighbor table information is discussed later in the section.

```
routerA#show ip route
Codes:   C – connected,  S – static,  I – IGRP,  R – RIP,  M – mobile,  B – BGP
         D – EIGRP,  EX – EIRGP external,  O – OSPF,  IA – OSPF inter area
         N1 – OSPF NSSA external type 1,  N2 – OSPF NSSA external type 2,  E – EGP
         i – IS-IS,  L1 – IS-IS level-1,  L2 – IS-IS level 2,  * - candidate default
         U – per-user static route, o – ODR
         T – traffic engineered route

Gateway of last resort is not set

C        192.168.1.0   /24  [0/0]    is directly connected, Ethernet1
C        192.168.0.0   /24  [0/0]    is directly connected, Ethernet0
O        192.168.2.0   [110/2] via 192.168.0.2,00:01:10, Ethernet0
O        192.168.3.0   [110/2] via 192.168.0.3,00:01:20, Ethernet0
O        192.168.4.0   [110/2] via 192.168.0.4,00:01:25, Ethernet0
O        192.168.5.0   [110/2] via 192.168.0.5,00:01:13, Ethernet0
```

Figure 8-43 Router output after OSPF is configured.

Summary of Single Area Configuration

Although the **network** command appears a little hairy at first, note how few commands were required to configure this network to run OSPF. Without additional configuration, a DR and BDR are elected, the flooding of LSAs occurs, the SPF algorithm runs, the route table is populated, and the system is ready to forward packets. This of course is a best-case scenario. The commands to cover network types that require additional configuration, alter the router ID, router priority, and other optional commands relating to OSPF configuration are shown after the following multi-area configuration is examined.

```
routerA#show ip ospf neighbor

Neighbor ID    Pri   State          Dead Time   Address        Interface
192.168.2.1    1     FULL/DROTHER   00:01:03    192.168.0.2    FastEthernet0
192.168.3.1    1     FULL/DROTHER   00:01:13    192.168.0.3    FastEthernet0
192.168.4.1    1     FULL/BDR       00:01:34    192.168.0.4    FastEthernet0
192.168.5.1    1     FULL/DR        00:01:08    192.168.0.5    FastEthernet0
```

Figure 8-44 Using the **show ip ospf neighbor** statement to see who got elected DR and BDR.

Multi-area Model (Standard Area)

Figure 8-45 depicts the model used for configuring OSPF in a multi-area environment.

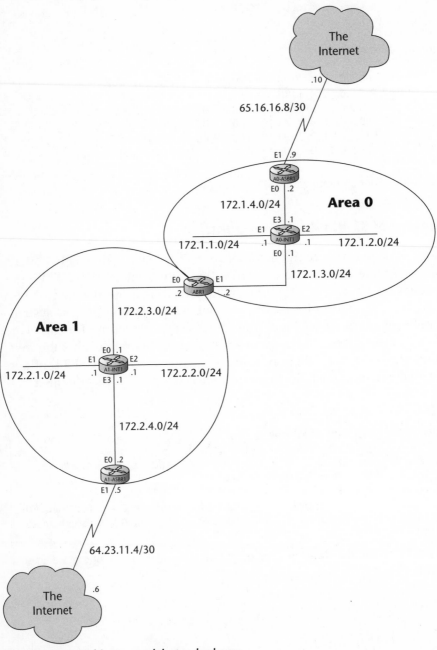

Figure 8-45 Multi-area model, standard area.

Given that there are two ASBRs providing Internet access, and one of the ASBRs is in a non-zero area, a standard area is a wise configuration. An NSSA area is the other option, but let's assume that some of the networks in area 1 are (metrically) closer to the ASBR in area 0. In this case, you want the detailed external routing information that is delivered to a standard area.

Initial Configuration—No Routing Protocol Yet

```
A0-INT1#configure terminal
A0-INT1(config)#interface fastethernet 0/0
A0-INT1(config-if)#ip address 172.1.3.1 255.255.255.0
A0-INT1(config-if)#exit
A0-INT1(config)#interface fastethernet 0/1
A0-INT1(config-if)#ip address 172.1.1.1 255.255.255.0
A0-INT1(config-if)#exit
A0-INT1(config)#interface fastethernet 0/2
A0-INT1(config-if)#exit
A0-INT1(config-if)#ip address 172.1.2.1 255.255.255.0
A0-INT1(config)#interface fastethernet 0/3
A0-INT1(config-if)#exit
A0-INT1(config-if)#ip address 172.1.4.1 255.255.255.0
A0-INT1(config-if)#exit

A0-ASBR1#config term
A0-ASBR1(config)#interface fastethernet 0/0
A0-ASBR1(config-if)#ip address 172.1.4.2 255.255.255.0
A0-ASBR1(config-if)#exit
A0-ASBR1(config)#interface fastethernet 0/1
A0-ASBR1(config-if)#ip address 65.16.16.9 255.255.255.252 (1)
A0-ASBR1(config-if)#exit

A1-INT1#config t
A1-INT1(config)#interface fastethernet 0/0
A1-INT1(config-if)#ip address 172.2.3.1 255.255.255.0
A1-INT1(config-if)#exit
A1-INT1(config)#interface fastethernet 0/1
A1-INT1(config-if)#ip address 172.2.1.1 255.255.255.0
A1-INT1(config-if)#exit
A1-INT1(config)#interface fastethernet 0/2
A1-INT1(config-if)#exit
A1-INT1(config-if)#ip address 172.2.2.1 255.255.255.0
A1-INT1(config)#interface fastethernet 0/3
A1-INT1(config-if)#exit
A1-INT1(config-if)#ip address 172.2.4.1 255.255.255.0
A1-INT1(config-if)#exit

A1-ASBR1#configure terminal
A1-ASBR1(config)#interface fastethernet 0/0
A1-ASBR1(config-if)#ip address 172.2.4.2 255.255.255.0
```

```
A1-ASBR1(config-if)#exit
A1-ASBR1(config)#interface fastethernet 0/1
A1-ASBR1(config-if)#ip address 64.23.11.5 255.255.255.252 (2)
A1-ASBR1(config-if)#exit

ABR1#configure terminal
ABR1(config)#interface fastethernet 0/0
ABR1(config-if)#ip address 172.2.3.2 255.255.255.0
ABR1(config-if)#exit
ABR1(config)#interface fastethernet 0/1
ABR1(config-if)#ip address 172.1.3.2 255.255.255.0
ABR1(config-if)#exit
```

(1) /30 assigned address from ISP.

(2) /30 assigned address from ISP.

As you can see, the initial configuration of all five routers is quite straightforward. Only the IP addresses have been configured on the interfaces, but that is all that's required before configuring OSPF for this particular multi-area model.

Configuring OSPF

```
A0-INT1(config)#router ospf 1
A0-INT1(config-router)#network 172.1.0.0  0.0.255.255 area 0 (1)

A0-ASBR1(config-router)#network 172.1.4.2 0.0.0.0 area 0 (2)
A0-ASBR1(config-router)#default-information originate metric 10 metric-
type 1 (3)
A0-ASBR1(config-router)#exit
A0-ASBR1(config)#ip route 0.0.0.0  0.0.0.0 e1 (4)

A1-INT1(config)#router ospf 1
A1-INT1(config-router)#network 172.2.0.0  0.0.255.255 area 1

A1-ASBR1(config)#router ospf 1
A1-ASBR1(config-router)#network 172.2.4.2 0.0.0.0 area 1
A1-ASBR1(config-router)#default-information originate metric 10 metric-
type 1
A1-ASBR1(config-router)#exit
A1-ASBR1(config)#ip route 0.0.0.0  0.0.0.0 e1

ABR1(config)#router ospf 1
ABR1(config-router)#network 172.2.3.2 0.0.0.0 area 1
ABR1(config-router)#network 172.1.3.2 0.0.0.0 area 0
```

(1) all interfaces configured with subnets of 172.1.x.x join area 0.

(2) only the interface configured with 172.1.4.2 joins area 0.

(3) propagates the default route throughout the OSPF system.

(4) sets a default route pointing to the ISP.

Explanation (Standard Area)

Router A0-INT1

Placing this router in area 0 makes it a backbone router. This is an internal router (all interfaces within the area), so a mask is applied to the network command that assigns all interfaces into area 0.

Router A1-INT1

This is also an internal router, so a mask is applied to the network command that assigns all interfaces into area 1. Notice that nothing special was done to make the area a *standard* area. This happens by default when an area is created with a non-zero number.

Router ABR1

An ABR will always require at least two network statements because one interface will join area 0 and the other interface will join a non-zero area, in this case area 1. A very tight mask was applied to each network statement because there is no need for the mask to encompass more than the single address used at each interface. Notice that no special command was issued to make the router an ABR. This happened automatically by virtue of configuring the router's interfaces into at least two different areas *under the same OSPF process*.

Routers A0-ASBR1 and A1-ASBR1

Routers become ASBRs when a redistribution command is executed. In this case, the special OSPF command for redistributing default routes, **default-information originate**, is what caused the two routers to take on the role of ASBR.

The bigger question is: Why only redistribute a default route and why was the path type (the keyword on the Cisco IOS is *metric-type*) set to type 1 on the command line? Because both routers are connecting to the Internet, the interface facing the ISP is not configured to run a routing protocol. Therefore, there *are* no routes to redistribute. And there needn't be. Well, almost. All that is required is to redistribute a default route on each ASBR. The default route is created with the **ip route** statement and is then redistributed throughout the OSPF system with the **default-information originate** statement.

The path type is set to 1 which is the E1 path type. Having the default route configured as E1 means the metric advertised with the route will increment as the route is advertised through the system. The route will reflect the cost of the additional interfaces traffic must pass through on the way to the ASBR.

Because this system has two ASBRs, it's helpful to use the E1 path type so that each OSPF router can determine the shortest path to the nearest Internet connection (ASBR). Each router will receive two candidate default routes, one from each ASBR. The default route with the lowest metric will be installed. In case the route to the Internet goes down, each router will run SPF again and install the remaining default route.

Router Output After OSPF Configuration

In Figure 8-46, router A0-ASBR1 has learned of all the networks in the system. The only network it is not aware of is 64.23.11.4, which was not advertised. OSPF is not running on the router interface that 64.23.11.4 is connected to, nor was the route redistributed into the system. Router A0-ASBR1 was told about a default route that leads to 64.23.11.4, but it rejected the route because its administrative distance value (110) was higher than the administrative distance of the directly connected default route (0). This is a good opportunity to underscore that a route's *metrics* only apply when comparing routes learned by the same process. In this case, an OSPF learned route was compared to a directly connected network, so administrative distance values were used for the comparison. Finally, note the last entry in the route table. The 0.0.0.0 network is being advertised to other OSPF routers thanks to the **default-information originate** command.

```
AO-ASBR1#show ip route
Codes:   C – connected,  S – static,  I – IGRP,  R – RIP,  M – mobile,  B – BGP
         D – EIGRP,  EX – EIRGP external,  O – OSPF,  IA – OSPF inter area
         N1 – OSPF NSSA external type 1,  N2 – OSPF NSSA external type 2,  E – EGP
         i – IS-IS,  L1 – IS-IS level-1,  L2 – IS-IS level 2,  * - candidate default
         U – per-user static route,  o – ODR
         T – traffic engineered route

Gateway of last resort is 65.16.16.10 to network 0.0.0.0

65.0.0.0 is subnetted, 1 subnets
C        65.16.16.8 is directly connected, Ethernet1
172.1.0.0 is subnetted, 4 subnets
C        172.1.4.0 is directly connected, Ethernet0
O        172.1.1.0 [110/2] via 172.1.4.1,00:02:32, Ethernet0
O        172.1.2.0 [110/2] via 172.1.4.1,00:02:32, Ethernet0
O        172.1.3.0 [110/2] via 172.1.4.1,00:02:32, Ethernet0
172.2.0.0 is subnetted, 4 subnets
O IA     172.2.1.0 [110/4] via 172.1.4.1, 00:02:32, Ethernet0
O IA     172.2.2.0 [110/3] via 172.1.4.1, 00:02:32, Ethernet0
O IA     172.2.3.0 [110/4] via 172.1.4.1, 00:02:32, Ethernet0
O IA     172.2.4.0 [110/4] via 172.1.4.1, 00:02:32, Ethernet0
S* E1    0.0.0.0/0 [0/0] via 65.16.16.10, 00:02:22, Ethernet1
```

Figure 8-46   Router A0-ASBR1 after the SPF algorithm has run.

It's pretty much the same drill for router A1-ASBR1 as shown in Figure 8-47. Of course, the router installed a default route pointing to *its* closest Internet connection, which is through its directly connected interface.

```
A1-ASBR1#show ip route
Codes:   C – connected,  S – static,  I – IGRP,  R – RIP,  M – mobile,  B – BGP
         D – EIGRP,  EX – EIRGP external,  O – OSPF,  IA – OSPF inter area
         N1 – OSPF NSSA external type 1,  N2 – OSPF NSSA external type 2,  E – EGP
         i – IS-IS,  L1 – IS-IS level-1,  L2 – IS-IS level 2,  * - candidate default
         U – per-user static route, o – ODR
         T – traffic engineered route

Gateway of last resort is 64.23.11.6 to network 0.0.0.0

64.0.0.0 is subnetted, 1 subnets
C         64.23.11.4 is directly connected, Ethernet
C         172.2.4.0 is directly connected, Ethernet0
O         172.2.1.0     [110/2] via 172.2.4.1,00:04:10, Ethernet0
O         172.2.2.0     [110/2] via 172.2.4.1,00:04:10, Ethernet0
O         172.2.3.0     [110/2] via 172.2.4.1,00:04:10, Ethernet0
172.1.0.0 is subnetted, 4 subnets
O IA      172.1.1.0     [110/4] via 172.2.4.1, 00:04:50, Ethernet0
O IA      172.1.2.0     [110/4] via 172.2.4.1, 00:04:50, Ethernet0
O IA      172.1.3.0     [110/3] via 172.2.4.1, 00:04:50, Ethernet0
O IA      172.1.4.0     [110/4] via 172.2.4.1, 00:04:50, Ethernet0
S* E1     0.0.0.010     [0/0] via 64.23.11.6, 00:02:22, Ethernet1
```

Figure 8-47   Router A1-ASBR1 after the SPF algorithm has run.

The two internal routers in each area, as depicted by Figures 8-48 and 8-49, now list all networks within the autonomous system. Neither router is aware of the 65.16.16.x networks. Instead, they have each received advertisements indicating the availability of two candidate default routes. Each router has installed the default route closest to it.

The ABR is of course aware of all routes that have been advertised into either area 0 or area 1 as shown in Figure 8-50.

Notice that all subnets of both the 172.1.0.0 and 172.2.0.0 are fully enumerated, not only at the ABR, but throughout the system. No aggregation of routes occurs without additional configuration. The commands to perform route summarization and other commonly used OSPF commands are described after the following stub area configurations are presented.

```
A0-INT1#show ip route
Codes:   C – connected,  S – static,  I – IGRP,  R – RIP,  M – mobile,  B – BGP
         D – EIGRP,  EX – EIRGP external,  O – OSPF,  IA – OSPF inter area
         N1 – OSPF NSSA external type 1,  N2 – OSPF NSSA external type 2,  E – EGP
         i – IS-IS,  L1 – IS-IS level-1,  L2 – IS-IS level 2,  * - candidate default
         U – per-user static route, o – ODR
         T – traffic engineered route

Gateway of last resort is 172.1.4.2 to network 0.0.0.0

172.1.0.0 is subnetted, 4 subnets
C        172.1.1.0 is directly connected, Ethernet1
C        172.1.2.0 is directly connected, Ethernet2
C        172.1.3.0 is directly connected, Ethernet0
C        172.1.4.0 is directly connected, Ethernet3
172.2.0.0 is subnetted, 4 subnets
O IA     172.2.1.0 [110/3] via 172.1.3.2, 00:04:10, Ethernet0
O IA     172.2.2.0 [110/3] via 172.1.3.2, 00:04:10, Ethernet0
O IA     172.2.3.0 [110/2] via 172.1.3.2, 00:04:10, Ethernet0
O IA     172.2.4.0 [110/3] via 172.1.3.2, 00:04:10, Ethernet0
S* E1    0.0.0.0/0 [110/1] via 172.1.4.2, 00:02:22, Ethernet3
```

Figure 8-48   Router A0-INT1 after the SPF algorithm has run.

```
A0-INT1#show ip route
Codes:   C – connected,  S – static,  I – IGRP,  R – RIP,  M – mobile,  B – BGP
         D – EIGRP,  EX – EIRGP external,  O – OSPF,  IA – OSPF inter area
         N1 – OSPF NSSA external type 1,  N2 – OSPF NSSA external type 2,  E – EGP
         i – IS-IS,  L1 – IS-IS level-1,  L2 – IS-IS level 2,  * - candidate default
         U – per-user static route, o – ODR
         T – traffic engineered route

Gateway of last resort is 172.2.4.2 to network 0.0.0.0

172.2.0.0 is subnetted, 4 subnets
C        172.2.1.0  is directly connected, Ethernet1
C        172.2.2.0  is directly connected, Ethernet2
C        172.2.3.0  is directly connected, Ethernet0
C        172.2.4.0  is directly connected, Ethernet3
172.1.0.0 is subnetted, 4 subnets
O IA     172.1.1.0  [110/3] via 172.2.3.2,00:04:10, Ethernet0
O IA     172.1.2.0  [110/3] via 172.2.3.2,00:04:10, Ethernet0
O IA     172.1.3.0  [110/2] via 172.2.3.2,00:04:10, Ethernet0
O IA     172.1.4.0  [110/3] via 172.2.3.2,00:04:10, Ethernet0
S* E1    0.0.0.0/0  [110/1] via 172.2.4.2, 00:02:22,Ethernet3
```

Figure 8-49   Router A1-INT1 after the SPF algorithm has run.

```
ABR1#show ip route
Codes:   C – connected,  S – static,  I – IGRP,  R – RIP,  M – mobile,  B – BGP
         D – EIGRP,  EX – EIRGP external,  O – OSPF,  IA – OSPF inter area
         N1 – OSPF NSSA external type 1,  N2 – OSPF NSSA external type 2,  E – EGP
         i – IS-IS,  L1 – IS-IS level-1,  L2 – IS-IS level 2,  * - candidate default
         U – per-user static route, o – ODR
         T – traffic engineered route

Gateway of last resort is 172.2.3.1 to network 0.0.0.0

172.1.0.0 is subnetted, 4 subnets
C        172.1.3.0  is directly connected, Ethernet1
O        172.1.1.0  [110/1] via 172.1.3.1, 00:04:10, Ethernet1
O        172.1.2.0  [110/1] via 172.1.3.1, 00:04:10, Ethernet1
O        172.1.4.0  [110/1] via 172.1.3.1, 00:04:10, Ethernet1
172.2.0.0 is subnetted, 4 subnets
C        172.2.3.0  is directly connected, Ethernet0
O        172.2.1.0  [110/1] via 172.2.3.1, 00:04:10, Ethernet0
O        172.2.2.0  [110/1] via 172.2.3.1, 00:04:10, Ethernet0
O        172.2.4.0  [110/1] via 172.2.3.1, 00:04:10, Ethernet0
S* E1    0.0.0.0/0  [110/2] via 172.2.3.1, 00:02:22, Ethernet0
```

Figure 8-50   Router ABR1 after the SPF algorithm has run.

Stub Area Configuration

In Figure 8-51, area 1 has no ASBR, so some form of stub configuration for the area may still allow for optimal routing. There are two ASBRs attached to area 0. Because one ASBR provides a path to another autonomous system and a second ASBR provides the Internet connection, the routing solution must include advertising the EIGRP routes into area 0. That way the default route is saved for the ASBR connected to the Internet. The EIGRP routes need not be propagated into area 1 however. Area 1 can live with a default route representing all external networks, with the two ABRs routing externally bound packets appropriately.

The inter-area destinations are a different matter. Because one ABR may have a shorter path to certain area 0 networks compared to the other ABR, it is not wise to configure area 1 as totally stubby. A stub area is the best choice here. External routes will be represented as a default route propagated in a type 3 (summary) LSA, while intra-area routes will be fully enumerated in type 3 (summary) LSAs.

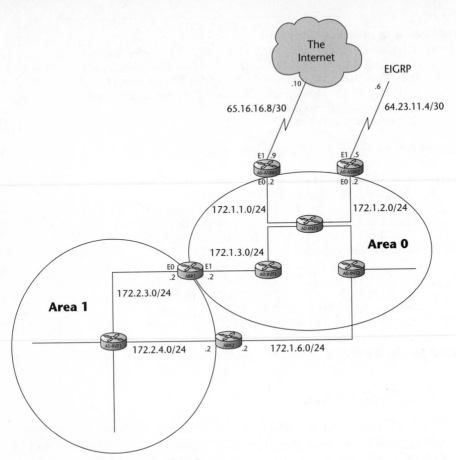

Figure 8-51 Multi-area model, stub area.

Three key configurations must be performed to configure this model:

- Configure A0-ASBR1 to advertise a default route into area 0.
- Configure A0-ASBR2 to advertise the EIGRP routes into area 0.
- Configure area 1 as a stub area.

When configuring an area as any form of stub area (stub, totally stubby, or not-so-stubby), all routers within the area require additional configuration. The following router commands will cover the OSPF configuration for the ASBRs, the ABRs, and the internal area 1 router. All other routers are configured as previously described in this section.

```
A0-ASBR1(config)#router ospf 1
A0-ASBR1(config-router)#network 172.1.1.2 0.0.0.0 area 0
A0-ASBR1(config-router)#default-information originate metric 10
A0-ASBR1(config-router)#exit
A0-ASBR1(config)#ip route 0.0.0.0  0.0.0.0 e1
```

```
A0-ASBR2(config)#router eigrp 100
A0-ASBR2(config-router)#network 64.0.0.0
A0-ASBR2(config-router)#exit
A0-ASBR2(config)#redistribute eigrp 1 metric 10 subnets
A0-ASBR2(config)#router ospf 1
A0-ASBR2(config-router)#network 172.1.2.2 0.0.0.0 area 0

ABR1(config)#router ospf 1
ABR1(config-router)#network 172.1.3.2 0.0.0.0 area 0
ABR1(config-router)#network 172.2.3.2 0.0.0.0 area 1
ABR1(config-router)#area 1 stub

ABR2(config)#router ospf 1
ABR2(config-router)#network 172.1.6.2 0.0.0.0 area 0
ABR2(config-router)#network 172.2.4.2 0.0.0.0 area 1
ABR2(config-router)#area 1 stub

A1-INT1(config)#router ospf 1
A1-INT1(config-router)# network 172.2.0.0 0.0.255.255 area 1
A1-INT1(config-router)#area 1 stub
```

Explanation (Stub Area)

A0-ASBR1

This router has been configured almost exactly as it was in the previous standard area example. A default route is created with the **ip static** command and then redistributed with the **default-information originate** command. The only difference in this case is that the path type (metric-type) has not been specified, leaving is at the default of E2. Because there is only one router advertising a default route, there is no need to include the cost of the route from the internal source router to A0-ASBR1.

A0-ASBR2

This router has the EIGRP routing process enabled with autonomous system number 100 for any interface configured with a subnet of the 65.0.0.0. That's a very wide address range, but there is only one interface on this router that falls under it, so EIGRP gets enabled on E1, and the router starts learning whatever EIGRP routes are being advertised across the link. Meanwhile, interface E0 gets enabled for OSPF, and the EIGRP learned routes are injected into OSPF process 1 with the **redistribute** command. A metric of 10 is assigned to all EIGRP learned routes, the path type is left at the default of E2, and all subnets of any learned routes are advertised with the **subnets** keyword.

ABR1 and ABR2

The **area 1 stub** statement causes a default route to be injected into area 1 that represents the path to all external locations. When packets from area 1 reach either of the ABRs, they will be forwarded to either A0-ASBR1 or A0-ASBR2, depending on the destination address. More specifically, if the ABR's route table does not have an entry for the external address listed in the packet (an EIGRP network), the default route will kick in and forward the packet to the Internet router.

NOTE The *area 1 stub* statement must be executed on all routers within area 1. This action sets the E-bit in the options field of the Hello packet to 0, which causes the router to not accept any type 5 (external) LSAs.

Totally Stubby Area Configuration

In Figure 8-52, area 1 has no ASBR. Some type of stub area should work here and still allow optimal routing. Since there is only one connection to area 0 through ASBR 1, a totally stubby area will work just fine—as long as the ABR supports it. Let's suppose the ABR is a Cisco router, so the area will be configured totally stubby.

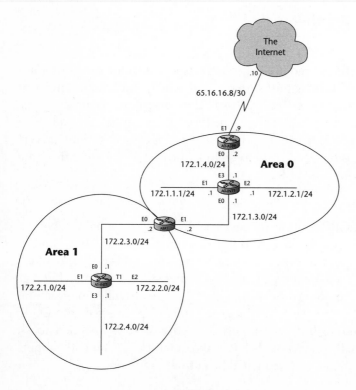

Figure 8-52   Multi-area model, totally stubby area.

The following router commands will cover the OSPF configuration for just the area 1 routers:

```
ABR1(config)#router ospf 1
ABR1(config-router)#network 172.1.3.2 0.0.0.0 area 0
ABR1(config-router)#network 172.2.3.2 0.0.0.0 area 1
ABR1(config-router)#area 1 stub no-summary
A1-INT1(config)#router ospf 1
A1-INT1(config-router)#network 172.2.2.0 0.0.255.255 area 1
A1-INT1(config-router)#area 1 stub
```

Explanation (Totally Stubby Area)

As you can see, all that is required to configure an area as totally stubby is to add the keyword **no-summary** to the stub area statement. (Gee, for all the talk about totally stubby areas, there isn't even a totally stubby command—what a gyp.) The **no-summary** keyword suppresses the advertisements of type 3 (summary) LSAs that normally carry intra-area routes. Instead, just the single type 3 (summary) LSA carrying a default route will be propagated into the area.

Note that only the ABR requires the Cisco proprietary **no-summary** keyword. All other area routers are configured simply as **stub**. This is why only the ABR need be a Cisco router.

Not-So-Stubby Area Configuration

In the version of the multi-area model depicted in Figure 8-53, the simplicity of a default route pointing to the Internet router in area 0 is desirable, but area 1 has a connection to another autonomous system—thereby nixing the idea of a stub or totally stubby configuration for the area. Therefore, the area will be configured as NSSA. The NSSA type permits the benefit of receiving type 3 (summary) LSAs from the ABR, as well as receiving a default route from the ABR that points to external networks, yet also allows the routers within the NSSA to learn of specific external networks from a locally attached ASBR.

The Big Picture for NSSAs

Before digging into the NSSA commands, let's take a step back for a moment. Because of the flexibility of allowing an ASBR to be attached to a stub area, the NSSA type has more configuration options than any other stub area type—for example, there is a *totally stubby* version of an NSSA. Here is a summary of the various configurations possible with the NSSA type:

- Configuration option A
  - ABR advertises type 3 (summary) LSAs into the area.
  - ABR injects a default route into the area.
  - NSSA ASBR advertises specific external networks into the area.

- Configuration option B
  - ABR injects a default route into the area (totally stubby, NSSA).
  - NSSA ASBR advertises specific external networks into the area.

- Configuration option C
  - ABR advertises type 3 (summary) LSAs into the area.
  - ABR injects a default route into the area.
  - NSSA ASBR injects a default route into the area.

- Configuration option D
  - ABR injects a default route into the area (totally stubby, NSSA).
  - NSSA ASBR also injects just a default route into the area.

In addition, any of these configurations may either allow or disallow the propagation of external routes learned by the NSSA ASBR into the backbone. This makes for a very flexible area type. The model shown in Figure 8-52 will be configured according to configuration A. Then just the commands to configure the other NSSA alternatives will be shown.

```
ABR1(config)#router ospf 1
ABR1(config-router)#network 172.1.3.2 0.0.0.0 area 0
ABR1(config-router)#network 172.2.3.2 0.0.0.0 area 1
ABR1(config-router)#area 1 nssa

A1-INT1(config)#router ospf 1
A1-INT1(config-router)#network 172.2.0.0 0.0.255.255 area 1
A1-INT1(config-router)#area 1 nssa

A1-ASBR(config)#router rip
A1-ASBR(config-router)#network 64.0.0.0
A1-ASBR(config-router)#exit
A1-ASBR(config)#router ospf 1
A1-ASBR(config-router)#network 172.2.4.2 0.0.0.0 area 1
A1-ASBR(config-router)#area 1 nssa
A1-ASBR(config-router)#redistribute rip metric 1 metric-type 2 subnets
```

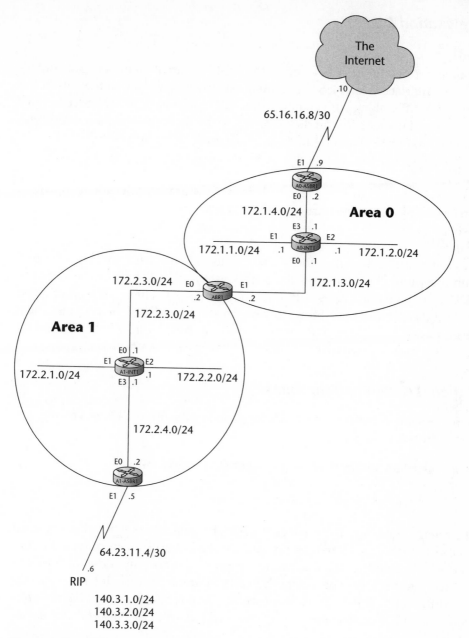

Figure 8-53   Multi-area model, NSSA.

Explanation (NSSA)

ABR1

Of note here is the **nssa** keyword used with the **area** command. All routers with an interface in an NSSA area must use the **area x nssa** statement. In the case of the ABR, along with enabling the ABR to receive type 7 (NSSA external) LSAs, this statement also alerts the router to the fact that it must convert type 7 LSAs into type 5 (external) LSAs, and advertise them into area 0.

A1-INT1

The only thing unique here is the inclusion of the **area x nssa** statement, which is required by all routers participating in the NSSA.

A1-ASBR

This router connects to the other autonomous system, so it must be configured with the protocol running on the other system, which is RIP. The **network 64.0.0.0** statement activates RIP only on interface E1. Then OSPF is activated on E0 and configured as NSSA. However, no type 7 (NSSA External) LSAs will be propagated until the RIP routes are redistributed into the OSPF routing process, which the **redistribute** command takes care of.

Optional NSSA Configurations

Here are some common commands for enacting the optional NSSA configurations alluded to earlier.

Make the NSSA Totally Stubby (Configuration Option B)

```
ABR1(config-router)#area 1 nssa no-summary
```

The **no-summary** keyword makes the ABR behave just as when this keyword is used to make a stub area totally stubby: the advertisement of type 3 (summary) LSAs into the NSSA area are suppressed, and only a default route is injected into the area. The model shown in Figure 8-52, since it has only a single ABR, would benefit from this feature. *Only the ABR requires the **no-summary** keyword in the statement, and of course, the router must support the keyword.*

Make the NSSA ASBR Inject a Default Route in Lieu of Advertising Individual Routes (Configuration Option C)

```
A1-ASBR (config-router)#area 1 nssa default-information originate
A1-ASBR (config-router)#exit
A1-ASBR (config)#ip route 0.0.0.0  0.0.0.0 e1
```

The **area 1 nssa default-information originate** command executed on the ASBR will suppress the propagation of type 7 (NSSA External) LSAs, and instead inject a default route into the NSSA. *The default route must be listed in the route table of the ASBR or no default route will be propagated.*

Make Both the NSSA ASBR and the ABR Inject a Default Route (Configuration Option D)

Note that configuration D is simply a combination of configurations B and C employed on the same NSSA. In this case, two candidate default routes will be injected into the NSSA. Each router in the NSSA will of course install the default route with the lowest advertised metric. This is an unusual configuration, but if both ASBRs in the system connect to the same set of external networks, it might be a viable option. This is yet another example of how flexible OSPF can be.

Suppress the Conversion of Type 7 LSAs to Type 5 LSAs at the Border

The default behavior of an NSSA is to convert all type 7 (NSSA External) LSAs into type 5 (external) LSAs at the Area Border Router and propagate the externally learned networks into the backbone. The generic **summary-address** command, which is used to manually summarize a range of networks, has an option that applies to this situation. If the **summary-address** command is issued with the **not-advertise** keyword (applies to OSPF only), the range of networks in the statement are not advertised into the backbone. The **summary-address** command is therefore executed at the NSSA ABR.

```
ABR1(config)#router ospf 1
ABR1(config-router)#network 172.1.3.2 0.0.0.0 area 0
ABR1(config-router)#network 172.2.3.2 0.0.0.0 area 1
ABR1(config-router)#area 1 nssa
ABR1(config-router)#summary-address 64.0.0.0 0.255.255.255 not-advertise
```

The **summary-address** command uses the same inverse mask that the OSPF **network** command uses. Here, the entire 65.0.0.0 network and its subnets are suppressed from being advertised into area 0.

Suppress Both Type 7 LSAs and a Default Route from Being Propagated From the NSSA ASBR

This final twist in the NSSA configuration arsenal seems a bit strange at first. Why would you want to suppress both type 7 LSAs and a default route at the NSSA ASBR? This concept would be helpful if an NSSA ASBR was doing double-duty as an ABR.

In Figure 8-54, the ASBR, rather than being a separate router attached to some internal NSSA router, is simply an interface of the ABR. In this case, the routers in the NSSA really only need the default route injected by the ABR by virtue of the area being configured NSSA. The default route already being injected into area 1 by the ABR would accurately forward *all* externally bound packets to the ABR, where they would either be sent to the ASBR interface or to the area 0 interface depending on the destination address in the packet. In that case, the ASBR need not propagate type 7 LSAs or a default route into the NSSA. They just aren't needed.

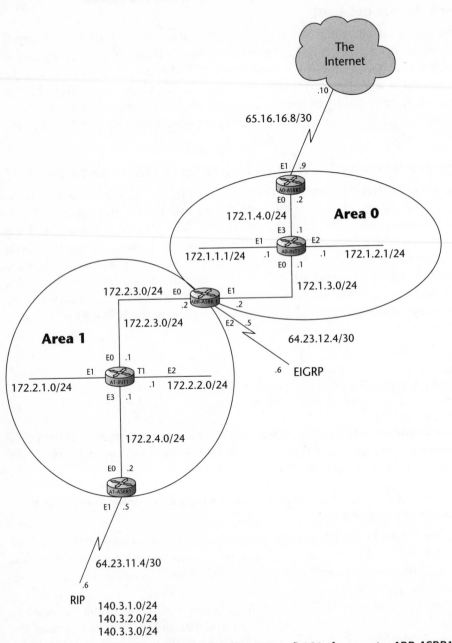

Figure 8-54 NSSA not requiring type 7 (NSSA External) LSAs from router ABR-ASBR1.

Because there is an ASBR hanging directly off area 1 (A1-ASBR1), the area must be configured as NSSA if it is desirous to make it a stub area. Type 7 LSAs are needed from A1-ASBR1, but not from ABR-ASBR1. The syntax of the **area nssa** statement in the following example achieves the desired result:

```
ABR-ASBR1(config)#router rip
ABR-ASBR1(config-router)#network 64.0.0.0
ABR-ASBR1(config-router)#exit
ABR-ASBR1(config)#router ospf 1
ABR-ASBR1(config-router)#redistribute rip metric 1 metric-type 2 subnets
ABR-ASBR1(config-router)#network 172.1.3.2 0.0.0.0 area 0
ABR-ASBR1(config-router)#network 172.2.3.2 0.0.0.0 area 1
ABR-ASBR1(config-router)#area 1 nssa no redistribution
```

ABR-ASBR1 will still propagate type 5 (external) LSAs into area 0, but thanks to the **no redistribution** keyword, the NSSA will not receive type 7 LSAs from this router. If it is desired to also suppress type 3 (summary) LSAs from area 1, the previously discussed **no summary** keyword can be appended to the statement, making it totally stubby (assuming the router vendor supports it), like this:

```
ABR-ASBR1(config-router)#area 1 nssa no redistribution no-summary
```

Now ABR-ASBR1 will advertise nothing into area 1 except a default route. A1-ASBR1 will still advertise external routes into area 1, which will also be advertised into area 0 through the ABR, which will convert type 7 to type 5 LSAs. These could be suppressed of course with the filtering command shown earlier.

Other Common OSPF Commands

Here is a listing of typical OSPF commands. Reference will be made to a previous network diagram when feasible, to help set a context for the usage of the command.

Configuring Inter-area Summarization

The network model previously shown in Figure 8-45 will be used as an example for configuring summarization. Recall that summarization of OSPF routes can only be done at an area border, and that summarization is OFF by default. The route table for A0-INT1 (previously shown in Figure 8-47) lists each network in area 1. The **area x range** statement summarizes inter-area networks, as follows:

```
ABR1(config)#router ospf 1
ABR1(config-router)#area 1 range 172.2.0.0 255.255.0.0
```

The 1 in the statement indicates the area whose routes should be summarized. The address following the **range** keyword specifies the summary address. The mask following the address is a conventional subnet mask that identifies the network portion of the address. Here, all subnets of the 172.2.0.0 (172.2.1.0/24, 172.2.2.0/24, etc.) are summarized as a single address, 172.1.0.0, as shown in Figure 8-55. It will take only a single type 3 (summary) LSA to advertise area 1's networks to area 0.

> **NOTE** Since the entire range of 172.2.0.0 is being summarized in this example, it is assumed that all subnets of 172.2.0.0 are reserved for use in area 1.

Conversely, area 0's routes can also be summarized before they are advertised to area 1, as follows:

```
ABR1(config)#router ospf 1
ABR1(config-router)#area 0 range 172.1.0.0 255.255.0.0
```

Configuring External Summarization

Recall that summarization of external routes can only be done at an ASBR, and that external summarization is OFF by default. In the NSSA model (previously shown in Figure 8-53), some number of RIP routes were injected into the OSPF system. Figure 8-56 shows an example route table in area 0 before external summarization.

```
AO-INT1#show ip route
Codes:  C – connected,  S – static,  I – IGRP,  R – RIP,  M – mobile,  B – BGP
        D – EIGRP,  EX – EIRGP external,  O – OSPF,  IA – OSPF inter area
        N1 – OSPF NSSA external type 1,  N2 – OSPF NSSA external type 2,  E – EGP
        i – IS-IS,  L1 – IS-IS level-1,  L2 – IS-IS level 2,  * - candidate default
        U – per-user static route,  o – ODR
        T – traffic engineered route

Gateway of last resort is 172.1.4.2 to network 0.0.0.0

172.1.0.0 is subnetted, 4 subnets
C        172.1.1.0  is directly connected, Ethernet1
C        172.1.2.0  is directly connected, Ethernet2
C        172.1.3.0  is directly connected, Ethernet0
C        172.1.4.0  is directly connected, Ethernet3
O IA     172.2.0 0  [110/3] via 172.1.3.2, 00:01:05, Ethernet0
S* E1    0.0.0.0/0  [110/1] via 172.1.4.2, 00:01:12, Ethernet3
```

Figure 8-55 Router AO-INT1 after summarization has been configured.

```
A1-INT1#show ip route
Codes:   C – connected,  S – static,  I – IGRP,  R – RIP,  M – mobile,  B – BGP
         D – EIGRP,  EX – EIRGP external,  O – OSPF,  IA – OSPF inter area
         N1 – OSPF NSSA external type 1,  N2 – OSPF NSSA external type 2,  E – EGP
         i – IS-IS,  L1 – IS-IS level-1,  L2 – IS-IS level 2,  * - candidate default
         U – per-user static route,  o – ODR
         T – traffic engineered route

Gateway of last resort is 172.2.3.2 to network 0.0.0.0

172.2.0.0 is subnetted, 4 subnets
C        172.2.1.0  is directly connected, Ethernet1
C        172.2.2.0  is directly connected, Ethernet2
C        172.2.3.0  is directly connected, Ethernet0
C        172.2.4.0  is directly connected, Ethernet3
140.3.0.0 is subnetted, 3 subnets
O E2     140.3.1.0  [120/10] via 172.2.4.2, 00:01:16, Ethernet3
O E2     140.3.2.0  [120/10] via 172.2.4.2, 00:01:16, Ethernet3
O E2     140.3.3.0  [120/10] via 172.2.4.2, 00:01:16, Ethernet3
S* E1    0.0.0.0/0  [110/1] via 172.2.3.2, 00:01:20, Ethernet0
```

Figure 8-56   Router A1-INT1 before external summarization.

Whereas internal route summarization is performed with the **area range** command, external summarization is performed with the **summary-address** command. However, the command is also entered in router configuration mode, and the address/mask syntax is the same. To summarize the external networks in the example, the **summary address** command is added before the routes are redistributed, as follows:

```
A1-ASBR1(config)#router rip
A1-ASBR1(config-router)#network 64.0.0.0
A1-ASBR1(config-router)#exit
A1-ASBR1(config)#router ospf 1
A1-ASBR1(config-router)#network 172.2.4.2 0.0.0.0 area 1
A1-ASBR1(config-router)#area 1 nssa
A1-ASBR1(config-router)#summary-address 150.23.0.0 255.255.0.0
A1-ASBR1(config-router)#redistribute rip metric 1 metric-type 2 subnets
```

Now that A1-ASBR1 is summarizing the external routes before redistributing them, an examination of internal router A1-INT1 reflects the change (see Figure 8-57).

```
AO-INT1#show ip route
Codes:   C – connected,  S – static,  I – IGRP,  R – RIP,  M – mobile,  B – BGP
         D – EIGRP,  EX – EIRGP external,  O – OSPF,  IA – OSPF inter area
         N1 – OSPF NSSA external type 1,  N2 – OSPF NSSA external type 2,  E – EGP
         i – IS-IS,  L1 – IS-IS level-1,  L2 – IS-IS level 2,  * - candidate default
         U – per-user static route, o – ODR
         T – traffic engineered route

Gateway of last resort is 172.2.3.2 to network 0.0.0.0

172.2.0.0 is subnetted, 4 subnets
C        172.2.1.0  is directly connected, Ethernet1
C        172.2.2.0  is directly connected, Ethernet2
C        172.2.3.0  is directly connected, Ethernet0
C        172.2.4.0  is directly connected, Ethernet3
O E2     140.3.0.0 [120/20] via 172.2.4.2, 00:01:34, Ethernet3
S* E1    0.0.0.0/0 [110/1] via 172.2.3.2, 00:01:20, Ethernet0
```

Figure 8-57   Router A1-INT1 after external summarization.

Injecting a Default Route at the ASBR

An ASBR can advertise individual external routes, summarize those routes before advertising them, or simply advertise a default route that represents the path to the external networks. The first two options were covered earlier in this section. Here is how the network model previously shown in Figure 8-51 would be configured to inject a default route at A1-ASBR1:

```
A1-ASBR1(config)#router rip
A1-ASBR1(config-router)#network 64.0.0.0
A1-ASBR1(config-router)#exit
A1-ASBR1(config)#router ospf 1
A1-ASBR1(config-router)#network 172.2.4.2 0.0.0.0 area 1
A1-ASBR1(config-router)#area 1 nssa
A1-ASBR1(config-router)#default-information originate metric 1 metric-
type 1
A1-ASBR1(config-router)#exit
A1-ASBR1(config)# ip route 0.0.0.0  0.0.0.0 64.23.11.5
```

NOTE It should be noted that a default route is only desirable in this model if A1-ASBR1 also provided Internet access. Otherwise, any router installing a default route to A1-ASBR would lose its ability to forward packets to the Internet. So, for the purposes of this example, let's pretend that both ASBRs have Internet access and that both routers are connected to the same RIP network.

The difference in advertising a default route rather than redistributing the RIP learned routes is in simply using the **default-information originate** and **ip route** command rather than the **redistribute** command.

Forcing the Router ID

If a loopback address is configured, it will be used to establish the OSPF Router ID regardless of the value of the LAN/WAN interfaces. It is recommended that you force the Router ID to a specific address by configuring a loopback interface. This results in assured uniformity and continuity of router IDs. Loopback addresses never go down, do not need to be altered if the network addressing is changed, and don't cause the router to retransmit its link-state database if the ID is changed. Here's how to do it:

```
RouterA(config)#interface loopback 0
RouterA(config-if)#ip address 192.168.0.1 255.255.255.0
```

Altering Default Costs

The various ways to alter the cost of routes are referenced on page 286. Here is the syntax to employ the commands referenced in the text.

Interface Bandwidth

The default bandwidth for an interface varies according to media type. To alter the default bandwidth:

```
routerA(config-if)#bandwidth xx (1)
```

where:

(1) x is specified in Kbps.

Media Type Cost

The default cost assigned to a media type is 100. To alter this default cost:

```
routerA(config-if)#auto-cost reference-bandwidth xx (2)
```

where:

(2) x is specified in Mbps.

Interface Cost

There is no predefined default cost assigned to an interface. To directly alter this cost:

```
routerA(config-if)#ip ospf cost x (3)
```

where:

(3) x = 1-65535

Cost of a Summary Route Advertised into a Stub Area

The default cost of a summary route advertised to a stub area is 1. To alter this cost:

```
ABR1(config-router)#area x default-cost y (4)
```

where:

(4) x = area number; y = a value for cost

Cost of Redistributed Routes at an ASBR

The default cost of all redistributed routes at an ASBR varies according to the routing protocol whose metric is being translated. To alter the default cost:

```
ABR1(config)#router rip
ABR1(config-router)#default-metric x (5)
ABR1(config-router)#redistribute ospf 100
```

where:

(5) x = a value for the metric

Cost of a Redistributed Route at an ASBR

To alter the default cost of a single redistributed route at an ASBR:

```
ABR1(config-router)#redistribute rip metric x (6)
```

where:

(6) x = a value for the metric

Cost of a Default Route Advertised by an ASBR

To alter the default cost of a default route advertised by an ASBR:

```
ABR1(config-router)#default-information originate metric 1 (7)
```

where:

(7) x = a value for the metric

Cost of a Default Route Advertised by an ABR

To alter the default cost of a default route advertised by an ABR:

```
ABR1(config)#router ospf 1
ABR1(config-router)#network 10.0.0.0
ABR1(config-router)#area 1 stub
ABR1(config-router)#area 1 default-cost x (8)
```

where:

(8) x = the cost for the area. The default value is 1

Altering Default Timers and Router Priority

Most of the timers in OSPF can be changed, but proceed with caution.

Hello Packet Frequency

The default frequency of Hello packets is 10 or 60 seconds. To alter the default:

```
routerA(config-if)#ip ospf Hello-interval x
```

Interval Before Declaring a Neighbor Dead

The default interval for how long a router waits for Hello packets before declaring a neighbor dead is four times the Hello interval. To alter this default:

```
routerA(config-if)#ip ospf dead-interval x
```

Acknowledgement Wait Time

The default for how long a router waits for an acknowledgement to an LSA before resending it is 5 seconds. To change this default:

```
routerA(config-if)#ip ospf retransmit-interval x
```

Traverse Time

The default estimated time for an LSA to traverse a link is 1 second. To change this default:

```
routerA(config-if)#ip ospf retransmit-delay x
```

OSPF Topology Detection Time

The default delay between when OSPF detects a topology change and begins an SPF calculation is 5 seconds. To change this default:

```
routerA(config-router)#timers spf spf-delay x
```

Minimum Time Between SPF Calculations

The default minimum time between SPF calculations is 10 seconds. To alter this default:

```
routerA(config-router)#timers spf spf-holdtime x
```

DR and BR Election Priority

To alter a router's priority for getting elected as a DR or BDR:

```
routerA(config-if)#ip ospf priority x (9)
```

where:

(9) x = 0-255

Show Commands

OSPF Information

To show general information about an OSPF process:

```
routerA#Show ip ospf x (10)
```

where:

(10) x = process ID

OSPF Process

To show details about the OSPF process on a specific interface:

```
routerA#Show ip ospf interface x (11)
```

where:

(11) x = name of interface, like ethernet 0

Link-State Database

To show the link-state database of a router:

```
routerA#Show ip ospf x y database (12)
```

(12) x = process ID; y = area ID

Neighbor Infomation

To show the neighbor information:

```
routerA#Show ip ospf neighbor
```

ABRs and ASBRs

To show the ABRs and ASBRs a router is aware of:

```
routerA#Show ip ospf border-routers
```

LSAs Requested

To show a list of LSAs that have been requested:

```
routerA#Show ip ospf request-list
```

LSAs Awaiting Acknowledgement

To show a list of transmitted LSAs that are awaiting acknowledgement:

```
routerA#Show ip ospf retransmission-list
```

Summary Address Information

To show a list of all summary address information for an OSPF process:

```
routerA#Show ip ospf summary-list
```

Configured Virtual Links

To show information regarding configured virtual links:

```
routerA#Show ip ospf virtual-links
```

Notes

1. The interior routing protocol IS-IS is similar to OSPF and was developed around the same time. Although IS-IS is not widely used, it is in use on some ISP backbones.

2. When multiple routers interface to a common subnet, LSAs on the subnet are instead forwarded to a single DR, which will then propagate the LSAs to each router sharing the link.

3. OSPF maintains additional tables beyond the ones described here, but the most commonly discussed tables are listed here.

4. The finite state machine was defined in Chapter 7 on page 190.

5. An interesting extension to OSPF to demonstrate its extensibility is a newer class of LSAs termed "opaque" LSAs. See RFC 2370.

6. Due to the sometimes complex nature of configuring OSPF for NBMA, the command reference does cover this advanced topic.

7. A detailed look at the SPF algorithm and the population of the route table will occur in a subsequent section (page 198). The explanation will make the most sense after a full treatment of area types, router types, and LSA types.

8. If the downed DR or BDR comes back online, it is *not* restored to its former role. Elections are only held if a DR or BDR is missing. For those familiar with Windows NT Domain Controllers, the DR and BDR election process works in a similar manner.

9. Cisco routers employ a fifth area type, which will also be discussed.

10. In fact, even a single area configuration requires the numeric designation of the area to be 0. An area can conceivably be linked to area 0 via another area with a technique known as a Virtual Link. This contingency will be covered later.

11. An area can conceivably be logically linked to area 0 via another area with a technique known as a Virtual Link. This contingency will be covered later.

12. Just to be clear, if summarization was not enabled in area 0, any summarized networks it learned of from other areas would remain summarized, but networks within area 0 would not be summarized as they are advertised to other areas.

13. Of course, even if the ASBR is configured with this option, stub areas will receive only a default route. This is by design.

14. Be advised that summarization of non-OSPF routes can occur only at the ASBR. If not initially summarized at the ASBR, such routes will not be summarized at an ABR.

15. The E-bit in the options field of Hello packets is set to 0 when an area is configured as stub, totally stubby, or not-so-stubby.

16. In case there is any confusion about how the external route types 1 (E1) and types 2 (E2) would come into play here, they only affect how the metric would be reported from the ASBR to routers in area 0 and standard areas. ABRs injecting default routes into any form of stub area are unaffected by the setting. The metric an ABR reports to a router within a non-zero area is simply the cost from the ABR to the router receiving the default route.

17. Take care when configuring an NSSA ASBR to inject a default route into an NSSA. By definition, an NSSA will also receive a default route from the ABR. The routers within the area will accept the default route with the lowest metric only. Be sure that you don't accidentally cut the area off from external routes only available through the backbone.

18. OSPF can emulate the function of the autonomous system number by enabling two OSPF processes on the same router, and configuring an interface into each system. The redistribution command is then used to redistribute routes from one system to another. Special care must be taken to avoid routing loops by using distribution lists and the other tools mentioned in the chapter on redistribution.

19. When all "don't care bits" (.255) are used in the mask, the corresponding bits in address for the statement are essentially placeholders, and are set to 0. For example, in the statement `network 192.168.0.0 0.0.255.255 area` x, the third and fourth octets of the address are set to 0, corresponding with the "don't care bits" in the third and fourth octets of the mask.

CHAPTER 9

External Routing Protocols in Brief

Overview

In this chapter, external routing protocols are explored. This class of protocols is generally referred to as Exterior Gateway Protocols (EGPs). The chapter covers the following EGP topics:

Up until now, *Interior* Gateway Protocols have been studied; that is, the routing protocols that run inside an autonomous system. Ultimately however, the many autonomous systems deployed throughout the world need to connect to each other. There's a familiar name for a worldwide network of autonomous systems talking to each other; they call it the Internet. The current External Gateway Protocol (EGP) used to tie the autonomous systems of the Internet together is the Border Gateway Protocol (BGP).

Our coverage of external routing protocols will not be as in-depth as the treatment of the internal routing protocols in previous chapters. Many network engineers may go through their entire IT careers and not deal directly with BGP, because with certain exceptions (as noted later), most organizations don't run BGP. They instead point default routes to their ISPs, which *are* running BGP. The main purpose of this chapter is to contrast exterior routing protocols to their interior counterparts and to give you a general familiarity with the default EGP for Internet routing; BGP. If you require in-depth knowledge of BGP (for industry certification, employment with an ISP, working for a large enterprise that runs BGP, or just general curiosity), you will do well to purchase one of the many books dedicated to BGP. Please don't read this chapter and then apply for a job with your friendly neighborhood ISP stating that you "know BGP." The fact is, you probably need to have more routing experience to configure BGP than any other routing protocol. This is due to the complexity of BGP, the fact that it is manually configured to a much greater degree than other routing protocols, and the impact on the Internet as a whole if BGP is misconfigured.

Internal versus External Routing Protocols

The requirements of an *inter*-autonomous system routing protocol differ significantly from the requirements of an *intra*-autonomous system. While OSPF, EIGRP, or even RIPv2 fulfill the dynamic routing requirements within a company, enterprise, government, or educational institution, these protocols are not engineered to handle the thousands of networks forming the Internet.

Even if an interior routing protocol *could* scale to handle such a number of networks, the current crop of internal routing protocols don't have the traffic shaping features to facilitate routing on the Internet. Routing between autonomous systems is handled by a number of companies, and these organizations participate in the inter-autonomous system routing process through service agreements. Service agreements specify a number of responsibilities, including the specific routing traffic each carrier must handle, which are implemented through *routing policies*. Routing policies involve security filtering and other types of filtering that autonomous systems under the same administrative umbrella don't have to deal with. An external routing protocol used to manage Internet traffic must be designed so that it can be tuned to accommodate the implementation of such routing policies.

Brief History of External Gateway Protocols

Although the Internet of today is composed of thousands of separate autonomous systems, this was not always the case. In ancient times (1980s), when the Internet was still the ARPANET, there was no distinction among autonomous systems. ARPANET at that time was one big internetwork under a single routing administration. A distance vector routing protocol called the Gateway-to-Gateway Protocol (GGP) was used to route traffic. Every router had to maintain a route to every destination network. GGP was basically an interior routing protocol.

As ARPANET grew, it was discovered that GGP was unable to scale in size. In 1982, RFC 827 introduced the concept of dividing the single ARPANET internetwork into a number of *autonomous systems*. The first exterior gateway protocol to tie together these autonomous systems was the Exterior Gateway Protocol or EGP. EGP allowed a group of internetworks to be assigned an **autonomous system number** or **AS number**, which uniquely identified it. Routing between the autonomous systems was handled by EGP. Within an AS, the local administrators were free to employ whatever methods they preferred to route traffic. Initially, GGP was the interior routing protocol of choice, but RIP quickly took over as the defacto interior routing protocol of the time.

Although the deployment of autonomous systems and EGP solved several problems, EGP itself was only a stop-gap to a true external routing protocol. EGP had several limitations. For example, the protocol required manual configuration of all routes and had no native mechanism for determining optimal routes or preventing routing loops. Furthermore, EGP was designed with the assumption that the internetworks it connected were attached to a single backbone. As ARPANET evolved away from a backbone architecture and into the mesh network now known as the Internet (see Figure 9-1), it became clear that a full-blown routing protocol that could scale well, implement routing policies, and prevent routing-loops was required. In 1989, RFC 1105 defined just such a protocol with the first release of BGP. The rest of the history of EGPs is really about the evolution of BGP, whose story is told in the following section.

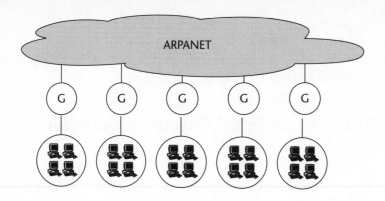

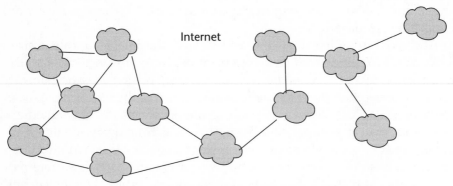

Figure 9-1   The backbone-based ARPANET evolved into the AS-based Internet.

BGP—King of External Routing Protocols

Since its initial deployment in 1989, BGP has proved itself a workable solution for interdomain routing. This section is devoted to helping you understand the architecture of BGP, how it has survived the explosive growth of the Internet, and further clarifying how BGP differs from the popular interior routing protocols RIPv2, EIGRP, and of course the recommended IGP for the Internet, OSPF.

BGP Backgrounder

BGP is now the principal routing protocol used to connect autonomous systems across the Internet. The protocol has been updated several times since its initial release in 1989 as an experimental protocol. The current version is BGP-4, released as RFC 1771 in 1995.[1] Among several changes in version 4 was full support for CIDR. Table 9-1 shows the basic characteristics of BGP.

Table 9-1 Routing Characteristics of BGP

Metric	Composite metric
Interior or Exterior?	Exterior
Distance vector or Link-state?	Path vector
Singlepath or Multipath?	Singlepath[2]
Broadcast or Multicast?	Multicast
Flat or Hierarchical?	Hierarchical[3]
Classful or Classless?	Classless (BGP-4)

When to Use BGP

BGP is an inter-autonomous system routing protocol, so its primary use is by the companies that facilitate inter-autonomous system routing; that being ISPs. As has been pointed out many times throughout this book, most organizations connect to an ISP and simply employ default routing to forward packets bound for another autonomous system. There are exceptions however. Some organizations do run BGP. This mostly occurs when the organization utilizes more than one ISP and BGP allows them to configure redundant links for auto-failover as shown in Figure 9-2.

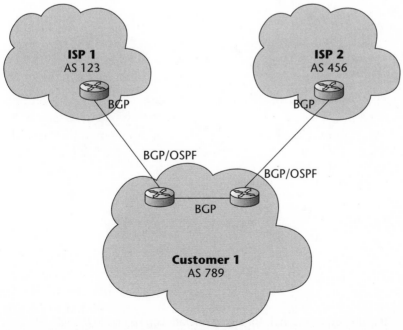

Figure 9-2 Some companies may use BGP if they connect to multiple ISPs.

On the other hand, if a company is simply multi-homing to a single ISP for redundancy as shown in Figure 9-3, BGP is not necessary.

Other Uses for BGP

Another possible use for BGP is by a multi-national organization wishing to tie together geographically dispersed segments of their business. The company may assume that there would be something to gain by breaking up the inter-network into multiple autonomous systems and using BGP to route between the ASs. This has been done, but you should also be aware that OSPF is a capable contender for very large networks, configured as either a single AS or as multiple ASs redistributing routes to each other. We will not go into a full comparison of the two approaches here, except to note that BGP is a complex enough protocol that it might be wise to consider it the *last* solution as opposed to the *first* solution for solving routing problems.

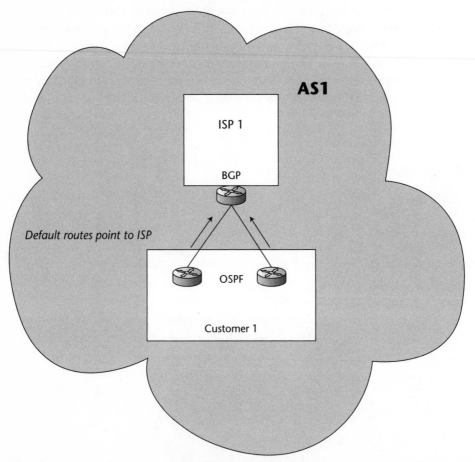

Figure 9-3 BGP is not required simply for a fault tolerant connection to a single ISP.

How BGP Works

As has been alluded to, BGP operates quite differently from interior routing protocols. BGP is considered a **path vector** routing protocol. What does that mean? BGP is actually a distance vector protocol in that BGP routers advertise *routes*, not *network links* as OSPF does. However, BGP does not use the typical distance vector methods of route selection such as bandwidth, hop count, delay, and so on. Instead, BGP keeps the full path to a destination by maintaining a list of autonomous systems that packets must pass through to reach a target network. Thus the moniker: *path vector* routing protocol.

In lieu of conventional metrics, BGP applies a variety of **attributes** to each route it learns. The purpose of attributes is to allow **routing policies** to be implemented. Routing policies allow control over what routing prefixes are distributed between interconnected ISPs and between ISPs and their customers. This feature allows BGP to be deterministic; meaning an administrator can exert granular control over what routes are accepted or rejected, and set a preference of one route over another to a particular network. Routing policies are the name of the game in interdomain routing. There are many players that take part in routing on the Internet, and the various companies such as Sprint and MCI create service agreements with each other that are implemented through routing policies. It is the ability to shape traffic through path attributes that is at the core of what makes BGP so different from interior routing protocols. It is not uncommon for a policy file to be several thousand lines long in a backbone ISP.

BGP Terminology

BGP has some unique terminology associated with it. Some of the terms refer to characteristics unique to BGP, while other terms are simply new names for a feature present in other routing protocols.

BGP Router Roles: Speakers, Peers, and Border Gateways

Any router configured to run BGP takes on the role of BGP **speaker**. The router advertises, or *speaks*, the routes it is aware of. BGP speakers that form a connection with each other for the purpose of exchanging routing information are known as BGP **peers**. BGP speakers that form peer relationships with BGP speakers in other autonomous systems take on the additional role of BGP **border gateway** routers.

ROUTING PROTOCOLS VS. AUTOMOBILES
If you were to compare routing protocols to cars, then you might say that RIPv2 is like an old, well maintained VW bus; it will get you from point A to point B, but it doesn't keep up well on the big Interstates. OSPF is like a Honda Civic; very well engineered and quite economical. On the other hand, BGP is kind of like a formula race car; you can tune every aspect of such a vehicle from carburetion, to gearing, to suspension setup. BGP has the right stuff for fine-tuning inter-autonomous system routing.

EBGP and IBGP (External BGP and Internal BGP)

BGP operates in two distinct modes. When communicating between autonomous systems, External BGP (EBGP) is used. Within an AS, BGP enabled routers use Internal BGP (IBGP) to communicate. The differences between the two modes of operation are few, but important. For example, routes learned through IBGP have preference over the same routes learned from EBGP. This is somewhat analogous to OSPF areas, where a route learned from within the area is preferred over the same route learned from either another area or external to the system. Subsequent examples will illustrate other differences.

NLRI (Network Layer Reachability Information)

The NLRI refers to the IP prefix (i.e. 17.2.3) and prefix length (i.e. /24) of each route being advertised by a BGP speaker.

Path Attributes

Every route advertised in BGP has a number of attributes, or *path* attributes, associated with it. A route's attributes are critical to conveying and applying routing policies, and are discussed further in this chapter.

RIB (Routing Information Base)

BGP keeps routing information in a database known as the RIB, or Routing Information Base. The RIB has three parts, which may be stored in a single database, or three separate databases, depending on the vendor's implementation of BGP.

Raw routing information received by a BGP speaker is stored in an information base known as Adj-RIBs-In (Adjacent Routing Information Base In). This is a listing of all routes the BGP speaker is aware of, and are referred to as **feasible routes**.

Routes in Adj-RIBs-In are processed by applying the routing policies to each route. This results in the route table used by BGP, known as the Loc-RIB (Local RIB).

Finally, routes chosen to be advertised to a BGP speaker's peers are stored in Adj-RIBs-Out (Adjacent RIB Out). This is where any aggregation of routes occurs (BGP prefers the term *aggregation* over *summarization*).

BGP Confederations

BGP confederations allow a single AS to be broken into smaller ASs. Confederations were introduced well after the first BGP RFC was published to solve a problem whereby the protocol did not scale well in large autonomous systems (the current RFC for BGP Confederations is 3065).

The scaling problem of BGP results from the fact that every BGP speaker within an autonomous system must form a peer relationship with every other BGP speaker. A direct connection to every speaker is not required, but a full mesh of every BGP speaker in the AS is. With confederations, a full mesh is created within the confederation, not to each speaker within the confederation. Each confederation must then be able to reach every other confederation.

BGP Path Attributes

Integral to BGP are path attributes. Every route known to BGP has a set of attributes associated with it that are passed along with the route. Path attributes convey routing information, but just as important, they also convey routing policies.

AS_PATH

The AS_PATH attribute is utilized by EBGP for interdomain routing. The attribute contains the full path to the destination network (see Figure 9-4). That's a rather surprising statement, because interior routing protocols normally do no such thing (although OSPF certainly knows the full path to a destination within an area via its topology table). However, this is a list of autonomous system IDs, not network IDs. At a glance, this would appear to be source routing, but in fact traffic may or may not pass through the ASs specified in the attribute, depending on routing policies and other factors. Rather, the AS_PATH attribute is BGP's mechanism for preventing routing-loops. If a BGP router receives a routing update that includes its own AS number in the AS_PATH attribute, it knows that accepting the route would create a loop and the update is therefore rejected.

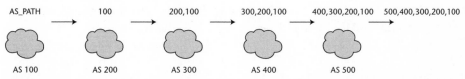

Figure 9-4 As a route is advertised, it accumulates a list of autonomous systems the advertisement has passed through.

NEXT_HOP

The NEXT_HOP attribute specifies the IP address that packets should be forwarded to. Naturally the value of this attribute will be updated each time the route is advertised. The specified address will normally be the interface of the router the route was learned from, but in the case of two IBGP routers exchanging a route within another AS, the address will be the interface of the EBGP router the route was learned from.

ORIGIN

The ORIGIN attribute is one of several attributes used to evaluate which route to use for forwarding traffic to a particular network. Three possible values exist: IGP, EGP, and Incomplete. If the value of the ORIGIN attribute is IGP, it means the route was learned from an interior routing protocol, and the route therefore is contained within the local AS. Such routes get a higher preference than routes with an ORIGIN attribute of EGP or Incomplete. A value of EGP for the ORIGIN attribute indicates the route was learned from an EBGP router (learned from another AS) and has the next highest precedence for route selection. Finally, a value of Incomplete means that the origin of the route is unknown, such as a redistributed route, and thus has the lowest precedence.

MULTI_EXIT_DISC

MULTI_EXIT_DISC, as in Multiple Exit Discriminator (MED), is an optional attribute that can be used by EBGP speakers to tell another AS which path to use when there are multiple links between the ASs. The MULTI_EXIT_DISC attribute basically acts as a metric to set a preference for one path over another. The attribute can be set to a particular value for routes advertised across one link and set to another value for routes advertised over a redundant link. The corresponding AS will then send traffic to the originating AS over the link where the routes with the lowest-value MULTI_EXIT_DISC attribute were learned. Keep in mind that like any attribute, MULTI_EXIT_DISC can be applied to a single route or a group of routes.

Also note that although the MED is a way for one autonomous system to suggest to another autonomous system how to route traffic, it is only a suggestion. For example, if an ISP used the MED to say, tell another ISP to send west-coast traffic through a west-coast interconnect and east-coast traffic through an east-coast interconnect, no ISP would accept such a command because it lets a competitor say how traffic flows within the ISPs network. Rather, MEDs are generally used when an ISP has two routers on the same LAN as another ISP to tell the other ISP which of the two routers to use.

LOCAL_PREF

The LOCAL_PREF attribute is an optional attribute used only within an AS (IBGP). Like MULTI_EXIT_DISC, the value can be manually set to prefer one path to a destination over a different path to the same destination. Although LOCAL_PREF is only used internally, it can be applied to both internal routes as well as routes to networks in other ASs.

ATOMIC_AGGREGATE and AGGREGATOR

The ATOMIC_AGGREGATE attribute is active when a route to be advertised has been summarized (aggregated). The presence of this attribute indicates to downstream BGP routers that the route has been aggregated and should not be de-aggregated. The AGGREGATOR attribute is used to indicate which autonomous system and which router performed the aggregation.

COMMUNITY

The BGP COMMUNITY attribute is a handy little tool for simplifying the application of routing policies. It provides a means of applying an attribute to a group, or *community* of routes, rather than set the attribute on each route.

The Autonomous System Revisited

BGP connects autonomous systems together, so it's important to understand exactly what an autonomous system is. In relation to interior routing protocols, an autonomous system is often defined as a collection of networks under common administrative control. Quite often a single organization, like say WidgetCO, is considered an autonomous system regardless of how large or small it is.

In relation to EGPs though, a more precise definition of autonomous system is encountered: a collection of networks under common administrative control *and sharing a common routing strategy*. The latter part of the definition is critical with BGP. The administrator of an autonomous system takes on the responsibility of employing a routing strategy (vis-à-vis routing policies) that encompass all networks the AS may come to learn of. In the world of EGPs, an AS is usually an ISP, and can include more than a single organization, as illustrated in Figure 9-5. Each ISP forming an AS is responsible for routing to and from its customers and may also be required to route transit traffic passing through to other autonomous systems.

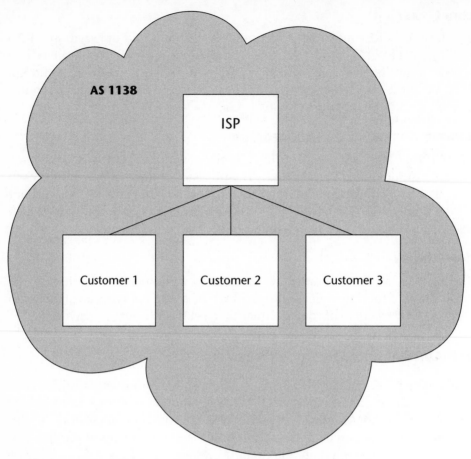

Figure 9-5   Many companies may come under the umbrella of a single AS.

Autonomous System Numbering[4]

Just as IP networks must be identified by a unique IP address, autonomous systems running BGP must be identified by a unique **AS number (ASN)**. The same assigning authority that allocates IP addresses allocates autonomous system numbers. In America for example, the authority is ARIN. Autonomous system numbers are 16-bit numbers ranging from 1–65535.

The numbers 1–64511 are designated as public ASNs. Any autonomous system connecting to the Internet core must have a public ASN. The numbers 64512–65535 are designated as private ASNs, and may be used for various purposes such as private peering between two ISPs, but can never be used on the public Internet. There is work in progress to double the size of the ASN number allocation, because over half of the public pool has been exhausted.

NOTE Every IP subnet used within an autonomous system must be associated with the ASN assigned.

BGP Peer Sessions

BGP operates by BGP-enabled routers forming *peer* relationships with other BGP routers, through which *network reachability* information is exchanged. This is the Network Layer Reachability Information (NLRI) for each route, which is composed of the IP prefix ID and length, along with the attributes for the route. A BGP router may have a peer relationship with one or more BGP speaking routers.

Routing neighbors are not discovered automatically in BGP. Each pair of BGP speakers that will exchange routing information must be configured by hand. This is by design. Peer relationships are only established between organizations doing business with one another.

Peer sessions between BGP speakers commence with the opening of a TCP connection between the routers. Unlike OSPF, which uses its own proprietary mechanism for assured delivery, BGP relies on TCP for reliable communications. TCP sessions use port 179. Upon initialization of a TCP session, a pair of BGP speakers exchange the entire contents of their Adj-RIBs-Out database. After that, only updates are sent, and then only when the contents of Adj-RIBs-Out changes (known as triggered updates). The TCP session stays open with keep-alive packets. If the connection is terminated, the initialization process starts over.

NOTE Like conventional distance vector routing protocols, BGP uses split horizon. Routes learned through an interface are not advertised out the same interface.

BGP Path Determination (Decision Process)

Because BGP does not incorporate the traditional metrics of interior routing protocols, how is one route selected over another when there are multiple paths to the same network? This is one place where routing policies come in. BGP stores all learned routes and their attributes in Adj-RIBs-In. This is raw, unprocessed routing data. Routes to be installed and/or advertised go through a three-part process as described next.

Three-Phase Decision Process

The three-phase decision process is described in this section.

Phase 1: Calculate the degree of preference for each route in Adj-RIBs-In

For routes learned from an *internal* peer, the degree of preference is calculated based on policy information, or in lieu of a policy the preference is calculated based on the LOCAL_PREF attribute. For routes learned from an *external* peer, the degree of preference is calculated strictly based on policy information. This process returns a set of **feasible** routes that are acted on in phase 2.

Phase 2: Install the best route to each destination into Loc-RIB

Each feasible route is first checked to see if the next hop router specified in the NEXT_HOP attribute is reachable. If the next hop is not reachable the route is dropped. Then the AS_PATH variable is checked to be sure the route is not looped. Qualified routes are then installed to Loc-RIB based on the following criteria:

- If there is only one route to a particular destination, it is installed into Loc-RIB.

- For multiple routes to the same destination, install the route with the highest degree of preference as calculated in phase 1.

- For each instance where multiple routes to the same destination remain (because they have the same degree of preference), a set of tie-breaking rules are engaged. The algorithm iterates through a series of steps that eliminates routes. The algorithm terminates when only one route to the destination remains.

    - **Shortest AS path:** Select the route with the smallest value for the AS_PATH attribute and eliminate all other routes. If more than one route has the same smallest value, continue the tie-breaking process.

    - **Origin number:** Select the route with the smallest value for the ORIGIN attribute and eliminate all other routes. If more than one route has the smallest value, continue the tie-breaking process.

    - **MULTI_EXIT_DISC:** Select the route with the smallest value for the MED attribute and eliminate all other routes. If more than one route has the smallest value, continue the tie-breaking process.

    - **EBGP versus IBGP:** If at least one of the candidate routes was received via EBGP, remove from consideration all routes that were received via IBGP. If more than one route has the smallest value, continue the tie-breaking process.

    - **Interior cost:** Select the route with the smallest metric based on the cost of reaching the next hop and eliminate all other routes. If more than one route has the smallest metric, continue the tie-breaking process.

    - **BGP identifier:** Select the route with the lowest BGP identifier, and eliminate all other routes. If more than one route has the lowest BGP identifier, continue the tie-breaking process.

    - **IP address:** Eliminate all routes except the one with the lowest peer IP address.

Phase 3: Route dissemination

Select which routes in Loc-RIB will be advertised. This selection process is based on configured routing policy. Any configured route aggregation also takes place here.

Decision Process Wrap Up

Vendor specific implementations of BGP may employ additional attributes or even add options to the decision process. For example, the Cisco IOS allows multiple routes to be installed into Loc-RIB. Cisco also adds a WEIGHT attribute that allows an administrator to easily force one route to be selected over another.

Sample BGP System

Figure 9-6 illustrates a slice of a BGP system as it fits into the hierarchy of the Internet.

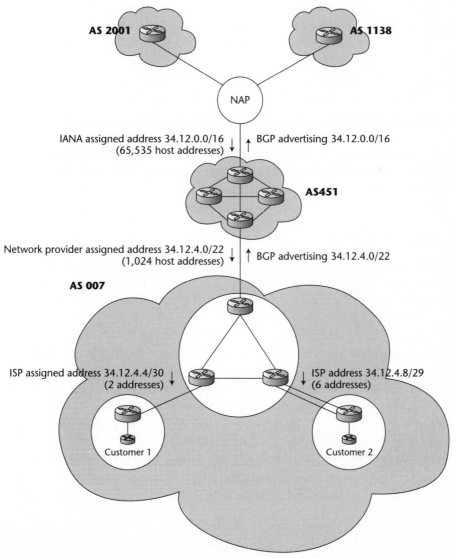

Figure 9-6   The big picture of BGP operation.

Note the following about Figure 9-6:

- Starting at the top, three autonomous systems running BGP are connecting to the core of the Internet at a Network Access Point (NAP). Each AS is public peering with each other AS and exchanging routes through EBGP.

- Network provider AS 451 is private-peering with AS 007, a local ISP, again exchanging routes via EBGP.

- All the autonomous systems are using IBGP internally to propagate routes learned through EBGP.

- The ISP is providing Internet access to two customers. BGP is not used any lower on the hierarchy in this model. Each customer is using default routing to forward packets with unknown destinations to the ISP. BGP is therefore not required at this level, even for the customer with the redundant connection.

- Finally, note the hierarchy in the addressing of the networks. AS 451 received a CIDR block of 65K plus addresses, to reassign as it sees fit. The ISP has been assigned about a thousand of those addresses, and only needs to allocate a very few addresses from the pool to satisfy the needs of these two customers. The customers use private addressing within their networks and therefore only require the addresses for the link to the ISP.

The Future of BGP

To keep BGP current with the ever evolving Internet, additional RFCs supplement the BGP-4 specification. Technologies such as IPv6, multicasting, and VPN support have been added to the core BGP specification. Issues such as security are always being examined.

On the other hand, there is talk that BGP will ultimately be replaced or radically revamped. Although BGP is successfully holding up the Internet, it has its problems. It can be slow to converge (on the order of minutes, not seconds), policy dissemination is imperfect, and it is a relatively insecure protocol. Some drafts of a new inter-autonomous system routing protocol have been created, but replacing BGP is a huge endeavor because it cannot simply be taken offline and replaced with another protocol. For that reason, the next generation inter-autonomous system may roll out in an evolutionary, not revolutionary manner.

Notes

1. As we went to press, RFC 1771 was being obsoleted. The new standard was in draft form and did not yet have an RFC number. See the appendix for a link to the draft document.

2. Some implementations of the RFC defining BGP utilize multi path routing.

3. Hierarchical in the sense that BGP follows the roughly hierarchical structure of the autonomous system based Internet, but not hierarchical as in OSPF, which incorporates a distinct two-level hierarchy.

4. RFC 1930 was created to clear up confusion about AS numbers.

CHAPTER 10

Redistribution and Default Routing

Overview

The topics of route redistribution and default routing have been saved until after the routing protocols were covered because it's easier to discuss these topics if you already understand something about the mechanics of routing protocols.

Default routing has to do with configuring a router to forward packets when a destination network is not found in the route table. Normally, if a router can't find a path for a packet, the packet is dropped. Default routing helps prevent that scenario by providing a path to forward such packets in hopes that another router will have more information about the packet's destination. The default routing facility can be used to great advantage in managing the size of route tables and the bandwidth used by routing updates.

Default routing, in and of itself, can be configured without any routing protocol. But if it is desirable to have the default route shared with other routers, a routing protocol must get involved. When a default route, or in fact any route, is made known to a routing protocol that did not natively discover the route, it is known as *redistribution*.

Of course, the most common use of redistribution is to import routes learned by other routing protocols. Routing data known to one protocol can be redistributed into another routing protocol, and vice versa. These external routes are then advertised by the native routing protocol.

Be advised that redistribution is generally considered an advanced topic. Its coverage in this book is mainly to familiarize you with what redistribution is and some of the issues surrounding the implementation of redistribution.

The following topics are covered in this chapter:

Route Redistribution

Route redistribution refers to the process of importing routes learned from other sources into a particular routing protocol. The source may be routes known to another routing protocol, a statically entered route, or directly connected routes where the interface is not enabled for the native routing protocol.

When you're redistributing routes learned by another routing protocol, it is typical to configure the foreign routing protocol on a border router connected to the other system. Both the native and the foreign protocols run on a single router, thus laying the groundwork for routes to be redistributed into the AS. Redistribution can be one-way or two-way. Even when multiple routing protocols are enabled on a router, redistribution does not usually occur automatically, as illustrated in Figure 10-1.[1] Redistribution must be specifically configured.

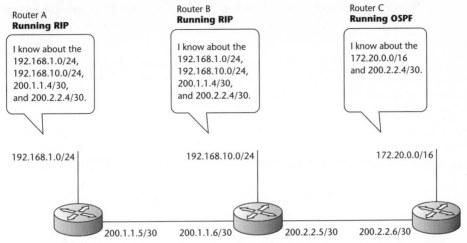

Figure 10-1 Routing protocols don't share learned routes with each other by default.

Be advised that route redistribution can be a complex issue. No real standards exist for redistribution, so you need to rely more on the experience of others. Lack of proper planning when configuring redistribution can result in anything from sub-optimal routing, to routing holes, to routing-loops. This treatment of redistribution is only an introduction to the topic. If you need to configure redistribution, be sure to learn all you can about the specifics of redistribution for the routing protocols in use. See the appendix for recommended reading.

The Need for Redistribution

In a perfect world, all networks would run the same routing protocol. Intra-domain routing has different requirements of a routing protocol than inter-domain routing, so in a slightly less-than-perfect world, maybe two routing protocols would be in use : an interior protocol and an exterior protocol; like BGP and OSPF. Alas, in this much less-than-perfect world, networks sometimes need to absorb routes from foreign routing protocols.

Here are some reasons for running multiple routing protocols.

- An organization is migrating from one routing protocol to another.

- Two organizations need to share routes with each other, but each organization runs a different routing protocol.

- A large, geographically dispersed organization might run both an interior routing protocol and an exterior routing protocol to tie together the disparate branch offices.

- An organization is running multiple *routed* protocols: IP, IPX, and Appletalk. Only EIGRP supports all these routed protocols, so unless EIGRP is in use throughout the system, multiple routing protocols may be required.

Figure 10-2 cites a network model where two autonomous systems want to share routing information. The systems are physically connected, but each routing domain is running a different routing protocol. In this case, each system's border router must be configured to run the foreign routing protocol before routes can be dynamically learned, as shown in Figure 10-3.

After the corresponding routing protocol and configuring redistribution are activated, routes are shared with the opposing system.

Static routes can be redistributed as well. The most common example of this is the static default route examples in the subsequent section on default routing. But any static route in a router's route table can be redistributed.

All the common interior routing protocols are capable of redistribution (RIP, IGRP, EIGRP, and OSPF). The ubiquitous exterior routing protocol BGP is capable of redistribution as well.

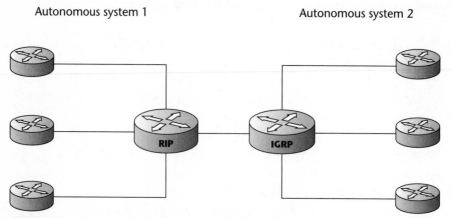

Figure 10-2 Example of the need to redistribute routes between domains when running dissimilar routing protocols.

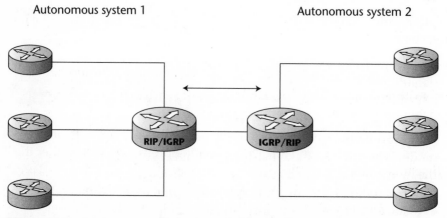

Figure 10-3 Route propagation occurs only after configuring redistribution.

Redistribution Issues

As alluded to earlier, route redistribution must be done with care. If not properly configured, convergence will be slowed and/or routing-loops may develop. For example, say a router is running both RIP and EIGRP. RIP learns of routes known to EIGRP because they have been redistributed into RIP. RIP begins to advertise the EIGRP learned routes along with its normal routing updates. If the EIGRP routers are also configured to learn and redistribute RIP routes, eventually the RIP routers will learn about their own routes again through EIGRP. These are far less favorable paths to the networks within the RIP routing domain. This scenario can sabotage routing, so there are a variety of mechanisms available to ensure redistribution works smoothly. Let's have a cursory look at each available method.

Metric Translation When Redistributing Routes

As you have garnered from earlier reading, every routing protocol has its own unique set of metrics for determining the best path to a network when multiple paths exist. But what metric should be applied to a route injected from another routing protocol? Because the routing protocol did not discover the routes itself, the metric for the external route cannot be used because it is probably not compatible with the native routing protocol. For example, RIP uses *hop count* as the metric. A network three hops away would have a metric of 3. Conversely, OSPF uses bandwidth for the metric. That same destination network may have a metric of, say, 1020 under OSPF. Therefore, injecting a route with a metric of 3 into OSPF would tremendously skew the route selection process. Because of this fact, metric conversion is a prime consideration when redistributing routes.

Setting a Metric for Redistributed Routes with a Cisco Router

Metric translation can occur globally or locally. You set the metric with the following commands:

- **default-metric:** Used in router configuration mode to globally set a default metric for redistributed routes. This value can be overridden for a specific route.

- **redistribute,** with optional keyword **metric *x*:** The **redistribute** command is used to redistribute routes. It is used in router configuration mode. When the leyword **metric** is used in the redistribution statement, the metric of the external routes being redistributed is set. This form of setting a route's metric takes priority over any other method for setting a metric for the route.

See the full-context examples for each routing protocol.

Special Administrative Distance Values for Redistributed Routes

Routes redistributed from certain routing protocols may be assigned a different administrative distance number than normal. As you can see from Table 10-1, EIGRP and BGP have a different administrative distance value when learned externally. As you will recall from the treatment of administrative distance, routes with lower administrative distance values are chosen over routes with higher values. For example, externally learned EIGRP routes are not trusted as much as directly learned EIGRP routes. Also see the subsequent section on route tagging.

Table 10-1 Administrative Distances

ROUTE	DISTANCE
Directly connected interface	0
Static route	1
EIGRP (summary routes)	5
BGP (external)	20
EIGRP (internal)	90
IGRP	100
OSPF	110
IS-IS	115
RIP	120
EGP	140
EIGRP (external)	170
Internal BGP	200
Unknown	255

Route Tagging

Routes injected into one protocol from another protocol can be *tagged*—marked with unique identifiers noting their source. This allows other routers to identify the redistributed routes as having been redistributed, and accept, discard, or otherwise rank the route accordingly. The routing protocol must support this feature.

Distribution Lists

Distribution lists are used to filter specific routes when redistribution takes place. Distribution lists are a form of access lists (a filtering mechanism provided by the Cisco IOS) applied to routing updates.

Route Maps

Route maps are access lists on steroids. Route maps make it possible to test for certain conditions and branch one way or another based on the condition. When route maps are used with distribution lists, route filtering can be managed in a very granular fashion.

Default Routing

The concept of a default route (also known as a default gateway) is quite straight forward. A default route provides a way of saying *none of the above*. If there is no entry in the route table matching the destination address of a packet, rather than drop the packet, it can be forwarded to the address specified by the default route entry. Default routing was first mentioned in Chapter 2, when it was noted that workstations usually rely on default routes to forward packets off the local network. Routers may or may not employ a default route depending on the configuration of the network. In point of fact however, if a network is connected to the Internet, default routing is very likely in use. Would you want to import the entire routing table for the Internet? Most ISPs don't even do that.

Default routing doesn't happen automatically. Packets with no matching route are normally dropped and an ICMP *Destination Unreachable* message is returned to the sender. Furthermore, even if a default route is established packets may still be dropped if default routing is not configured properly.

When to Use Default Routing

There are several reasons for configuring a default route:

- Internet access
- Provide a path to another autonomous system without importing the routes of the other system
- Stub routers that only have a single entry and/or exit point
- Minimize router updates and/or minimize the size of route tables

Accessing the Internet

Internet access is the most obvious reason to use default routing. It is not practical to populate a route table with every possible network a user may need to reach. Therefore, a typical approach is to have all the networks within the autonomous system populated into the route tables, and then configure a default route to direct all externally bound traffic to the organization's border router—the router interfacing the autonomous system to the outside world. The border router in turn would have a default route pointing to the interface connecting to the organization's ISP. Any packet not destined for somewhere in the organization finds a path leading it out of the system, as illustrated in Figure 10-4.

In this model, routers B, C, and D each have a default route pointing to router A. Router A in turn, has a default route pointing to the Internet.

Routing Packets to Other Autonomous Systems

Sometimes it's necessary to route packets to a different autonomous system, but it is not desireable to have the networks of the other system redistributed into the local system's route tables. In this case, a default route could be used for externally bound packets. The default route would forward packets to the local organization's border router, which may or may not be populated with the routes to the other system, depending on the network configuration.

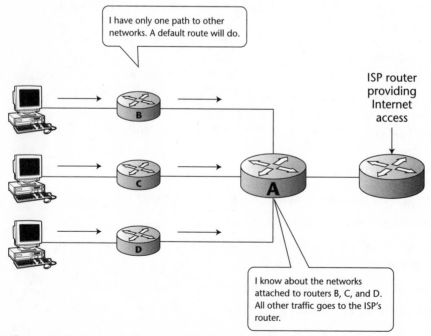

Figure 10-4 Arrows indicate the direction of packets along the default route.

If the border router was only connected to the target organization's border router, a default route might work there as well. If on the other hand, the border router also connected to an ISP for Internet access, it would be necessary to populate the border router's route table with the networks to the other autonomous system and save the default route for directing unknown traffic to the Internet. This could be accomplished by either running the routing protocol of the target organization on the border router and performing redistribution, or by creating static routes that point to the other system.

Using Stub Routers

In the model shown in Figure 10-4, routers B, C, and D are stub routers. Meaning, they have only one interface connecting to the rest of the network. Regardless of whether router A had an external connection or not, the route tables of the stub routers could be populated with nothing more than a default route pointing to router A. This model is sometimes termed a *hub-and-spoke* configuration.

Minimizing Network Traffic and the Size of Route Tables

As you will notice in all the aforementioned examples, route tables—and the network traffic associated with populating and maintaining them—are minimized to one degree or another when default routes are employed. Moral of the story: default routing is yet another tool the network engineer has for optimizing routing.

When Not to Use Default Routing

Default routing works best when there is only one path to or from a network (no routing decisions need to be made). In the modified model in Figure 10-5, redundant links have been added. Populating routers B, C, and D with just a default route is no longer appropriate because each router has multiple paths to the other networks. In this case, a well-designed routing solution would populate all routers with the routes to all internal networks. Whatever routing protocol was in use would choose the best path among whatever routes were available at the time. The routers could still employ a default route for Internet access, as long as the internal networks were listed in the route tables.

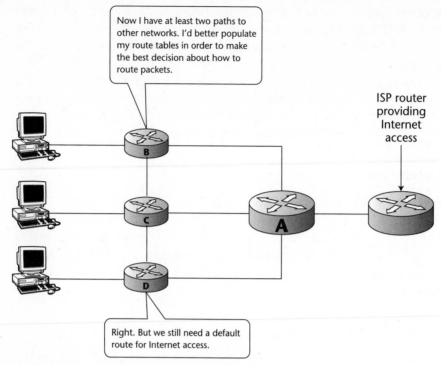

Figure 10-5 Redundant links and default routes don't mix.

Configuring Default Routing

Using a Cisco router as an example, there are two different methods for configuring default routing. One method is to set what's known as a **static default route** using the **ip route** global configuration command. This is simply a static route entry specifying a wild card network, which receives all traffic that doesn't find a match in the route table. This command is not supported by all routing protocols however. There is also the **ip default-network** global configuration command, which can be used by certain routing protocols. Both commands achieve similar results, but there are nuances in the way each is configured. Figure 10-6 provides a reference model for configuring both methods of default routing.

Initial Configuration of Routers

An initial configuration of the network is first performed using EIGRP as an example. Then two examples will be presented illustrating the two methods for configuring default routing (only the configuration for routers A and B will be enumerated).

```
routerA#config-term
routerA(config)#ip classless
routerA(config)#interface serial 0
```

```
routerA(config-if)#ip address 66.77.88.5 255.255.255.252
routerA(config-if)#exit
routerA(config)#interface fastethernet 0
routerA(config-if)#ip address 192.168.3.2 255.255.255.255
routerA(config-if)#exit
routerA(config)#interface fastethernet 1
routerA(config-if)#ip address 192.168.4.2 255.255.255.255
routerA(config-if)#exit
routerA(config)#interface fastethernet 2
routerA(config-if)#ip address 192.168.5.2 255.255.255.255
routerA(config-if)#exit
routerA(config)#router eigrp
routerA(config-router)#network 192.168.3.0
routerA(config-router)#network 192.168.4.0
routerA(config-router)#network 192.168.5.0
routerA(config-router)#exit
routerA(config)#

routerB#config-term
routerB(config)#ip classless
routerB(config)#interface fastethernet 0
routerB(config-if)#ip address 192.168.0.1 255.255.255.255
routerB(config-if)#exit
routerB(config)#interface fastethernet 1
routerB(config-if)#ip address 192.168.3.1 255.255.255.255
routerB(config-if)#exit
routerB(config)#router eigrp
routerB(config-router)#network 192.168.0.0
routerB(config-router)#network 192.168.3.0
routerB(config-router)#exit
routerB(config)#
```

The route tables for the configuration after they have converged are depicted in Figures 10-7 and 10-8.

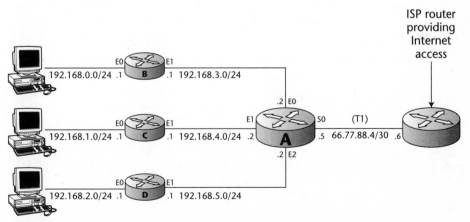

Figure 10-6   Reference model for configuring default routing.

```
routerA#show ip route
Codes:   C – connected,  S – static,  I – IGRP,  R – RIP,  M – mobile,  B – BGP
         D – EIGRP,  EX – EIRGP external,  O – OSPF,  IA – OSPF inter area
         N1 – OSPF NSSA external type 1,  N2 – OSPF NSSA external type 2,  E – EGP
         i – IS-IS,  L1 – IS-IS level-1,  L2 – IS-IS level 2,  * - candidate default
         U – per-user static route, o – ODR
         T – traffic engineered route

Gateway of last resort is not set

      66.77.88.4/30 is subnetted, 1 subnets
C         66.77.88.4  [0/0] is directly connected, Serial0
C     192.168.3.0/24 [0/0] is directly connected, Ethernet0
C     192.168.4.0/24 [0/0] is directly connected, Ethernet1
C     192.168.5.0/24 [0/0] is directly connected, Ethernet2
D     192.168.0.0/24 [140/307200] via 192.168.3.2, 00:00:10, Ethernet0
D     192.168.1.0/24 [140/307200] via 192.168.4.2, 00:00:10, Ethernet1
D     192.168.2.0/24 [140/307200] via 192.168.5.2, 00:00:10, Ethernet2
```

Figure 10-7   Router A before default routing is configured.

Notice the statement **Gateway of last resort is not set** in the printout of both routers. The obvious conclusion is that this is where a configured default route (default gateway) would show up. Often true . . . but not always, as these examples will show.

```
routerB#show ip route
Codes:   C – connected,  S – static,  I – IGRP,  R – RIP,  M – mobile,  B – BGP
         D – EIGRP,  EX – EIRGP external,  O – OSPF,  IA – OSPF inter area
         N1 – OSPF NSSA external type 1,  N2 – OSPF NSSA external type 2,  E – EGP
         i – IS-IS,  L1 – IS-IS level-1,  L2 – IS-IS level 2,  * - candidate default
         U – per-user static route, o – ODR
         T – traffic engineered route

Gateway of last resort is not set

C     192.168.0.0  [0/0] is directly connected, Ethernet0
C     192.168.3.0  [0/0] is directly connected, Ethernet1
D     192.168.1.0  [90/332800] via 192.168.3.2,00:01:10, Ethernet1
D     192.168.2.0  [90/332800] via 192.168.3.2,00:01:12, Ethernet1
D     192.168.4.0  [90/307200] via 192.168.3.2,00:01:12, Ethernet1
D     192.168.5.0  [90/307200] via 192.168.3.2,00:01:12, Ethernet1
```

Figure 10-8   Router B before default routing is configured.

NOTE If you are wondering why router A has not been configured to advertise the 66.77.88.4, there really is no point. Although 66.77.88.4 is the link to the Internet, simply advertising the route is not enough to coax the stub routers into directing Internet bound traffic to it. In truth, whether or not the route is ultimately advertised is based on which of the two methods are employed for default routing. Read on.

At this point, all the routers know about all the internal networks. However, the Internet is still unreachable by the stub routers, and even by the border router for that matter. Any packet bound for a network other than the six internal networks will be dropped because there is no entry for destinations other than the local networks in the route tables. Thus, a default route must be added to enable Internet access.

The most likely place to configure the default route is router A. Why? Because a routing protocol will do the job of advertising the default route. Giving router A a default route negates the need to manually configure it on the other routers. Let's start with an example of creating a default route with the **ip route** command.

Example 1: Default Route with the ip route Command

The **ip route** command is just a general statement for adding a static route. Here's the syntax:

```
routerA#config-term
routerA(config)#ip route 0.0.0.0 0.0.0.0 s0
```

REDISTRIBUTION TIP FOR STATIC DEFAULT ROUTES

In general, static routes are not automatically advertised to other routers (redistributed). To redistribute static routes, the *redistribute static* command must be issued in global configuration mode, as shown in the redistribution section of this chapter.

The exception to the rule is with static default routes, but only in one case. Note in configuration example 1 that either the *interface name* or the *IP address* of the interface can be used with the *ip route* command on Cisco routers. If the name of the interface is used ("e0"), the route is automatically redistributed by the routing protocol. Instead, the actual IP address of the interface could be used, like this:

```
ip route 0.0.0.0 0.0.0.0 66.77.88.5
```

In this case, the route is not redistributed unless the *redistribute static* statement is also issued. If you have a static default route that you don't wish to redistribute to other routers, use the latter form of the command. Having the two forms of the command is extremely useful for controlling which static routes are redistributed.

However, specifying the network ID as 0.0.0.0 with a mask of 0.0.0.0 is what makes it a static *default* route. 0.0.0.0 is basically a wildcard address that matches any destination address. When the router fails to find a match for a destination network within the table entries, the matching algorithm will "fall through" to the wild card route, which matches any destination address.

The output in Figure 10-9 shows that the Gateway of Last Resort is now set. Packets bound for 0.0.0.0 (any network not in the route table) will exit out interface S0. Internet bound packets now have a valid path out of the system if they reach this router.

An additional entry also appears in the table; a static route entry. Note that the static route listed at the bottom of the table is tagged with an asterisk (*) indicating it is a candidate default route. A candidate default route is one that is advertised as a *potential* default route for other EIGRP routers. Whether or not the route is actually used by the routers is based on how many other candidate default routes they have to choose from, in addition to any default route that may have been statically configured locally. The router can employ only one default route, although it can keep others standing by if the current default route goes down. The choice is based on metrics and administrative distance, just as it is with any other route. If the installed default route fails, a backup default route from the list of candidates can be installed in its place (if one even exists).

An examination of router B's route table in Figure 10-10 shows how it handled the advertisement of the default route after recalculating its route table.

```
routerA#show ip route
Codes:  C – connected,  S – static,  I – IGRP,  R – RIP,  M – mobile,  B – BGP
        D – EIGRP,  EX – EIRGP external,  O – OSPF,  IA – OSPF inter area
        N1 – OSPF NSSA external type 1,  N2 – OSPF NSSA external type 2,  E – EGP
        i – IS-IS,  L1 – IS-IS level-1,  L2 – IS-IS level 2,  * - candidate default
        U – per-user static route, o – ODR
        T – traffic engineered route

Gateway of last resort is 66.77.88.6 to network 0.0.0.0

     66.77.88.4/30 is subnetted, 1 subnets
C        66.77.88.4    [0/0] is directly connected, Serial0
C     192.168.3.0/24    [0/0] is directly connected, Ethernet0
C     192.168.4.0/24    [0/0] is directly connected, Ethernet1
C     192.168.5.0/24    [0/0] is directly connected, Ethernet2
D     192.168.0.0/24    [140/307200] via 192.168.3.2,00:00:10, Ethernet0
D     192.168.1.0/24    [140/307200] via 192.168.4.2,00:00:10, Ethernet1
D     192.168.2.0/24    [140/307200] via 192.168.5.2,00:00:10, Ethernet2
S*    0.0.0.0/0 [1/0] via 66.77.88.4
```

Figure 10-9 Router A has been given a default route using the **ip route** statement.

```
routerB#show ip route
Codes:  C – connected,  S – static,  I – IGRP,  R – RIP,  M – mobile,  B – BGP
        D – EIGRP,  EX – EIRGP external,  O – OSPF,  IA – OSPF inter area
        N1 – OSPF NSSA external type 1,  N2 – OSPF NSSA external type 2,  E – EGP
        i – IS-IS,  L1 – IS-IS level-1,  L2 – IS-IS level 2,  * - candidate default
        U – per-user static route,  o – ODR
        T – traffic engineered route

Gateway of last resort is 192.168.3.2 to network 0.0.0.0

C    192.168.0.0    [0/0] is directly connected, Ethernet0
C    192.168.3.0    [0/0] is directly connected, Ethernet1
D    192.168.1.0    [90/332800] via 192.168.3.2,00:01:44, Ethernet1
D    192.168.2.0    [90/332800] via 192.168.3.2,00:01:45, Ethernet1
D    192.168.4.0    [90/307200] via 192.168.3.2,00:01:45, Ethernet1
D    192.168.5.0    [90/307200] via 192.168.3.2,00:01:46, Ethernet1
D*   0.0.0.0/0 [90/0] via 192.168.3.0, 00:01:46, Ethernet1
```

Figure 10-10   Router B has received and accepted a default route.

Router B has been provided with a path to the Internet without the need for reconfiguration (as have routers C and D). As with router A, notice that not only has a Gateway of Last Resort been set, but router B is in turn advertising the default route in its updates. Downstream routers running EIGRP will be made aware of a candidate default route as well. Pretty cool.

Summary of the *ip route* Command

Here's what you should remember regarding the **ip route** command.

- Static default routes work as described in the previous example for EIGRP and RIP.

- OSPF can make use of static default routes, but redistribution of the default route is not automatic, and furthermore, must be configured differently from other routing protocols. See the default routing section in the OSPF chapter (page 295) and a configuration example (page 314).

- IGRP does not support static default routes. IGRP does not understand the 0.0.0.0 network; therefore, default routes cannot be propagated with the **ip route** statement. However, IGRP (as well as EIGRP and RIP) can use the second method for default routing as described next.

Example 2: Default Route with the ip default-network *command*

The other way to create and propagate a default route is with the **ip default-network** command. Unlike the **ip route** command, which provides a path through network 0.0.0.0 to the actual gateway router, the **ip default-network** command usually propagates an actual network number.

The key difference with this method is that the network specified for the default route must be in every router's route table.[2] This will require a slight alteration to the base configuration of the network model at router A. The following statements must also be be added to the configuration:

```
routerA(config)#router eigrp
routerA(config-router)#network 66.0.0.0
routerA(config-router)#exit
routerA(config)#
```

Because all routers need the network ID of the default route listed in their route tables, the best way to make that so is to propagate the 66.0.0.0 throughout the system. With the network now being advertised, router A is configured for a default route by executing the **ip default-network** command:

```
routerA#config-term
routerA(config)#ip default-network 66.0.0.0
```

Notice that the statement does not include a network mask. A mask is not used with the **ip default-network** command. Now let's examine the router output in Figure 10-11.

```
routerA#show ip route
Codes: C – connected,  S – static,  I – IGRP,  R – RIP,  M – mobile,  B – BGP
        D – EIGRP,  EX – EIRGP external,  O – OSPF,  IA – OSPF inter area
        N1 – OSPF NSSA external type 1,  N2 – OSPF NSSA external type 2,  E – EGP
        i – IS-IS,  L1 – IS-IS level-1,  L2 – IS-IS level 2,  * - candidate default
        U – per-user static route,  o – ODR
        T – traffic engineered route

Gateway of last resort is not set

*       66.77.88.4/30 is subnetted, 1 subnets
C  *    66.77.88.4   [0/0] is directly connected, Serial0
C       192.168.3.0/24 [0/0] is directly connected, Ethernet0
C       192.168.4.0/24 [0/0] is directly connected, Ethernet1
C       192.168.5.0/24 [0/0] is directly connected, Ethernet2
D       192.168.0.0/24 [140/307200] via 192.168.3.2, 00:00:10, Ethernet0
D       192.168.1.0/24 [140/307200] via 192.168.4.2, 00:00:10, Ethernet1
D       192.168.2.0/24 [140/307200] via 192.168.5.2, 00:00:10, Ethernet2
```

Figure 10-11 Router A has been given a default route using the **ip default-network** command.

The route table looks different from the earlier example with the **ip route** command. To begin with, the Gateway of Last Resort entry shows no gateway set. This is due to the fact that router A is itself the gateway. The **ip route** statement in the previous example specified the interface address of the next hop router, but the **ip default-network** statement specifies a network; which is directly connected. Packets arriving at this router, finding no matching address in the route table, will be forwarded out interface Serial 0 because of the default route entry in the route table. This point also addresses the other difference in the output: there is no 0.0.0.0 candidate default route. Rather, the asterisk is next to the 66.0.0.0 network, indicating that it's the candidate default route.

Let's see how router B's route table has been influenced after a routing update by examining the output in Figure 10-12.

Router B now has a Gateway of Last Resort set. Additionally, the router is also advertising the candidate default route to its neighbors. With just the two commands entered at router A, every router in this system now has a route to the Internet.

```
routerB#show ip route
Codes: C – connected,  S – static,  I – IGRP,  R – RIP,  M – mobile,  B – BGP
       D – EIGRP,  EX – EIRGP external,  O – OSPF,  IA – OSPF inter area
       N1 – OSPF NSSA external type 1,  N2 – OSPF NSSA external type 2,  E – EGP
       i – IS-IS,  L1 – IS-IS level-1,  L2 – IS-IS level 2,  * - candidate default
       U – per-user static route, o – ODR
       T – traffic engineered route

Gateway of last resort is not set

*     66.77.88.4 is subnetted, 1 subnet
D  *     66.77.88.4  [90/793600] via 192.168.3.2, 00:01:22, Ethernet1
C     192.168.0.0  [0/0] is directly connected, Ethernet0
C     192.168.3.0  [0/0] is directly connected, Ethernet1
D     192.168.1.0  [90/281600] via 192.168.3.2,00:01:23, Ethernet1
D     192.168.2.0  [90/281600] via 192.168.3.2,00:01:23, Ethernet1
D     192.168.4.0  [90/307200] via 192.168.3.2,00:01:16, Ethernet1
D     192.168.5.0  [90/307200] via 192.168.3.2,00:01:17, Ethernet1
```

Figure 10-12   Router B has a default route to network 66.77.88.4.

Summary of the *ip default* Command

Here's what you should remember regarding the **ip default-network** command:

- This is the only way to set a default route if you want to have the route propagated by IGRP.

- OSPF handles default routes in a special way and does not use the **ip default-network** command. See the default routing section in the OSPF chapter (page 295) and a configuration example (page 314).

- Be sure each router has a path to the network specified by the Gateway of Last Resort statement. Exception: RIP will propagate the default route as 0.0.0.0, negating the need to have the network indicated by the default route residing in any table except the router directly connected to the specified network.

- Be sure to specify a classful address in the **ip default-network** statement. A subnet address will not be recognized and the default route will not be set.

Notes

1. The exception is IGRP and EIGRP, which automatically share routes with each other by default.

2. This statement is true for IGRP and EIGRP. RIP does not actually require the route to be listed in any other router's route table to propogate the default route because RIP will advertise the route as 0.0.0.0.

Where Do You Go From Here?

This is an introductory book, so naturally there is a lot more to know about routing. This appendix will give you an idea what more you can study.

The Routing Protocol in Your Environment

It pays to learn everything you can about the routing protocols in the network environment where you work. If you're like the author, you will want to get your hands on all the books written about those routing protocols. No single reference ever has everything there is to know about a particular technology. All it takes is finding one critical piece of information relative to the *emergency of the moment* that, in itself, pays for the book. Study the RFCs related to the protocol and then study the routing vendor's implementation of the RFC.

Multicast Routing

With the popularity of the Web, multicasting (transmitting data to a group of hosts) has become a hot item. You will be well-served to know about how multicasting works, and which routing protocols and networking equipment support multicasting the best.

Security

As everyone knows, security is a key issue of 21st century networking. Learning about security as it relates to network routing, means learning about access lists, Virtual LANs (VLANs), packet encryption, and Virtual Private Networks (VPNs), for a start.

Redistribution

As stated in Chapter 10, redistribution must be approached with caution. If you need to redistribute routes into your network, study this topic some more, and be cautious with the metrics you set on redistributed routes. Fully understanding redistribution means understanding *access lists*, *route maps*, *route tags*, and *distribution lists*.

On-Demand Routing

On-demand routing (ODR) was noted in Chapter 2. If you employ static routes on your network, it would be of benefit to research the benefits of ODR, a newer technology that may prove to be more versatile than static routes.

IPv6

Although it may be years until it's fully deployed, IPv6 is coming. It's wise to start learning it, even if your shop is not running IPv6 protocol stacks yet.

MultiProtocol Label Switching

MultiProtocol Label Switching (MPLS) is a more recent technology that may have future importance. MPLS uses a variety of network information to assist in traffic engineering, Quality of Service (QOS), and Class of Service (COS).

Recommended Reading

We recommend that you pick up a copy of one or all of these books to further your knowledge of network routing:

- *Routing TCP/IP volumes I & II*, Jeff Doyle, Cisco Press, ISBN 1-57870-041-8, 1-57870-089-2

  Put simply, this is the Bible of IP routing. This comprehensive two-volume set should be on your bookshelf. The book was revised to a second edition in 2005, so watch the edition number when ordering. There is a great deal of granular information, such as a full treatment of IPv6, OSPF packet formats, and OSPF Virtual Links. The bulk of the second volume is devoted almost entirely to BGP.

- *Troubleshooting IP Routing Protocols*, Faraz Shamim, et al, Cisco Press, ISBN 1-58705-019-6

  This is an excellent resource for down-and-dirty troubleshooting. There are lots of examples of failed routing scenarios and how to fix them.

- *CCNP Routing*, Clare Gough, Cisco Press, ISBN 1-58720-001-5

  This is one of the better-written books in the Cisco Press lineup. There are a few mistakes here and there, but the topics are well-covered. It includes a great treatment of redistribution and good treatment of OSPF over Frame Relay. We recommend it even if CCNP certification is not your goal.

- *Computer Networks*, Andrew Tanenbaum, Prentice Hall, ISBN 0-13-066102-3

  This is a great primer on networking. It covers a wide variety of networking topics and is very detailed.

RFCs Related to Routing

RIPv2

2453, 1582, 1721, 1724, 2082, 2091

OSPF

2328, 2370, 2740, 3101, 3623, 3630, 3883, 4136, 4203, 4222

BGP

4271, 1657, 1997, 2385, 2439, 2547, 2796, 2918, 3065, 3107, 3392, 3765, 3882

IGMP

1112, 2236

VLSM

1878

IPv6

2460, 2461, 2462, 2463, 2464, 2675, 2711, 3041, 3122, 3513, 3587, 3633, 3646, 3697, 3736

IP

791

CIDR

1518, 1519

Subnetting

950

VLSMs

1009

Route Summarization

1518

DHCP

1541

BOOTP

951, 1395, 1497, 1532, 1542

Broadcast on Subnets

919, 922

Requirements for IPv4 Routers

1812

DVMRP

1075

TCP/IP utilities

1739

EIGRP White Papers (Proprietary Protocol, No RFCs)

Do a Google search on the following:

Loop-free Routing using Diffusing Computations

A Unified Approach to Loop-free Routing Using Distance Vectors or Link States

Web References

IP Address Allocation

Internet Corporation for Assigned Names and Numbers (ICANN):
`www.icann.org`

IANA (Internet Assigned Numbers Authority): `www.iana.org`

Number Resource Organization: `www.nro.net`

North America ARIN: `www.arin.net`

Europe, RIPE NCC: `www.ripe.net`

Asia Pacific APNIC: `www.apnic.net`

Latin America LATNIC: `www.latnic.net`

Africa AfriNIC: `www.afrinic.net`

Internet Standards Bodies

`www.ietf.org`

`www.isoc.org`

`www.w3.org`

www.ansi.org (click on Internet Resources)

www.ifla.org

www.webstandards.org

Macro View of the Internet

www.caida.org/analysis/topology/as_core_network

Initial Setup of a Router

www.opennet.ru/soft/cisco-configuration.html

www.swcp.com/~jgentry/topo/cisco.htm

www.sdnp.undp.org/rc/areas/tech/setup/cisco-geta2.html

Other Sites of Interest

www.tcpipguide.com/free/

www.hottrainingmaterials.com

Administrative Distance Table

ROUTE	DISTANCE
Directly connected interface	0
Static route	1
EIGRP (summary routes)	5
BGP (external)	20
EIGRP (internal)	90
IGRP	100
OSPF	110
RIP	120
EIGRP (external)	170
Internal BGP	200
Unknown	255

Quick-and-Dirty Subnetting— No Calculator

The key to subnetting "quick-and-dirty style" is via a trick known as the *magic number*. Once you determine the magic number in a subnetting problem, everything else is child's play. See for yourself.

Follow these steps to subnet a /24 address (former class C) with no binary numbers and no calculator:

1. Determine the number of networks (subnets) needed.

    This example uses the address 192.168.1.0:

    (a) Count on your fingers, starting at two, doubling the number for each finger until you get the number of subnets you need (1 finger = two subnets, two fingers = 4 subnets, and so on).

    (b) Subtract 2 from the result, and if you still have enough subnets, that is the number of binary digits to borrow. If not, you're one finger short, so just borrow 1 additional bit.

    Example for 6 subnets: 1 finger = 2; two fingers = 4; three fingers = 8. Subtract 2 (8-2 = 6) and you know that borrowing 3 bits will provide enough subnets.

2. Determine the magic number.

   Start at the number 256 and cut it in half for each bit you borrowed. This gives you the magic number! The subnet mask and all subnet addresses come from this number. That's why it's called the *magic number*.

   Example with 3 borrowed bits: 128, 64, 32. (32 is the magic number).

3. Determine the custom subnet mask.

   Subtract the magic number from 256.

   Example: 256-32=224. 224 is the custom subnet mask for the fourth octet (255.255.255.224).

4. Determine the first subnet number.

   Easy: the magic number *is* the first subnet number (192.168.1.32).

5. Determine successive subnet numbers.

   Just add the magic number to the previous subnet number.

   Example: The previous subnet number was 192.168.1.32. Adding the magic number to 32 = 192.168.1.64. The next subnet number is 64+32 = 192.168.1.96, then 96+32 = 192.168.1.128, and so on.

6. Determine the last subnet number.

   Subtract the magic number from the custom subnet mask.

   Example: 224-32 = 192 (192.168.1.192)

7. Determine the host IDs and broadcast address for any subnet:

   - The number of host IDs per subnet is always the magic number – 2.
   - The first host ID is always one greater than the subnet number.
   - The last host ID is always two less than the next subnet number.
   - The broadcast address is always one less than the next subnet number.

     Example using subnet 192.168.1.32 (255.255.255.224):

     - There are 30 host addresses (32-2=30).
     - The first host number is 192.168.1.33 (32+1).
     - The last host number is 192.168.1.62 (64-2).
     - Broadcast address is 192.168.1.63 (64-1)

This technique works for any classful or classless address. Just remember to borrow from the correct octet.

Subnetting Helper Sheet

	Network address to subnet			
	Default subnet mask			
	# of networks required			
	# of hosts per network			
	# of bits borrowed			
	Custom subnet mask			
	Subnet IDs	**1st Host ID**	**Last Host ID**	**Broadcast Address**
1				
2				
3				
4				
5				
6				
7				
8				
9				
10				

Index